THE HOUSATONIC

RIVERS OF AMERICA

THE
HOUSATONIC

CHARD POWERS SMITH

Illustrated by Armin Landeck
Foreword by Erik Hesselberg

LYONS
PRESS

Guilford, Connecticut

An imprint of The Rowman & Littlefield Publishing Group, Inc.
4501 Forbes Blvd., Ste. 200
Lanham, MD 20706
www.rowman.com

Distributed by NATIONAL BOOK NETWORK

British Library Cataloguing in Publication Information available

Library of Congress Cataloging-in-Publication Data available

ISBN 978-1-4930-4016-2 (paperback)

∞™ The paper used in this publication meets the minimum
requirements of American National Standard for Information
Sciences—Permanence of Paper for Printed Library Materials,
ANSI/NISO Z39.48-1992.

To the Farmers of the Valley

on whom the rest of us depend

Foreword

In his journal on August 20, 1846, Henry Wadsworth Longfellow grumbled, "It is difficult to write in this house, so closely is it shut in with trees." Only a year before at Elm Knoll, the stately manor house of his father-in-law, Nathan Appleton, Longfellow penned "The Old Clock on the Stairs," using a French poem for pattern and Elm Knoll's big timepiece for material. But now, the words would not flow. "I find it quite impossible to write in the country, the influences are soothing and slumberous," Longfellow complained. Seeking a change of scene, the poet set out for a walk along the Housatonic River winding through the flatland of Pittsfield, Massachusetts, not far from the Appleton estate. English colonists called it "the Great River," but that first visit Longfellow only saw, "A shallow brown stream, not very clear." However, two days later—August 22nd—is feelings changed. "Drove to Stockbridge and came upon the Oxbow. . . .Up the hill we went from which the view is so fine; beneath wound and circled upon itself the slow Housatonic through meadows fair, forming the Oxbow." Longfellow would return again and again to the spot over the next twenty years. Whether it was British actress Fanny Kemble in the 19th century fleeing an abusive marriage, or celebrities of today seeking refuge from the hustle of Hollywood, the "Place beyond the Mountains," as Native Americans called the Housatonic Valley, has always been a haven for those who want to escape. Writes Chard Powers Smith in *The Housatonic; Puritan River*:

Whether as a cause or as a result of its continuing pristine state, an impressive number of people have, from the earlier days, followed the intellectual pursuits in the valley, theologians, political philosophers, miscellaneous writers, educators, scientists, artists and musicians who have come here to escape from the outer world's too insistence reminders of change full time.

Artists and celebrities of all types continue to settle in the Housatonic Valley. In the Kent-Cornwall-Sharon area, Henry Kissinger, Reagan biographer Edmund Morris, William F. Buckley, and Lynn Redgrave all have or had homes.

Writers especially have been lured by the region's rustic beauty. In 1850, Nathaniel Hawthorne rented a farmhouse in the Berkshires and was so taken with the "static grandeur of the mountain scene," he feared he would not be able to work there. Six miles distant in Lenox, Massachusetts, Herman Melville was toiling away on his epic *Moby Dick.* Hawthorne and Melville met at a picnic in the Berkshires in the summer of 1850, when during a hike up a mountain a thunderstorm forced the giants of American literature to take shelter "in a crevice under a ledge that barely gave them cover." After, the two meet often at Melville's farm, known as "Arrowhead," where one of their practices was "to lie in the hay in the barn and discuss the universe . . ."

Fanny Kemble first came to the Berkshires in 1832, a guest of the literary luminary Catharine Sedgwick, whose mansion on the terrace by the river in Stockbridge was a gathering place for celebrities of the day. Kemble bought an estate in Lenox she called "The Perch." It was her refuge. "A happy valley indeed—the Valley of the Housatonic," she wrote, "locked in by walls of every shape and size, from grassy knolls to bold basaltic cliffs. A beautiful little river wanders singing from side to side in the secluded Paradise."

The Housatonic was part of the landmark "Rivers of America Series," launched in 1937 by Rinehart and Company. The idea, developed by Constance Lindsay Skinner, was inspired—to tell the story of America through its rivers and the people who lived along their banks. Skinner, a poet herself, thought poets and novelists were best suited to tell America's story, not historians. She recruited for the series top literary figures like Robert P. Tristram Coffin, Henry Seidel Canby, Carl Carmer, and Henry Beston. Originally planned to run 24 volumes, the series was so popular it was extended to 64 volumes published over 37 years. Among the classics were, *Everglades*, *River of Grass*, by Marjory Stoneman Douglas, and Paul Horgan's *Great River: The Rio Grande in American History*, winner of the Pulitzer Prize for History in 1955. *The Housatonic* was published in 1947, the 31st in the series. Flowing 150 miles from its northernmost source on the flanks of Mount Greylock in northwestern Massachusetts to the marshes of Stratford, Connecticut, on Long Island Sound, the Housatonic is a small river. It drains about 1,950 acres—skimpy compared to the 11,260—acre watershed of the Connecticut River, its cousin 40 miles to the east. Nor does its story rival the epic grandeur of its neighbor to the west, the "Lordly" Hudson, whose "discovery" by Englishman Henry Hudson in 1609, sparked a century of warfare over the fur trade. And indeed it was the so-called "Beaver Wars" that pushed the peaceful Mohicans out of the Hudson and into the Housatonic valley. When the migrated, they came in from the West over the mountains, and the land where they settled became *Wussi-adene-uk,* "The Beyond-the-Mountain-Place," which through innumerable spellings became "Housatonic."

In the pattern of other Rivers' books, *The Housatonic* traces the geology, culture, and commercial history of the river valley, with a focus on people rather than events. There is the story of the Dutch explorer Adriaen Block, the first European to come upon the Housatonic in the spring of 1614. Block, who also explored the Connecticut River that same trip, had been ousted from the Hudson River following a clash with a rival Dutch fur trading company. In the fray, his flagship *Tyger* was burned to the waterline. He built a new boat, a 44 ½ foot sloop he christened *Onrust,* piloting the vessel up the East River through the whirlpool currents of Hell Gate, where the tides rush in and out of Long Island Sound. Sailing eastward along the coast, Block came upon the Housatonic, which he named "River of the Red Hills," presumably from the sand dunes of Stratford Point. The Mohicans, meanwhile, called the marsh-fringed lagoon *Cuph-eag,* the Shut-in-Place. In 1639, the first English settlers arrived under the ministry of the forty-year-old Reverend Adam Blakeman, some thirty families, half from old England, the rest from Wethersfield on the "River Connecticut," under whose auspices the plantation was being undertaken.

Chard Powers Smith (1894-1977) published more than a dozen books of fiction, poetry, and history, much of it about New England. He lived in Cornwall, Connecticut, with its picturesque covered bridge over the rushing river, which he often paddled in his canoe. He saw in the Housatonic's tumultuous flow and ever-changing surface, a timelessness and symbol of "eternal truth." "Signally among the rivers of America today," he writes,

> The Housatonic and its valley combine these qualifications as symbols of the truth that men seek and sometimes find . . . This value of a river as a symbol of eternal truth is increased if the valley through which it flows likewise suggests permanence behind change, if the hills are wide and gracious under the sky, especially if man's cupidity has violated them but little, so the forest retains its seeming timelessness, while within it the trees turn their cycle of seed and growth and decay.

Smith studied law and he tries to make the case that the English obtained title to the aboriginal lands that would become the "new plantation at Pequannock," by fair and honorable means. The swath of coastland that would become Stratford was acquired by the "right of conquest," he maintains, having been seized in the aftermath of the Pequot War of 1638. The 80 or so survivors of the "Mystic Massacre" on May 26, 1637, when 400 to 600 men, women, and children were slaughtered, fled westward along the coast, making a final stand in Fairfield's Saco Swamp. The battle was known as the "Great Swamp Fight." Before leveling their muskets at the reeds, the soldiers, under Captain John Mason, who had led the Pequot slaughter, this time allowed women and children to surrender, along with 200 or so Pequannock Indians. However, Smith neglects to mention that the captives would soon be shipped to the West Indies as slaves to work the sugar plantations. Of this unhappy episode, he concludes, "So, at the outset, the Lord punished the enemies of his Chosen People."

Smith's view of Indigenous peoples is paradoxical—at times praising their "great human spirit" while disparaging their primitive "Stone Age" culture. "[Native Americans were] generally faithful to their larger, treaty undertakings but not above petty pilfering. . . . Picturesque in dress, but filthier in person than any animals . . . affectionately generous, and yet at the same time sub-humanly cruel."

Of the Mohicans in particular he writes:

Though the men were of splendid physic, they were an unwarlike, submissive, and pessimistic people. Their solution of emotional problems was suicide, normally by leaping from a cliff into the arms of the Great Spirit, after singing a hymn to apprise him of their approach . . . The women, squat, deformed—and frequently sterile—from overwork, cultivated corn, squashes, and a few beans with wooden hoes. The men raised tobacco, but were otherwise above manual labor.

On the other hand, *The Housatonic* staunchly defends the Puritan settlers, whom Smith describes as the first "Seekers of Truth," and whose reputation for bigotry and intolerance is largely the fault of "blackwashing historians who make a profession of detracting New England," The real Puritan, writes Smith,

Was not, as is now universally believed, primarily interested in anybody else's conduct. Conduct was a secondary matter to him . . . The Warrant for the accusations of intolerance which has fondly been pinned on the Puritans by America's Europe-flattering apologists is largely derived from a work of irritated fancy touchingly fictitious 'Blue Laws of Connecticut . . . Of all the accomplishments of the Puritan-baiters, none is more groundless than the reputation they have given them for religious intolerance.

The Housatonic attempts to present the history of the valley as a 300-year struggle between the "Lord" and the "Devil"—a narrative frame that gets tedious at time. This is partly compensated by the book's freshet of facts and lively depictions of the valley's colorful personalities, like the pugnacious Ethan Allen, whom court records tell us did on at least one occasion: "strip himself to his naked body, and with force and arms, without law or right, did assail and strike the person of George Cadwell . . ." Another picturesque character is the Salisbury iron master, Samuel Forbes, whom everyone referred to as "Captain," though he held no military rank. "One thing about him seems certain, his surviving portrait. By its evidence he surely wore the ugliest face that ever covered a human soul."

Industry flourished along the Housatonic in the 19th century, and the valley's manufacturing history is richly detailed. We learn that in Derby, at the head of tidewater, was set up the first factory in America for hoop skirts; also the first factory

ARGUMENT

Puritan River

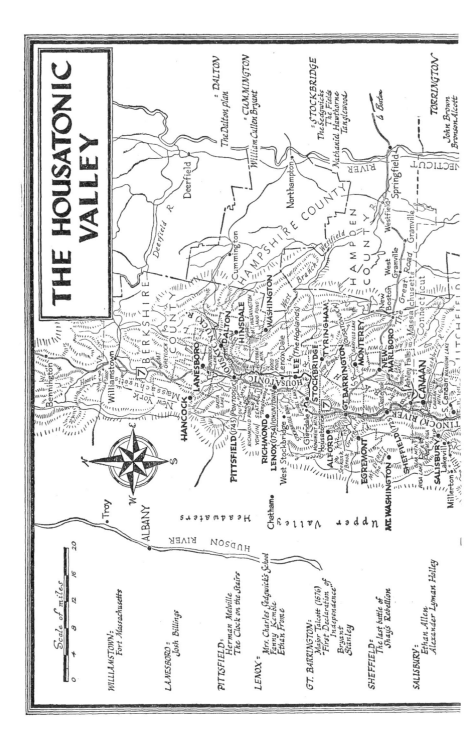

THE HOUSATONIC VALLEY

Scale of miles
0 4 8 12 16 20

WILLIAMSTOWN:
Fort Massachusetts

LANESBORO:
Josh Billings

PITTSFIELD:
Herman Melville
The Clock on the Stairs

LENOX:
Mrs. Charles Sedgwick's School
Fanny Kemble
Ethan Frome

GT. BARRINGTON:
Major Talcott (1676)
"First Declaration of
Independence"
Bryant
Stanley

SHEFFIELD:
The last battle of
Shays Rebellion

SALISBURY:
Ethan Allen,
Alexander Lyman Holley

DALTON
The Dalton plan

CUMMINGTON
William Cullen Bryant

STOCKBRIDGE
The Sedgwicks
The Fields
Nathaniel Hawthorne
Tanglewood

TORRINGTON
John Brown
Bronson Alcott

LITCHFIELD
George III melted
First law school
Miss. Pierce's school
The Beechers

MORRIS
Morris Academy

BETHLEHEM
Joseph Bellamy
First Divinity school

WASHINGTON
Marbledale
= ROXBURY

WOODBURY
Orenaug Rocks

BRIDGEWATER
First mail orderhouse

Ethan Allen
Seth Warner
Remember Baker

DERBY
Edward Wooster
Genl. Humphreys

MILFORD
Robert Treat
The Regicide Goffe
Whalley

New Haven (Quinnipiack)
Boston Post Road

ORANGE
Milford Pt.
Cupheag
PURITANS
MILFORD (WEPAWAUG) (1639)
Charles I. (Milford I.) (Poquehaug)

PURITANS ARRIVE 1639

Long Island Sound

Hartford
Farmington

NEW HAVEN COUNTY

LITCHFIELD (1719)
(The Greenwoods)
Thomaston
Waterbury
Watertown
MORRIS
BETHLEHEM
WASHINGTON (1705) (WEANTINOG)
WOODBURY (1705)
ROXBURY
BRIDGEWATER
SEYMOUR
ANSONIA
Naugatuck
Oxford
DERBY (PAUGASSET) (1655)
Stevenson Dam

SOUTHBURY
SHELTON (RIPTON) (1705)
GEORGE WASHINGTON BRIDGE, 1802
Trumbull
BRIDGEPORT (1639)
STRATFORD RIVER
STRATFORD
Stratford Pt.

GREAT STRATFORD
MONROE
NEWTOWN (QUANNEAPAQUE) (1705)
Bethel

VOYAGE OF THE "UNRUST" 1614

Tide water

HOUSATONIC
CORNWALL
GOSHEN
WARREN
KENT
SHERMAN
NEW MILFORD (1705)
POTATUCK
BROOKFIELD (1686)
NEW FAIRFIELD
DANBURY (PAHQUIOQUE)
Brewster
Ridgebury
S. Salem
Bedford

Norwalk
Westport
Southport
Fairfield
Saugatuck

New York-Boston Post Road
CONN. FAIR. R.
Port Chester
Rye
White Plains
to New York

Greenwich–Boston Post Road
Stamford

Millbrook
Amenia

Lower Vat.

The Allen family
Dudley Town
Mission school
General Sedgwick

TENMILE RIVER:
"Hideous High Mountain"
(1694)

SCATACOOK:
"First Indians" (1500?)

SHERMAN:
Roger Sherman

NEW MILFORD:
Waramaug's palace
Fishing cove
Goodyear's Island
Tobacco

SANDY HOOK:
Charles Goodyear

DANBURY:
Tryon's raid
General Wooster

SHELTON:
Commodore Isaac Hall
Indian fort

SOUTHPORT:
Great swamp fight (1637)

STRATFORD:
Dr. Samuel Johnson
The Stratford rappings

NORWALK:
Cession of Potatuck lands
(1638)

Puritan River

IN TIMES of war or other turbulence men frequently look out at the cosmos or into their own hearts, searching for some fixed reality they can call God, some rock to anchor to beneath the shifting surfaces of life. For this purpose, no symbol is better than that of a great river, whose surface of easy or tumultuous flow is forever changing and unstable, never for two successive instants comprising the same atoms and electrons, yet to the eye and the ear it is always the same.

The value of a river as a symbol of eternal truth is increased if the valley through which it flows likewise suggests permanence behind change, if the hills are wide and gracious under the sky, especially if man's cupidity has violated them but little, so that the forest retains its seeming timelessness, while within it the trees turn their cycle of seed and growth and decay.

The symbolic value of a river is further strengthened if the population of its valley consists of men who exhibit some elements of stability, some moral affinity with eternal truth behind the shifting business of their lives. The populations of cities rarely suggest this permanence, for their very essence is of change, the fun of the sheep-stampede after material fashion. But a population of farmers, working the same ground and often occupying the same houses their ancestors have worked and occupied for many generations, such a population contributes its part to the sense of timelessness of the stage it occupies. The farms, scattered at easy intervals over the hills and little valleys, are part of a truce which man has long reached with nature, by which each

5

serves the other and both survive. The forest and its deer and man and his cattle subsist together from the same soil, and the same rule of birth and death within the continuity of life controls them all.

Finally, this symbolic value of a river and its valley is further humanized for the observer if he happens to know, as a matter of record, that many thousands of men have sought truth in this valley down the centuries, that some of them have approached, as nearly as men may, to the central Light that is God, and that others have come into some earthly reflection of that light in philosophical, political, moral, scientific or aesthetic understanding.

Signally among the rivers of America today, the Housatonic and its valley combine these qualifications as symbols of the truth that men seek and sometimes find. Grooved twenty miles wide for a hundred and fifteen crow-flight miles southward through the uplands of southwestern New England, the main valley is carved by tributaries into labyrinthine lesser valleys among steep-sided ranges known as the Berkshires in Massachusetts and the Litchfield Hills in Connecticut.

Down this 115-mile valley, the river itself, because of its windings, pours about a hundred and sixty miles from its triple headwaters in the horseshoe of mountains around Pittsfield to its harbor in Long Island Sound between Bridgeport and New Haven. In volume it is of the second order, smaller than the Connecticut, forty miles to the east, or the Hudson forty miles to the west. Yet it is large enough to suggest the power and majesty of the cosmos, and the first colonists of its banks, men who had seen bigger streams, called it the Great River.

Geologically it is an old river, the irregularities of its bed mostly smoothed back by aeons of flow, so that it is relatively uniform in moderately rapid current, only four natural "great falls" and one unnavigable rapids remaining.

The quality of the surrounding hills also is that of geologic antiquity, in distinction from the jagged and rainbow-garish grandeur of younger, unmellowed peaks. Here nature

with the weathering tools of a hundred million years has
modeled a graceful ocean of mountains undulating back in
any direction under forests haze-purple in summer and red
and gold in autumn, autumn which is more colorful here
than elsewhere, because the steep tilt of the slopes shows off
all the trees to advantage, like millions of clustered, titanic
bouquets. Here from any point, high or low, there is a
spacious and satisfying view, a view over hills and valleys
wide enough to stir the imagination, yet small enough and
with horizon curves graceful enough to contain it within
the limits of a place and a meaning. Here the spirit not only
flies out toward infinity but it goes full circle and returns
to finite repose.

As there is composure in the river and the hills, so there
is composure in the people, mostly Yankee farmers, who inhabit the valley. Here the equation has long been reached
between population and the capacity of the soil. It has become a region apart from the common restlessness of America.
It has become a country where people stay. The basic stratum
of farmers and villagers stays, while on the surface strangers
come in for the summers or for a few complete years,
strangers from the cities, most of whom are seeking the
peace of the scene as a background for intellectual effort,
creative, academic or interpretive. Not only in the natural
beauties of the river and the mountains, not only in the
composed culture of the native farmers, but in the long
record of its contributions to the total of human achievement, this ancient valley is an inspiration to the exercise of
the best faculties of man.

The region as delimited for the purpose of this book
contains all the tributaries of the river except two, the
Naugatuck, which is the largest, and the Tenmile, which
is one of the largest. I have excluded these, partly because
they both break in from outside through the roughly
parallel ranges that otherwise neatly contain the valley;
and I have excluded them especially because the histories
of these two collateral valleys are so different from that
of the rest of the Housatonic watershed that to include

them would be to sacrifice continuity. It would be to recount the annals of three separate regions instead of a single, fairly homogeneous one. I have included as properly in "The Valley" the towns on all the other tributaries, but I have given most attention to the doings of those towns which actually border on the main stream.

The river and valley divide naturally into four parts from north to south, namely the Headwaters, the Upper, or

Massachusetts, part, the Lower, or Connecticut, part, and Tidewater.

The Headwaters consists of three branches fanning out symmetrically to the west, the north, and the east of the city of Pittsfield in the southern part of which they join and the river properly begins. The West Branch is the smallest and curves in for some eight miles from the sizable lake called Richmond Pond. The East Branch is the longest, the largest in volume, and appropriately carries the name of the river all the way to its source. This is in a lost lake called Mud Pond in the bleak, scrub-covered uplands of Washington

Township in Massachusetts, precisely on the height of land where the booster locomotives leave the trains they have helped up the long grades from either east or west. This lake and its shore line of scrubby woods are the more desolate for being kept perpetually in flood by a big beaver dam across the outlet that starts off the river with its first fall. From there down to Pittsfield, it drops from nearly sixteen hundred to a thousand feet elevation in about eighteen river miles. It is a fast mountain stream which used to turn the once considerable mills of Hinsdale, and still does contribute a good part of the power to the big paper and other mills of Dalton.

The Middle, or North, Branch of the Headwaters is immediately the outlet of big Pontoosuc Lake, just north of Pittsfield City, and back of that is its inlet, called Town Brook, coming down from New Ashford through Lanesboro. It assembles from three big springs on a hill called Brodie Mountain, and by the time it dives under near-by Route 7 it is a gay, racing stream. But in its gravelly bed under the concrete bridge it performs the remarkable feat of disappearing from the face of the earth into subterranean courses. About a hundred yards to the east a series of springs boiling up in a cow pasture suggests the return to the light of the lost river. From there on it heads southward in a leisurely way.

The interest of the North Branch is less in the stream than in Pratt Hill, a spur of Greylock two miles southeast of the stream's rising, that is the true head and beginning of the long chute of the Housatonic Valley. From Pratt Hill the great groove down through the highlands, scarcely ten miles wide in these upper reaches, is spectacularly visible southward over Pittsfield for about a third of its entire length, the Massachusetts third which I call the Upper Valley. On the left another spur of Greylock runs south to merge, after it is penetrated by the East Branch, into the eastern rampart of the valley, at first long October Mountain, one of the biggest of the Hoosacs, and afterwards the Beartown Mountains, the

Green Mountains, and other names that change in almost every new township.

On the right are the taller Taconics, visible even under normal haze for thirty miles down to 2,300-foot Mt. Everett, or "The Dome," just north of the Connecticut line. With Monument Mountain, jutting out from the Beartowns to overlap it, it forms a sort of titanic gateway through which the river spills southward into the Lower Valley, the crest of whose eastern wall, Canaan Mountain, is visible over Monument on clear days.

Besides the eastern and western walls, there are visible from Pratt Hill the remnants of a medial range that once ran down the center of the valley and still puts up respectably large hills down through Lenox. The one in the foreground is called Constitution Hill in commemoration of a famous bonfire and celebration which Lanesboro staged there in honor of its illiterate delegate whose speech before the Massachusetts Constitutional Convention of 1787 is said to have carried the day for the Union. Ten miles farther southward, South Mountain pre-empts the middle of the panorama, then Yokun Seat and Baldhead running down into Lenox. There can be seen the first transverse horizon, the first abrupt drop in the central level of the valley, the first of the huge, geologic steps by which it descends to the sea. Above this horizon extrude the heads of Monument and Everett, sloping down to each other to form the gateway to the South.

For the most part the thirty-three air-line miles of the Upper Valley, especially the part south of Monument Mountain, are wide and flat, the mountains set far back on both sides, rising on the average about fifteen hundred feet above the valley floor. The river drops from a thousand-foot elevation in Pittsfield to about six hundred in Canaan, Connecticut, but since most of this drop is taken in a few, brief reaches, especially those which turn the paper mills in Lee, Housatonic, and Rising, the stream for most of this phase is sluggish and meandering. Indeed, it winds almost double the amount of its actual progress southward, frequently turning all the way back and biting into itself to make little islands.

Here in the flatlands is one of the best agricultural sections of the valley, which means one of the best in New England.

The third part of the river and the valley, which I shall call the Lower River and the Lower Valley, begins at the Great Falls at Falls Village, in Canaan, Connecticut, about six miles south of the state line, and runs with only one major bend for some fifty-five crow flight miles down to Derby and Shelton, picking up many tributaries and increasing in width from about fifty to a hundred yards. Throughout this stretch the mountains stand in close to the river that here runs by their picturesque precipices and through their gorges with a uniformly rapid current flecked with white

water, though with only four falls and one rapids that require carries by canoers and fold-boaters in normal times. In rainy seasons, especially spring and fall, when the leaf covering is gone, the cliffs along the river, and along the distant mountains where they are visible, are draped with white bridal-veil falls of little streams and freshets, the nearer ones rustling high up the precipices like a forest wind. The drop at river level is from about six hundred feet at Falls Village to the tide at Derby, and in the last reach the flow is wide and deep and majestic. In the whole Lower Valley there are on the river only three industries large enough to be called factories, with a dozen or more hidden back in the hills.

The fourth, or Tidewater, part of the river begins at industrial Derby and Shelton, where the gorgeous bluffs at

the confluence of the Housatonic, the Naugatuck, and the
ocean tides are ubiquitously disfigured and vilified by chimneys, smoke and slums. From here down, the river widens
between sycamore trees, salt marshes and fertile peneplanes
for thirteen tidal miles to its good harbor at Stratford, and so
between Milford and Stratford Points to Long Island Sound
and the sea.

Of the four parts of the valley, the central two, namely,
the Upper Valley and the Lower Valley, constitute together
about ninety of the valley's hundred and fifteen miles of
over-all length. It is in this main central stretch, neglecting
both the Headwaters and the Tidewater, that the qualities
of the region are most apparent, the combination of graceful, wooded mountains and cultivated, wholly agrarian lowlands, of quiet wilderness surrounding long-settled farms
and the villages that serve them.

In the past, these conditions have been approximated
in other river valleys in the East; but there is no other river
valley in the populous parts of the country where they are
preserved today to the degree that the Housatonic Valley
preserves them. The region is unique in having been occupied
and farmed for three hundred years, in being closely flanked,
east and west, by two of the earth's most highly industrialized districts, in itself possessing the resources that at least
equally invited exploitation, yet in having resisted it in a
contest of forces that make up the drama of its history.
Twenty miles to the east the Naugatuck Valley clanks and
reeks with "progress." Forty miles to the west the beauty of
the Mohawk Valley and much of that of the Hudson Valley
have disappeared under cities, smoke, chimneys, garish highways, dumps, billboards, and summer slums. Between and
above them, the Housatonic, with water power greater than
one and equal to the other, pours down its marble bed between iron hills, bordered by one of the two oldest real railroads in New England, one that was built to reach its
superior resources. And still the Housatonic remains almost
as undeveloped by industry and commerce, its minerals almost as hidden under forests, and its valley as green, agricul-

tural, and thinly populated as in the eighteenth century. Not a municipality of six thousand occurs in the main, central valley, and there are only twelve factories on the hundred and twenty river miles with hundreds of unused power sites between Pittsfield and Derby. Only the hills and the farms and the little villages remain, sequestered, scarcely changed from what they were when the white men first settled here to worship Truth in their fashion.

Whether as a cause or a result of its continuing pristine state, an impressive number of people have, from the earliest days, followed intellectual pursuits in the valley, theologians, political philosophers, miscellaneous writers, educators, scientists, artists and musicians who have come here to escape from the outer world's too insistent reminders of changeful time. Some have been born here, but more have immigrated in maturity, and many have been merely regular summer residents. The valley is less a cradle than a workshop for seekers of truth. For the large proportion of them in its population, it can claim a very high place in America.

At the arbitrarily taken dates of 1820 and 1860, I have compared, with respect to the number and proportion of people in the *Dictionary of American Biography*, the valley of the Housatonic with that of the Charles. Since the latter contained Cambridge and Boston, I presumed that it would embrace the most distinguished population in New England and so, at the dates taken, in America. In the population of the Housatonic Valley I included seasonal residents who either owned or regularly rented property there, or who are known to have done some of their best work there. For the year 1820, the Charles Valley shows more than double the proportion of distinguished residents than the Housatonic Valley does, Boston being then small and the Charles Valley rural. But in 1860, when Boston was a big city and the Charles Valley had quadrupled in population, the still rural Housatonic region drew abreast of its eastern rival, where it has since approximately remained.

In the second table the figures for distinguished people are taken from *Who's Who* for 1940. The Housatonic Valley clearly leads the entire United States, as it does New York and Chicago. It is a trifle behind the Charles Valley and well behind the smallish city of New Haven, where the *Who's Who*-filling university has a greater infleuence on the ratio of distinction to general population than is the case in Boston. If the inquiry be confined to the long, central, cityless reach of the Housatonic Valley between Pittsfield and Derby, then its proportion of distinction exceeds that of any other region examined.

	1820			1860		
	Popu-lation	No. in Dic. Ameri-can Biog.	No. per 10,000 in Dic. Amer. Biog.	Popu-lation	No. in Dic. Ameri-can Biog.	No. per 10,000 in Dic. Amer. Biog.
Housatonic River Valley	73,570	71	9.7	96,323	97	10.
Charles River Valley	83,133	184	22.2	312,483	305	9.8

1940	Population	No. in Who's Who	No. in Who's Who per 10,000
Housatonic Valley,	212,063	208	9.8
Entire U.S.	134,146,298	31,752	2.4
Chicago	3,396,808	1,346	4.0
New York	7,454,995	5,110	6.9
Charles River Valley	1,264,327	1,360	10.8
New Haven	160,605	222	13.8
Housatonic Valley excluding Headwaters, Tidewater, and Danbury	65,525	173	26.4

Looking back over the record of three hundred years, it seems impossible to seize upon any single cause as *the* reason why the forces of growth have here so effectively resisted the forces of destruction, why, in spite of inviting natural resources, the example of neighboring regions, and the tendencies of the industrial age, the beauty of the landscape, the strong intellectual tradition, and the stable agrarian economy without either squalor or great wealth have remained. The contest has often been close, though in the past the opposing forces were rarely aware of each other and their rivalry. Today they are very much aware of the issue, and, strengthened by the most recent immigration, the forces that desire to preserve the valley are probably the stronger. For another century or more the valley may well remain what the Indians first called it, "Hous-aton-uck," the *Place-beyond-the-mountains*, the place where you climb up over the Litchfield Hills or the Berkshires and come down into a wide land where the symbols of eternal truth lie quietly around you yet, and the Great River still flows untroubled by the values of the outer world.

In view of these qualities, I might have given this story of the Housatonic the subtitle "River of Truth." But, because the Puritans were the first truth seekers here and started the tradition of the valley flowing, and because their affirmative qualities have been in large part preserved both in the native Yankees and in the successive invasions of intellectuals, I have called it *Puritan River*. The word "Puritan" has for so long been used negatively, and ignorantly, to denote blue-nosed intolerance that it is time to recall its real and affirmative significance. The essential quality of the Puritan was that he lived in, or hoped he lived in, what he called the State of Grace. In Calvinist theology this meant that he had been assigned a part, however tiny, in the magnificent cosmic drama of the creation, the fall of man, his redemption and salvation. In immediate fact it meant that he was a Platonist, finding reality in an idea in his mind or imagination, and directing his life in accordance with the idea.

Besides its Platonic quality, there were at least three important features of this "inner light," this "heart religion," this domination of life by an idea, which continue to distinguish it today in those who follow it in their fashion. First, it was attainable only through disciplined thought— every Puritan was, in his degree, an intellectual. Second, it was an individual matter, having nothing to do with any priest, bishop or other authority. Third, the satisfactions accompanying the grasp and application of the inner idea were likewise in the mind, and were in contrast to the gratifications of sense and vanity in the material world. All three of these qualities have distinguished the residents of the valley in the past and continue to distinguish them, whether they are ministers, farmers, villagers, merchants, writers, educators, scientists, painters, sculptors or musicians.

In passing I would like to record a few specific protests against the strange reputation latterly given the Puritans by blackwashing historians who make a profession of detracting New England. To begin with, the real Puritan was not, as now universally believed, primarily interested in anybody else's conduct. Conduct was a secondary matter with him. It was important only as an indication of the presence or absence of the State of Grace, for it was the latter upon which the qualification for church membership was based. Once you had achieved that state, it was presumed that your conduct would take care of itself. It was only in the two main periods of Puritan decay—one between about 1675 and 1725, and especially the final one called "Victorianism" —that the descendants of the Puritans concerned themselves with conduct for its own sake and so became touched with smugness, propriety, snobbery, and the ensuing hypocrisies.

The warrant for the accusation of intolerance which has been fondly pinned on the Puritans by America's Europe-flattering apologists is largely derived from a work of irritated fancy touching the fictitious "Blue Laws of Connecticut," composed by one Reverend Samuel Peters, an Episcopal minister, a Tory, and a faintly picturesque liar. He was used a little roughly by the Sons of Liberty in 1774—he claimed

that his robe was torn—fled to England, and composed his
authoritative work.[1] He makes much of capital crimes and
"bloodie" cruelty generally. A few facts in rebuttal will
suffice.

In 1602 England had 31 capital crimes; and the number
gradually increased to 223 in 1819. In 1656 Massachusetts
and New Haven colonies had 16 each, and Connecticut
Colony 14; and the number decreased thereafter in all three
colonies. Of the other American plantations, New York and
Virginia, while more moderate in this respect than England,
were less so than the Puritan establishments.

As for witchcraft, the delusion of it possessed the whole
Occidental world in the sixteenth, seventeenth, and part of
the eighteenth centuries, during which time it is estimated
that there were a hundred thousand executions in Europe,
perhaps one in five hundred of the average population during
the period. Until 1697, when the mania ended in America—
though not abroad, there were either nine or eleven executions in Connecticut, one of the doubtful ones being of
Goody Bassett of Stratford, the only case in the valley. During the same period there were thirty-two executions in
Massachusetts, making a maximum total of forty-three, or
one in about seven thousand of the average population of the
two colonies.

In the matter of "cruel and unusual punishments," the
Puritans were also much farther advanced out of medieval-
ism than the mother country, and somewhat more liberal
than New York and Virginia. The same was true of the use
of torture to extract evidence. Nowhere in America were
the Nazi horrors of the British Star Chamber even remotely
rivaled, least of all in the New England colonies.

Of all the accomplishments of the Puritan-baiters, none
is more groundless than the reputation they have given them
for religious intolerance. Here, as in all things, they can be
truly pictured only against the background of their times,
not ours. Religious toleration as we know it today was upheld

---

[1] For a thorough examination of Peters's famous forgery, see *The True-Blue
Laws of Connecticut and New Haven*, by J. Hammond Trumbull, 1876.

by no state in the early seventeenth century. The Puritans did not flee from ghastly legalized persecution in England in order to establish that yet unknown principle—which one of their number, Roger Williams, was going to be the first to promulgate and practice. Nor did they claim that their settlements were havens for any sects but their own. They undertook certain privation and possible violent and early death in order to worship God in their own way, and once they had hewn out their settlements, they asked only to be let alone. There was plenty more wilderness available. Let the Quakers and Ranters and Baptists found their own settlements, instead of meddling with those who had already established theirs with great hardship.

The British law the Puritans fled from was far more cruel to heretics than the laws they adopted. It imprisoned all nonconformists, banished them after three months if they did not make public confession and submission, and killed them "without benefit of clergy" if they failed to obey the sentence of banishment or returned after their initial departure.

The laws of Virginia and New York against heresy were milder than those of Great Britain, but more stringent than those of New England. Massachusetts, like Virginia, killed Quakers who, having been twiced banished, returned the third time. Connecticut—which incidentally included all of the settled part of the Housatonic Valley until after religious tolerance had become universal—never had any law against heresy at all. The extent of intolerance, as actually practiced by all the Puritans against people of different faiths, was stated in the law of New Haven Colony. It recognized freedom of private conscience, but forbade "broaching, publishing or maintaining any dangerous errour or heresie, or shall endeavour to draw, or seduce others thereto," the punishment being normally fine or banishment. That is, every man's private belief was his own affair, but when he began to *preach* any unorthodox "errour" and so threatened what the Puritans at great pains and danger had built, then they invited him either to desist or to leave.

In passing, it may be worth noting why the Puritans, like the rest of the Anglo-American world, were particularly severe against Quakers. The reason was that in the seventeenth century the Quakers were something quite different from the promoters of peace and brotherly love who are now universally admired. Their quietism did not appear till a century after, and in the period of Puritan settlement they were, for the most part, an ignorant and militant sect whose members made a practice of attending other meetings—especially Puritan meetings—for the avowed purpose of disrupting them. To this end they habitually violated ordinary decorum, keeping their hats on, heckling the minister, and sometimes breaking into his sermon to harangue the congregation. It is understandable that this made them unpopular.

In our modern intolerance of the founders of our country, we would do well to inform ourselves concerning the times in which they lived. We would also do well to recall that they actually believed in and tried to live by a great religious faith. They were as tolerant as they could be and maintain their integrity. We, having no faith, can be tolerant of anything except faith, with a tolerance that is empty.

But the importance of the record of the Puritans is not to rebut their detractors; it is to remind us of their positive contributions to America and the world. By the 1620's, when they began coming to America, their principle of religious individualism was already expanded to include political individualism. In the earliest expressions of the first American Puritans and in the governments they founded, the doctrine is established that no man is to be governed but by his consent, that government comprises a contract or "covenant" between the rulers and the governed, and that when the former break the contract the latter have the right to take up arms in defense of their freedom. By the middle 1630's, Massachusetts and Connecticut had embodied these principles in instruments which, after that of their neighbor Plymouth Colony, were the first of America's series of written constitutions. Between these instruments and the correspondence of the men who drew them we find all the basic doctrines and much of the language of the great documents of a century and a half later.

At the same early period the theory of individualism was being applied as local democracy, first, in the religious congregationalism and, second, in the expansion of the principle to the town meeting where likewise majority vote prevailed. The now popular assumption that until some quite recent date all of New England except Rhode Island was theocratic—that is, limited the vote to church members—is contrary to fact. Massachusetts, the largest colony, had universal male suffrange, with a small property qualification, in town matters, but in colony elections limited the vote to church members until 1690. Connecticut, the second largest colony, allowed universal male suffrage in all respects from the beginning, was in fact founded in protest against the theocracy of Massachusetts. New Haven had thoroughgoing theocracy until 1665, when it united with Connecticut and accepted the latter's liberal constitution. Actually, there was no organized settlement in the Upper, or Massachusetts, part of the Housatonic Valley until more than thirty years after that colony's abandonment of theocracy. Wherefore, with the exception of Milford which, between 1643 and 1665, unwillingly and with reservations followed the New Haven theocracy, the suffrage in the valley was never limited except by the very small property qualification which was universal in America till the early nineteenth century. It is true that the popularly elected magistrates, the chief civil officials, were often drawn from the congregationally elected Seven Pillars of the Church, the chief ecclesiastical officials. But this was by free choice, and if the people wanted a magistrate or member of the Assembly or any other official who was a Quaker or an Episcopalian or an atheist, as they often did, they got him.

Of only slightly less importance than the spiritual and political legacies of the Puritans was their intellectual legacy. For them religious experience was not only an emotional but also an intellectual affair, and was possible only after a thorough understanding of the nice complexities of Calvinist

theology. The bulk of the colonists came from the educated
classes—four-fifths of the families of Connecticut were entitled to coats of arms. What is almost incredible today is that
these people—many of whom we would call "intellectuals,"
coming from comfortable homes and not at all accustomed
to physical hardship—lived in perpetual, mortal danger on
their tiny frontiers, spent all their secular, waking hours in
the crudest labor, and then, assembling twice on Sunday and
once on lecture-day—usually Thursday—in an unheated,
usually windowless, log meetinghouse with slabs for seats,
not only endured but insisted upon one- to two-hour sermons of the utmost scholastic refinement. Out of this eagerness and vitality came most of the American educational
tradition, which fact the detractors of the Puritans have not
been able wholly to conceal.

The Puritan plantations generally had schools going as
soon as churches and before anybody was well under cover.
The earliest colonial enactments of Massachusetts, Connecticut and New Haven contain maximum requirements for
the education of children and apprentices at home. By 1640,
each of the three colonies required every plantation to maintain a school, and before long the governments were prescribing all details regarding them. "Grammar" or "Latin"
—what we might call high—schools were required in towns
of a hundred families in Massachusetts and in the county
towns of Connecticut, and many smaller towns maintained
them without compulsion of law. Although the local school
law enforcement was often inadequate, nevertheless, by 1700
the two colonies that governed the valley did have systems
of universal, compulsory, free, elementary education, with
secondary education available for a tiny fee.

Meanwhile, Harvard had been flourishing since 1644, all
the towns of New England sending voluntary contributions
"for the maintenance of poor scholars"—recognizing that
higher education was not a luxury for the rich but should be
available "to such young plants worthy for His [Christ's]
service" as should be thought "meet and worthy." In 1701
the "collegiate school," shortly to be called Yale, was founded

and became the college for the youth of most of the valley. The Reverend Israel Chauncey of Stratford at the river's mouth declined the first presidency, but the Reverend Samuel Andrew of Milford across the river was the second president, and the Reverend Timothy Cutler of Stratford the third. The fourth president, the Reverend Elisha Williams, was not from the valley, but he did have a part in the valley's first major struggle between Puritan idealism and Puritan greed.

In the matter of Puritan, and subsequently Yankee, greed, we come to the negative quality of the founders in the celebration of which the detractors of Puritanism find themselves on partly solid ground. Puritanism was an aspect of the Renaissance, and so was identified with economic as well as religious and political individualism, with the rise of the middle class and the enshrining of the profitable virtues of industriousness, parsimony and shrewdness in trade and finance. Almost without exception, the early Puritan divines preached to their congregations that the earth was the Lord's garden and that He desired them, His Chosen People, to develop its fullness to the glory of Himself and their own prosperity. The application of this injunction was indeed necessary to bare survival in the beginning, and it remains harmless enough today among rural Yankees whose farthest economic dream is to accumulate enough to pay the mortgage and leave something to bury them. There is nothing reprehensible in a shrewd swap when the exchange of an animal or a crop may mean the difference between plenty and too little on the family board next winter. There is something endearing in the Yankee inconsistency that will trim you when challenged to a deal, but will devote hours and days to "helping" you as a neighbor and refuse pay for it, and will fill your kitchen with rich food when your wife is ailing.

But under the spectacular temptations of the industrial revolution and the opening of the West, it was the original, simple shrewdness that saw the long chance and became the worst of Yankee and American traits, the competitive desire for wealth and power, not as a means of survival but for their own sakes, the pursuit of them as the objects of life, and, in the extremity of urban degeneracy, the admiration of those who possessed them, whether or not they also possessed intelligence and virtue. Encouraged by science, and adapting the old Puritan idealism to its uses, this lust for power has accomplished America's material conquest of the earth, and her current efforts at spiritual suicide, which may or may not prove successful.

But while the Puritan vices of greed and shrewdness have been having their innings, the Puritan virtues of individualism, intellectuality and life in service of some idea or other have also survived in numerous forms and groups. Most evidently they have survived in the rural Yankee. In his individualism in politics, in his unwillingness to organize even for his own obvious interest, in his entire independence of anybody's opinion of him, in his courtesy such as is possible only in one who is inwardly self-sufficient, in his incapability of being bribed or bought—in all these respects his individualism is evident and has been sufficiently celebrated. His essential intellectuality and his devoted idealism are less evident, for typically he is not educated beyond high school, and, while he probably goes to church and behaves himself tolerably well, he is not usually religious in any orthodox sense.

He is, in fact, a pretty close replica, not of the real Puritans who were in the State of Grace, and belonged to the Church, but of what might be called the Quasi Puritans, those who in fact comprised a majority of most of the Puritan communities. These were people of Puritan leanings who went to church regularly and professed the doctrine, but who for one reason or other stayed outside the formal fold during the early, strict period when the conditions of admission were severe. Under the perpetual challenge of the pulpit and their neighbors, they were driven to study and puzzle their way into their own private and miscellaneous convictions about God, grace, truth and all ultimate values, and to order their lives accordingly.

By the Revolutionary period, when orthodox Puritanism had shriveled beyond recognition, it had created a civilization every member of which, beginning in youth, thought his way into some private conviction about life and the world, one which he might or might not choose to share with his neighbors. According to his lights, he went through an intellectual process by which he arrived at the psychological equivalent of the State of Grace. This secret light, this relic of Jonathan Edwards's "heart religion," varied as widely as individual capacity and training. It might be as pretentious as a religious, philosophical or moral system. It might be the battle hymn of a crusade. Or it might be no more than a private conviction about conduct or politics, or maybe the love—or the hatred—of a lifetime. But, whatever it might be, it made its possessor permanently sufficient against the world, indifferent to its opinion of him, and brought down on him the chronic scorn of extroverts who move by external action from transient satisfaction to transient satisfaction.

But while the rustic Yankee recalls his Puritan ancestor in his greed—of the harmless, swapping variety, in his individualism, in his essential intellectuality and idealism, he has acquired through the centuries an important quality, the legacy of sophistication, which his forebears did not possess. The proper Puritans were seldom if ever troubled by what they called levity and we would call humor. They believed their Bible in every literal detail. Solemnly they believed that they were themselves the Chosen People of God, that rocky and icy New England was the new Promised Land whither He was leading them, and that the New Jerusalem would descend in glory as soon as they were well established on the new and golden shore. It was the material of major tragedy when, after they had indeed established themselves by dint of great courage, not only did the New Jerusalem fail to descend but the second and third and fourth generations turned from the complete and literal faith of their fathers and grandfathers.

But with this "sliding off" during the second half of the seventeenth century, the basic seriousness, the zeal for truth, was in fact neither weakened nor lost. Instead, there grew over its pith an earthy crust, a crackly shell, a realization of the incongruity between literally unknowable truth and the all too literal faith and professions of the fathers. In this sense of incongruity there began to appear somewhere along in the eighteenth century that humor whose possession a century later was to distinguish the Yankee from his ancestors. The Yankee is a Puritan soul and a Puritan mind, but tinctured for three gradual centuries by the poison of worldly understanding, a poison whose only antidote is laughter, a laughter as profound as the basic illusion that must be preserved in spite of the superficial understanding. In the tremendous intellectual honesty of the Puritans lay the foundation of that Yankee humor which is so bitterly profound because grounded in a faith that is never quite lost, so universally wise because it contains the living tragedy of human aspiration, so skeptical at once of the rewards of virtue and of vice, of poverty and riches, of the world and heaven, skeptical of everything except its own integrity and a quiet, unutterable and smiling faith that somewhere there is a Reason. In passionate individualism, intellectual aspiration, spiritual conviction, industriousness and shrewdness we find the complete Puritan. And if, without destroying these qualities, we sadden them all with great humor, we get the complete Yankee.

Actually, the modern Yankee and his secret god is but a sorry relic of his gigantic ancestors with their heroic expectation of a perfect and divinely ruled world. A closer suggestion of the passionately held and openly declared idealism of the original Puritans, and the equally consecrated Quasi Puritans, is to be found in other passionate and open idealisms—political, philosophical, aesthetic or scientific—whether they are of a religious color or not. Thus it is that, while the Yankee farmers of the Housatonic Valley maintain an essential Puritan integrity as against their industrial and commercial neighbors over the hill, yet it is those, whether natives or outsiders, who down the ages have openly pursued some form of truth in the valley, who are the proper heirs of the strength and the idealism of the first settlers. It is they who have fought the long war of Puritan idealism against the Puritan greed, essentially the conflict between the Lord and the Devil, that has been the drama of America, and so, in microcosm, the drama of the valley. In the country as a whole that drama continues unresolved. But in the valley one complete production of it, possibly a preview of the whole, has been completed, with the forces of the Lord triumphing and those of the Devil got firmly under the heel.

This drama of the valley, which is the theme of this story, divides naturally into five acts, in each of which the Lord and the Devil appear respectively in slightly different roles.

In the First Act, the Lord thunders as the true Puritan God, the architect of the cosmic theater and the author and producer of its drama, while the Devil whispers of wealth in cheap land to be had from the Indians.

In the Second Act, the Lord appears as the Rights of Man, while the Devil, still whispering of profit in cheap land, delights to confuse the new liberty with irresponsible license.

In the Third Act, the war is bitter between the new science and industrialism that are beginning to destroy idealism in the rest of America and the great surge of humanitarianism that shows itself in the valley in the reform of education and in America's first age of indigenous literature.

In the Fourth Act, the Devil enters in the guise of new wealth that has been accumulated outside the valley, and makes his sublest attack in terms of gentility, the tallyho, and the Switzerland of America, while the Lord resists in a display of detached, scientific inventiveness. The final failure of the Devil in this act would seem to depend little on the victory of idealism, but rather on the irrelevant chance that most of the great fortunes in the valley crumpled, for extraneous reasons, after 1929.

The Fifth Act is less a drama than an epilogue, a final seal upon the victory of the Lord, the triumph of idealism. The triumph was intimated before 1920, and by 1930 the valley was the scene of a powerful invasion of writers, musicians, painters, educators and miscellaneous intellectuals, people mostly of small means buying up the old Puritan farms, many for summer homes only, but more and more of them staying out the winters and growing into the lives of the townships.

In these people, more numerously and convincingly perhaps than at any other time in two centuries, we see the valley being rededicated to the pursuit of truth. Most of them know what great wealth did to America in the past hundred years, and they are determined that their votes and their increasing influence in the communities will be used in the interest of themselves and their farmer neighbors against any further attempt of the Devil to despoil the valley. The curtain of America's first complete drama is falling now, coming down on the valley as the same haven for hungry souls that it was when the first shipload of Puritans landed in 1639. The Great River is still the same symbol of the change within unity that is the truth of the universe, the symbol that anyone may still read here without the confusion of smoke or traffic or the awareness of misery around him. It is too early to guess whether in future centuries America may again seek truth in terms of the Puritan God, the Mind of the cosmos. If that time comes, the Great Valley and its people will be ready and rehearsed to start the drama over. The Great River will become again in literal fact, as in tradition and psychological fact, a Puritan River.

The Promised Land

The First Billion and a Half Years

NEW ENGLAND has never quite forgotten that in the old days it was a separate continent. The old days were the first five and most of the sixth day of Biblical creation. Or, if you prefer, they were almost all of a billion and a half years of geologic history which the scientists find recorded in the rocks. It is only in the last fifty million years or so that New England has accepted the inevitable and joined the unwieldy continental union which we call North America.

The old continent of New England went north into Canada about as far as the present St. Lawrence River, and south to include Long Island. Its eastern shore was a good way out in what we call the Atlantic, and sometimes its western shore included most of modern New York State. The scientists call it Acadia, because that is a pretty name, or perhaps because they lack proper respect for New England. To the northwest, beyond a stretch of ocean, was another little continent which they call Canadia. To the southwest was another named Appalachia.

From the earliest geologic time, western Acadia, where the valley was to be, has been "the place beyond the mountains." From the age of fire and steam, when the earth's crust was cooling into shape, it remained restless over this upland. Every twenty or thirty million years, either the underlying fire or the lateral pressure of the contracting earth's crust would heave up volcanic peaks five or six miles into the sky. Then the volcanoes would quiet down, the broken crust would lie jagged in upended fragments, and for a quiet aeon frost and water would whittle down the giants, spilling out the sediment in strata that filled the valleys and lay eastard and westward over lowlands and out over the ocean floor. Then another period of fire and shrinking crust would thrust up mountains again, and the whole process would be repeated. October Mountain, Monument, Bear, Everett, Riga, Canaan, Sharon, Skiff, and the hundreds of others are the worn stumps of what were once the loftiest mountains in the world. Throughout these ages, the drainage of Acadia's western highland was into either the western or the eastern ocean. There was no ancestral, north-and-south Housatonic Valley where a great river ran into the southern sea.

During most of the billion and a half years of the old days there was life of sorts around Acadia or upon it. For the first billion years it was all in the sea or in the rivers, with a little greenery groping into the air along the shores. During this time, the fish got such a head start that the Yankees haven't yet been able to catch them all. After a billion years, real forests and flowering plants began to cover the gray rocks, and the oldest fossils in New England are of some of the latter from the western mountains where the valley was to be. Certain fish experimented with breathing air, and out of these amphibians reptiles emerged that ran on the land and forgot the water entirely. The old days ended picturesquely with the dinosaurs, the biggest animals that ever lived. They left their footprints and bones here and there in Acadia, but there is no evidence that they ever carried their ponderosity up into the western mountains. After the dinosaurs were exterminated—by what process is still in doubt—the new days, the epoch of recent life, dawned with little mammals that suggested their modern descendants. On the Biblical analogy, the sixth and last day of creation began.

This end of the old days and dawn of the new occurred about fifty million years ago. Geologically, it was marked by a very special mountain uplift which involved few if any volcanic eruptions and was not a local affair in Acadia. It likewise involved Canadia and Appalachia, generally the whole eastern part of the great new continent whose coast line it lifted out of the ocean. From southern Appalachia, in modern Alabama, to northern Acadia, in modern Quebec, it was as if some earth-huge Titan put his hands on the carpet of the earth's crust about two hundred miles apart and pushed them steadily together for perhaps a million years. The carpet, much of which had before been on the ocean floor, bowed up in a thousand-mile-long welt running exactly northeast and southwest. The welt was the whole Appalachian ridge, the backbone of eastern North America. It shed off the sea between Appalachia and Acadia and Canadia forever, and lifted its western slope far out to drain the ocean from the great plains and complete the rough outlines of the big continent. The high point of the new range was in New York, a little west of where the primordial Berkshires had been. Everywhere from the new heights, new rivers began to pour southeast to the Atlantic, the beginnings of most of the great rivers of the eastern seaboard today, the Santee, the James, the Potomac, the Rappahannock, the Susquehanna, the Delaware, the Connecticut, the Merrimack, the Kennebec, and among them, the Housatonic.

In the beginning, the Housatonic was a straight river flowing southeast all the way, and the lower third of the modern stream, traveling southeast from the big bend at Scatacook in northern Sherman, still runs in its primeval, fifty-million-year-old bed. Above the big bend, the original upper reaches came straight down from the northwest, far over in New York State beyond the future Hudson Valley. For a precarious age, it looked as if one of New England's big rivers was going to be sourced in New York. But the primitive Hudson, then a mere tributary of the Delaware, took care of that. Nibbling its way headward, it broke through the banks of the Housatonic and stole its headwaters. What had before been the biggest tributary of the Housatonic, running south out of Massachusetts to join it at Scatacook, became the main stream that has since boiled around the big bend there. Deprived of its original sources, the Housatonic became a smaller river, as its old shore lines high along the hills below Gaylordsville bear witness. But it became exclusively a New England river, and the geologic honors of both New York and New England were saved.

Meanwhile, the promised land has swarmed increasingly with life. At first it was a tropical jungle, with the diminutive

ancestors of tigers, elephants, rhinoceroses, tapirs, horses and dogs. Later, as the climate grew cooler, the forest took its modern form, and the animals began to look like moose, deer, wolf, bear and bison, while the monarchs were the mastodon and the saber-toothed tiger.

A million years ago, the Glacial Ages began. For four periods of about a hundred thousand years each, the valley lay under an ice sheet at least a thousand feet deep. Between the glaciations there were long temperate periods when life returned. The weight and slow flow of the glaciers did not alter the topography of the region. But it did scoop off the precious topsoil from the hills and dump it into the ocean south of Long Island that until very recently was part of the mainland. Having scraped off the soil, the ice sandpapered and scratched the underlying granite, deposited piles of gravel here and there, and scattered everywhere the billions of boulders that the Yankees have hauled out of the ground and piled into walls.

It was only twenty thousand years ago that the fourth ice sheet was all gone, and the time since has been too short for much topsoil to weather out of the rocks. The landscape was taking its complete modern aspect, and the new forest teemed with the creatures man has known, including the vanished heath hen, passenger pigeon and wild turkey. In migration time, the flocks of pigeons overshadowed the sun and made a fluttering twilight in the forest. Waterfowl and fish crammed the streams and ponds, and every spring lamprey eels and solid shoals of shad ran up the river and its tributaries. Otter and beaver were plentiful. A vast natural larder and wardrobe was preparing.

There is no evidence that the valley—or any other part of America—ever cradled any of the primitive ancestors of Man. That grave responsibility was left to the more experimental, old world. After he finally entered this continent from the west, New England was probably the last region to accept this strange, nervous creature. No one knows just when he slipped through the mountains into the valley of the Housatonic. But if the rock-recorded, geologic time is an hour, it was less than a thousandth of a second ago. It was late in the twilight of the sixth day of Biblical creation. And here the analogy of Genesis breaks down. Having set man in New England, the Lord neither rested nor let him rest.

Heathen in the Land

THE FIRST human beings to inhabit the valley were the heathen of the Mohican family of the great Algonkin race. They did not come in search of truth, but were driven out of the Hudson Valley. Those who entered the upper Housatonic region were probably expelled by the Dutch, in the first half of the seventeenth century, those of the lower valley by stronger Indians, at an earlier but not remotely earlier date. They brought with them one great human quality, the recognition of a Great Spirit informing all things, whom they would rejoin after death in the Happy Hunting Grounds far to the southwest. Otherwise, they were a paradoxical people: generally faithful to their larger, treaty undertakings, but rarely above petty pilfering; magnificent in courtesy and picturesque in dress, but filthier in person than any animals; capable of great fortitude under physical suffering and strain, yet without self-control in eating, drinking and gambling; affectionately generous, and at the same time subhumanly cruel.

Though the men were of splendid physique, they were an unwarlike, submissive and pessimistic people. Their solution of emotional problems was suicide, normally by leaping from a cliff into the arms of the Great Spirit, after singing a hymn to apprise him of their approach. Bryant immortalized the legend of the maiden who leapt from the escarpment of Monument Mountain, after her betrothed was killed in battle. Two young chiefs destroyed themselves in the same way from Mt. Tom in Litchfield. An old sagamore, his land in future Bethlehem having been sold to the English by younger chiefs against his will, climbed to the lofty summit of Nonewaug Falls, chanted his death song and jumped. An Indian girl, having been refused by her family to the brave she loved, and being already bedecked for her enforced marriage to another, ran to the summit of Squaw Rock in South Britain and leapt to her death. Having no doubt that at their death they would be welcomed by the Great Spirit, the chief concern of the river Indians during their bodily lives was with Hobbamocko, the Evil Spirit who, they believed, would ultimately destroy their world. Their principal festivals were horrid orgies to propitiate him, during which the frenzied powwows or medicine men threw their possessions and sometimes their children into the flames.

The river Indians lived in villages ranging from two or three up to a hundred or more families. The normal family occupied a hide wigwam, while the hereditary sachems and nonhereditary sagamores had houses, sometimes a hundred feet in length, framed of bent saplings and covered with bark. Occasionally, several families occupied a long house with a chief, and ceremonial dances were held in their halls in the winter. On defensible high ground near their principal settlements, the sachems and sagamores usually maintained palisaded forts.

The Indians were in the Stone Age of culture, and their livelihood was by hunting, fishing and crude agriculture. The women, squat, deformed—and frequently sterile—from overwork, cultivated corn, squashes, and a few beans with wooden or stone hoes. The men raised tobacco, but otherwise were above manual labor. In the autumn they burned the underbrush out of the forest, both to clear the view for hunting and to fertilize for planting. Each spring all the tribes came downriver to catch shad anywhere below the Great Falls at New Milford, which was the top of their run. Thence they proceeded down to the Sound, where they spent the summer digging shellfish on the beaches of Milford and Stratford, feasting on them and making wampum from their shells. After the English came, black wampum beads—made from the eye of the hen clam—passed current in the settlements at three for a penny. Twenty-four acres on Milford Point were virtually covered with discarded clamshells. On the Stratford side of the river, just above the railroad bridge, a large heap of them remains today, having somehow escaped use for either road building or fertilizer.

All the Indians of the valley were one people in physique, language, law, customs, and way of life generally. When the white men appeared, there were at least six fairly well-organized tribes in the Connecticut part of the valley, but only the remnant of one in the Massachusetts part. Although each of the tribes in the Lower Valley was gathered round its own sachem at his "Great Wigwam" or "Council Fire," and although each hunted and planted in a more or less distinct region, yet each made traditional claims roughly to all the land on both sides of the river from the sea to its source.

A plausible explanation of this is that all the tribes represented fairly recent emigrations from a common center —traditionally Scatacook in Kent—and that each group, in moving to a new domain, carried with it all the laws and claims of the parent tribe. Wars of succession were avoided because the hereditary sachems, whose power was absolute and who personally "owned" all their respective tribes' hunting grounds, were all related to each other, constituting a horizontal royal family cutting across the tribal divisions, and they alone understood and applied the traditional laws. The sachems kept in close touch with each other and consulted and acted together on matters of importance. The colonists learned early that, in order to get a good deed to a large tract, it was desirable to get on the deed the marks of as many sachems as possible. The sachems were like brothers, each delegated to rule over his part of the land of their single father, who no longer existed.

The confusion of tribes is further simplified when it is understood that in a philological sense the Indians of the valley were not divided into tribes at all, that they had no generic tribe names. The apparent tribe names were no more than the names of the places where a subdivision of the main tribe lived. The Indians living around the ford were called in their language "The Fords," those near the cleared field were "The Cleared Fields," those at the narrows were "The Narrows," those at the falls were "The Falls," and so forth. When an Indian moved his family from the ford to the cleared field, he was no longer a "Ford," but became a "Cleared Field." Only the sachems were more or less fixed at their little capitals, and around them the "tribes" were fluid. Incidentally, a fact that tended to keep all the Indians unified was their common trek every spring over each other's trails to the fishing grounds down the river, and every summer to the shellfishing grounds on the beaches of the Sound.

Of the six tribes in the Lower Valley, the *Wepawaugs* were centered in the region east of the mouth of the river, at the *Weepwoi-auk*, the "Crossing-place," the ford in modern Milford village across the little river that enters the Sound just east of the Housatonic. With its Anglicized pronunciation and spelling, the stream retains its original name.

Across the Great River, the *Pequannocks* were centered around the *Pauquun-auk*, or "Cleared-land-place," a large and important cornfield in the center of modern Bridgeport. Like the Wepawaugs, the Pequannocks are remembered by the little stream that flowed through their region, the Pequannock River of the modern map.

Above the Wepawaugs on the east bank of the river were the *Paugassets*, whose council fire was at the *Paug-as-et*, the "Water-at-rest-narrow-place." (There were two locative suffixes in the Mohican language, one spelled -auk, -aug, -ac, -uk or -uck, the other -ut or -et.) The *Paug-as-et*, where the river widens from the narrows into quiet, tidal water, was at Derby Neck, occupied by the modern city of Derby which was known by its Indian name until quite late in the white man's history.

On the west bank of the river, above the Pequannocks and opposite the Paugassets, were the *Potatucks*, the inhabitants of the *Powntuck-uck*, the "Falls-place," the region around Derby Falls, modern Shelton. Potatuck is the most important Indian name in the Lower Valley, because there are so many powntuck-ucks, so many falls-places. Either the first or the second Indian settlement in the valley is supposed to have been at the *powntuck-uck*, the great falls, at Bull's Bridge, wherefore the tribe there also called itself the Potatucks. There was at least one other powntuck-uck that gave its name to a subtribe that inhabited not only the vicinity of future Newtown, but also, across the river, the larger region running up the Pomperaug and Shepaug rivers as far as Bethlehem and Litchfield. Though the Great River itself had other local names, its commonest Indian name in the Lower Valley was Potatuck, the River-of-the-Falls-Place. Certainly it retained this name for the thirteen river miles from Derby or Shelton Falls to the sea, though this reach was of quiet, tidal water. With one exception, it is the nearest to a generic name that the Indians bequeathed to the valley. It is remembered in the Lower Valley only in the musical little *Pootatuck River* that pours over its weir in Sandy Hook village in Newtown, and then down its hemlock gorge to the Great River.

The fifth considerable tribe of river Indians was centered some thirty river miles above the Paugassets of Derby and the Potatucks of Shelton. These were the *Weantinocks,* the dwellers at the *Wean-adn-auk,* the "Winds-mountain-place," the place where the river winds around Long Mountain in New Milford. In spite of the rich Indian association with this region, the name has disappeared from the modern map.

The sixth considerable tribe in the Lower valley, when the English came, were the *Weataugs,* Weataug being the name for the Salisbury region, forty to fifty miles north of Weantinock on the border of modern Massachusetts. The meaning of Weataug is uncertain.

Besides the six main tribes, there was a subtribe of the Pequannocks, with whom the earliest white settlers had intimate dealings. These were the *Cupheags,* who lived at *Cuphe-ag,* the "*Shut-in-place,*" the harbor, modern Stratford.

In conformance with the Indians' own legends, it is generally agreed by local historians that they first entered the Lower Valley from the west at Scatacook in southern Kent, about a mile below the original Potatuck, or Falls Place, at Bull's Bridge. The Indian name was *Pishgach-tig-ok,* the "Divided-broad-river-place," the place where a tributary comes into the broad river, specifically the place where the modern Tenmile enters the main stream. It is one of the richest spots in the valley for Indian relics. There is dramatic value in the supposition that the Indians first entered the valley here through the break in the mountains that lets in the Tenmile from New York State; for it was to the general reservation, set aside here by the Colony of Connecticut in 1752, that all the Indians of the Lower Valley gradually contracted, and it is certain that at this point their culture is at this moment coming to an end.

Their resounding place names, usually with the croaking locative suffix, were the most permanent contribution of the river Indians to the valley. Besides *Potatuck, Wepawaug, Pequannock,* and *Scatacook,* which have been mentioned, there are many others that survive on the modern map.

There is a historical paradox between the fact that the Upper Valley, the Massachusetts part from Canaan northward, was at one time populous and the fact that it was almost deserted when the English began to come in during the early eighteenth century. One of the largest concentrations of Indian graves and relics in the whole valley has been found in a small area on the river in Great Barrington village, an area—not a specific building—that was by tradition the central capital or "Great Wigwam" of the neighboring Indians from the earliest times down into the period of English settlement. Yet in 1694 a traveler, crossing the river at this point, wrote in his diary that the place had been "formerly inhabited by Indians," implying that it was then deserted; and, forty years later, it was recorded that the sachems Umpachene, residing with four other families at Skatecook in northern Sheffield—spelled differently from Scatacook in Kent, and Konkapot, living with an equal number of families at Wnahtu-kook, just south of present Stockbridge village, were the only Indians in the whole region between these points.

The traveler's information that the place was "formerly inhabited by Indians" presumably came either from somebody's living memory or from surviving relics of the flimsy, former Indian village which thirty years would obliterate. In either case, it would seem that the exodus had occurred not many years before. Conjecture suggests one of the closing episodes of King Philip's War, in the late summer of 1676, when a band of two hundred fugitive Indians was overtaken and almost annihilated at the ford of the river within the Great Wigwam locality. It may well have been at that time, either before or during the battle, that the local Indians, being unwarlike and not allied with Philip, decamped to join their kin over the Taconics in the Hudson Valley, and so left their capital deserted.

Whatever may have been the prehistory of the original Indians of Berkshire County, Massachusetts, which contains the whole of the Upper Valley, they yet performed the service of establishing the principal and most enduring place name in the valley. When they immigrated, they came in from the west over the mountains, and the place where they established became *Wussi-adene-uk*, the "Beyond-the-Mountain-Place," the country beyond the mountains. The Indians accented the first syllable, and, allowing for the elision that would have occurred at the outset, the original pronunciation would have been close to Wúsadenuk or Wúsatenuk. Through innumerable spellings by the whites—including Westenhook —Westonock— Hooestennuc—Awoostenok—Ansotunnoog —Ousetonuck—Ousatunick—Housatunack—House of Tunnuck (!)—Housatonac—and with the transference of accent to the third syllable, it has reached its modern form, Housatonic. As late as 1859, Princess Mahwee, the last pure-blooded survivor of the Scatacooks in Kent, said that it should be pronounced *Hóu*setenuc.

Like Potatuck, the place name was transferred to numerous features of the region it described. The traveler in 1694 said the place where he crossed the river—otherwise identified as the Great Wigwam—was called "Ousetonuck." Thus the place name was attached to the principal village in that place. And, at the coming of the whites, the Indians of the Upper Valley were known as the Housetonucks, the people who lived in the place beyond the mountains. It was not until the eighteenth century that the name flowed downstream to become generic for the whole River, replacing "Potatuck," "the Great River," and the other Indian and English names that had been used in the Lower Valley.

Outside of surviving place names, the only peculiarly local contribution of the valley Indians to the white man's culture was the baskets of the vestigial, conglomerate tribe at Scatacook in Kent and Sherman. With their ornamental curlicues, these baskets have remained until very recently a source of income for the remnant of the tribe. The numerous other and more valuable legacies of the Indians were universal throughout New England, and not peculiar to the valley: their real science of medicinal herbs, many examples of which survive in modern pharmacy; the mysteries of maple syrup; the whole culture of corn, from planting—"when the leaf of the dog-wood was the size of a squirrel's ear and the first leaf of the oak as large as his foot"—to roasted corn-on-the-cob, succotash ("suktac"), ground meal, corn cakes, and numerous other preparations; the use of bark dyes; the more than two hundred Indian words in the modern American language. A possible survival of the Indian feast of spring was the old Yankee Strawberry Festival. And the white man's Thanksgiving is suggestively reminiscent of the Indians' "corn feast," a gluttonous orgy of thanks to the Earth and the Life Spirit after the harvest was in.

With the exception of the legendary suicide of the maiden on Monument Mountain, the Indian stories that have come down in history or legend belong to the period after the white man's coming in the seventeenth century, and some of them will be recounted in later chapters. At this point in the story of the valley, the period of transition from the Age of the Indians to the Age of the English, it remains only to state a few generalities about the relatively happy relations between the races in this region.

It is true that when the heirs of the weaker culture

came in contact with the stronger the Indians usually degenerated into alcoholics, beggars, petty thieves, and more or less picturesque local characters. Yet, it cannot be said that in the gradual acquisition of the land by the whites, and in their treatment of the Indians generally, there was more than sporadic and exceptional injustice. The behavior of the colonists in settling can be questioned only by denying that a population of not over three thousand natives should have been asked or *permitted* to sell for use their three thousand square miles of wilderness, very little of which they used and none of which they developed. The "natives" themselves had appropriated the territory not many generations before, without paying anything for it. In every case, the colonists acquired the land by means that were legal, by both Indian and English law; and, in every case but one, they got it by fair purchase.

The price scale of between one and ten cents per acre of wilderness, whether paid in money or in excellent tools, weapons, and blankets, was the same scale that the purchasers applied in subsequent resales among themselves. And the Indians often got especially good bargains in collateral terms, such as the reserved right to hunt or plant on the land or much of it, along with other stipulations, which the colonial governments and most of the individual colonists always respected. Important among collateral terms were those dealing with defense. Although the valley Indians undoubtedly feared and hated the English, they had an even greater hatred and fear of their predatory neighbors, the Mohawks to the northwest and the Pequots to the east. Both of these strong tribes exacted regular tribute from the valley, and made additional, sporadic raids there for good measure. Consequently, a frequent stipulation in many of the contracts of sale was that the white purchasers would protect the sellers against the Mohawks and the Pequots, and this the English certainly did.

It can hardly be supposed that individual colonists, who were sharp enough in dealing with one another, would have any reticence about driving sharp bargains with the filthy savages. But their propensities in this direction were repressed by the wise and humane laws of the governments they maintained. Individuals were forbidden by law to buy land from the Indians without authorization by the General Court, and before such authorization was given the court would look minutely into the particular colonist's need of the land, the adequacy of the purchase price, and the remaining resources for self-support of the Indian or Indians involved. In the majority of cases it was the Indians themselves who instigated the sales, with their usual lack of self-control pressing deeds and mortgages on the settlers in return for desired items, whether useful tools, useless baubles or—when it could be bootlegged to them—firewater. There were, of course, scamps who circumvented the law and imposed on the Indians' childishness. But they were few, and they were disciplined when caught.

The generally conscientious treatment of the Indians by the English was commendable in an age when Europeans of all sects recognized either the Lord or the Devil in any unusual phenomenon, and when anyone addicted to curious practices was instantly suspected of being a wizard or a witch, a servant of Satan. The colonists had no doubt from the beginning that the Indians were the get of the Devil, and they loathed them anyway for their filth, their drunkenness and petty thievery and pilfering. Nevertheless they tried their trespasses, larcenies and murders in the courts, giving them the benefit of the same rules that they enjoyed themselves. They did ostracize them socially and biologically. They did try to keep liquor and firearms from them, for the protection of both races. And they did limit their right to alienate land. But outside of these impositions they gave them equal rights under equal laws, including access to the schools. The failure of the Indian in the valley was principally his own, a dissatisfaction with his own Stone Age culture in the presence of the wonders the white man brought, and a desire to acquire the white man's ways, yet an inability to accept the discipline that the stronger culture implied. In consequence the Indian experienced an increasing self-contempt and need to escape into the only world where reassurance remained, the world of alcohol.

The Indians of the valley shared with their immediate successors one great quality, otherworldliness, life in eternity instead of in time. Like the Puritans, the Indians looked on this life as a vale of tears. But their methods of dealing with the problem were different. The Indian merely did what he could to propitiate Hobbamocko, the Evil Spirit who was responsible for all terrestrial difficulties. The Puritan went ahead vigorously to make the best of a bad situation. The vast amount he has accomplished in economic, materialistic terms is now suspect. But if there is any virtue in the activities that distinguish man from the animals, namely, his elaborate works of the imagination in philosophy, art and science, then the Indian culture was justly supplanted by the Puritan one that involved equal mysticism, a more inclusive morality, a wider science, and a more active curiosity and enterprise. The Indians should, and will, be remembered for their religion, some of their arts and sciences, and the integrity of many of their leaders. Yet their culture was of a scope so limited as to be unqualified long to play a part in man's progress toward adjustment to the cosmos. Its passing was pathetic, but in the valley of the Housatonic it was not tragic in any universal sense.

In economic terms, the Indians were the greatest of the animals, able to merge into the natural beauty of the valley and survive, leaving it unchanged, the mountains still stately under their forests, the falls plunging from the cliffs with undiminished power. The Indian lacked the mental force either to build or to destroy. The white man came with the power to do either, and history's judgment of him will depend on the final balance he attains between these conflicting tendencies. Along most of the rivers that he has populated he has destroyed the natural beauty and replaced it with industrial piles of no significance in spiritual, intellectual or aesthetic terms. But along the Housatonic, his favorable score is still high. In the ninety-mile stretch of the central valley, he has put up a dozen or so factories that offend the landscape today. He has robbed the great falls of their water to turn his dynamos, and has left their rocks smooth in the sun under the remembered flow. But, on the whole, he has left the peaceful stateliness of the region unchanged. The electricity that he makes here he sends far out of the valley to run factories and slums in other places. In compensation for the small havoc he has wrought, he has contributed in the valley literatures, theologies, works of art and music, and scientific discoveries such as were hardly intimated in the wilderness's dream.

The Indian was part of that older dream, with its sure virtues and limitations. If the white man's dream of religion and poetry and science proves to be a better dream, and if it survives his dynamos and factories, then it will be well that he has prevailed. But, if it is not a better dream, or if it is forgotten in his commerce and his greed, then his destructive tendency will have exceeded his creative one. In that case, he is Hobbamocko, the Spirit of Evil, who, as the Indians feared he would do, has overcome the world.

The Lord's Scouts

What was probably the second seagoing ship built in North America was appropriately christened the *Onrust*, which in English means "Restless." In the summer of 1613, while the Dutch explorer Captain Adrian Block lay at anchor in New Amsterdam—now New York—harbor, the flagship of his fleet of four was destroyed by fire. The following winter he built the *Onrust* to replace it. The new flagship was forty and a half feet long and eleven and a half wide. In the spring Captain Block took it on a maiden voyage which turned out to be of diplomatic importance. He sailed up the East River, through Hell Gate and into Long Island Sound, which he called the "Great Bay." Besides its claim to be an early ancestor of all American ships, the little *Onrust* has the incidental distinction of being the first vessel that is known to have touched the shore of Connecticut.

The first, or one of the first, places that Captain Block put in was *Cuph-eag*, the Shut-in-Place (Stratford Harbor) where the Great River flowed in. Doubtless the gigantic white bird swimming up the harbor caused consternation among the Indians who at that season would have been clamming and musseling along the beach. In his log Captain Block called the river the "River of the Red Hills," probably from the sand dunes of Stratford Point. He also reported that it was "about a bow-shot wide," implying that he explored no farther inland than the tidal marshes at the river's mouth. Proceeding eastward, he mapped the whole coast of Connecticut and, with the usual modesty of explorers, claimed for Holland a vast country northward which included most of New England. Within a few years the Dutch contracted their claim westward to the Connecticut River. But the remainder of it, inherited by the colony of New York after the English took it from the Dutch in 1670, was the cause of much litigation and some bloodshed, and was not cleared from all of the Housatonic region for two centuries and a half after Captain Block made his sovereign gesture.

After this glimpse through the clouds of prehistory, they close again over the Housatonic until July of 1637, when the Indians of the valley got their first close view of the white man in action. His entrance was convincing, but hardly suggestive of his fealty to the Prince of Peace. For two months, the Pequot war had been raging along the Thames and the Connecticut to the east. In organized reprisal for their unprovoked forays, murders and torturings, six hundred of that savage tribe had been killed and their villages destroyed. The survivors, some eighty warriors with twice as many old men, women and children, fled westward across the Connecticut, the Quinnipiack, and the Housatonic, and made a stand in the Saco Swamp in Fairfield. Captain Mason with his small force of Connecticut and Massachusetts men pursued them.

Since all the River Indians hated and feared the Pequots, the white men in passage were welcomed by Ansantawae, sachem of the Wepawaugs, in his Great Wigwam at modern Milford. Across the river, however, in Stratford and Fairfield, the Pequannocks were in a sorry case. Under Indian law, the Pequots claimed their land by a previous conquest, and, for some years, had been exacting tribute from them. As a subject people, they were bound to aid their conquerors, and as a practical consideration they feared them more than they did the little-known English. Consequently, about two hundred of the neighboring Pequannocks joined the Pequots in the swamp. But, after the first day of the Great Swamp Fight that followed, they had a change of heart and took advantage of the offer of the English to spare the lives of any who came out and surrendered. Some of them, mostly women, were made slaves, and the rest fled a dozen miles upriver to the fort of their kinsmen at Potatuck.

Because of the behavior of the Pequannocks in the Great Swamp Fight, the Connecticut colonial government thereafter treated this tribe's land west of the river as conquered territory as far north as Potatuck. This was the only tract in the valley that was originally acquired otherwise than by fair purchase. Both the Pequannocks and the Potatucks, presumably under the compulsion of the English, accepted for their sachem Okanuck, the son of Ansantawae who had befriended them. So, at the outset, the Lord punished the enemies of His Chosen People. And so there were seeded a resentment in the Pequannocks and the Potatucks and a qualm of conscience in the English, that made Stratford and, later, Shelton the only sites of bitter feeling between the races in the whole valley.

The later misunderstandings about the title to the former Pequannock lands in Stratford and neighboring Fairfield were not due to any illegality in the original acquisition. The right of conquest was recognized by both Indian and English law, and in this case seems to have been specifically confirmed by the sachems of the Pequannocks and their neighboring tribes. Owing, however to persisting uncertainty about the title, the Connecticut General Court, twenty-two years after the Great Swamp Fight and twenty-one years after the subsequent negotiations, required affidavits from men who had taken part in the latter:

> Being desired [wrote the Reverend John Higgison, late pastor at Guilford, in 1659] to expose what I remember concerning the transaction between the English of Coneckticott and the Indians along the Coast from Quilipioke [i.e., Quinnipiack or New Haven] to the Manhatoes about the land the substance of what I can say is briefly this: that in the beginning of the yeare 1638, the last weeke of March Mr. Hopkins and Mr. Goodwin, being imployed to treat with Indians and to make sure of that whole tract of land in order to prevent the Dutch and to accomodate the English who might after come to inhabite there, I was sent with them as an interpreter (for want of a better) we having an Indian with us for a guide,

acquainted the Indians as we passed with our purpose and went as far as about Norwalk before we stayed. Coming thither on the first day we gave notice to the Sachem and the Indians to meet there on the second day that we might treat with them all together about the business. Accordingly on the second day there was a full meeting (as themselves sayd) of all the sachems, ould men and Captains from Milford to Hudson River. After they had understood the cause of our coming and had consulted with us and amongst themselves and that in as solemn a manner as Indians use to doe in such cases they did with an unanimous consent express there desire of the English friendship, their willingness the English should come to dwell amongst them and professed that they did give and surrender up all their land to the English sachems at Coneckticott it being not long after the English Conquest and the fear of the English being upon them; it being moved amongst which of them would goe up with us to signifie this agreement and to present their wampum to the sachems at Coneckticott; at last Waunetan and Wouwequock, Paranoket offered themselves and were much applauded by the rest for it. Accordingly those two Indians went up with us to Hartford, not long after there was a comitee in Mr. Hooker's barne, the meeting-house then not buylded, where they two did appere and presented their wampem; (but ould Mr. Pinchin one of the magistrates there then) taking him to be the interperator, then I remember I went out and attended the business no further. So that what was further done or what writings there were about the business I can not now say, but I suppose if search be made something of the business may be found in the records of the court, and I suppose if Mr. Goodwin be inquired of he can say the same for substance as I doe and William Cornish at Saybrooke who was there.

The affidavit of Nicholas Knell confirmed what Mr. Higgison said, and added that he remembered "the payment of money to the Indians as gratuity for the gift."

The affidavit of Thomas Stanton made the point that the Pequots had previously conquered the territory of the Pequannocks and considered it as theirs, so that it passed to the English by the conquest of the Pequots; and he added that the Pequannocks "did intreat Mr. Hopkins and Mr. Haynes [then magistrates] that some of the English would come and dwell by them that so they not be in fear of their enemies, the uplanders [the Mohawks?] and that the English should have all their land only providing them some place for planting; which I think is but a reasonable request, and I hope you will atend rules of mercie in that case; not that they shall be their owne carvers what they will and wherefore their exorbitant humour will carry them to disposes you and your houses. Experience proves it; give an Indian an inch and he will take an ell . . ."

Altogether, there is little doubt that the English acquired the Stratford territory by legal conquest, and it is probable that the sachems, less than a year after the Great Swamp Fight of 1637, "the fear of the English being upon them," confirmed the acquisition by gift, or by sale for a token figure. Yet a few years later, when the English had duly "atended rules of mercie" by leaving them land for both planting and fishing, the natives began to question the original acquisition. At the same time, the consciences of the colonists were troubled about it, for at first single settlers, and presently the colonial government, obtained new cessions of the same land by purchase for good consideration. Nevertheless, the "exorbitant humour" of the Indians having been aroused, they continued to make a racket of their claims, and generally there was bad blood about it for half a century, leading sometimes to open hostility, though never to war. The Stratford difficulties were an example of the effects of a process which, though legal, is against universal human conscience. And, legal or not, it shows the inconclusive results of conquest by a supposed "master race."

For English and practical purposes, the military expedition of 1637 was the discoverer of the coast west of the Connecticut River. It led to the settlement of New Haven in 1638 and of the first two plantations at the mouth of Great River a year later. Meanwhile and thereafter those heroes of greed and adventure, the trappers and traders, were pushing up into the wilderness. By 1642 Messrs. Wakeman, Goodyear and Gilbert of New Haven had sailed or paddled thirteen miles up the river and built a trading post at Paugasset, or Derby. In 1644 Goodyear paddled or poled up thirty miles farther of mostly fast water and built a large post on what is still called Goodyear's Island, just below the Lover's Leap rapids and the big Fishing Cove at Weantinock, or modern New Milford. How much farther these adventurers penetrated is matter of conjecture. There is no record of exploration above New Milford until the 1670's.

The entrance of Awanux—the English—into the Upper Valley, as at Milford and Stratford, was to the sound of their muskets making good a punitive expedition. In 1676 King Philip's War, which had convulsed all of New England, ended with the death of the brilliant Wampanoag sachem. In August, Major John Talcot, with a body of Connecticut soldiers and friendly Indians from the Connecticut River, pursued a party of two hundred Indian fugitives along the Indian trail—later the "Great Road"—from Westfield to Albany, which crossed the "Ausotunnoog River" at a ford at the Great Wigwam, future Great Barrington. On the level bank of the river just west of the ford and within the region of the Great Wigwam—the spot now marked by a stone between the river and the big brick schoolhouse—the Indians made their encampment. Here Talcot attacked them at dawn, killed twenty-five, captured twenty and routed the rest, many of them "sorely wounded, as appeared by the dabbling of the bushes with blood, as was observed by them that followed—a little further." One story glorifies the slaughter with the information that the river was reddened by it. A later account adds that "there were sundry lost besides the forty-five forementioned, to the number of three score in all; and also that a hundred and twenty of them are now dead of sickness." As already suggested, it may have been at the time or just before Major Talcot's victory that the Housatonic Indians vacated the Great Wigwam and the surrounding territory.

Less than in the case of the Great Swamp Fight, thirty-nine years earlier and seventy-five miles to the south, was this first flourish of power related to the later colonization by the English. The Upper Valley remained an unsettled wilderness where Dutch from the Hudson were presently

trading energetically with the local Indians—or what was
left of them. By 1685 a group of these enterprising Dutchmen were already taking deeds from the natives, usually in
the form of the foreclosure of mortgages for moneys advanced to the savages. In 1705 these early grants were con-
solidated in the Patent of Westenhook, in which the colony
of New York granted to a syndicate, composed mostly of
Dutchmen, a vast tract including part of the Lower Valley
in future Litchfield County in Connecticut and all of the
Upper Valley in future Berkshire County in Massachusetts.
The basis of the grant was the claim of New York, previously
that of New Amsterdam, to all land west of the Connecticut
River. There used to be a philological heresy to the effect that
"Westenhook"—which happens to mean "western corner"—
was originally applied by the Dutch to the region, and that
it was the Indian way of pronouncing it—"Hóusatonuc"—
that gave the name to the river. The fact is that the Dutch
prospectors in 1685 referred specifically to "the creek called
Westenhook" as a name already established, and they used
the "creek" as a landmark in their deeds. Obviously, the
Indian name was older, and "Westenhook" was the Dutch
way of spelling it.

Illustrative of the vagueness of boundaries in the early
grants is a Great Barrington legend, without date or authen-
tication. A Dutchman proposed to purchase—presumably
from the Westenhook patentees—a tract of land running as
far eastward from the Hudson as a man could run in day,
and the contract was duly signed. To enlarge his bargain
the purchaser employed a famous Indian runner, who between
dawn and sunset covered the forty miles from the Hudson
to the Housatonic in Sheffield, including the passage of the
Taconic Mountains.

The legalities of the conflicting English and Dutch
claims in western New England derived from the grandiose
gestures of the early explorers—the English Cabots had
claimed to the Pacific—and from Indian deeds that were
readily repudiated, for a consideration, by later Indians.
Practically, what mattered was the actual possession, clearing

and cultivation of the land claimed. With half a dozen exceptions, the Dutch failed to confirm their Indian grants by actual settlement. But for the trading post, the trapper's cabin, a few scattered settlers, and a remnant of Indians, the Upper Valley remained uninhabited till the 1720's, when organized colonies from the east began seriously to make good the English claims. They recognized the holdings of those Dutch who had actually settled, but as for the enormous claims of the Westenhook Patent, they referred to the claims of the Cabots as more than a century older than those of Block. And they naturally got a new set of deeds from the Indians.

Meanwhile, in 1694, the Reverend Benjamin Wadsworth, a young minister of Boston, afterwards a president of Harvard, recorded his impressions of the Upper Valley. He was accompanying certain commissioners of Massachusetts and Connecticut to a treaty convention at Albany with commissioners from other colonies and the Five Nations of New York, the little cavalcade being escorted by a guard of sixty dragoons under Captain Wadsworth of Hartford. The Reverend Benjamin confided to a diary the irritation of his metropolitan sensibilities by the ruggedness of the region, which was later considered one of the most picturesque in the world.

The party set out from Westfield for Albany by the old Indian Trail, "the nearest way thro' the woods; . . . The road which we traveled this day was very woody, rocky, mountainous, swampy; extreme bad riding it was. I never yet saw so bad traveling as this was." It took them five days to reach the valley where, on August 10th, "we . . . took up our lodgings, about sundown, in the woods, at a place called Ousetonuck formerly inhabited by Indians"—that is, at the Great Wigwam, the ford in future Great Barrington, the scene of Major Talcot's fight eighteen years before. "Thro' this place runs a very curious river, the same which some say runs thro' Stratford, and it has on each side some parcels of pleasant, fertile intervale land. . . . The greatest part of our road this day was a hideous, howling wilderness . . ."

Having completed their mission in Albany, the commissioners returned by a southern route through Kinderhook, Claverack, Taghkanick, Kent, Woodbury and Hartford. After leaving "Turconnick," they rode twelve or fifteen miles, "on our left a hideous high mountain"—possibly any of the main Taconics of which the Reverend Mr. Wadsworth of Boston had now seen plenty, perhaps—as claimed by one local historian—a particularly bold escarpment that rises a thousand feet sheer near the source of the Weebatuck (Tenmile) River in New York. A few hours after passing the "hideous high mountain," the party reached "Ten miles" River, "called so from its distance from Wyantenuck, runs into Wyantenuck. . . . Wyantenuck river is the same that passeth thro' Ousetonnuck; it is Stratford river also."

Here we have a glimpse at the transitional nomenclature of the Great River. In the lower, tidal reaches, the period of discovery, exploration and pioneering is long past. The English are more than fifty years established at Stratford and they have attached the name of their place to the river, supplanting both the Indian Potatuck and the Great River of the first white settlers. In the central span, the Indians, retreating before colonization, have concentrated at Weantinock, or New Milford, and some whites, visiting them there, have accepted and reported their local name for the river. In the upper reaches, "Ousetonnuck" is still simply the name of a place in the English vocabulary, though both the Indians and the Dutch have already applied it to the river. This supercilious young minister records what appears to be the white man's first discovery of the fact that the river at Ousetonnuck is the same as that at Weantinock and Stratford. Twenty-five years later the name of that obscure "beyond-the-mountains-place" will have flowed down to entitle the whole stream.

PART I

The Land and the Lord (1639-1761)

The First Two Tribes (1639-1657)

Some time in the spring or early summer of 1639, an unknown vessel bearing an unknown number of Puritans, under the ministry of the forty-year-old Reverend Adam Blakeman, approached the entrance to Stratford Harbor. There could hardly have been over thirty families of them, and it is not known whence they came, beyond the fact that the Reverend Mr. Blakeman himself came directly from Old England, that part of his following was from his former flock there, and that another part was from Wethersfield in Connecticut Colony under whose auspices this plantation was being undertaken. Doubtless the Devil—with the authority of Calvinist doctrine—had whispered to some of the settlers of the chances of enhancing land values and of trade with the Indians. But the effective cause, without which the plantation would not have been attempted, was their determination to risk their lives and their property in order to live in accordance with an idea and a faith.

Between the long, low natural sea wall of Milford Point and the dunes of Stratford Point, the ship entered the mile-and-a-half diametered harbor. On the western, or Stratford, side, they dropped anchor in the mouth of a tidal inlet—later called Mac's Harbor—and put ashore on its northern beach. Undoubtedly their first act as a community was to

59

kneel on the beach while the Reverend Mr. Blakeman gave thanks to the Lord who in His mercy had predestined them for a safe landing. The gulls wheeled and screamed overhead. From the near forest a few Cupheag Indians watched. On the outer points boomed the surf of three thousand miles of ocean, cutting them off from the homes they had left forever.

Six months later, in the late fall of 1639, the cold twilight of any dawn fell on the village—then called Pequannucks—in its first phase, at once a triumph of fanatical energy and an example of the havoc that civilization wreaks when it first touches the wilderness. Throughout the night, as through all the nights and days, there had been no silence, for the wolves never stopped their racket of hunting moose and deer in the forest, right up to the palisade round the settlement. In the first, gray light, the high platform of the watchhouse stood in bleak outline on Watch House Hill—modern Academy Hill—the cold sentry at his post with loaded musket, powder horn and shot bag, the frost crackling on the planks when he shifted his feet. In the lower shadow the rectangle of the clearing lay faintly visible under light snow, a quarter of a mile north and south and half as wide, the eastern side on the harbor and the other three sides palisaded with logs, the watchhouse standing against the northern wall that traversed its hill. Down there in the darkness, at the western and southern gates, at the platforms at the corners of the stockade, and along the harbor, the other members of the watch kept their vigil. They took their turns by roster from Sergeant Nichols' Train Band, which was the male community between sixteen and sixty in its military aspect.

Descending from the watchtower on the hill, the twilight fell on the snow-whitened, thatched pyramid that was the roof of the little log meeting house, already built near the point where the congregation had landed six months before. Then rapidly the still unfleshed skeleton of the whole village came out of darkness.

Two parallel streets—modern Elm and Main—ran south

from the little common around Watch House Hill, their
frozen mud pitted from boots and hoofs; and along these were
ranged the twenty-five or so ugly, one-room, lean-to, log
and clay huts with their big, squat, mud chimneys. Behind,
in the long, narrow homelots, the stumps of the ruined
forest stood out of the snow, some of them blackened and
still smoldering. Among the stumps were the split-rail cattle
pens, the ricks of wild hay from the marshes outside the
stockade, a few miniature log barns rising, the big woodpiles,
some patches of corn stubble from last summer's first, meager
planting that had been attempted only within the stockade.

From the huts came the mumble of morning prayers and
the passage from God's Holy Word, then thumpings and
voices. The oiled parchment windows glowed sallow from
blown-up hearth light and out of the chimneys bluish plumes
rose and leaned westward together on the gray wind. Slab
doors swung open on their leather hinges, and figures, with
wooden or birchbark pails, tracked out to the cowpens. The
new watch assembled and tramped round, relieving the old.
The cowkeepers drove a dozen, assembled cattle up to the
common on Watch House Hill to eke out the last blades and
shoots of freezing growth. Men in linen shirts and knee
breeches of homespun from England or deer-hide already
dried—the knee breeches baggy to permit being reversed
when the seat was worn—men in homespun caps or broad
"sugar loaf" hats, and wide-toed, big-buckled shoes, congregated in the streets, carrying their tools, greeting each other
as "your Honor" for high officials, "master" or "goodman"
for freemen, first names for servants. Under their communi-
tarian socialism, most men were officeholders and the great
majority property owners; universal, male democracy was
founded in the assumption of universal, male, proprietary
responsibility. The work of the day began, the rhythmed
snarl of long saws over the sawpits, the slash of adzes, the
whack of mallets on pegs, the shouts to the oxen drawing in
logs, the occasional musket shots from outside the palisade
where the boys were foraging in the forest against starvation.

At sundown on Saturday, which was the beginning of

the Sabbath, a hush fell over the village, as over the rest of New England. The cooking for the next day was done, the wood carried in. Nothing remained for Sabbath activity, but the guard and the animal chores. At eight o'clock on Sunday morning the drum rolled the first summons, and at ten the second and final one. Men in weekday attire with homespun capes added and women in capes and hoods came out of their hovel doors that seemed too small for them and walked solemnly over the frozen mud to the heatless, windowless meeting house. The women took their places on the slab benches on the right, the men on the left, the armed, Sabbath guard from the train band in the rear. For an hour they bowed to the Reverend Mr. Blakeman's prayer, then listened with complete attention to the difficult, scholarly sermon, while he turned the hourglass twice, and, if it was Communion Sunday, the Lord's Body froze before the pulpit.

In the interval between the afternoon service and the end of the Sabbath at sunset, each family sat on the benches and chests or on the hearth before the fire in its one-room hut, while the father reread the texts of the day, discoursed on the sermon and applied it, as might be, to each of them present. At his signal, the mother set out the cold beans and corn bread and, after thanks to God for His blessings, they partook of it on wooden trenchers. As the light of the sunset faded in the paper windows, they put the victuals away and each knelt on the dirt floor at his private prayers. The hearts of the young silently confessed to God the multitude of their sinful thoughts that kept them unworthy of His grace whose attainment was all their ambition. The father and mother, in their respective corners, likewise searched their hearts with agonized sincerity, and confessed in prayer what they found there of cupidity and vanity and licentiousness, of jealousy and malice toward their neighbors, of every evil tendency that jeopardized the Covenant of Grace they had entered into with their God.

The darkness deepened and the dying fire hissed in the otherwise unlighted silence. Each heart felt, for the moment, unburdened of its sins and worthy to glorify the God of creation. From the surrounding cosmos, where He was enacting His stupendous drama, His peace gathered and entered that house, bringing with it a joy in His mercy that was the greatest of all joys and an immediate earthly reward and sufficient compensation for the discomfort and suffering of being there. Outside in the cold, the wolves howled and the watch stood round the little rectangle of the palisade, protecting their idea against the world. Down from unknown, forested distances to the north came the Great River. Westward for unknown thousands of miles stretched a continent.

Owing to the loss of Stratford's records before 1650, the exact time of its settlement in 1639 is not known, but it was probably a month or two ahead of that of Milford on the other side of the mouth of the Great River. Of all the Puritan plantations, Milford best exemplified that method of settlement by religious schism, imperial growth by ecclesiastical cell subdivision, which for at least the first century was a stronger force than economic greed in the expansion of New England. The truculent future Yankees of Milford went through three schisms before they put down roots. To begin with, they followed their Reverend Peter Prudden out of England to Boston in 1637, more or less in the company of another Puritan group under the Reverend John Davenport. Next, both groups found the then theocracy of Boston too confining for them, and in 1638 they moved to New Haven, recently discovered and recommended by Captain Underhill, who had noticed the harbor on the way to the Great Swamp Fight the year before. Then, in early 1639, Prudden's group fell into divers differences with the majority, or Davenport, group in New Haven, notably on the question of theocracy, the determination of the majority to limit the vote to church members. In the spring Mr. Prudden's followers bought a small tract of land ten miles to the west from Ansantaẁae, chief of the Wepawaugs, embracing the old sachem's former Council Fire where the little Wepawaug River flowed into its long, narrow harbor. The transfer was by a combination of English and Indian ritual; on the one hand, the delivery of a deed bearing the sachem's mark and, on the other hand, the twig and turf ceremony by which Ansantawae took up a sod, thrust a twig in it and handed it to the English.

Having bought their tract in the spring, the Wepawaugites did not move until August, thus probably letting Pequannocks—Stratford—across the main harbor get the honor of being the first plantation on the Great River. But if they lost a race of which they were unaware, the Wepawaugites were for that the better prepared for their enterprise. They came with their church all organized, the Seven Pillars already chosen. And, perhaps uniquely among pioneer settlements anywhere, they brought with them their combined dwelling, tabernacle and government house, all cut, notched, bored and ready to raise. They sent it round from New Haven by water while most of the pioneers walked the ten miles, driving their cattle. And their first act was to raise this common house and cover it with another unique distinction for a pioneer building, clapboards and shingles. It was large enough to house the forty-four families of the original settlement while they were building their own huts and houses outside, at the same time functioning as a meeting house and a town hall. It stood just west of where the Weapawaug spilled into the top of its narrow harbor. The present Town Hall of Milford is the fourth on the almost identical site.

During the following winter, 1639-40, they laid out the village. The common was modern Broad Street, spanning the two hundred yards between the Wepawaug River and West End Brook. A pair of residential streets ran north along the respective sides of each of these streams; or, more precisely, each of two wide, residential streets contained a sizable all-purpose stream running down the middle of it— a suitable convenience for people who were not troubled by notions of sanitation. Along these streets sixty-five home-lots were laid out, averaging three acres each. At a town meeting that March—1640—it was agreed with Mr. William Fowler, one of the Pillars, "that he shall build A Mill and A house for it and doe all the work to her for stones [that is, millstones] and Iron-worke and all other Materials fit for her; and substantially done and to be goeing By the last of September." Mr. Fowler carried out his pressing assignment, and the committee in charge set his "towle" at three quarts of grain for every bushel brought to be ground. In addition to building the mill, housing it and cutting the stones, Mr. Fowler that summer built a dam, creating back of the town house the pond which shortly became what it remains today, the picturesque center of the town's group of public buildings.

The condition of retaining a homelot in Milford was that a "substantial house" be built on it within three years. Most of the houses went up during 1640 and, because the villagers had the common house for suitable temporary quarters, they were able to take their time and make the construction indeed "substantial." As distinguished from the situation in most settlements where it was necessary to take hurried cover under logs, mud and thatch, many of these first houses of Milford were framed, clapboarded and shingled one and a half to two and a half stories high around a huge, central stone chimney in the pattern that was to be orthodox in New England for two centuries.

In its leisurely fashion, Milford reached mature form in 1641. A roughly circular stockade of twelve-foot logs was built around the village and a train band established—as in all the settlements, every able-bodied man between sixteen and sixty—under Captain John Astwood. South of the village the common land was apportioned for cultivation, the young surveyor being one Robert Treat, not yet a freeholder but destined to become the most picturesque figure in Connecticut in the seventeenth century.

The third achievement of that year was the erection of the meeting house on the knoll on the upper bank of Fowler's millpond. This appropriately was the most commanding site in the village, looking down over the pond, the town house, the village and the central common, all in the stockade, and outside the stockade southward across the farmland to the Sound and westward to the harbor of the Great River, the marshes along its southern reaches, the great sycamores that marked its course as it narrowed inland toward Derby. Like the town house, that first meeting house is survived today by its third successor on nearly the same site. More than most villages, modern Milford, centered around its pond, now nicely parked, and its town hall and First Church of Christ, now lofty and magnificent, suggests its bleak beginnings of three centuries ago.

Even that first meeting house was magnificent for its time. It was forty feet square, framed in heavy timbers and covered with unpainted clapboards like the common house. It was two full stories high under a pyramidal roof with a bell-less bell tower at the peak. The casement windows of both stories were fitted with the luxury of diamond glass. Within, at the head of the central aisle, the lofty pulpit was reached by its winding steps that embraced the slightly elevated deacon's seat in their curve. The most desirable pews, occupied by the town dignitaries, were those on either side of the pulpit and facing it along the north wall. The next most desirable ones were the central ones, flanking the center aisle. The poorest pews were the raised ones along the side wall facing, not the pulpit, but the center of the church. All the pews at the outset were rough-hewn benches. But for the lack of a bell, a gallery, and musket racks behind the guards' seats at the rear, deficiencies that were eventually filled in Milford, this meeting house was typical of the more substantial ones in New England throughout the seventeenth century.

It is a fair guess that by the time Milford's meeting house was completed, not a grown tree remained anywhere within either its stockade or that of Stratford five miles away across the river. By the end of 1641, Stratford doubtless had a few framed houses too and, but for Milford's better public buildings, the two settlements presented the same crude aspect. Between the buildings there was mud, broken only by a few shrubs round the houses, and the withered gardens of the homelots. Everywhere the gray mud not yet softened with green, and the yellow of raw timber not yet weathered into gray.

In the annals of the two colonies during the next dozen years, four events are of historical consequence:

In 1643 Milford, requiring protection against the Dutch, surrendered its previous independence and joined the New Haven Confederation, accepting perforce and conditionally the theocracy which it had not practiced before.

In 1645 Stratford's meeting house got the first bell in Connecticut.

In 1648 Moses Wheeler of Stratford got the first concession for a ferry across the Great River—a raft with a pair of oars at each end. This Wheeler, incidentally, was a giant, hated Indians and made himself hated by them. One morning, when he was in his cellar, a group of Indians appeared in the hatchway suggestively armed with tomahawks. Picking up a half-empty cider barrel, Mr. Wheeler said, "Let's all have a drink," and himself drank from the bung. The Indians thought the barrel was full, lost their nerve before such strength, and departed.

In 1651 occurred the supposed hanging of "Goody" (Goodwife) Bassett for a witch on Witch Rock in Stratford, the only execution for witchcraft in the valley.

Throughout this early period Stratford was in a continuous state of tension with the Indians, as was Fairfield to the west of it, because of the refusal of the new generation of natives to recognize the English acquisition of the land by conquest. The trouble was aggravated by the cattle and swine of the whites straying into the Indians' planting field—Bridgeport—and by the Indians' weakness for stealing the crops of the whites, so that an armed guard was always maintained around all fields. Between 1644 and 1649 there were three cold-blooded murders by Indians in Fairfield, two of them of women. The three murderers were properly arrested, and, after two of them had escaped, the third was brought to trial and executed. The General Court at Hartford rejected a motion to declare war, a measure which, by depriving the Indians of civil rights, would have greatly helped the colonists. In 1656 a Mr. Ludlow of Fairfield confirmed his title to a large tract by purchasing it and taking a regular deed, "although Mr. Ludlow had been in possession of it for nearly seventeen years." Encouraged by this success, all the Indians of Fairfield and Stratford began to clamor for payment for their former land, starting a series of conferences, treaties, repudiations by the Indians, purchases, repurchases, and generally bad blood on both sides which continued for thirty years more. Meanwhile, on the opposite side of the Great River, the Milfordites, having purchased their land at the outset, lived at peace with their native neighbors.

The years 1656 and 1657 mark respectively the end of the first phase of colonization in the valley, and of pure Puritanism. In 1656 the Reverend Peter Prudden died, and the Milford that he left behind him was an age away from the pioneer village of only seventeen years before. The danger from the heathen and wolves had all but retired over the northern horizon and, given a proper industriousness, every family in town was on a comfortable subsistence basis, its manpower bringing in and its womanpower finishing all its necessities of food, shelter and clothing.

The dawn light of a May Sabbath first struck the belfry that still wanted a bell to rival Stratford's. In the twilight below, the sentries no longer looked out at the forest but over miles of open pasture and fields corrugated by spring plowing, the whole checkerboarded with fences of stone or split rails, with farms in their closes and with orchards in bloom. In the village proper the yellow oblongs of light along the dark streets came no longer from wakened hearths shining through oiled skins or parchment but from rush candles behind real casement windows with diamond panes. The dwellings that took shape around these windows out of the dawn mist were sizable, clapboarded structures housing their great chimneys, varying from a story in height to the lofty salt boxes recently built by Magistrate Robert Treat and a dozen others.

As the light grew, low palings of pickets appeared before many of the houses. In the little front yards imported grass was already growing, and lilacs in bloom and other shrubs were mounting to the second stories against the weathered clapboards. In the rear of the old homelots, the stumps had rotted into the soil of big gardens, already plowed and partly planted, while behind them young orchards were in full pink and white bloom and the first sunlight made them murmurous with bees at their predestined mission of refilling the half-empty cider kegs in the cellars.

At the southern fringe of the village, the last features to come out of the sea mist were the masts of ships, the warehouses, the lines of oystermen's shacks. Around the pond between the town house and meeting house lay a small green where there was no useful planting. Here and in some of the little front yards young trees grew unmolested, trees that had been left as seedlings when the ground was cleared and were now outfanning their duster tips over the lower gables, baby trees that were to outlast every man-made structure and become the first village elms of New England.

Comparable to the change in the appearance of the village was that in the appearance of the people. The Lord's and the Devil's admonition to tend the former's garden had transformed almost all the householders into substantial farmers with a few hundred good acres outside the palisade where they raised all needful clothing and food except rum. On the other hand, they produced exportable crops of hides, furs, horses, cattle, pork, beef, mutton, fish, flour, corn meal, barrel and pipe staves. A half dozen big merchants and shippers such as the Bryans were rich even by European standards. At ten o'clock, when the drummer boy rolled the final summons to meeting from the meeting house belfry, the families that emerged from the houses—the man and wife in front, the former carrying his musket, and the children behind—were those of a prosperous village. Several men wore long red coats over plush waistcoats and breeches. A few had expensive "beaverettes" in place of the old sugar loaf hats. Many wore shoes of buff leather, with silver buckles adorned with garnets, and slashes revealing gay red or green stockings. The wealthy ladies had red or blue cloaks with hoods and elegant shoes of red morocco, flowering russet, silk, velvet or damask. The poorer people still wore long, homespun coats and cloaks, the men woolen caps or sugar-loaf hats, but most of them were also able to display red stockings and elegant silver buckles on their square-toed shoes. Only the poorest wore heavy boots that made an unseemly thumping as they entered the meeting house.

But the great and significant change was in the minds and hearts of the congregation when it assembled. The majority of those present were of a generation that had grown up in the seventeen years since the first settlement, years in which the risk of starvation or violent death had decreased while comfort had increased. The immigrant parents of these children, being in constant danger, had felt themselves utterly in God's hands, and accordingly had been utterly humble in their lives and under the ministration of His vicar. But with the youngsters—the oldest of them now in their thirties—the adventure of physical living had been less risky, and in consequence their religious necessity had been less desperately passionate. No less serious and responsible than their elders, they yet felt qualified to arrive at their own opinions upon ultimate matters. Especially at this time, when a successor to Mr. Prudden had not been selected and the visiting minister was on trial, they listened to his sermon with a frankly critical attitude. Sometimes their criticism took a form that called on the tithingman—in charge of discipline in meeting—to use his long rod with its knob for drowsy gentlemen and its feather for equivalent ladies. The Calvinist individualism which had always characterized a man's relation with God, but had not sanctioned any questioning of settled doctrine, of the opinion of the congregation, or of the Lord's anointed minister, this individualism was now invading all these dangerous fields. The youngsters were going so far as to question the parental congregation in its infallible control of church membership. And with that change the first of America's major social tragedies was being enacted.

Under Puritan theology there were two sacraments, baptism and holy communion, the first celebration of the latter being also the occasion of the communicant's joining the church and entering thereby into the State of Grace which was the prerogative of the elect. Baptism occurred in infancy, and the condition of it was that the parents be church members. Communion, or union with the church, was voluntary, but with two precedent conditions: the individual must be baptized and he must, before admission, stand a severe inquisition on the part of the entire congregation as to the validity of his conversion or regeneration.

This inquisition many of the young generation, however anxious they might be to join the church, now declared themselves unwilling to meet. Knowing every member of the congregation with village thoroughness, they questioned the holier-than-thou assumption that the Lord had commissioned them to express His will as to the redemption of all and sundry. Prayerfully, young men concluded that their own inmost conscience was as fit to pass upon their eligibility for church membership as was a majority of the church members.

Fathers who had sacrificed everything in order to raise their sons in the hope of the immediate establishment of the Holy Commonwealth, the New Jerusalem on earth, now saw their boys refusing even to qualify for the elect. As parents they were defeated, while in larger terms their idea of the Holy Commonwealth was evaporating before the fact of an all too secular commonwealth. This was the beginning of the Great Puritan Decline.

The decline became official in 1657 with the adoption

of the Halfway Covenant by a synod of ministers, its subsequent recommendation by the General Courts, and its adoption in some form by many congregations. The immediate crisis impelling the Synod of 1657 into its unorthodox position was the fact that large numbers of the younger generation who had refused to qualify for church membership under the old ordeal were now presenting their own children for baptism, and baptism was for none but the children of church members. Not only were thousands of babies being left in Calvinistic, infant damnation, but, since the unbaptized could under no circumstances join the church, in another twenty years there would be almost no church left to join. The Halfway Covenant provided that baptized infants could, on reaching years of discretion, merely "own the covenant" and thereby qualify themselves for church membership and their children for baptism. Of the two Puritan sacraments, baptism and communion, such people would experience only the first. They were only "halfway" to grace. Theirs was the Halfway Covenant.

Thus, as throughout its history, the Church of Christ, by refusing to die at its spiritual guns, saved itself and its influence as a secular institution. The congregations were no longer communities of saints who had attained Heavenly Grace here and now, but missionary societies urging the unregenerate to qualify by good works for redemption in a postmortal hereafter, snobbish societies of the leading families who undertook to run the towns. In the form of church courts they began to examine and censor the life of the citizenry and to earn their future reputations. The proposed site of God's Holy Commonwealth shifted back from New England to heaven. The enrollments of the churches increased. And the "noblest" large-scale experiment ever tried in America was over.

The Next Seven Tribes (1655-1743)

FOLLOWING the arrival of the first two tribes in 1639, it took a hundred and thirty-two years for sixteen more separate tribes, or plantations, of the Chosen People to occupy the rest of the Promised Land, which they eventually did clear to the three tips of the river's headwaters in Washington, Lanesboro and Richmond. In some of these settlements the avaricious motives of the Devil seemed to outweigh the impulse to worship the Lord. Also, increasingly there appeared the new motive of American social individualism, the desire to move out into frontier elbowroom free from the older and already crowded settlements. But generally throughout this colonizing era the prevalent motive was the religious one. For most of the people most of the time the controlling interest of life continued to be in God and His cosmic drama.

Third Tribe, Paugasset, or Derby (1655-1665)

The third tribe consisted of five families from Milford who in 1655 drove their oxcarts ten miles up the Indian trail to settle on the heights at Paugasset. Below, the Housatonic, the Naugatuck and tidewater convened between mountainous bluffs in a titanic, slow whirlpool. In its natural state this was surely the most magnificent site on the river, as it would be today if the industrial cities of Derby and Shelton could be deleted and the Naugatuck cleansed of the sewage of its industrial wealth. Appropriate to the future of the vicinity, the plain motive of the original settlement was the Devil's, for most or all of the five families bought shares in the trading post already established there by some New Haven people. Nevertheless, they continued to make a persuasive show of being good Puritans, most of them making every Sabbath the twenty-mile round trip to attend their old church in Milford, though the law with its five-shilling fine did not require them to go so far.

It is plain that all did not go smoothly between Milford and her northern daughter. During the period of first settlement there occurred an obviously hostile though obscure event referred to in local history as "the incident of Parson Prudden's pigs." Also, Milford for a long time forestalled Paugasset in its efforts to get independent township, and in 1659 the "Wolf-killer" Edward Wooster asked the General Court whether he should seek from New Haven or from Milford the bounty for seven wolves destroyed. In 1660 the Paugassetites started the shipbuilding industry, which was to flourish for almost two centuries. In 1661 Edward Riggs sheltered the regicides Goffe and Whalley in his palisaded house while they were being moved from the famous Judges' Cave in New Haven to the house of Micah Tompkins in Milford, where they were successfully concealed for three years.

Fourth Tribe, Woodbury (1665-1685)

After the death of their first minister, the Reverend Adam Blakeman, in 1665, Stratford split in two on the issue of the Halfway Covenant, the conservatives immediately ordaining the Reverend Israel Chauncey and the liberals, or Halfwayites, ordaining three years later the young Reverend Zechariah Walker. There followed some years of acrimonious squabbling, mostly epistolary, at the height of which one "loving brother" wrote to another in the opposite camp: "It seemeth our greatest difference is what is our difference."

In 1670 the General Court of Connecticut enacted in dignified annoyance that "it shall not be offensive to this Court if Mr. Walker and his Company doe meet distinctly elsewhere." Accordingly in April, 1673, the first contingent

of the Walker schism, being fifteen families complete with
children and worldly goods, passed Paugasset with rafts and
canoes, bound for the tributary Pomperaug sixteen miles
farther into the wilderness up the Great River. Four or five
miles up the small stream they had bought from some Indian
chiefs, sight unseen, an allegedly large and fertile valley.
Early on what was probably the third day of their journey,
they passed the mouth of the Pomperaug as being too small
according to the instructions they had from the Indian
sellers. Four miles farther up they climbed the larger Shepaug,
including lofty Roxbury Falls, wandered lost for a day in
the Roxbury region, and were finally led by the Lord southward through the wilderness into their excellent valley,
which they immediately recognized from the top of Good
Hill. What they had not been apprised of, they saw also in
the middle of the valley a fortified and occupied Indian village on a natural pinnacle which they later called Castle
Rock. This led to a conference in which three conflicting
views were advanced, each of them soundly puritanical. One
proposal was that they first kneel down and thank the Lord
for having led them to this valley and then await His advice.
The second was to go down immediately and attack the Indians. The third was to return to Stratford and sue the chiefs
who had sold them the land. The pious view prevailed, and
when, after thanks, they went down into the valley they
were not disturbed.

For three years thereafter they lived a migratory existence in their new domain, occupying tents in the summers,
laying out and clearing the ground, building a mill for their
grain, worshiping in the gorgeous, uplifted, natural temple
of the Orenaug rocks, clearing by order a highway down to
Paugasset, and returning to Stratford for the winters while
the Indians stole the grain they left hidden in log cribs.
During King Philip's War in 1676, the development was
suspended for fear of disaffection among the local Indians
and because Woodbury, like the other towns in the valley,
sent more than its quota of men to the colonial forces. In
1677, after the peace, they completed permanent settlement

along wide Woodbury Main Street as it is today, building several stockaded houses in place of a palisade round the whole mile-long village. In 1681 the impossibility of agreeing on a place for a meeting house required a reference to Magistrate Nathan Gold of Fairfield and Colonel Robert Treat of Milford who was now deputy governor of Connecticut. The place "pitched upon" was near the grave of the sagamore Pomperaug who had ruled the region, and across the street from Drum Rock where the Masonic Temple now stands. The site of the meeting house is today occupied by a small barn, while that of Pomperaug's grave is marked by a fitting bronze tablet on one of the characteristic outcrops of his one-time domain.

During the period of Woodbury's schism and settlement, the chief event elsewhere, other than King Philip's War, was the absorption of New Haven, including Milford, into Connecticut Colony in 1665. In the same year the colony was divided into four counties, of which New Haven and Fairfield were divided by the Housatonic, each having a fringe of towns in its watershed.

In 1673 Paugasset changed it name to Derby and was incorporated as a town. Not till 1682 did that rich little settlement build a church, and then a wretched shanty in a section appropriately called the Squabble Hole, a shanty hardly larger than a deckhouse on one of the merchantmen being built in the flourishing shipyards below.

In 1680 Stratford, having greatly increased in population in spite of the defection of the Woodburyites, built its second church, this time on Watch House, now Academy, Hill. The new structure was graced with high-backed pews.

In 1681 Connecticut Colony reached a new agreement with all the sachems having any claim to the Stratford lands, repurchasing them all and taking a new blanket deed for the whole tract, which included most of modern Shelton. This ended the petty clashes in Stratford proper, but the Indians in their fort at Potatuck across the river from Paugasset remained sulky, and delayed the settlement of Shelton until the eighteenth century.

Fifth Tribe, Pahquioque, or Danbury (1685-1708)

In the spring of 1685 seven families from Norwalk and one from Stratford made their way twenty-five miles northward through the woods with their possessions, bought from the friendly Indians Pahquioque, the "open plain" on the tributary Still River, and typically marked each of the three corners of the survey by "a rock" and the fourth by "an ash tree." They built their cabins in two rows along Town Street, which is today lower Danbury Main Street where it ends at South Street.

The local historian says the early inhabitants were famous for piety. On the other hand, there is no evidence that they organized their church until 1695, and, though they built an early meeting house, its date, location and description are not on record. Furthermore, the Devil's motive is intimated from the beginning by the fact that they and their "open plain" became immediately famous for excellent beans, which they hauled to market down to the older towns on the Sound, thereby earning the name of Beantown. When, in 1687, they applied for a township, their own choice of a name was the humble one of Swampfield, from the great swamp, now drained, that used to parallel Town Street to the east. The same note of humility is heard in the assertion in the application that "there are twentie families at Pahquioque and more desirable persons acominge." Robert Treat, being now governor of Connecticut Colony, thought the name "Swampfield" undignified, and saw to its incorporation under the name of a village in Essex called Danbury. A few days after signing the incorporation, the governor managed the famous Charter Oak incident whereby the already "ancient" rights of Connecticut were preserved.

In 1690 Stratford passed an ordinance that was novel surely in New England, probably in the British Empire, and possibly in human history: ". . . Voted, that from the middle of March next to the middle of May next no sow that have had pigs or hath pigs, shall be suffered to goe upon the commons or streets, but by the owners shall be shutt up [the reason for this daring enactment is anti-climactic] for the preservation of the increase of our flock of sheep, to save our lambs."

During this period there was founded the legend of Captain Kidd's burying treasure on Milford Island, the sands of which have since been thoroughly and fruitlessly mined. To the fact that he visited Milford village at least

once there is credible evidence in the form of a letter written in 1699 by a young lady:

. . . Aunt Prudence has told you of the visit from Capt. Kidd, from the craft wh. was seen to come in the harbor at 7 of the clock in the evening. He stayed in the house till in the early morning and sat all the night by the fire with Jacobeth and Tomas Welsh carrying himself in an uncivil and bold manner. I told Aunt Prudence that he will come to trouble in the sinful way, wh. he has done,—for Zecharaiah White has told us all about him. . . . I want to tell you, cousin Thankful, what he did: when he came in the room he put his arms around my waiste, and kyssed me, wh. made Jacobeth laugh and Tomas Welsh cough. Jacobeth says that Capt. Bob is not so bad as the folks say. . . . I overheard Jacobeth say that Kidd was going on a long cruise, and that he had left some things with him. I am going to tell Aunt Prudence all about it, and find out what they are. . . .

Your cousin, Patience Tuttle.

In addition to the stories that caused the overturning of Milford Island, the legend of Kidd's having buried treasure on Stratford Point became so persistent that in 1850 a company was formed and some miles of sand were plowed on the outer stretch of beach still called "The Gold Diggings."

In 1702 the old family quarrel between Stratford and Woodbury was composed when, upon the death of the latter's minister Mr. Walker, the now aged Reverend Israel Chauncey of Stratford came up to officiate at the ordination of Woodbury's new minister, Mr. Joseph Stoddard.

Meanwhile, in 1701, the War of the Spanish Succession had begun in Europe, releasing in America what is sometimes called the First French and Indian War, but which was virtually the beginning of a single, sixty years' struggle between the British and the French for the mastery of the Continent. American hostilities opened in February, 1704, with the French-led sneak raid and massacre at the Massachusetts frontier town of Deerfield. The minister there, carried off prisoner and later ransomed, was John Williams, a member of the Williams family that was later closely identified with the history of the Housatonic Valley.

After the Deerfield massacre Woodbury and Danbury became outpost towns with garrisons and several stockaded houses. Also, the Connecticut General Court passed repressive measures on the local Indians, because of the difficulty of distinguishing them from the marauders from Canada who were roaming the frontiers in small scalping parties. Each town was to assign limits for its Indians, which they would pass at their peril, and they were offered a £10 bounty for any enemy Indian they captured. White men, both military and civilian, were offered a £5 bounty for the scalps of male enemy Indians. Not long after his ordination in Woodbury the Reverend Mr. Stoddard, from the large palisaded house the town built him, shot dead two Indians he saw lurking in his garden.

Doubtless Mr. Stoddard's hunting of Indians caused no more stir in Woodbury than an episode involving tea that occurred in his solid, seventeenth century mansion. A package of the herb was sent to the minister, being the first to reach this frontier township, with the injunction that it was to be used only for sickness or on very special occasions. Shortly, it appears, the parson's two daughters were overwhelmed by the vices of curiosity and frivolity, for they invited their respective swains to a tea party in one of their bedrooms, providing furtive access thereto by a ladder. Being uninformed in the preparation of tea, the young people boiled it violently at the fireplace, emptied it into a pewter platter, leaves and all, and drank it like soup. The fate of the daughters and the swains is not of record.

Mr. Stoddard seems to have been possessed of an amiable vagueness to which, in some part, it would be charitable to attribute his brutal murder of the two Indians. Several times on Sunday morning his wife asked him to mind the baby, and, when he took it, went off to church. One of the deacons knew what it meant when she appeared alone, wherefore he slipped out of church, reported at the parsonage, himself took the baby and held it while Mr. Stoddard went and held the service.

The picture of Mr. Stoddard approaches completeness with the tale of his Newfoundland dog which, if at large, would follow its master to church, proceed up the aisle at elephantine leisure, mount the pulpit steps to a landing part way up, turn there and sit down facing the congregation, and remain so throughout the service. At length Mr. Stoddard commanded his several small sons to confine the dog and see that it did not happen again. The next Sabbath the dog came up the aisle a little later than usual, with the parson's second-best coat on, buttoned over his back with the forelegs through the arms, the parson's second-best wig on his head, and an old pair of the parson's spectacles on his nose. At home, after church, all the boys denied guilt except the youngest, who was duly whipped. Years later he told his father that they had all done it together but that he, as the youngest, was selected to take the punishment for which they had prepared him by putting sheepskin in his pants.

A major scandal in Parson Stoddard's time was an application in 1708 by Woodbury's Jonathan Taylor to the General Assembly for a divorce. He proceeded to prove that his wife had tried to kill him, had been otherwise violent, had some time since deserted him and gone to New York Colony, and was now living openly with one John Allen, a Negro. The General Assembly generously granted the application.

Woodbury—as well as other colonies!—makes claim to the famous Indian-Puritan episode that is supposed to have occurred about this time. After two of the settlers had spent the evening in the house of one of them disputing the question of predestination, the guest rose to go home and, as he did so, looked to the priming of his musket. "Why do you do that?" asked the host. "If it is predestined that an Indian is to shoot you, you cannot prevent it." "True," said the other, "but if it is predestined that I am to shoot an Indian I must be ready." By modern psychology that was a rationalization of a practical intent. Actually it revealed the center of the indomitable energy of the true Puritans. In all their hardships and dangers they were working, not for themselves but for the glory of God; they were God's agents to carry out His plan which had been foreordained since before the beginning of the world.

Sixth Tribe, Quanneapague or Newtown (1705-1720)

Having cast off Woodbury to the thunder of schism, Stratford next mothered Newtown so gently that it is impossible to find the motive behind the settlement. Since the region, at first called Quanneapague, was mostly inside the frontier line of Woodbury and Danbury, the fact that the war with the French and Indians was going on does not seem to have deterred the settlers. In 1705 a group of Stratford men bought the town from the Indians, and in 1708 the General Court—already called the General Assembly—gave the residents town privileges. In 1710 there were twenty-two proprietors who took their "pitch" of land, and in 1711 the village was laid out about as it is today. In the same year

efforts—unsuccessful until 1714—were begun to call a minister. In 1720 the first meeting house was roofed and put into
use, but it was not finished until many years later.

Seventh Tribe, Weantinock, or New Milford (1705-1720)

In New Milford the hills within and bounding the
valley begin to get higher, the river swifter, and the whole
landscape more rugged and mountainous. The center of the
town is a sort of elliptical bowl, three miles long by a mile
wide, where the drama of the Indians and the whites was
played out for twenty-five years with maximal credit to
both sides. The mile-wide valley plain, through which the
modern, contracted river winds, is the former bottom, as
the flanking hills are the former banks, of the enormous,
ancestral Housatonic. A hundred feet or so up each of these
hills, and at the same level, are two wide river terraces of
the ancient stream. On the western of these, called Indian, or
Fort, Hill, the Indians had their village and fort of Weantinock. On the eastern shelf, called Town Hill, the whites
made their village. Thus the two civilizations faced each other
across the mile-wide "Indian Field," which was the name of
the central valley plain. Three miles downriver stood the
divided mountain above the "great falls," Metichawan, where
the Lover's Leap Rapids had eaten their gorge, and where
the sachem Waramaug had his palace.

There were early unauthorized purchases from the Indians in the Weantinock region, leaving the unexplained,
prehistoric name of Gallows Hill in southern New Milford,
and the large log house of one John Read in the original
village. In 1705 the General Assembly wiped out all earlier
titles—Mr. Read fought the matter for years—by granting
a syndicate of 111 "adventurers" under the leadership of
the ubiquitous Colonel Treat, the right to purchase 50,000
acres from the Indians. Since very few of the adventurers
ever adventured upriver into this northern wilderness and
there was a lively speculation in the rights, this was the
first plantation on the river founded frankly as a business

speculation. The price paid the Indians was about a cent an acre, and the prices realized by the adventurers averaged about a cent and a half. The Indians retained the right to harvest apples in the Indian Field and to fish at Metichawan.

Most of the actual settlers are said to have taken to the wilderness for purposes of religious freedom. The first was a John Bunyan of a man named John Noble of Westfield, Massachusetts. In 1706 he bought several tracts from the rich Bryans in Milford, and, in spite of Weantinock's being outside the frontier and the war raging, he reached it by Indian paths, bringing with him his eight-year-old daughter Sarah "to cook his victuals for him." He built his first cabin at the foot of Fort Hill, right under the Indians' noses. Later the same summer he built a second and larger log house on Town Hill, at the foot of Aspetuck Hill, a little west of the already deserted house of John Read and at the head of the future New Milford green, then a thick swamp. In the autumn of the same year he entertained a company of travelers who wanted to reach Albany, some hundred and twenty-five miles to the northwest without a house between or any trails but those of the Mohawks. Leaving his daughter with an Indian squaw, Noble guided his guests to their destination and returned after three weeks, finding his little girl well, happy and fixed forever in the affections of the Indians.

Settlement in force did not occur till after the peace of Utrecht in 1712, in which year and until 1715 town meetings were held in Milford. In 1714 there were fourteen cabins around the quagmire of the future green. In 1712 the settlers had organized their church and called the Reverend Daniel Boardman, whose subsequent and sincere friendship with the great sachem Waramaug was a pattern of proper relations with the Indians. In 1716 he moved into residence, and services at first were held in the deserted Read house. In 1719 they voted the meeting house, but it was not occupied for seven years and not finished for twelve.

Meanwhile, in the older part of the valley, the Reverend Samuel Andrew, third minister at Milford, had, in 1717, become the third president of Yale, holding the post till

1718 when he was succeeded by his son-in-law, Timothy Cutler, of Stratford. In the year that Mr. Andrew became president of Yale, a group of Anglicans in Stratford set up the first Episcopal church in New England, though their action was illegal and they were subject to fine for failure to attend the orthodox Congregational church. They had a weapon, however, in a long-smoldering disposition of Parliament to punish Connecticut for too much independence generally, and an eagerness on the part of the Church of England to appoint a bishop over all of New England. The Connecticut General Assembly in 1708 cagily passed the niggardly Toleration Act, permitting the Episcopalians to worship as they saw fit, but still requiring them to pay taxes for the support of the Congregational establishment. Thus did the Puritans in their decadence admit the church that had persecuted them, and with it the seeds of Toryism.

In 1710 died Robert Treat of Milford, certainly the most prominent and useful citizen of Connecticut in the seventeenth century; the commander of the colony's troops during King Philip's War and second in command in New England; governor of Connecticut for thirteen years; hero of the Charter Oak incident; leader of an expedition to the far southwest, and founder there of Newark, New Jersey. But for all his ability, Treat was a man of action and not properly in the puritanical, intellectual tradition of the valley.

In 1719 Danbury built its second meeting house, a substantial one at the corner of modern Main and West streets.

In 1720 Derby, now flourishing between shipbuilding and the West Indian trade, likewise built itself a meeting house less shameful in diminutive size than the original one had been. The minister was the Reverend Daniel Humphreys whose son David was to be distinguished in the Revolution. The chief parishioner was Colonel Johnson, who was much beloved by the local Indians, raised and commanded several detachments of them for the French wars, and whose home address was in Sodom Lane.

In 1717 Ripton (later called Shelton) was set off as a

separate parish, though remaining until 1789 a part of the town of Stratford.

Eighth Tribe, The Greenwoods, or Litchfield (1719-1724)

By the Peace of Utrecht in 1712 the Five Nations of New York, including the Mohawks, were acknowledged to be British subjects. This released the first westward emigration from settled New England, and specifically caused the opening of the "Western Lands" of Connecticut, comprising most of modern Litchfield County, where the presence of the dangerous Mohawks had discouraged pioneering before. The region was then called "The Greenwoods" because of its growth of colossal pines, the name being applied particularly to future Litchfield Township, because that was nearer to civilization and so better known. Forty years after the whole territory was settled, President Stiles of Yale, riding through Norfolk and Canaan, measured a pine fifteen feet in girth and counted four hundred annual rings in a cut one.

Litchfield Township was sold in 1719 at Hartford, to which town that part of The Greenwoods had been given previously. The method and conditions of sale were those followed, with slight variations, in the settlement of the rest of the valley thereafter, both in Connecticut and in Massachusetts. The land was divided into sixty shares, or rights—in this case about 785 acres per right—and fifty-seven of these were disposed of at public sale. Of the remaining three, one was to be given to the first minister absolutely, one reserved for the support of the first and succeeding ministers, and one reserved for the support of the school. The shares were bought blind, and afterwards the purchasers drew lots for the order of selection of their tracts. Only a fraction of each share was "pitched" at the original drawing, and in later drawings the order of selection was reversed, so that the division was fair in the long run. Speculation was discouraged by three conditions of sale: every purchaser must within three years build a habitable house at least sixteen feet square; he must live in it for three years after its completion;

for five years thereafter he could not sell or lease; if he broke or failed to fulfill any of these conditions, his title was forfeit.

Settlement began in 1720, with three families, and three years later there were forty-seven adult male inhabitants. The original layout of the village was as it is today, the modern green being then called Meeting House Street, modern North Street then Town Street, and modern South Street, running out of Meeting House Street approximately opposite Town Street, being then called Town Hill Street. Because of the famous beauty of Litchfield today and the opinion sometimes heard that such greens and elm arcades were "planned" by the founding fathers, the actual origin of Litchfield's plan is worth noting.

The highways meeting at the Center were originally even wider than they are today—sixteen, twelve and eight rods, respectively—"more," writes the honest, local historian, "for the convenience of the cattle than for the delight of residents and strangers." Here, as in every new settlement where the threats of Indians and wolves were still real, the plan was to enclose for protection as much common pasture land as possible within the line of huts, still keeping them near enough together to comprise a united system of defense. A second reason for the wide street was to provide a drill field or training ground for the train band, but this could be provided outside the village as well as in its central common. In the early days the identification of the "street" with the public highroad as an avenue for transportation and communication was not important, because both transport and communication took the easiest route, whether over public or private land. Any aesthetic motives for the wide streets were wholly nonexistent. Typically of other early settlements, the great avenues of Litchfield became, soon after they were denuded of trees in the beginning, thick alder swamps where the water collected on the underlying hardpan. Through these bushes and stands of marsh grass wound cattle paths, footpaths and presently cartways, two of the latter in each great street tending to follow the line of the front of the houses. Stories of children and strangers getting lost in the jungles of these "streets" were not unusual. The only motive for clearing them was to improve the pasture or the training ground, which latter was in the western part of Meeting House Street, where the village gathered on the annual Training Day to watch the wonderful convolutions of the plumed soldiers.

Litchfield called its minister in 1721, voted its meeting house in 1723, and raised and completed it three years later. It stood in the middle of Meeting House Street opposite the end of Town Hill—modern South—Street.

In 1722 fresh French and Indian troubles broke out in eastern Massachusetts and Maine, and the Massachusetts governor and Council declared war independently, though Great Britain was at peace with France at the moment. The trouble spread westward, and now it was Litchfield and New Milford that were the frontier towns, selected houses being palisaded and garrisoned. During the next two years one Litchfield man was captured and escaped, one was stealthily murdered and scalped in his field, and two strange Indians were shot, the bounty on their scalps being now increased to £20. In 1727 the scare passed. The local Indians were at least superficially friendly, keeping the colonial order that they must stay within their prescribed limits at their peril. Their limits included Litchfield's highest hill which, because any local Indian was called "Tommy Indian," became known as Mount Tom.

In 1722 New England had rocked when President Cutler of Yale, along with Tutors Browne and Samuel Johnson, professed episcopacy, were dismissed, and went to England where they received Anglican ordination and D.D.'s. In 1723 they returned as missionaries, Dr. Cutler becoming rector of the newly organized Christ Church in Boston and Dr. Johnson of the parish of the same name in Stratford. In 1724 the latter congregation built an Episcopal church, the importation of one Samuel Folsom to do the metalwork setting the stage for America's best Cinderella story, which will be recounted later.

Ninth Tribe, Sheffield (1725-1743)

In 1725 a committee authorized by the Massachusetts General Court bought from the Sachem Konkapot and other Housatonic Indians the southwestern corner of Berkshire County, an area about eight miles wide with the river flowing through the middle of it, and lying northward from the Connecticut line approximately as far as modern Stockbridge village. The price was "Four Hundred and Sixty Pounds, Three Barrels of Sider and thirty quarts of Rum." From the beginning, the tract was divided into the Lower and Upper Townships by an east-west line crossing the Great River at a point where the Great Bridge was presently to be built for the Great Road from Boston to Albany, and where U.S. Route 7 crosses the Great River today at the northern end of Great Barrington village. At the time of the original survey, the Great Road still swung half a mile south to cross the Great River at the ford at the Great Wigwam where Major Talcot had destroyed the fugitive Indians at the end of King Philip's War fifty years before.

In 1726 shares in the Lower Township were sold in Springfield. One of the purchasers was Matthew Noble of Westfield, a worthy kinsman of John of Westfield and New Milford. Matthew had already explored the region and, having bought his tract, repeated the feat of his cousin, taking in with him his sixteen-year-old daughter Hannah to keep house for him. Riding into the wilderness, carrying a feather bed on the horse behind her, she was the first white woman in Berkshire County.

The new settlers met with and returned some violence on the part of a few Dutch who had titles under the old Westenhook Patent, were in at least seasonal residence and had done a little building. Civilities were exchanged between the governors of Massachusetts and New York, and the difficulty was settled by a recognition of such Dutch claims as had actually been developed.

In 1722 the Lower Township was incorporated as Sheffield. Two years later it voted, raised and finished its church and ordained its first minister. The vote for the raising is more explicit in some respects than any found in the records of other towns:

Voted to Set the meeting House on a Certain Nole of Land—which is In the Street or Highway.

Voted to allow three Barrels of Good Beare towards or for the Raising of the meeting house.

Voted to allow twenty Gallons of Rhumb towards or for the Raising of the meeting house or for the towns use.

Voted to allow twenty pounds of Sugar to go with the Rhumb and Obadiah Noble and Ensign Ashley were made choice of to Dool out Drinks to Strangers or Towns People and also to receive the money likewise Ensign Ashley to serve as Pinman.

Voted to allow no drink to the Labourers after they are Dismist from Labour. . . .

At the ordination in October, 1735, two important names make their first appearance in the valley. Among the assisting ministers were the Reverend Samuel Hopkins of West Springfield and the Reverend Jonathan Edwards of Northampton.

Meanwhile, after the opening of the region in 1725, the northern, or Upper, Township, from modern Great Barrington village north to modern Stockbridge village, had lain in an unorganized and lawless state, without even so much orderliness as would be given by a division and sale of lots. It had, in consequence, become a paradise for tax dodgers and all kinds of criminals centered around the fastnesses of Monument Mountain. In 1736 the northern half of this area was enclosed in the new township of Stockbridge. But this left the southern half, including the mountain, as wild as ever, a plague to the decent people in the northern part of Sheffield, who were under the additional hardship of having to ride six miles down to Sheffield Center to church. Soon after the incorporation of the town they began to agitate for separate parish rights, with the lawless region to the north incorporated with them so that they could bring the rascals there under control.

In 1742 this northern strip of Sheffield, locally called Housatonuck from its ancient name, already had two hundred inhabitants and had taken upon itself to build and maintain its own separate school. In that year its inhabitants won their fight and became the North Parish of Sheffield, the badman's land to the north being incorporated with them. They set out with a promising rush, building their church at once on the old common on the east of the river, gracing it with a "belfree" that was not roofed for three years and never got a bell. For a year they "hired preaching," then, in '43, called the young Reverend Samuel Hopkins, nephew of the divine of the same name who had assisted at the ordination in Sheffield. The young man was destined to become one of New England's great theologians, and incidentally the hero of Harriet Beecher Stowe's *Minister's Wooing*. As this time, being just out of Yale, he was studying with Jonathan Edwards in Northampton, where the messenger from Sheffield's North Parish found him. A few days later the Lord accredited the call, and they rode back over the mountains into the rugged country that forty-seven years before had so offended the sensibilities of another young minister with its "hideous high" mountains.

Young Hopkins, less finicky but physically frail, found himself equally tired. The second night out on the old Great Road he wrote in his diary:

> I went to bed after midnight, and after I was abed was much troubled with gnats, which are very tedious here; they kept a smoke by the door all night . . . but this did not keep them off, but they came all around and into my bed, so . . . I did not lie there but about four hours, and slept I believe not one. The people of the house seemed to be after the world, and not to savor of religion any more than the heathen. . . . Came to Tunnick at 11 o'clock, am kindly received and well accomodated to all appearance.

After preaching a few Sabbaths, Mr. Hopkins recorded that the congregation consisted of "very wicked people." On August 1st he wrote: "Took a walk through the woods, and as I returned went into the tavern, found a number of

men there, who I believe had better been somewhere else.
Some were disguised by drink. . . . The circumstances of
this place seem to be more and more dreadful to me: there
seems to be no religion here; if I did not think I had a call
here I should be quite discouraged." Two years later, in 1744,
the minister tried to have the two or three taverns closed.
"Some are offended at me," he wrote sadly in his diary, "yea
even rage at me."

Making allowance for the sensibilities of the young divine,
who was unaccustomed to addressing the Lord otherwise
than from the refined appointments of New Haven and
Northampton, making allowance further for the fact that
the parish was temporarily embarrassed by the ruffians from
its northern section who had just been brought within the
law, admitting also that the chief motive for the carving
of the parish out of Sheffield had been religious, admitting
all this, yet in this frontier settlement that was going to be
Great Barrington there is already a suggestion of a worldliness greater than in the downriver settlements. The intimation is found less in the alcoholic status of the bar flies
than in the economic status of the respectable. In spite of
the original sale of shares in Sheffield having been under safe-
guards against speculation similar to those applied in Connecticut, land grabbing had got well under way in the fifteen
years since the settlement. Even at this early date all the land
in North Parish on the west of the river was in the hands
of three men. The social note of big landowning, henceforth
to characterize the settlements of future Berkshire County,
was already struck. In the mud and drunkenness of embry-
onic Great Barrington the existence of a small, landed, ruling
class was already inferring that wealth rather than godliness
was the chief aim of existence. Before long the same class
was to establish in the region a pattern and tradition of
pseudo-aristocratic, worldly charm instead of piety. And
at the same time there was founded among the commonality
in the taverns a proportionately more watchful jealousy of
their rights, and a quicker readiness to violence than in the
Connecticut towns. As between the inhabitants of the Lower

and the Upper Valley, the latter were to be the less godly and stable, and correspondingly the more colorful and explosive.

At the outset, however, and even while Mr. Hopkins was inditing his complaints, the original, responsible element in Housatonuck remained in control. In 1752—only two years after their southern neighbors of Sheffield proper—they built their own independent grammar, or high, school. Yet twelve years later this quixotic municipality was fined for not maintaining a teacher even in its elementary school!

During the period of the settlement of Sheffield, Milford in 1728 built its second meeting house on the original site, with a spire ninety feet high, a bell better than Stratford's, and a clock. Citizens living outside the village were not taxed for the clock "on account of the distance they lived from the church and could not see the clock anyhow." In the same year of 1728 Derby built a school building, apparently its first.

In 1730 the Connecticut General Assembly licensed Peter Hubbell to run a ferry across the Great River between Newtown and a point in Woodbury—presently to be in Southbury—near the mouth of the Pomperaug.

In 1731 New Milford finished its meeting house, which had been used in an unfinished condition for five years, and the following year it was found necessary to buy a drum to summon the faithful to meetings. At this time New Milford also had a school building, the earlier date of its completion not being of record.

In 1731 Southbury was incorporated as a separate parish. In 1732 it called and ordained the Reverend John Graham, who from 1732 to 1736 carried on a famous battle of pamphlets with the Reverend Samuel Johnson of Stratford on the question of episcopacy.

In 1737 New Milford built the first bridge across the Housatonic above Derby, a long, covered structure at the site of the present Bennitt Street Bridge which did service till the flood of 1802, which carried it away.

In 1710 the boundaries of Woodbury had been increased

by the "North Purchase" of approximately the later towns of Bethlehem and Washington. In 1734 lots were sold and the region spelled "Bethlem" in the early records was promptly settled. In 1738 Bethlem asked the General Assembly for and received "winter privileges," the right to hire their own minister and hold their own services from November to March, instead of riding the six miles down to the parent church in Woodbury. Bethlem made good use of its winter privileges, for it hired young Joseph Bellamy, just out of Yale. In 1739 it became a separate parish, and Mr. Bellamy accepted a permanent call, holding services in a barn until 1744.

Judea—future Washington Township—and Roxbury were carved out of Woodbury as separate parishes in 1741 and 1743, respectively. Already had been born Roxbury's triumvirate of prodigious first cousins, Remember Baker, Seth Warner and Ethan Allen.

In 1743 the Sherman family invaded New Milford, the older brother William building in that year the first separate store building in town. Young Roger went on into the northern part of New Fairfield, afterwards named for him.

1743 was a year for ecclesiastical architecture in Stratford. The Episcopalians got the six-foot, gilded weathercock which still turns to the wind on Christ Church; and the Congregationalists countered with a mammoth new meeting house on the common—Academy Hill—with a spire a hundred and thirty feet high, forty feet nearer heaven from grade than any other edifice in the valley.

But throughout this period from the mid-twenties to the early forties the most interesting feature is the rise in religious interest. Ever since the beginning of the Puritan decline in about 1660, a consistent attack from all the pulpits up and down the valley had been directed at the dissoluteness and indifference of each new generation of youth—the period having been that of the Restoration in England. But now a religious unrest, some kind of reawakening, becomes widely perceptible, evidencing itself both in increased membership and piety in the established congregations and in experimentation in new directions and the demand for ever-wider tolerance.

In 1708 the Episcopalians had won the right to worship according to their ritual, but they were still compelled to pay taxes for the support of the established church. In 1727 Daniel Shelton, the richest citizen of Stratford's Ripton Parish, went to jail in protest against this tax. Soon thereafter the Connecticut General Assembly relented and passed a law that the church taxes of Episcopalians should go to the support, not of the orthodox Congregational churches, but of their own establishments. Presently the long-abhorred Quakers and Baptists got the same concession. In 1726 and 1727 the unprecedented number of thirty-six persons joined the church in New Milford. Then, after the completion of the church building in 1731, nineteen, mostly young people, "fell away" into Quakerism over a period of eight years. It is symptomatic of the broadening tendency of the times that New Milford's minister, the Reverend Daniel Boardman, used to attend the Quaker meetings that were stealing his parishioners.

In 1732 Newtown, where Dr. Johnson of Stratford had been holding occasional services since 1724, organized an Episcopal church and had a rector assigned. In 1737 Derby did the same; the Roxbury region of Woodbury in 1740; New Milford in 1743. In 1740 the Episcopalians of Ripton Parish in Stratford built their own church. Outwardly, this swing to Anglicanism would seem to indicate a surrender of individualism. But this particular movement expressed rather a reassertion of individualism, bolstered to be sure by an increasing number of English immigrants in the population. With the hindsight of two centuries we can already see great doings afoot, doings that were to begin with religion and end with epic politics, that were to begin by tolerating the Anglican Church and end by pitching it out, all for the same, politically individualistic reasons.

The religious ferment of the twenties and thirties at last boiled over in the Great Awakening of '40-'41. Theologically, this was a revival of original Puritanism, a revolt against the compromise of the Halfway Covenant. Socially and politically, it was an expression of rising libertarianism. By restoring individual, emotional religious experience as the condition of church membership, in place of the now almost universal, purely formal qualification of "owning the covenant," the people asserted their independence of the plutocracy which had come to control not only the economy but the churches also.

Oratorically, the chief leader of this religious debauch, this strange emotional epidemic, the only one of its kind in the history of New England, was the Englishman George Whitefield who landed in Boston in 1740, added fuel to the already raging flames, and became America's first great revivalist. Theologically, the center of the movement was Jonathan Edwards of Northampton, who as early as 1734 had engineered a full-scale dress rehearsal in his own congregation, and in 1740 started the region-wide revival by a series of guest sermons, the first in Boston.

As distinguished from Whitefield, Edwards was no orator in the artistic or rhetorical sense. He had a high, weak, overrefined voice, spoke monotonously with his elbow on the pulpit and his chin in his hand, and employed neither gestures nor modulation of expression. What he did possess was the complete consecration of a mystic, one of the great theological intellects of all time, an absolutely humble and absolutely comprehensive Christian humanity, and along with these a commanding stature and a handsome face. What he believed in was "heart religion," justification and regeneration through a spiritual revelation of God to the individual mind and emotions, a process involving a long period of contemplation and prayer. What he got, all over New England, was a sudden crop of hysterical, wholly unintellectualized outbursts from thousands of troubled spirits who had been groping for light in the increasing worldliness of the age and at the same time had been resenting the control of their towns and their churches by the increasingly exclusive plutocracy.

Edwards never doubted the validity of many of the conversions. But when, following the tour of Whitefield in 1740, he encountered on every side screamings, faintings, convulsions, contortions and trances, he desisted from his evangelical labors and considered more carefully than ever the nature of true religious experience. While the fire he had helped to kindle raged around him, he quietly wrote and published in 1741 *The Distinguishing Marks of a Work of the Spirit of God,* and thus joined with the "Old Lights," or conservatives, in extinguishing the fire.

Theologically, Edwards was of the "New Lights," the believers in individualistic instead of social and formal religion. But like all first-rate intellects he saw the virtues and the evils on both sides of the fence and so, eventually, was condemned by both schools. Through his doctrine of "heart religion" and individually achieved grace he restored dignity to the little man in the pew and elevated him to spiritual equality with the educated ministry which was socially identified with the rich. Yet, ten years later, the very common people he had honored dismissed him from his church, because of his blood, marital and educational kinship with the landed, ruling class of western Massachusetts. And at the same time that ruling class spat him out of its mouth for his adventures in "enthusiasm."

Religiously, the Great Awakening was a violent death spasm of true Puritanism whose healthy life had ended eighty years before, leaving it in a coma. The eventual significance of the spasm was the harvest of new sects in the beginning of the nineteenth century. The immediate significance was the strengthening of the political motivation of life that was arising to replace the declining religious one. The humble parishioners whom Edwards had elevated would shortly forget their spurious religious excesses, but they would not forget their elevation. Twenty and thirty and forty years later, the thousands of quietly fanatical men who would be willing to die in pursuit of liberty would be repeating the psychological pattern they learned in the strange, noisily fanatical days of the Great Awakening.

The conflict aroused by the Great Awakening between

the Old Lights and the New Lights split New England in two. By 1742 the controversy was so severe that Jonathan Law of Milford, then governor of Connecticut, issued a proclamation calling for a day of fasting and prayer because of "The Unhappy Divisions and Contentions which still prevail . . . in the Doctrines and Practice of Religion." Joseph Bellamy of Bethlem, now the leading preacher of the valley, was in favor of Edwards's heart religion and against the Halfway Covenant, as were also the Reverend Messrs. Stoddard of Woodbury, Graham of Southbury, and Judd of Judea—now Washington. Bellamy, likewise following Edwards, who had been briefly his tutor at Yale, was opposed to the excesses of the New Lights. In late 1739 or early 1740 Edwards had invited him up to Northampton to preach. He was so impressed by the young man's performance that afterwards they talked together in the center of the church for a long time, oblivious to the departing congregation, and later walked out in the snow leaving at least Edward's hat. Thus began a close friendship between Bellamy and Edwards which remained affectionate and active while they both lived.

In 1744 Bethlehem finished its meeting house. About the same time they built near by a parsonage for Mr. Bellamy, which he later incorporated in the fine mansion that remains the most prominent feature of the village. The tiny, two-room building still preserved in the back yard was Bellamy's study. With this for a classroom and his house for dormitory he began in the 1740's systematically to receive and teach candidates for the ministry, and thus established the first divinity school in America. The enrollment averaged about twenty "sirs," as divinity students were called. To exercise them in preaching, Dr. Bellamy used to lend them out to neighboring parishes as guest preachers, and would take along the whole school to hear each performance, that they might all criticize it together afterwards. The cavalcade of black-coated, black-hatted youths, with Dr. Bellamy and the preacher of the day at the head, was a common sight in and around Bethlem till near the end of the eighteenth century.

Though the controversies stirred up by the Great Awakening continued in a war of ministerial pamphlets up till and through the Revolution, the popular interest was obliterated by the new excitement of the War of the Austrian Succession, in America the Second French and Indian War, 1744-48. It was symbolic of the change that when William Pepperell of Kittery, Maine, got a commission as commander of the expedition against Louisburg, Whitefield the revivalist happened to be visiting him and supplied the motto for the expedition's flag—"Nil desperandum Christo duce." Once again Constantine advanced the cross before the legions. The Light of Religion became the Light of Liberty.

The End of the Heathen

ON THE WHOLE the relations between the English and the Indians were in terms of the better qualities of each race, responsibility and humanitarianism on the part of the former and loyalty and long memory on the part of the latter. The cases of ruthless greed, on the one hand, and of cruelty and vindictiveness, on the other, were exceptional. A Litchfield story, supposed to have occurred during the flare of French hostilities in the 1720's, contains the whole picture of the relations between the races, both for better and for worse.

According to this tale, a strange Indian, giving every sign of hunger and weariness, appeared in a Litchfield tavern, asked to be trusted for a little food and was refused by the landlady, with insulting remarks about filthy, shiftless Indians. A white man who had been listening told the woman to feed the Indian at his expense, which she proceeded to do. When he had eaten, the Indian told the white man the story of creation, recounting how God made the world, the light, the waters and land, the grass and trees, the beasts and birds and fishes, pausing after each separate creation to look at it and say "It's all very good." Finally he made woman and looked at her and "no dare say any such word." Many years later this same white man, while crossing the wilderness between Litchfield and Albany, was captured by northern Indians, taken to their village on the St. Lawrence and saved from torture and death by an old squaw who asked for him in place of her son who had been killed in the war. About a year later, while the man was at work in the forest, he was approached by an Indian whom he did not recognize and led away secretly to a point where the savage had hidden two muskets, ammunition and provisions. The Indian led him southward through the forest for many days, and one day took him to an eminence whence he saw below him the settlement of Litchfield. "Now I pay you," said his guide. "Go home." With that the Indian turned and disappeared in the forest.

Looking back, it is easy for us to see that the only way in which the Indian culture could have been preserved was that it should never have come in contact with white culture. But from the point of view of the early eighteenth century, it would have seemed quite possible for the barbarians to carry on if they—that is, their sachems—could retain the ownership of a sufficiently large tract upon which they could move with the dignity of full legal right. And the possibility of survival would have seemed especially good if the Indians were under a wise leadership that could restrain their impulses to run to the white man and mortgage their land and their souls for a pair of pants, a mirror or other bauble.

Such a leadership the Indians of the Lower Valley enjoyed under Waramaug, "a man of uncommon powers of mind, sober and regular in life, who took much pains to suppress the vices of" his people. Beginning in about 1680, this great sachem, whose origin is obscure, ruled from a Council Fire in the Paugasset-Potatuck (Derby-Shelton) region, where the former Wepawaugs, Pequannocks, Paugassets and Potatucks were reblending into a single tribe. In about 1700 they retreated before the whites still farther northward to Weantinock (New Milford) where, mingled with the related tribe already there, Waramaug, heir of all the sachems of the Lower Valley, kept them together in the last phase of their independent culture through the remaining thirty-five years of his fifty-five-year reign. The domain to which he held unquestioned title, for the support and pleasure of not over six hundred Indians, comprised approximately the modern townships of Sherman, New Milford, Bridgewater, Roxbury, Washington, and parts of

Litchfield and Warren. The capital and central fort was at Weantinock on the terrace of Guarding Mountain, westward across the river and about a mile distant from modern New Milford village.

Waramaug did not himself live at Weantinock, but chose a site two miles to the southeast on the verge of the western precipice of the river's canyon that was shortly to be called the Lover's Leap Canyon. Here, above the perpetual rumble of the falls of Metichawan and the great rapids in the gorge that not even an Indian could navigate in floodwater, he built his "palace," which was the wonder of the age. It was a long house of the usual dimensions for a sachem, a hundred feet by twenty, the walls thatched with huge slabs of specially selected bark that were carried in from miles around on the backs of the builders. Seeming to recognize the traditional claim of the southern sachems to dominion over the whole river to its source, the best artists from all the tribes were sent by their sachems and sagamores from far up and down the river to work many months on the interior decorations. The walls of the main Council Room were adorned with portraits of the sachem himself, his family, his principal councilors and judges. The smaller rooms were painted with beasts, birds, reptiles and insects, "down to the ant and the covey-fish."

In about 1705 the English, with their always attractive proposals to buy, approached Waramaug, and he made a threefold deal with them to the advantage of all. For the Indians he retained absolutely their fishing rights, their village and fort at Weantinock with the hills westward into future Sherman, and a large strip of his eastern domain running northeastward to and around Bantam Lake in future Litchfield. To the English he sold absolutely a tract comprising part of New Milford township east of the river and including the site of the village. The rest he sold conditionally, retaining for the Indians the right to hunt, fish, plant, build and live on it, all the rights of ownership except that of alienation. Under this arrangement, until the great chief's death in 1735, the two races lived amicably in their respective villages scarcely a mile apart on the eastern and western river terraces, with their common river and their common planting ground between. During the period there is no record of any clash or even of hard feeling, while Waramaug himself gained a reputation for tact, ability, and integrity which survives in tradition to this day. For this happy, if temporary, solution of the race problems, a share of the credit must also be given to the white leader of New Milford, the Reverend Daniel Boardman, who was Waramaug's close, personal friend and called him "that distinguished Sachem, whose great abilities and eminent virtues, joined with his extensive domain, rendered him the most potent prince of that or any other day in this colony. . . ."

There is no convincing evidence that Waramaug accepted Christianity to the point of being baptized, but he did spend much time studying the doctrine with Mr. Boardman, and he was sufficiently impressed to send for his friend when he was dying and to ask him to pray for his soul. Waramaug's wife, like most of the Indians, deplored the chief's interest in the alien religion, and was determined that he should not die outside the influence of the faith of his fathers. Accordingly, when Mr. Boardman had gone to the sickroom in the palace she summoned a distinguished powwow, stationed him at the door and bade him proceed with the appropriate rituals. These consisted in writhings, grimaces and bellowings at the top of the Indian's lungs, so that the Christian minister, kneeling at the bedside, had to raise his own voice in order that the dying sachem might hear his prayer. Soon both were shouting with all their strength, and the Indians in the vicinity, favoring their champion, gathered behind him to watch the contest. The rumble of the falls and the rapids below the cliff was overwhelmed by the immediate hubbub. By Mr. Boardman's account he prayed steadily for three hours, till at last the powwow gave up with a tremendous yell, fled down the hill, and "never stopped till he was cooling himself up to his neck in the Housatonic." It does not appear whether this clash of vitality proved immediately fatal to the dying old man who was already too weak to prevent it. In any event he was prepared by respectively accredited ministers for reception by either the Great Spirit or the Christian God. It is possible that, being a man of imagination, he saw no ultimate distinction between them.

Waramaug was buried on the summit of the hill on the eastern side of the Lover's Leap Canyon, higher than the hill on the western side where his palace was, but equally within hearing of the thunder of the rapids that shook the mountain in times of flood. It was a magnificent situation, with an open

view downriver over the Fishing Cove and Goodyear's Island to the lower country that the Indians had already relin-·quished, and upriver to the still populous village at Weanti-nock, and farther northward over the hills that had been Waramaug's to the limit of sight. His grave, like his life, was unique in combining Indian and Christian elements. Its out-standing feature was a monolith eight or ten feet high, split out of solid rock and upended, suggesting white workman-ship and an effort to raise a real monument. Around this, to a height of five or six feet, small stones and trinkets were piled in the usual Indian manner, each item a memorial contribution by some passer-by. The monument stood until some time in the 1880's, when a family from Bridgeport bought the site and built a pseudo castle on it, the stones of Waramaug's monument being utilized in the foundation and chimney of the shabby pile. Meanwhile the largest lake in his old domain became a more permanent monument by being named for him; and in 1852 a private school in near-by New Preston also was given his name.

After Waramaug's death in 1735 the Weantinocks began increasingly to move up the valley to the congregated remnant of all the river tribes at Scatacook in northern Sherman and southern Kent. But the tradition of friendliness with the New Milford people continued well into the nineteenth century, as long as the Indians made their annual migrations downriver to exercise the fishing rights they had reserved in the "Waramaug," or "Good-Fishing-Place" below the rapids. As a matter of unwritten right, they always stopped with the old families on the way, sleeping in the barns in the summer and in the houses in the winter, entertaining the children in the evening with their stories. And as a matter of duty while they enjoyed hospitality, they did the heavier chores and repaired the baskets that had been bought from them.

Waramaug's reign at Weantinock constituted the only successful attempt in the valley to keep the Indian culture alive and distinct. Comparable was the more artificial enterprise of the reservation at Scatacook in Sherman and Kent, where the Indians are supposed originally to have entered the valley on the western side of the Great River where the Tenmile flows in. There the important element of Indian independence was missing. The land had first been bought by the colony and was given back only in the pleasure of the colonial government, whose virtual wards the Indians became. The result was that they degenerated only a little less rapidly than those who lived in the white settlements.

Even before Waramaug's death, Gideon Mauwehu, a man of Pequot descent, was gathering the remnants of the river tribes to this ancestral site. In 1738, when Kent began to be settled by the English, there were about a hundred Indian families around the union of the rivers. The whites began immediately to buy their land, and Mauwehu, although he was recognized as the sachem, seemed powerless to prevent it. In despair he appealed to the Connecticut General Assembly, and in 1752, when the Indians were reduced to twenty families, they got a grant of two hundred acres of tillable land along the river and two thousand acres of hunting land in the mountains adjoining to the west. This caused an increase in the tribe until it was able to furnish a hundred warriors in the Revolution, their chief job being to transmit messages from Stockbridge downvalley to the Sound by drumbeats and signal fires.

After the Revolution the hybrid tribe continued its decline, until by 1800 there remained only thirty-five individuals, most of them half-breeds, drunkards and beggars. The immediate cause of the decline of the Scatacook Reservation was the fact that Mauwehu and others of the leaders went Christian and departed. The basic fact was that the weaker culture could never survive the faintest contact with the stronger, except under the leadership of such men as Waramaug and Mauwehu, men of a type that could not be counted on to appear in every generation. Eunice Mauwehu, granddaughter of the original sachem, and the last of the pure-blooded Indians, died in 1864 at the age of one hundred.

The attempt to keep alive the Indian culture was, by whatever means, bound to be a failure. A second general way of dealing with this race problem was to attempt frankly to Anglicize the Indians, to absorb their culture, and ultimately their race, out of existence. To accomplish this, there was a natural method, that of encouraging the Indians to join the white settlements and live like the whites; and there was an artificial method, that of proselyting them actively with schools and missions. Of these, what I have called the "natural method" was by all odds the quickest and surest way of hurrying the natives into degeneracy. The local histories of all the river towns are rich in anecdotes regarding these remnant Indians who stayed behind in the white settlements after their tribes retreated northward, anecdotes universally built around rum, poverty, squalor, genuine humor, and the sadness of a vanishing race.

There was old Chuse, son of Gideon Mauwehu, who lived for many years in Derby and loved to sit beside a fine spring that flowed from a rock near his wigwam by the highway. Periodically, in the hearing of a passer-by, he would lean over, drink from the spring, then praise it in a loud voice, adding that if only there were another spring of rum beside it he would be perfectly happy.

There was Molly Hatchett who lived in a twelve-foot-square house built for her on the river by the Indian agent in Derby. She was tall, erect and powerful, habitually wore a white blanket shawl and a man's hat and carried a hatchet. Like most of the Indians, she made and peddled fancy baskets, and she customarily presented newborn babies with basket rattles containing six kernels of corn or, if there were more than six children in the family, with a corresponding number of kernels. Like her brethren, she subsisted on rum to the extent that she could get it.

There was Tom Wallops, who was a cavalryman in the Revolution and afterwards owned a little farm with a cabin in New Milford, where he imitated the whites and bore himself with an air of superiority to other Indians. On Thanksgiving, he and his squaw having nothing to eat but hominy and rum, he seated himself and required her to serve him a feast of many courses which consisted of alternately bringing on the bowl of hominy and the bottle of rum, each being removed while the other was enjoyed. One summer Tom found it necessary to replenish his stores from the cornfield of his neighbor, Captain Zalmon Read, who eventually lay in wait to catch him and reported the procedure. About midnight Tom came from his house with his basket, mounted the fence and sat on the top rail, surveying his neighbor's cornfield. "Lot," he said presently, addressing the field, "can Tom have some corn?" Then he would reply for the field, "Yes, Tom, take all you want."

A cider miller in Kent once dismissed two Indian beg-

gars with the promise that he would give them all the hard
cider they could carry away in a bushel basket. The following
winter the Indians reappeared with a bushel basket which
they had sealed by alternately dousing it in the river and
letting it stand, till it was coated with ice. The miller kept
his promise.

The only natives who seem fully to have adjusted themselves to the conquering culture were the descendants of one
of the early New Milford sachems whose name the whites
spelled sometimes as Cocksure, sometimes as Corkscrew, but
which by the middle of the eighteenth century had been
dignified to Cogswell. This family eventually spread up and
down the Lower Valley, supplying several respected artisans
and local office holders, and a lieutenant in the Civil War.
At least one of its scions is now living comfortably in the
West.

Perhaps the basic reason for the inability of the Indians
to blend respectably into the conquering race was the unwillingness of the English to marry them, due to the religious
prejudice against them as the agents of Satan and the
stronger, social prejudice against them as filthy, irresponsible, self-indulgent children. The seeming impossibility of
happy miscegenation reached tragic proportions where the
Indians involved were individuals of the highest quality.

Both the most picturesque and the least substantiated
of these legends is the Pocahontaslike story that is supposed
to have given the name of Lover's Leap to the western precipice of the gorge below Waramaug's palace. According to the
story, one summer day in the years before the whites had
come up to Weantinock to settle, the great chief's daughter
Lillinonah discovered a paleface youth lost and hungry in
the forest. She took him to her father, pleaded for and saved
his life, and when the first snow flew obtained the chief's
consent to their marriage. The boy said he must return to his
people for a little while, but that he would return shortly.
The winter dragged through and he did not return. By May,
Lillinonah was in a dangerous decline, and Waramaug decreed that she should marry a certain promising young saga-

more. On the wedding day, Lillinonah's maidens decked her in her finest beads and feathers, but just before the ceremony she slipped down to the river and, pushing out in her little canoe below the falls of Metichawan, headed downstream toward the canyon and the great rapids thundering through it with the power of the spring flood. When she was already in the gorge and nearing the heavy whirl of waters that would be her doom, her true white lover appeared on the cliff above, leaped down the hundred-foot precipice, and so joined her in the arms of the Great Spirit.

A fully authenticated, interracial tragedy occurred in Woodbury. Waramaukeag was the young, handsome and respected sachem of the Potatuck Indians in that township. Being disposed toward Christianity, he was accustomed to visit the Reverend Mr. Walker to hear his exposition of the doctrine. In the summer of 1687 the minister's seventeen-year-old niece paid him a visit and formed the habit of taking the pine- and hemlock-shaded walk up the Orenaug Rocks to the lofty solitude of Bethel Rock on the summit. Waramaukeag fell in love with her, but failed to win either the girl's or the uncle's consent to a marriage. One afternoon in Indian summer she took the accustomed path and was not seen alive again. The next day her body was found at the bottom of the precipice under Bethel Rock, bruised from the fall but not otherwise violated. She was decorously laid out, her blonde hair smoothed back, her dresses neatly arranged, altogether in a posture that could not have resulted from the fall. Near by was the mangled and twisted body of the young chief. What had happened before on the summit is not known. But local legend is charitable to the Indian.

Besides the natural method of absorbing the Indian culture by absorbing individuals into the white civilization, there was the artificial and conscientious method of proselyting them formally in missions. This method did produce a few score exemplary Christians, but in the main it only slowed up the descent into alcoholic squalor. In the Lower Valley the only organized mission work before the nineteenth century was on the part of the Moravians, a German sect claiming direct descent from the primitive Christian Church. In northeastern North America their central mission was in Bethlehem, Pennsylvania, and in 1740 one of their missionaries, Christian Henry Rauch, established himself at Shekomeko in New York, twenty miles west of Kent and Scatacook. Through the saintliness of his own life and those of his later helpers and successors, all of them living among the Indians in the Indian fashion and supporting themselves by their own labor, they made numerous converts, both at Shekomeko and at Scatacook. When, because of the persecutions of the rumsellers and others, both in Connecticut and in New York, who prospered through the weaknesses of the Indians, the missionaries were compelled to retreat to their main station in Pennsylvania, a score or more of the Scatacook Indians followed them.

A few years later the local attitude toward the missionaries became more friendly, and they returned and established themselves at Scatacook. By 1752 about a hundred and twenty Indians had been baptized there, virtually all the inhabitants, including the sachem Mauwehu, who at this time took Gideon for his Christian, baptismal name. A school and church were built and the congregation flourished for a few years. The mission was abandoned in 1763.

In 1741, when the Moravians first began preaching at Scatacook, they also visited an Indian village fifteen miles farther north at Wequodnoc in Sharon, on the shores of Indian Pond—called by the missionaries Gnadensee, the "Lake of Grace"—which lies on the boundary of Connecticut and New York. At some time in the forties a mission house was built here and also named Gnadensee, there being at the time twenty or thirty Indian converts. In July, 1749, David Bruce, the resident missionary, died, and the following is an excerpt from the Moravian records kept at Bethlehem, Pennsylvania:

Some English neighbors, to whom he had endeared himself, assisted the Indians in making preparations for interring the remains. The funeral service was attended by many friends. Joshua, son of Gideon [Mauwehu], of Pachgatgoch [Scatacook], delivered a discourse in Indian, reminding his hearers of all that their teacher had told them of the Savior's love, and many were the tears that moistened the dark cheek of that mourning and bereft assembly. The body was then put on two canoes, and carried over Gnadensee, the brethren and friends taking their way along the bank to the place of burial, amidst the singing of hymns. At the grave Brother Gideon offered a prayer. And thus was buried the first of our number among the hills and valleys of New England.

By this time Gideon Mauwehu, the supposed descendant of the fierce Pequots, had become a faithful assistant of the missionaries and a powerful preacher. Once another Indian threatened him with his gun, saying, "Now I will shoot you, for you speak of nothing but Jesus." "If Jesus does not permit you," said the old sachem, "you cannot shoot me." The assailant dropped his gun and soon thereafter was baptized.

After the death of David Bruce, the English of the neighborhood asked that another missionary be sent to Wequodnoc, and the mission continued to flourish, with a mixed Indian and white congregation. The last missionary was Joseph Powell at whose death in 1774 it was discontinued. In 1859 the Moravian Historical Society erected a monument to Bruce and Powell on a hill above Indian Pond, or Gnadensee, with a view down the valley of the Tenmile River to the hills of Scatacook and across into New York, overlooking the whole region where the Moravians carried on the only sustained and successful effort to Christianize the Indians in the lower part of the Housatonic watershed. Meanwhile the larger mission upriver at Stockbridge had provided the final resolution of the story of the Indians in the valley.

The Tenth Tribe—Stockbridge
(1734-1758)

THE DRAMA of the Stockbridge mission properly begins sometime between 1690 and 1700, with the distinguished Reverend Solomon Stoddard discovered in the midst of his also distinguished family. Dr. Stoddard was the leading liberal minister of New England, and his Northampton parish—just out of the valley to the east—was the richest in New England outside of Boston. The earliest intimation of forthcoming conflict is preserved in the legend that between Dr. Stoddard's powerful daughters Esther, who became the mother of Jonathan Edwards in 1703, and Christian, previously the mother of Israel and Solomon Williams, there was a lifelong coolness which unhappily boiled to a hotness between some of their children. More certain it is—though here also the original of the misunderstanding is obscure—that at an early period in Edwards's life there arose a difference between him and another Williams connection, Elisha, who had been his tutor at Yale. For whatever cause or accumulation of causes, by 1729 when Edwards at twenty-five succeeded his grandfather Stoddard as pastor in Northampton, there was already between him and his Williams kin a rift that was to have consequences of first importance for the valley, and indeed for the world.

Owing, perhaps, to having been latterly saddled with a royal governor and an appointed King's Council at the head of its government, Massachusetts was at this time bestridden by a sort of aristo-plutocracy, partly mercantile, partly landed, mostly both, a plutocracy in course of maturing into an aristocracy of dynasties whose power would be perpetuated by birth irrespective of wealth. In Hampshire and Hampden counties, which in 1729 comprised all of Massachusetts west of the Connecticut River, this already entrenched gentry, known locally as the "River Gods," included the Stoddards, the Woodbridges, the Dwights, and the Williamses. The last-named family was large, clannish and formidable, and most of its members possessed at least moderate ability. In the eighteenth century its most distinguished scion was Elisha, Edwards's tutor and afterwards rector of Yale, 1726-1739; and one of its insignificant members was Ephraim, Sr., who became its immediate representative in Stockbridge. Between these extremes there lay a formidable array of wealth and poverty, intelligence and stupidity, distinction and vulgarity, piety and worldliness, a clan most of whose members had nothing in common but the name and their loyalty to it. When in 1729 Edwards, a cousin not blessed with the name, succeeded his grandfather as minister at Northampton, he came under a half dozen pairs of already suspicious Williams eyes. When later he dared oppose the whole clan in bank, he brought down on himself a swarm of powerful hornets already seasoned by many worldly victories, while his lonely weapons were his utter innocence of the world, his utter fearlessness, his utter faith in the God he knew was guiding him.

The local history of the Stockbridge mission begins in 1734, when there was yet no North Parish at Housatonuck in Sheffield. There was the old Lower Township incorporated as Sheffield, running north to the Great Bridge to include Housatonuck, or the Great Wigwam, later North Parish, and still later Great Barrington village. And above that there was the Upper Township, a paradise for the irreligious and lawless, running as far north as the site of future Stockbridge village. That year of 1734 Jonathan Edwards's parish of Northampton was enjoying a revival, leading the current trend of New England back to piety. As part of the general stir of religious interest, in that year the Reverend Samuel Hopkins of West Springfield—uncle of the young divine of the same name who eight years later was to accept a call to Sheffield North Parish—and the Reverend Stephen Williams of Longmeadow directed an appeal to Colonel John Stoddard of Northampton, urging the organization of a mission for the conversion of the western, or Housatonuck, Indians. Colonel Stoddard, son of the late Reverend Solomon, was the leading citizen of Northampton, a prominent member of the Massachusetts Board of Commissioners for Indian Affairs, and the blood uncle, ardent supporter and most influential parishoner of Jonathan Edwards. He assembled a meeting at his house, and there the mission was born. Those present included the Reverend Mr. Edwards, the Reverend Stephen Williams and, first cousin to both, Israel Williams of Hatfield, known as the "monarch of Hampshire," the richest and most pretentious of Edwards's parishioners. As a result of the meeting, Colonel Stoddard went to Boston with a proposition, and returned with funds from the British Society for the Propagation of the Gospel in Foreign Parts. Thus Jonathan Edwards was in at the beginning of the Stockbridge mission. And so were the Williamses.

There followed meetings at the Great Wigwam, or Housatonuck, between the Reverend Messrs. Williams of Longmeadow and Bull of Westfield and the Indians under their sachems Konkapot, who already had a commission as captain from the governor of the colony, and Umpachanee, who similarly had been commissioned lieutenant. After four days of hesitation on the part of the Indians, the two ministers persuaded them to accept the philanthropy. On the nomination of Mr. Williams, a call to be missionary was sent to young John Sergeant, recently graduated from Yale and tutoring there at the moment, who had expressed a desire to be a missionary, though handicapped by a paralyzed left arm.

Reporting at once, Sergeant impressed the Indians from the start, and they brought in materials for a combined church and school, which was raised promptly at the Great Wigwam. Sergeant opened with twenty-five pupils and taught till December when he returned to Yale to complete his contract there, leaving Timothy Woodbridge of West Springfield in charge. In July, 1735, Sergeant came back to the Great Wigwam, was ordained at a great and colorful conclave of Indians and government officials at Deerfield in August, and, keeping Woodbridge as teacher, began work as pastor of the Indians in October. One of the first acts of his parishioners was to ask his permission to hold a native dance as an act of mourning for two Indians who had died. Sergeant consented, on condition that they promise not to get drunk. There was promise for the future in the fact that they kept their word.

During the ensuing winter the colonial government dedicated to the mission a tract, comprising approximately modern Stockbridge and West Stockbridge, carved partly out of the old Upper Township and partly out of the wilderness north of it. Subject to later subdivision among them individually, the whole tract was guaranteed to the Indians forever, except for one-sixtieth to go to Sergeant the minister, a sixtieth to Woodbridge the teacher, and a sixtieth to each of four white families whom Sergeant requested Colonel Stoddard to send in to settle and act as civilizing examples to the natives. The plan was to Anglicize them as a presumed help in the process of Christianizing them.

In May, 1736, the mission moved up and settled into the peaceful landscape where the lazy river meanders the rich meadows between the hills. At that time there were about fifty Indians in the mission, of whom forty were in the school, eleven were church members, and nine others were baptized. In July a delegation visited Governor Belcher in Boston, and in a fine speech Lieutenant Umpachanee, now baptized and christened Aaron, presented to the province fifty-two square miles of Indian land flanking the Great Road between Westfield and Housatonuck, besides an assortment of pelts. The governor ordered the pelts sold, the proceeds to be invested in books for the mission library, and in addition he presented the Indians with needed guns and blankets, along with his promise to see to the building of a church. After the conference, Sergeant and the Indians dined in state with the governor.

At the next meeting of the legislature he kept his word and obtained an appropriation for a meeting house, as well as a schoolhouse. The schoolhouse was built immediately, of bark, near Konkapot's house. The meeting house was dedicated on Thanksgiving, but it was not ready for use until 1739, almost three years later. In the meantime, it does not appear where Sergeant held his meetings; but it is plain that he held them, for a favored Indian named Metoxin got twenty shillings a year for blowing the summons to them on a conch shell, another present from Boston.

During that first year, Captain Konkapot and others of the Indians cleared their homelots and built themselves houses on the English plan, either on the "Plain" north of the river, where the modern village is, or on the Meadows south of the river. Timothy Woodbridge the teacher married a lady of West Springfield and built a house on the Plain, where Sergeant boarded with them till the following summer. Then he built for himself a house which was later incorporated into Jonathan Edward's house, commemorated today by the sundial on the property of the Riggs Institute.

By that summer of 1737 Sergeant had mastered the Housatonuck language and could preach without an interpreter. There were ninety Indians in the mission, of whom fifty-two were baptized, including Sachem Yokun of future Lenox and other northern Indians. The Society for the Propagation of the Gospel in Foreign Parts presented £60 for investment in agricultural implements. The Reverend Isaac Hollis of London promised £300 a year for the support of twelve Indian boys in a boarding school; Sergeant selected the twelve and took them into his new house where he taught them independently of Woodbridge's day school. The chaplain of the Prince of Wales—who was to be George III—sent a Bible. The loyalty of the Indians was completely enlisted by Sergeant. Already Woodbridge had taught many of them to write. Everything was going well. The only agent of the Devil present was one VanValkenburgh, a Dutchman who had been in residence before the English, whose title to 290 acres in the Meadows was, therefore, respected and who took advantage of his position to sell rum to the natives. It was certain, however, that in the long run money would be raised to buy out VanValkenburgh at his own figure. He was not a permanent threat.

If John Sergeant or his absolute counterpart could have lived for two or more Indian generations, and if in that time no other English had settled in Stockbridge to give the natives a sense of racial inferiority, while at the same time tempting them to sell anything and everything for liquor or baubles, it seems probable that there would presently have arisen a generation of young Indians who would have made the transition to white culture without going through a phase of degeneracy. But that both conditions should prevail was so unlikely as to be virtually impossible. There have been few men in America or anywhere else with Sergeant's missionary talent for enlisting the personal loyalty of barbarians. As to other Englishmen invading his little Eden, the irony is that it was Sergeant himself who asked Colonel Stoddard to have four families sent in to set an example of civilization to his charges.

It is claimed by some authorities that the leading man of the resulting quadrumvirate was deliberately chosen by Stoddard and the Commission on Indian Affairs in order to have a strong hand at this frontier post, in case the mission Indians began to show sympathy with the northern savages allied with the French. In view of the wisdom and kindness which Stoddard showed in other respects toward the mission and its Indians, a more credible explanation would be that the unfortunate choice was the work of the Williams clan—very possibly with complete innocence on the part of the good Reverend Stephen, who was genuinely interested in the mission and had made the excellent recommendations of Sergeant and Woodbridge.

It is not difficult to guess why the more worldly of the Williamses, of both eastern and western Massachusetts, were ready to conspire to send to a remote settlement a cousin and uncle whose greed had already stirred up a lawsuit in the family and whose lack of spiritual or intellectual refinement may well have been embarrassing to a family that was still less sure of its standing among the River Gods than were, say, the Stoddards and the Dwights. And because of the valuable and disinterested services the Williamses, especially Stephen, had already given the mission, it is at least natural that Colonel Stoddard should have accepted their recommendation, perhaps even without inquiry into the qualifications of their kinsman. By some such combination of circumstances the Devil managed to introduce a truly powerful agent into Eden, and the Indians' song of innocence became the white man's drama of good and evil.

It seems certain that Ephraim Williams was a man of smaller caliber than the one cousin, three nephews, and at least two sons of his who at various times supported him in the conflict of Stockbridge. Rather than a monster of evil, he was propably an ordinary, pompous, sordid mediocrity whose misfortune it was to come into collision with the great, and thereby to acquire a diminutive and unsavory immortality. There do not remain of him sufficient fragments of personality to put together a convincing portrait. There is the report of his continually indulging in lime-juice punch and wine. There are his petulant demands on his sons in his last years; and in the same letters there is evinced a genuine interest in agriculture. At the outset there is the faintly endearing picture of the forty-six-year-old "missionary," riding westward from Newton, Massachusetts, some hundred and fifty miles into the wilderness in June of 1737, carrying his two youngest children in panniers behind him on his horse.

But against these more or less human flashes we have the sordid fact that from the moment of his arrival Williams set about building up his power and prestige at the expense of the mission and of the Indians he was supposed to help to the light of Redemption. He was not even overbright in his machinations and, like the bad boy he was, was forever being caught cheating and having to be bolstered up by his influential kin in the outer world.

As he rode along the Great Road on that June day, Williams's cavalcade included his wife and her brother Josiah Jones of Weston, the head of the second of the four families who had been selected for the settlement. Whether any of Williams's older children accompanied him on the initial trek does not appear. The children of his first wife had been Ephraim Jr., who was now twenty-two and probably at sea at this time, and Thomas, now nineteen, who was to be a doctor. Of the seven children of his second wife, those who took an active part in the Stockbridge doings were Abigail who was now a predatory hussy of sixteen, Josiah who was fifteen, and Elijah who was a little boy. Ephraim Jr. was already rising in popularity and authority in the colony. From shortly after this time he made Stockbridge his official residence.

A year after Williams and Jones, the other two white families arrived, that of Joseph Woodbridge, brother of Timothy the teacher, and that of Ephraim Brown, who was replaced presently by his brother Samuel. Under the leadership of Williams, all four of the new white families built on the Hill above the Indians' Plain and Meadows, ostensibly to get the purer air and better view, actually to put and keep the Indians in their place. Williams himself was not to be hoodwinked by any brotherly love nonsense. He built his walls of solid timbers, in the manner not of ordinary dwellings but of garrison houses, fortifications. There was a well in the cellar, and he kept the place provisioned at all times against siege. Frowning down on the Plain, it was known as "The Castle." From the outset he was hated by the Indians, and presently by the whites also. But, being a Williams and the senior white man present, he enjoyed a deference which it took him several years of misconduct to destroy. In that year of 1738 the drama developed a little nearer to open conflict when Fate provided Jonathan Edwards with a new tie, a new demand upon his interest, in the mountain country to the west. In that year the province gave "Ministers' Grants" of 480 acres to each of seven of its most distinguished clergymen. Edwards got a strip which included about half of modern Lenox village, then wilderness six miles north of the Stockbridge mission.

In the mission the year 1738 was devoted to clearing and construction by both Indians and whites, several of the former achieving not only English houses, but well-fenced and stocked farms. Most of the natives were still leading industrious and sober lives, in spite of the fact that rum was to be had from VanValkenburgh and from several taverns not far away. Then came '39 with its three dramatic events, two of bright and one of dark omen.

Early that year the town was incorporated and named arbitrarily after a town in Hampshire, England. At the first town meeting in July, Ephraim Williams acted as moderator. The Indians being fully enfranchised, Captain Konkapot and Lieutenant Umpachanee were elected selectmen; Timothy Woodbridge the teacher, town clerk; and Josiah Jones, who despite his connection with Williams was always popular with the Indians, constable. The meeting imposed a penalty of £40 upon anyone who should bring liquor into Stockbridge for sale. At this time, or soon thereafter, the Indians surrendered their old tribal name of Housatonuck and began calling themselves officially the "Stockbridge Indians."

The second important development of that year was the completion, dedication and occupation of the log meetinghouse—on the site of the modern Field Memorial Tower. Then came the climax, "an occasion of great joy" to the Indians, and which, more than any other event except the arrival of Ephraim Williams, threatened their ruin. On October 8, 1739, in the presence of ninety Indians who "demeaned themselves with great dignity," John Sergeant married Abigail, Williams's eighteen-year-old daughter.

If Ephraim Williams can be dismissed as a crude and avaricious dolt who was out of his depth in intelligent, let alone in philanthropic, company, no such humble excuse can be found for Abigail. That she was a woman of attraction would appear from the fact that she led by the nose every man she set out to, except one. That she was a lady of taste was evident from the two mansions whose designs she either executed herself or closely supervised. That she was a lady of charm was evident from the complimentary report of her left by persons who did not know her well. Attraction, cultivated taste, charming and hospitable manners: it is certain that she possessed at least these positive qualities. And it is almost as certain that she used them to no purposes but her own advancement, and the domination of her environment. Though she married one great man, Sergeant, there is no indication that she either loved him or in any way sympathized with him or his filthy Indians. They were hardly wed before she issued her refusal to live in his little house on the Plain among his charges, and set him to building her

the exquisite, diminutive mansion on the aristocratic Hill, the house which has modernly been moved down into the village on the Plain and furnished as a museum. It is said that the paneling of the front door and the parlor was brought by ox team from Connecticut. However that may be, the construction of the house ran Sergeant into debt beyond the remotest possibility of payment from his £100 salary, a debt which, steadily increased by Abigail's personal extravagance, amounted ten years later to £700.

There is no telling how Ephraim Williams succeeded in nullifying the cardinal rules under which the mission was founded. One of these was that no white families were to be settled except those of the missionary, the teacher, and the four others introduced for exemplary purposes. A second rule was that each of these English planters should be entitled to one-sixtieth of the township—about 385 acres—and no more. A third was that no white man should buy land from the Indians who, but for the six-sixtieths allotted to the six white families, owned the rest of the 23,000 acres that comprised the town.

In spite of these rules, Williams in 1739, two years after his arrival, seems to have put over a wonderfully transparent deal. He induced "the clergy of the Connecticut Valley"— which included his cousin Stephen of Longmeadow and his nephew Elisha, then retired from Yale and in Wethersfield— to put up the money for the pious purpose of buying the 290 acres of VanValkenburgh, the rum-selling Dutchman. These good acres, long cleared and in production, were deeded to the Indians in return for 4,000 acres of their undivided land elsewhere in the township, land that was certain to be taken up at any moment. Williams's share was 900 acres. Two years later, in 1741, there were three new white families in residence. In 1744 there was a town vote which may or may not have been innocent. The Indians were directed "to lay out 1200 acres of land in one piece for themselves, and then the English proprietors to lay out the remaining part of their rights."

If this was a plot to limit the Indians to 1,200 acres it failed. But the final division in 1750 was almost as far from the original intention. At the time of settlement, 1,670 acres had been divided between thirteen Indian families. Now, 2,500 more were divided between fifty-five more Indian families, making a total of 4,170 acres for the natives. It is not plain how the remaining 16,500 acres in the town got out of the hands of the Indians, but presumably it was by sale to which all the Indians assented, exactly as in other plantations.

By 1750, the year of this division of land among the Indians, there were twelve white families living in Stockbridge. Ephraim Williams, Jr., who had traveled extensively in his youth, was now thirty-five and becoming one of the recognized leaders of the colony. In the second French War—

1744-1748—he had commanded a reinforcement sent to the siege of Louisburg, but had arrived too late to take part in the action. Immediately thereafter he had been put in charge of the colony's northern line of forts, of which the westernmost and the one of greatest concern to the valley war Fort Massachusetts, located just out of the valley in future Adams, some fifteen miles north of newly settled Pittsfield and a dozen miles more north of Stockbridge. In 1746 this outpost, having a garrison of twenty-two, including the second Williams son, Thomas the doctor, was attacked and burned by three-hundred French and Indians. The size of the garrison and the fact that the attack was a surprise has left some question as to the competence of young Major Williams, who was himself absent during the siege. However, it is plain that the government continued to hold him in respect for energy and intelligence, and good authority has it that in all his commands he was beloved by his men. He was elevated to the Governor's Council and held the position of sheriff of Hampshire County. At worst he was a tall, heavy, strikingly handsome, personally attractive, moderately competent man of the world. And at least once he was able to make a gesture of imagination and responsibility which would have been impossible for his father or his half sister Abigail.

By 1741 Sergeant, having frequent ministerial duties westward among the Mohawks and others of the Five Nations, and southwestward among the Delawares and Susquehannas, was finding it impossible to manage properly the boarding school provided for by Hollis in London, and began to agitate for a school building and a resident teacher. A board of trustees was selected for the boarding school, comprising virtually the same men who had originally organized the mission, including Colonel John Stoddard, Major Israel Williams, Reverend Dr. Stephen Williams and the Reverend Jonathan Edwards. Thus the Lord laid upon Edwards still another responsibility in the western place beyond the mountains.

The Great Awakening was now in full swing, and Edwards had on July 8th preached the famous Enfield sermon.

His remote cousin by marriage, the Reverend Stephen Williams, seems thus far to have approved of him. But his first cousin and parishioner, the "Monarch" Israel, had been annoyed by his enthusiasm from the beginning and his stepcousin Elisha was already attacking him in the current pamphlet war.

Owing at the outset to difficulties in raising money, and afterwards to the French War, the plans for the improvement of the boarding school did not materialize until 1747, when a good building was put up. The new teacher was Captain Martin Kellogg, who was a Williams appointee, a friend and connection by marriage of Elisha's, and who proved to be an incompetent man. Because of his unpopularity, the Indian boys began deserting the school, and Sergeant had trouble maintaining the student body of twelve which was the condition of the income from Hollis.

About this time still another development associated Edwards with the missionary work among the Indians. An occasional visitor to the mission during the forties was David Brainerd who, at the height of the Great Awakening in '41, had been expelled from Yale for opining that one of the tutors was not in the State of Grace. Jonathan Edwards had tried unsuccessfully to have the young man granted his degree, this being the first of several slaps Edwards was to get from his alma mater. Brainerd was a friend of Sergeant's and became a heroic, itinerant minister to the Indians, sending many to the mission and often stopping there himself. He became engaged to Jerusha Edwards, favorite daughter of Jonathan and "generally esteemed the Flower of the Family." In October, 1747, Brainerd died at the Edwards house in Northampton, having long continued his labors though stricken with tuberculosis. Four months later Jerusha, who had nursed him and taken the disease, followed him. Edwards took on the difficult and thankless task of editing Brainerd's papers.

In 1749 Stockbridge had the same plan it retains today, only the roads leading northward were still Indian paths. The recently finished road southward to Housatonuck, or

Sheffield North Parish—modern Route 7—crossed the river on a covered bridge painted red. Though Williams had succeeded in increasing the number of white families to twelve, the increase in Indian population was out of proportion. There were 53 Indian families in the village, comprising 218 individuals. Twenty of the families owned English houses and other farm buildings. Most of the youth understood English and many of them spoke it correctly. One hundred and twenty-nine out of the 218 had been baptized, and there were 42 church members. Sergeant had seen eight or nine of his flock die "with a good christian temper and a well grounded hope."

Sergeant himself had led a life of unbelievable hardship and activity. With his one good arm he had done most of the work on his little farm. He had preached two sermons a Sunday to the Indian congregation and two separate ones to the whites. He had taught in the boarding school, and had made many journeys each year among the western Indians. He had labored to raise money for the mission, and most trying of all, he had had to contest the interests—Williams interests among others—who told the Indians that he was depriving them of their rights in inducing them to give up drinking. On the whole he had been successful, seeing his charges increase in numbers, in piety and in civilized responsibility. Early in July, 1749, he was stricken with a "nervous fever," involving a "canker" in his throat. The Indians devoted a day to fasting and prayer for him. Once Sergeant rose from his bed to preach to them. On July 27th he died. The Indians filed a request with the village that they, when their time came, might be buried in a circle around him, so that at the resurrection they would first see him when they arose. One of them is credited with having composed his epitaph:

Where is that pleasing form? I ask; thou cans't not show:
He's not within, false stone, there's nought but death below.
And where's that pious soul, that thinking conscious mind?
Wilt thou pretend, vain cypher, that's with thee enshrined?
Alas, my friends, not here with thee that I can find;

Here's not a Sergeant's body, or a Sergeant's mind.
I'll seek him hence, for all's alike deception here,
I'll go to heaven, and I shall find my Sergeant there.

With the death of Sergeant, what might be called the
period of pioneer Christianity in the valley came to end, the
period when heroic ministers led their flocks, white or Indian,
out into the wilderness and suffered with them what hardships the human frame could endure, and sometimes more.
Alhtough all these early leaders—Blakeman, Prudden,
Walker, Stoddard of Woodbury, and the rest—were educated
men, yet their Christianity was perforce that of action, meeting and helping their charges to meet the immediate, practical trials of each day. Consequently they left behind them
no important body of recorded thought, no tangible contribution to the tradition of the valley.

Now that pioneering period is over. The downriver settlements are well established and men are beginning to find
leisure to lead the life of the mind and to record their observations. Already for some years the century-old town of
Stratford has been the seat of Samuel Johnson, America's
leading Episcopal minister, and his pamphlet controversies
with the Reverend John Graham of Southbury and others are
the most famous of this pamphleteering age. Now, in 1749,
Joseph Bellamy of Bethlem is about to publish his *True Religion Delineated,* the valley's first book that is to receive
world recognition and take a permanent place in the literature of theology. The introduction to Bellamy's book is to be
written by his friend Jonathan Edwards, and as the book
appears Edwards himself is to come over the mountains. With
his coming the ideational current of the valley rises to full
power. The rills coming down from the springs of the past
mingle. The River of History begins to roll.

In July, 1749, when Sergeant died, Jonathan Edwards in
his Northampton parish was already surrounded by the yap-
ping controversy that was to send him for peace into the
valley. The various pretexts used against him by the ignorant

have no relation to the story of Stockbridge and the river. As already indicated, they were rooted in the determination of the people, to whom he had given spiritual birth in the Great Awakening, to be rid of him because he was an aristocrat, one of the River Gods, the friend and protégé of Colonel Stoddard until his death, and afterwards the friend and protégé of Colonel Timothy Dwight, who inherited Stoddard's mantle of squiredom in Northampton. It was typical of Edwards that, while he carried always the deep hurt of his people's unchristian ingratitude, yet he carried too the suspicion that it was not their fault but his who in some way had led them unwisely.

Of closer relation to the history of the valley was Edward's now almost continuous controversy with his Williams kin, which controversy made its contribution to his dismissal. Ever since the Great Awakening he had been under pamphlet attack by Cousin Elisha. Now in the fall of '49, Edwards published his famous *Humble Inquiry* into the qualifications for church membership, summarizing his old arguments of the Great Awakening; and in April, 1750, Major Israel's brother, the Reverend Solomon, set out to compose a reply that would slay him. The ensuing exchanges covered two years. Meanwhile, in June, 1750, Edward's persecutors in Northampton accomplished his dismissal. Three years later one Joesph Hawley, the leader of the wolf pack, confessed to Edwards the unfairness of the "trial," where Edwards was never heard, published his confessions in the Boston papers, and begged Edwards's forgiveness. But by that time Edwards had climbed to a new plane, where his audience was not a parish, or New England, but the world.

Edwards was not long dismissed before he had calls from Canaan in the valley, from Lunenburg, Virginia, and from Scotland. But instead of considering any of these, he seems affirmatively to have sought the call to Stockbridge to replace Sergeant. Even before he was dismissed he went out to the mission to preach, and accepted a second invitation before he was called. The Williams interests were seeking the appointment of young Ezra Stiles, just graduated from Yale, and its future president. Abigail Sergeant, now a widow of twenty-nine, was zealous for him. But, after he had preached once at the mission, neither he nor the Indians were satisfied with his candidacy, and he was not called. Thereupon both the Indian and the white congregations agreed on the Reverend Samuel Hopkins from downriver at Housatonuck. He, being about three years older than Abigail, suited her even better than Stiles, and she is said to have suffered a nervous breakdown when he refused the call. When the call finally went to Edwards in '51, it was due in large part to efforts of his friend Bellamy of Bethlem and of his other former student Hopkins, who had turned down the job.

Even to a man of Edwards's prideless and humorless solemnity, it must have occurred that he was neither very much wanted nor very much suited for this position. He must have known that he was second choice for all and third for some, and that he owed the appointment to his friends. Perhaps he was not able to appreciate how ludicrously unqualified he was, how lamentably he lacked the personal touch that had been Sergeant's, what an absurd figure he, the finest American mind of the time, was going to cut every Sabbath standing before a small group of blanketed savages and warning them through an interpreter, "It is not good to get drunk." What he certainly did see was that a backwoods mission was hardly a place whence a pulpit voice battling for truth could be heard throughout New England. Yet, in spite of these obvious objections, he angled for the call and, when it came, accepted it with alacrity.

The reason was that he no longer considered himself a pulpit voice. After the doubts following his forensic success in the Great Awakening and the present doubts raised by his equally plain failure in Northampton, he was through with preaching and was convinced that the time had come to seek expression in another medium. From his youth he had cherished a determination someday to compose "a Particular Enquiry into the Nature of the Human Mind, with respect to both its Faculties—the Understanding and the Will—and its various Instincts, and Active and Passive Powers." His nearest approach to this objective so far had been the *Treatise Concerning Religious Affections* which he had turned out in 1746 and which was the one of his great treatises produced so far. But its subject had been only tangential to the main purpose he had in mind. He was now forty-eight years old and believed he was failing in physical stamina. He might not have many years left. His reason for going beyond the mountains and down into the valley was the same one which, since his day, has sent thousands of others after him—to find among the hills quiet and time to do the most ambitious work of his lifetime. His basic mood of pantheism always felt nearer to God in the wilderness. In Stockbridge the routine would be easy, and there would be few visitors dropping by with their demands on his time. In the center of the Plain there, with the easy-flowing river to the south, and the mountains standing guard all around, with the primeval forest everywhere sealing him off from settled New England, here in the great silences Edwards hoped to find and to be worthy of the universal, literary pulpit which had always been the object of his deepest desires.

At the beginning, this hoped-for resolution of his life seemed far from assured. Though the pastoral duties were less than in a large congregation, it looked as if the Williams opposition and other annoyances would pre-empt more of his energies than he otherwise conserved. In order to keep the Hollis Boarding School up to its necessary quota of twelve students, the Mohawks, at about the time of Sergeant's death, had been invited to join the mission. This some eighty of them had done in '50, living in tepees on the Meadows, their leader being the great chief Hendrick whose fate was later dramatically bound with that of Ephraim Williams, Jr. By '51 the Mohawks were dissatisfied with many things, especially with Captain Kellogg, the incompetent boarding school teacher and creature of Elisha Williams. In the summer of '51, when Edwards made a preliminary trip to Stockbridge, not intending yet to undertake any duties, he became involved with a commission sent out from Boston to pursue the Mohawks and try to get them back. He went with the commission to Albany, where a conference resulted in the return of some of the Mohawks, with recruits from the Oneidas and Tuscaroras, on condition of the appointment of a new boarding school teacher. The teacher appointed was Gideon Hawley, Edward's suggestion, representing a preliminary victory over the Williamses.

At about this time, and before Edwards was well dug in, Elisha Williams arrived from London, where he had got himself appointed a member of the Governing Board of the Society for the Propagation of the Gospel in Foreign Parts. Under the formidable power this gave him, he instantly founded an Indian girls' boarding school at Stockbridge with the Widow Sergeant as head mistress at £100 a year, which Elisha paid in advance, Abigail needing the money. In August Edwards was formally installed as missionary on a salary of £100 from the society, £6 13s. 4d. from the white congregation, and a hundred loads of wood from the whites and Indians together. His old church in Northampton was struck by lightning the moment he left town.

One of Edward's first acts in Stockbridge was to write the Commission for Indian Affairs in Boston, asking for a single, resident trustee to be appointed to supervise all the practical affairs of the mission and centralize the missionary's responsibility which was now divided between the commission, the society, the Indian congregation, the white congregation, the Hollis trustees and Hollis himself. While getting into the saddle, Edwards set to work on a counterreply to the attack on his *Humble Inquiry,* which his reverend cousin Solomon Williams had given the world many months before. In early October his daughter Mary married Timothy Dwight, Jr., son of Major Timothy, Edwards's Northampton friend, thus guaranteeing more closely than ever the help of that powerful agent in the outer world.

Edwards made Mary's marriage an occasion to ride out to Northampton and fetch back the formidable and dominantly female ranks of his family. It is perhaps a comment on Edwards's private, as distinguished from his public, character that, although his wife was stiff and severe, all seven of his daughters were irrepressibly high-spirited and gay, and had an eager, companionable love for their father. Jerusha, the fiancée of David Brainerd, had died four years before. Sarah, the eldest, had preceded her father to Stockbridge as the wife of Elihu Parsons, one of the recent settlers. Mary was to be left behind in Northampton. On October 10th, having duly given her away, Edwards marshaled the cavalcade of his remaining family and led it westward through the woods: Mrs. Edwards carrying the year-old baby Pierrepont; six-year-old Jonathan Jr., destined to carry on his father's theological fight long after it was lost; thirteen-year-old Timothy; and the four as yet unmarried daughters, beautiful, fragile Esther who was to be the mother of a beautiful, sensitive villain, and Lucy, Susannah and Betty, all sprightly and strong characters, each in her way. On October 12, 1751, these nine souls, all accustomed to relative luxury, sardined themselves gaily into the little house that Sergeant had built for himself alone on the Stockbridge Plain. The following year Edwards, harassed by a thousand petty controversies, enlarged it to the house that was long associated with his memory.

The year 1752 had seemed to start auspiciously with the arrival of Colonel Joseph Dwight—remote cousin of the Timothys—as resident agent of the Commission for Indian Affairs. Colonel Joseph had been second in command at Louisburg, where he distinguished himself for bravery. During '48-'49 he had been speaker of the King's Council. Doubtless he felt at the moment the need of a little cheap western land, but no one in New England would have questioned his integrity and ability. Edwards approved his appointment and hoped it would break the grip Williams had got on the whole mission in the two and a half years since Sergeant's death. Then all hope vanished when, a few months after his arrival, Abigail caught the general and married him. From that moment he was Ephraim Williams's man, one of his first duties being that of keeper of the boss's store, where liquor and other merchandise bought with government funds were sold secretly to the Indians. The spiritual reduction of this Samson ranks even higher than the financial ruin of Sergeant among Abigail Williams's achievements.

In the spring of '52 Edwards cemented the opposition against him by sending out to Colonel Timothy Dwight in Northampton his *Misrepresentations Corrected,* being his counterreply to Solomon Williams's attack on his *Humble Inquiry.* The melodrama in the air appears in his note to his friend:

Sir,

I have just sent the copy of my answer to Mr. Williams by my son Parsons, to be conveyed by you to Mr. Foxcroft [the printer]. I need not tell you that extraordinary Care had need be taken in the Conveyance. There are many Enemies who would be glad to destroy it. I know not how in the world it can well be got to Mr. Foxcroft's Hand, especially by Reason of the small Pox, but I desire you should do the best you can

J. E.

(The revelation of Edwards's worry about the "small Pox" is prophetic at this period of tension.) When the pamphlet appeared, Solomon Williams was so utterly and finally punctured that there was no further hope of peace between Edwards and any of the family. The job was the more perfect in that it was all factual and never descended to personalities. Not the Reverend Solomon—not even the great Elisha—had anything more to say on the theological issue on which Jonathan Edwards had been dismissed from Northampton and become involved in "a contention between me and most of New England."

The forces were now aligned for the valley's first cleancut conflict between the Lord and the Devil, between Idealism and Greed, between Spiritual and Material Truth: on the one side Edwards, the Indians, most of the local whites, and as foreign agents Colonel Timothy Dwight of Northampton, the Reverend Messrs. Joseph Bellamy and Samuel Hopkins of the valley, and generally the liberal wing of the New England clergy; on the other side the local Williamses, Colonel Joseph Dwight, and as foreign agents, the half dozen

Williamses who were powerful in Massachusetts, and the stuffed-shirt wing of the clergy, especially President Clap of Yale who delighted to harass the institution's first graduate of major distinction. As always, the forces of the Lord had the advantage of seeking nothing for themselves, while the forces of the Devil were handicapped by seeking nothing except for themselves. The letters with which Edwards began to bombard the provincial government were so candid and direct in their charges against Williams and Dwight that they would have driven honest men to bring suit, but the Williams attacks had to be furtive, taking the form either of whispering campaigns or of disingenuous and trumped-up charges.

In August, 1752, Edwards summarized the situation in a letter to the speaker of the Assembly, expressing a willingness to have the letter published. In his usual, wholly impersonal method of understatement he revealed that the Williams interests were creating profitable jobs for members of the family, that through the store government bounty was being distributed to the Williams-Dwight profit, that Mistress Dwight was performing none of the duties of the girls' boarding school except to collect the salary, expecting someone else to do the work at government expense, that Colonel Dwight was planning to take over the control of both schools and make his son—by a former marriage—master of the boys, that the attempt "to establish a Dominion of the Family of Williams's over Stockbridge affairs" was alienating the Indians, driving them away, and endangering not only the success but the peace of the mission.

It may well be that the Commission for Indian Affairs was not averse to a little graft inuring to two strong men who were willing to live in the wilderness and keep the Indians under control. But it was a different matter when it began to appear that they were not maintaining the desired control. This became apparent in the spring of '53 when Colonel Dwight was about to put into effect his scheme to assume the hegemony of both boarding schools, which meant the dismissal of the popular teacher Gideon Hawley and the installation of the colonel's son. The Indians' reaction to this consummation was persuasive. Mysteriously one night the boys' boarding school burned down. This alarmed the commission and evoked from it a complaint to Williams, which determined him upon strong measures.

Since the death of Sergeant, a new crop of whites, including Edwards's "son Parsons," had settled in Stockbridge. Most of them had bought farms, not on the Hill, but on the Plain where, although inferior to the Indians in population, they began to rival them in acreage. If Ephraim Williams could get hold of their land it should be sufficient, with his holdings on the Hill and elsewhere, to guarantee his economic control of the town. The subtler, more literate part of the plot he left to his compliant son-in-law, the colonel who, in his capacity of resident agent for the Indian Commission, was to write a detailed report upon the disqualifications of Edwards for the post of missionary. Such disqualifications did in fact exist. Although Edwards was an accomplished linguist in the classics, including Hebrew, and although he learned to understand the Housatonuck language, and his children spoke it like Indians, he never dared to preach in it. The more refined "infirmities"—the phrase Edwards's own—that made him inferior to Sergeant as a missionary were perhaps beyond the understanding of Williams and Dwight. The colonel went to work on his laborious report, and carried it to Boston about the time of the climax of midsummer, '53.

Williams set about his coup with the slyness of an elephant. He proposed to buy out all the white farmers on the Plain with such secret speed that the word of his venture would not get around until it was accomplished. So great would be the eventual profits that he was willing to pay any price the farmers asked.

He started one night after dark, threading his way over the Plain by the cattle paths, welcomed to dark house after house by the dogs. By sufficiently raising the price, he succeeded in buying out one man. But thereafter the going got slower and increasingly hopeless. With several farms in suc-

cession he wasted precious hours without effecting a purchase. By daylight he had not completed the rounds, and
those already approached met, compared notes, and reported
the now obvious purpose to those who had not yet been
honored.

From then on the calls were brief and to the point.
No more prospective victims would even listen to him. Long
before noon he had seen everyone. The result was one small
purchase in the bag. Already the village was alive with a
buzzing, among both Indians and whites. Presently an angry
swarm began to trend up the Hill toward the Castle. In
spite of his boasted fortifications and his provisions against
siege, Ephraim Williams, being sixty-two years old and a
man of pomp, rode out of town "very suddenly" and never
returned.

Colonel Dwight, already in Boston, read his report to
the commission, and had it rejected. Elisha Williams came to
Stockbridge and tried to bully Edwards into approving Abigail's appointment as headmistress of the girls' boarding
school, on threat of an unfavorable report to the London
Society for the Propagation of the Gospel. Ephraim Jr. organized in Boston a new whispering campaign against the
missionary. He bought all his father's lands in Stockbridge,
but, having duties in the French war, which was threatening
again, he leased the farm and castle on the Hill to his young
half brother Elijah and took his departure.

Old Ephraim in his hegira had fetched up in Deerfield,
whence he wrote Elijah demanding £100 a year "Equivalent" for his "Privileges" in his son's house: "viz—the House
Room, a Horse allways Kept, firewood fitted at the door;
and allso two acres of land at the door. . . ." After some
interesting instruction in orchard culture, he adds a list of
equally petulant but healthier demands: "I am more sensi-
ble of the want of aples than perhaps you may be aware
of. . . . I want the Red Jackit and blue millatary Britchis &
the Green old winter Jackit some good chease & the shrubb
. . . allso the thing I put over my head to keep my Ears warm
which I buttin under my chin. . . ."

The negative part of the climax of the drama of Stockbridge was over. The defeat of the Devil was complete. But the affirmative victory of the Lord was yet to be consummated. With the male Williamses out of the way, and with Colonel—now General—Dwight likewise in the north exercising over a brigade of men the command he could not exercise over his wife, Edwards for the first time found Stockbridge the wilderness retreat he had sought in the beginning. In that September of '53 the Seven Years' War was already raging, and it was about to break out in America, where it would be known afterwards as the Old French War. But here and now the fruitful silence of autumn was heavy on the hills and in the mists over the river. In its little farm buildings and tepees around him on the Plain and out across the Meadows, the Indian community was silent as usual, silent and friendly to Edwards. Farther off were the houses of the whites, many of them hidden over the Hill to the north. In his enlarged house, he was able to shut behind distant doors his family's gaiety, and there was silence in his four-by-eight study at the west end of the building, large enough only for a chair, many books and his unique hexagonal, revolving desk. From its window he could see his log meeting house among both of whose congregations there was at last repose. He was now able to spend at work a productive sixteen hours a day. At last the mountains around were become the cradle of peace he had hoped for. The "Particular Enquiry" which had teased him for years began to take shape. He started to write with the fever of a lifetime of contemplation and study pouring out into channeled expression. Up and down the valley the forest flamed into crimson and gold. The gray November rains came down the mountains, and December's wind and snow. The whiteness deepened, and the utter silence and the cold, isolating the settlement from the world. And in the silence a man's spirit burned secretly and grew more aware, and expanded to enclose time, and to fulfill its predestined potential by an act of its independent will.

Throughout the winter of 1753-54 the last war between

European powers for the possession of North America flamed along the horizons. On the frontier the tension was great, and every move of the Indians was watched with suspicion. In the spring two Scatacook Indians—recently arrived at the Stockbridge mission—were sapping in the Hoplands of future Lee, when they saw two white men—also strangers in the region—pass by, leading horses without bridles but with bark halters. This equipment being Indian, the two Scatacooks thought the horses had been stolen and pursued the whites who, upon being hailed, turned, shot one of the Indians and beat him to death. The culprits were pursued and caught, carried to Springfield and tried. One of them was acquitted and the other got off with a minimum punishment for manslaughter, this injustice being based on the difficulty of distinguishing a local from a northern Indian. The Indians in the region lapsed into an ominous sullenness. Weeks passed. In Deerfield old Ephraim Williams completed his part in the play by dying unnoticed.

More weeks passed. In the outer world the active war and in the Upper Valley the unhealthy tension continued. In August Jonathan Edwards, who was addicted to neither fear nor overstatement, wrote to the Assembly that the danger of an uprising was great. After much delay, the Assembly sent £20 to the family of the murdered Indian. This method had the justification of according with Indian law, but the amount was too little. Also, the half-Anglicized natives recognized it as an attempt not to do justice but to buy safety.

On August 28th a village in New York about ten miles northwest of Fort Massachusetts was destroyed by a large force of Canadian Indians. The news put the frontier on edge, and three days later the fringes of settlement north of Stockbridge were ordered to withdraw southward. The next day, being Sunday, September 1st, the Reverend Mr. Edwards had just opened the afternoon service of the white congregation when a parishioner from the northern part of town burst into the meeting house breathless. Interrupting the service, he explained that, hurrying late to church and passing the house of neighbor Chamberlain, he had surprised and frightened away two Indians who were in process of murdering the family. The victims so far were one child tomahawked, one baby's brains dashed out against the mantel, the hired man Mr. Owen wounded profusely and dying. Two other children were hiding in a feather bed, and the father and mother had prudently jumped out a window and escaped.

Though never identified personally, the two Indians were later found to have been Scatacooks taking blood for blood in accordance with their law. But to the nervous frontier, they were either Stockbridges rising or heralds of the northern enemy that had destroyed the New York village and now sweeping down on them with yells and scalping knives. Against Mr. Edwards's remonstrance and his personal calm, the meeting house was suddenly empty, and a race was in progress down the road to Housatonuck North Parish on the part of almost all the whites in town. With them went many of the squaws and children of the local Indians, who were just as astonished by the murders as the whites were, though their men behaved with more dignity. The aristocratic Dwights moved out with what baggage they could assemble quickly, Abigail not stopping to put shoes or stockings on little John Sergeant and merely leaving orders to the Negro slave London to bring along three-year-old Pamela Dwight—later the wife of Theodore Sedgwick and the mistress of New England's noblest slave. On this occasion the Negro was no braver than his white mistress for, having set out southward, fear overwhelmed him and, dropping little Pamela in a raspberry bush, he took to his unfreighted heels. An hour later Larry Lynch, an Irishman who boarded with the Dwights, was convoying the family silver at leisure when he discovered the child and restored her to the arms of her mamma.

Meanwhile, in response to the orders sent out the previous day, all of a small group of pioneers at Yokuntown (Lenox) and most of the more settled population at Pontoosuc (Pittsfield) were vacating their cabins and houses.

During the flight southward of the Yokuntown group, the little column was stalked by the very two bloodthirsty Scatacooks who were themselves in flight from their recent business in Stockbridge. Shooting from cover, they killed a Mr. Stephens and his horse, though "a young woman by the name of Percy" who was riding on the horse behind Stephens escaped "with the help of Mr. Hinsdale."

As the rumors of the "attacks" at Stockbridge and Yokuntown rippled outward, all of western Massachusetts rose in panic, pouring down through Stockbridge into Housatonuck North Parish, thence farther down into Sheffield proper, and even on into Connecticut where the recently settled northern towns took to their fortified houses. The Reverend Samuel Hopkins of North Parish wrote an account of the spectacle to his friend the Reverend Joseph Bellamy of Bethlem. From the facts that the panic had started at the opening of the Sabbath afternoon meeting in Stockbridge and that the reading of the psalm was still early in the normal service anywhere, it can be inferred that the Paul Revere who brought the news six miles southward to North Parish spurred his horse down the Monument Mountain road at a dangerous gallop.

On the Lord's Day P.M., [wrote the Reverend Mr. Hopkins] as I was reading the Psalm, news came that Stockbridge was beset by an army of Indians, and on fire, which broke up the assembly in an instant. All were put into the utmost consternation, men, women and children. What shall we do? . . . Not a fort to flee to, and few guns and little ammunition in this place. Some ran one way and some another; but the general course was to the southward, especially for women and children. Women, children and squaws presently flocked in upon us from Stockbridge, half naked and frightened almost to death; and fresh news came that the enemy were on the Plains this side of Stockbridge, shooting and killing and scalping people as they fled. Some persons presently came along bloody, with news that they saw persons killed and scalped, which raised a consternation, tumult and distress inexpressible. . . . Two men are killed, one scalped, two children killed and one of them scalped; but two Indians have been seen at or near Stockbridge, that we certainly know of. Two Indians may put New England to a hundred thousand pounds charge, and never much expose themselves, in the way we now take. The troops that came to our assistance are now drawing off; and what have they done? They have seen Stockbridge and eaten up all their provisions, and fatigued themselves, and that's all; and now we are left as much exposed as ever, (for I suppose they are all going.) . . .

Mr. Hopkins was wrong in his prophecy that the soldiers were "all going." What white citizens of Stockbridge had not fled had repaired to the protection of the house and the imperturbable faith of their minister. Thither also repaired the soldiers, presently marching up from North Parish. For a month, while a palisade was being built around their dwelling, transforming it into a fort for the village, the Edwards family housed a "great number" of them, others being billeted in the Williams castle and elsewhere. Most of the soldiers were drunken, destructive, ignorant and revoltingly insolent to the mission Indians. In October Edwards, in a complaining mood, submitted a bill to the colony for 800 meals, the equivalent of 24 hours' pasturage for 150 horses, and 7 gallons 1 quart of his rum; besides 180 meals for the workmen building the palisade, and 15 rods of new log fence which had cost him 10 shillings a rod.

But Edwards at this time deserves little sympathy for this diversion, either on his own part or on that of the world. The manuscript which had held his utter concentration for a year had gone off to Boston a little before the Chamberlain murders. On October 17, 1754, it was published by subscription. It was entitled *The Freedom of the Will*.

The climax of the drama of Stockbridge, the chief single drama of the valley in the colonial period, was now past. The forces of materialism and greed had been routed, and the forces of truth had triumphed in the issuance of the first of America's chief contributions to world literature and theology. By way of epilogue to the play, the final resolution occurred the following year, 1755, in a piece of dramatic justice that let the sun of history set with warmth and honor even on the enemy, even on the Williams clan.

By the governor's order Colonel Ephraim Jr. that year raised and commanded for the Lake George campaign a regiment drawn mostly from the valley. As was to be expected, any Williams who wanted a job was taken care of. The Reverend Stephen was chaplain, Ephraim's brother Thomas was surgeon, and his cousin (and Jonathan Edwards's) Colonel William of Pontoosuc was quartermaster; of the younger generation, a son-in-law of the Monarch Israel was a surgeon's mate, William the son of Colonel William was a surgeon's mate's assistant, and little Josiah, half brother of Ephraim, was an ensign.

It is supposed that Colonel Williams had for some time been troubled in conscience by the methods his father had used to amass large holdings in western Massachusetts, most of which had now come to young Ephraim either by purchase or by inheritance. On his own part, the colony had given him for his military and other services two hundred acres of land a little to the west of his now rebuilt Fort Massachusetts—a modest graft indeed and less than he deserved by the practices of the time. At camp near Albany a few evenings before the army moved, he had a prescience that this time his number was coming up, and he made his will, having a free hand in making his dispositions, for he had not married and had no dependents to care for. A few days later he and Chief Hendrick of the Mohawks, the most distinguished Indian who ever attended the Stockbridge mission, were jointly in command of the advance party south of Lake George when the detachment was ambushed by the French and their allies and both leaders were shot dead in the first volley. In his will Williams had provided that a free school should be established on his 200-acre tract west of Fort Massachusetts, and for the support of it he set up a trust fund consisting of virtually all the rest of his property. The town in which the school was to be located, the school itself, and the college it became forty years later were properly named after him. It is a coincidence that at the time Williams drew his will and was killed, Lord Amherst, whose

name was to attach to another college near by, was camped
with another army in Housatonuck.

For four years after Ephraim Williams, Sr., took his
hasty departure, and for three years after the publication of
The Freedom of the Will, Jonathan Edwards suffered no
serious interruption of his peace, his sixteen hours a day in
his study. Elijah Williams was still a youth, not at all the
worldly force he later became in the community. The last
dangerous enemies, the Dwights, moved down to Housatonuck, where Abigail caused her general, still commanding
a brigade in the Champlain campaigns, to build her the fine
mansion that is preserved today as the Bryant house. The
mission continued to be the place Edwards had hoped it
would be from the beginning, where the duties were little
exacting and he could devote most of his time to his writing.
In three years he turned out three more great treatises. During the same period the family was presumably at its happiest, the girls delighting in the absurdities of the father they
adored, the tremendous, six-foot-one, long-featured, gray-
eyed, absent-minded candor, coupled with the warm love
and perpetual concern for all of them.

A particularly absurd practice of Jonathan Edwards was
related to his failure as a breadwinner. Since it was impossible for a large family to live on what the Society for the
Propagation paid him, Mistress Edwards and the girls pieced
out the family income by making and selling fans and dress
patterns, both of which required heavy paper. And since
lighter, manuscript paper was hard to get, this was a bo-
nanza for Edwards. He customarily snitched all he could of
his women's article of commerce to write his sermons on,
and especially to write the notes which he made almost continuously during his waking hours. For the latter purpose he
customarily carried about considerable quantities of the fan
and pattern paper in his pocket, especially when he went
abroad. When, as often happened, he was invited to speak
or attend a council somewhere, he would spend the outward
journey—always on horseback—preparing his remarks. But
on leaving for the return journey he would instantly forget

where he was, leaving it to the horse to find the way home through the wilderness, often in the dark. As they jogged along, Edwards's mind would present him with a series of ideas worth noting. Tearing off a scrap from the paper in his pocket he would make a note, and would scracely have it finished before another would crowd for recognition. So the hastily scratched bits would be thrust back into his pockets, under the saddle, anywhere. At length, when every normal cranny was filled with them, he would start attaching them to his clothes with pins he foresightedly carried against this contingency. Finally his horse would deliver him at his door. Always oblivious of his appearance and speckled with scraps of paper, he would run with affectionate haste to greet his family, or with dignity to welcome the visitor who might be waiting.

Once, while taking a walk, he passed a boy at a stile in the northern part of town and paused to ask the youngster's name. An hour later he returned, found the same boy at the same place and asked the same question. "Sir," said the boy, "my name is the same as it was an hour ago."

Meanwhile, in the year *The Freedom of the Will* appeared, the brilliant and delicate Esther had married Dr. Aaron Burr, the president of Princeton. Earlier, at the height of her father's controversy with the Williamses, Esther had written in her girlish diary: "I think Mr. Dwight deserves to be Licked." In 1756, two years after her marriage, she returned to pay the family a visit, bringing her beautiful baby boy who one day was to be the beautiful bad boy of the baby Republic. During her visit, there was a quite valid Indian scare, the garrison having been reduced to a sergeant and five privates, and news arriving of the capture and torture of the two ranking officers at Fort Massachusetts. Almost everybody vacated Stockbridge again, begging the minister to go too, but he would neither leave nor permit his frightened daughter to do so. He did consent, however, to send the boarding school boys down to his friend Bellamy in Bethlem, a shift which, as it turned out, was the end of the boarding school, though the mission was to survive thirty years longer.

By 1757 Edwards had published *The Doctrine of Original Sin, The End for Which God Created the World,* and *The Nature of True Virtue.* There remained to be executed only one, and the most ambitious, of the works he had projected, the *History of the Work of Redemption*—virtually a history of the cosmos. He had completed the plan of this and had begun to write when his period of earthly creativeness came to an end. In September, 1757, his son-in-law Dr. Burr died, and the trustees of Princeton invited Edwards to succeed him as president. With great misgivings he accepted. In March, 1758, a month after he was installed, he volunteered for inoculation during a smallpox epidemic, and so died. Before the anniversary of Dr. Burr's death, Esther and Mrs. Edwards had followed their husbands out of the world. Edwards's friend Samuel Hopkins said, "Surely America is greatly emptied by these deaths."

The Land Filled (1737-1761)

JONATHAN EDWARDS was the last of the Puritans to cling to the belief that if he and his colleagues administered their stewardship successfully the New Jerusalem would descend forthwith on New England. The Stockbridge plantation is the last in which the motive for settlement is almost exclusively religious. Yet the eight more tribes that settled in the valley, motivated though some were by greed and others by the new quest for freedom, were all composed of dominantly religious people. The Lord was still leading His Chosen into the Promised Land.

Next after the settlement of Stockbridge was the appropriation of the rest of the Western Lands of Connecticut by a series of contemporaneous settlements. The Western Lands were the northwest corner of Connecticut, comprising most of future Litchfield county and including the Housatonic towns of Kent, Goshen, Cornwall, Canaan, Sharon and Salisbury. These towns, cut out of an almost unknown wilderness where the river rumbled down through its mountain gorges at an average level of five hundred feet above the sea, were sold off by the colony in 1737 and 1738, 300 acres having been first reserved out of each of them as "college land," which was given to Yale.

By the winter of 1739 there were a few cabins and town organizations in every township. That winter was a severe one, and the stories from each of the tiny settlements were about the same: infants dying of cold and hunger; cattle kept alive on venison broth; heroic measures by women,

while husbands were away foraging; men on snowshoe ex-
peditions for supplies, whipping each other all night to keep
from drowsing and freezing to death; epidemics of "nervous
fever." Later, the Reverend Solomon Palmer of Cornwall
wrote: "So great was the expense, fatigue and hardship that
I endured for the three first years, that I would not suffer
them again for the whole township."

Besides the usual bounties on wolves, at least Kent put
one on wildcats. Five bears were killed in Canaan in one day
in the first summer. In Cornwall, Deacon Benjamin Sedgwick, walking down to his woodlot, was surprised, knocked
down and bestridden by a bear, till his dog got the beast
by the tail. This diverted it sufficiently to allow the deacon
to spring up and divide its backbone with his ax. In Goshen,
on a "frosty morning," while the barefoot boy who had been
sent for the cattle looked on, a bear "took the sow in her
mouth, and carried her off, squealing bitterly; the pigs also
squealing and trying to follow." Later a neighbor tracked
the marauder through the swamp and, after finding the remains of the sow, "POW—he had put a ball right through
the head of the bear." As everywhere on the frontier, pigs
were privileged citizens. In its first town meeting Sharon,
having elected its officers, "farther voted that Swin having
a Ring in their noses Shall be accounted an orderly Creater."

Immediately upon settlement, each of these towns organized church and school, though not all of them had
church buildings until ten years after settlement and some
did not have school buildings till even later. In 1740 the
two-year-old baby Ethan Allen was carried by his family up
from Roxbury to their new home in Cornwall. Some years
afterward, it appears, the Cornwall schoolmaster, Master
Dean, fell asleep, whereat young Allen and others hoisted
him into the air by means of a tackle that hung in the
building they were using for a school. In the early 1740's
four insignificant members of the noble family of Dudley
settled on the big flat top of one of Cornwall's hills called
Coltsfoot, thus founding Dudleytown which, after a century of sprouting names of local, state and national distinc-

tion, was going to lapse into the status of one of the most utter and the most eerie of the ghost towns of New England. In 1747 Litchfield got its first Episcopal church and Woodbury its second orthodox meeting house which, by the report of the clerk of the church to the General Assembly, "for bigness, strength and architecture does appear transcendantly beautiful." In 1750 Roger Sherman joined his brother in New Milford to help with the store and to practice his own trade of cobbling, while studying law and publishing an almanac on the side. His prophecy of the weather for December 2, 1754, is a triumph of Yankee intellectual caution: "Freezing cold weather, after which storm of snow, but how long after I dont say."

Meanwhile, in '51, it was proposed to organize the old Western Lands into a county. Cornwall presented a strongly supported bid for the county seat, and after its case had been presented Litchfield's advocate complained that Cornwall's best argument had not been advanced. "If Cornwall is made the County Town," he said, "the expense of building a goal will be saved, for the rogues put in among the Cornwall hills can not get out again." Litchfield won, and the new county took the name of the county town. Two years later the courthouse was raised between Litchfield's meeting house and its school in Meeting House Street—now the Green— just opposite the end of Town Street—now North Street. Near the courthouse stood the whipping post and the stocks. With this organization of Litchfield County, the pioneer period of the Lower Valley comes to an end.

Before 1752 Pontoosuc—later Pittsfield—was the private property of Colonel Jacob Wendall of Boston, Colonel John Stoddard of Northampton or his heirs, and Philip Livingston of New York. In 1743 there was tentative pioneering, but the place was deserted again during the Second French War—1744-1748. In 1752 organized settlement was resumed and made permanent. Nathaniel Fairfield, on his way in from Wethersfield, Connecticut, hid three days in a hollow log while hostile Indians scoured the woods for him. Charles Goodrich came in with a cart and two horses, having to widen as he went the Indian path up from Stockbridge, and sitting up all the last night for fear of the Indians, keeping himself awake by eating apples. During the scare in '54 most of the population of Pontoosuc decamped, leaving their cabins. Among those who remained was Colonel William Williams who, being sent eighty soldiers from Connecticut and twenty from Massachusetts, constructed three forts, including the excellent Fort Anson on the high ground south of Onota Lake. After the war Colonel Williams built himself his fabulous "Long House," the most palatial dwelling in the valley in the pre-Revolutionary period. It was eighty feet long, two stories high, painted, gambrel roofed, and was entered at one end through double doors of twenty-six panels each, letting into a wide hall that ran the length of the building. On one side of this hall, likewise running the length of the building, was the "Long Room," where the regal colonel—forever complaining of debt, and with reason!—held court as probate judge and justice of the peace. The place was famous for its lavish paneling and wood carving, its lordly grounds, and its service of uniformed slaves. The colonel was able to raise and spend on his palace £1,373 17s 6d. During its construction the whole plantation built a small, barnlike, steepleless, belfryless, wholly unadorned meeting house at a cost of £40. Along with no other building but the substantial parsonage, likewise unpainted, it stood on the bleak hilltop which is now the park, surrounded by the stumps of recent clearing by fire. In front of it stood a single elm which had escaped destruction and duly became famous in local story. Colonel Williams lived until 1785, always busy in town and state affairs and always in debt. Not long after his death his now wealthy widow, being in her middle fifties, married a gentleman of twenty-nine, named Daniel Shearer. A few years later she had him in court for three alleged attempts to murder her: once by removing the curb around the well that she might, though she did not, fall in; once by loosening the planks over the cistern, whereby she did fall in but was hauled out by a servant; once by giving her an unbroken colt to ride to church, whereby she was thrown and broke her leg. She lived to be eighty-two, and after her death Mr. Shearer was faintly generous to the town with her money, and extremely vain of his generosity.

Throughout the fifties the overshadowing condition of the valley was war. The hasty departure of a pioneer group from Lenox in '54 has been recounted. Organized settlement was not resumed there until '62. In '54 two youthful pioneers in the exposed region of Lanesboro, north of Pittsfield, shot from ambush and killed two Indian chiefs of a party of Canadian Indians, possibly the party that had previously destroyed the village in New York and was now supposed to be on the way to massacre the small garrison and population at Pontoosuc. According to local legend, the death of the two chiefs saved the downriver settlements.

In the same year Salisbury had a small reign of terror, quite unrelated to the war but aroused by just Indian claims to certain land, and ending in the possibly fatal shooting of one Indian. Throughout the war every town up and down the river sent out most of its youth, and from every contingent there were many more losses by disease and hardship than by the muskets and scalping knives of the enemy. The Stockbridge Indians contributed a company of one hundred, which was all of its able-bodied braves.

During 1757 and 1758, British troops stationed in Stratford used the golden rooster atop Christ's spire as a target, and the ancient weather vane is still plentifully embossed with their bullet marks. Some of the same or similar British troops, being barracked in the Milford town house in the winter of 1757-58, got drunk and burned it down. The British government paid an insufficient indemnity of £50 toward a new town house, which was promptly erected.

Meanwhile, at the upper and lower limits of the valley the intellectual tradition was continuing. All of Edwards's definitive work was done during the war. In 1752 Dr. Samuel Johnson of Stratford had attained sufficient distinction to be offered the presidency of the new University of Pennsylvania. He refused it, but two years later accepted the same office at King's College—later Columbia—in New York.

In the autumn of 1760 came the news of the fall of Quebec and the end of the war. The courier reached Ripton Parish as the orthodox congregation was assembling for a baptism. A few moments later the minister, bemused by the news, declared solemnly, "I baptize thee Victory." And so Victory became the child's name.

Meanwhile, in spite of the war, settlement of the unoccupied corners of the valley was proceeding. By '61 New Marlboro and Tyringham—then including Monterey—were incorporated. Lee, Mt. Washington and Egremont were unincorporated districts, not yet under their permanent names. After the Indian anecdote already recounted, Lanesboro on the upper reaches of the Middle Branch of the river was deserted but for one man, till in 1781 his former copioneers returned. The same year another company pushed up the East Branch to found Dalton, which then included Hinsdale, and at about the same time the last of the pioneers settled in the uplands of Washington, where the East Branch rises in the spring above Mud Pond.

All the forty-seven future towns of the valley were now settled, and twenty of them were incorporated under their permanent names. A contemporary map shows the slow southward progress of the name of the river. Down as far as the big bend at Scatacook in Kent it was then called "Housatonic," but below that, according to the map, it was still called "Stratford River." Already a few deeds in New Milford, next below Kent, called it "Housatonic," but on most records it still retained one of its earlier names, "Great," "Stratford," or—the local New Milford name—"Weantinock."

The year 1761 properly marked the end of the pioneer era for the whole valley. With the fall of Quebec the year before, the menace of the French and their Indians was ended forever. From constituting an always threatened fringe, the plantations of the Upper Valley became the objects of eager immigration and leapt in a dozen years or so to populous maturity.

In 1761 Pontoosuc was incorporated as Pittsfield, and

Housatonuck, or Sheffield North Parish, was incorporated as Great Barrington. The "Barrington" came from a famous Puritan peer, the purpose of the prefix being to distinguish the place from Barrington, Rhode Island. An explanation of the selection of "Great"—instead of say "New"—for prefix is to be found in contemporary English practice. But, further, it must be remembered that here was a community long accustomed to grandiloquence in local nomenclature, a community living at the Great Wigwam where the Great Bridge carried the Great Road across the Great River. They could hardly be expected to tolerate less than verbal greatness in the name of their town.

And any modesty they might have retained was discouraged by the fact that in this same year of 1761 the colonial government not only incorporated Great Barrington as a town but named it the shire town of a new county, Berkshire County, the mountainous region of the west consisting mostly of the river towns. The organization of the valley was now complete. In both the Upper and the Lower Valley the people in the Place-beyond-the-Mountains now had their own courts and a sense of separateness and political integrity within their mountain walls. The Promised Land had been occupied and civilized. The earthly part of the original Puritans' dream had been fulfilled. But, alas, the New Jerusalem did not descend.

A few years after the final inrush of immigration which began in 1761, the over-all picture of the valley was that of a region whose population was almost exclusively rural, and which approximated in size the rural population of the same region today. The Connecticut census of 1774 and the Massachusetts one of 1776 show that, agriculturally speaking, the land had already reached its saturation point. The chief difference from the modern scene lay in the fact that many of the hilltops which are now deserted were still under cultivation in 1760, whereas many of the valleys where the best farms are today were then still swampy, miasmic, infested with bears and occasional wolves.

A clear demonstration of the fullness of rural population early in the latter half of the eighteenth century would require a comparison between the population then and the rural part of the population today, neglecting the modern villages and cities. But since the population statistics do not distinguish cities and villages from the towns containing them, such an accurate demonstration is impossible. To give approximate comparisons I have first listed the towns that remain rural today, containing no city or village of population of 1,000 or more, and I have compared their populations in the eighteenth century and in 1940. To complete the picture I have listed afterwards the towns that now contain cities or villages of 1,000 or more, and have likewise compared their populations in the eighteenth century and today.

One indication from this table is the rapidity of pioneer growth they represent, especially in the towns of northwestern Connecticut and of Berkshire County which in thirty or forty years have enlarged from a few cabins to settlements of a thousand citizens or more. Immigration after the end of the Old French War is not the only way of explaining this startling increase. The headstone of Mrs. John Buel, wife of one of Litchfield's original settlers, gives the following intelligence: "She died Nov. 4, 1768, aged 90; having had 13 children, 191 grandchildren, 247 great-grandchildren, and 49 great-great-grandchildren; total 410; 336 survived her." Contemporary was the Reverend Nathan Birdseye of Stratford who lived to be 103, rode horseback after he was 100, and had 163 living great-grandchildren when he died.

As already stated, the population of the valley in the latter half of the eighteenth century was almost exclusively rural. With two exceptions the villages and cities we know today did not exist. The "centers" of the towns were merely regions where a "street," usually called Town Street, was laid out and crossed by one or two other public "streets," sometimes also by a colonial highway. The town "streets" were areas a quarter of a mile to a mile long and ten to sixteen rods wide dedicated to town purposes, chiefly those of a common for the grazing of livestock—especially pigs—the

TOWNS REMAINING RURAL
TODAY, LACKING CITY OR VILLAGE
OVER 1,000

Connecticut	Population End Third Quarter 18th Century (Census 1774)	Population 1940
Newtown	2,229	4,023
Woodbury	5,313	1,998
Southbury	(Woodbury incl. South-	1,532
Roxbury	bury, Roxbury, Washing-	660
	ton & Bethlehem)	
Washington		2,089
Bethlehem		715
New Fairfield	1,308	608
Sherman	(N. Fairfield	477
	incl. Sherman)	
Kent	1,996	1,245
Warren	(Kent incl. Warren)	328
Goshen	1,111	778
Cornwall	974	907
Sharon	2,012	1,611
Salisbury	1,980	3,030
Canaan	1,635	551
North Canaan	(Canaan incl. N. Canaan)	2,304
Massachusetts	(*Census 1776*)	
Sheffield	1,722	1,709
Mt. Washington	259	57
New Marlboro	1,087	956
Egremont	671	463
Tyringham	806	213
Monterey	(Tyringham incl.	320
	Monterey)	
Stockbridge	907	1,815
West Stockbridge	370	1,062
Richmond	921	624
Lanesboro	1,434	1,321
Hinsdale	400 (est.)	1,235
Totals for Towns still rural	27,135	32,631

TOWNS NO LONGER RURAL,
CONTAINING CITY OR VILLAGE
OF 1,000 OR MORE

	Population End Third Quarter 18th Century (Census 1776)	*Population* 1940
Connecticut		
Stratford	5,555	22,580
Shelton	(Stratford incl. Trumbull, Shelton & Monroe)	10,971
Trumbull		5,294
Monroe		1,728
Milford	2,127	16,439
Orange	(Milford incl. Orange)	2,009
Derby	1,889	10,287
Seymour	(Derby incl. Seymour & Oxford)	6,754
Oxford		1,375
Danbury	2,526	27,921
Bethel	(Danbury incl. Bethel)	4,105
New Milford	2,776	5,559
Bridgewater	(N. Milford incl. Bridgewater & most of Brookfield)	537
Brookfield		1,345
Litchfield	2,554	4,029
Morris	(Litchfield incl. Morris)	606
Massachusetts	(*Census 1776*)	
Great Barrington	961	5,824
Lee	(Gr. Barrington incl. most of Lee)	4,222
Lenox	931	2,884
Pittsfield	1,132	49,684
Dalton	250 (est.)	4,206
Totals for Towns now industrialized, or otherwise containing city or village of 1,000 or more	20,701	188,359
Grand Totals	47,836	220,990

location of the meeting, town and Sabbath Day ("sabbaday") houses, a school, one or more ordinaries or inns and the
whipping post, the clearing of a training field for the exercises of the train band or militia on Training Day, and, incidental to these, a means of public passage to their fulfillment. The only one of these purposes that involved keeping
at least a part of one street mowed and drained, and so
faintly prophetic of the later green, was that of exercising
the train band. As already indicated, the common land other
than the training field tended, after being cleared, to lapse
into a swamp that was also the public dump, garbage heap
and cesspool. Great Barrington's Main Street was serrated
with ledges, at one point there being only a cart width of
passage in the whole muddy expanse. Between the ledges this
particular public domain was freshened by running streams.
These emptied into Ash Swamp, along the eastern side of
the southern reaches of the long street, Ash Swamp being a
noxious region where a squaw had once thrown her papoose,
since when it had been menacing with goblins and night
noises.

Along the borders of these town streets, where habitable,
there was usually a slight thickening of farms beyond the
normal saturation in the open town. Any wealthy families
who might have local or colonial authority were likely to live
in or near the Center for ease of transacting business, and
the same might be true of three or four other chronic officials.
There were no central stores or offices, all merchants and professional men, including the ministers and doctor, being
primarily farmers, with their places of secondary business in
their houses, often far outside the Center. Besides its public
buildings, the Center might have within a mile diameter a
dozen houses with their farm land around and behind them,
where an equal distance in the open countryside along a highway would have perhaps half the number.

These private dwellings of the mid-eighteenth century,
many of them beautifully constructed and surviving today,
crowded round by the modern, true villages, were usually
built along the boundary of the street or *on* it, in distinction

from the public buildings which were *in* it. In the attractive, well laid-out villages of today you need only look at the line of the mid-eighteenth century houses to see the wide limits of the muddy, brushy, more or less treeless, hog- and filth-infested morass that the street was then. Possibly a rich family with baronial aspirations would get permission to clear the portion of the street abutting its house and let the elms and maples grow there. Possibly neighbors, not to be outbaroned, would do the same, until someday, any time up to a century later, some genius would discover that here was a potential arcade of trees and a possible park for the baronial pleasure of all. So the planning of the modern green might begin. Outside of such sporadic gestures toward private parking, the eighteenth century Centers were unplanned, unbeautiful eye- and nose-sores. And they were only a trifle more populous than the open country, the two exceptions being the two oldest towns, Stratford and Milford, in each of which, in the extremity of danger in the beginning, all the dwellings had been huddled together in a single stockade.

In contrast to the insignificance of the eighteenth century town Centers as compared with the modern villages and cities, the open and everywhere hilly countryside at that time was dotted with farms and laced with roads almost as densely as it is today. In the Upper Valley, where occupancy was less than two generations old, the spectacle was still a crude one, being that of the devastation man works when he first touches the wilderness. Here the upland farms were not yet wholly cleared, and wide stretches of primeval forest covered the hills between the houses. In the clearings the cattle grazed and the corn grew among the charred·stumps of the original, pioneer burning, and few families had even started the epic labor of stoning the fields and pastures. The farmhouses were still mostly of logs, as were the outbuildings; and the barriers around the farm closes were of split rails or logs, with a barway for entrance. The roads, outside of the few maintained by the colony, were mere private paths or cartways through the forest from farm to farm, and finally to the Center.

Scattered through this landscape of ruined nature, and art not yet developed, there were a few substantial frame houses, mostly the mansions of the rich, such as the two of Abigail Williams that are preserved, the little one she made John Sergeant build her in Stockbridge and the big one she made General Dwight build her in Great Barrington, now miscalled the "Bryant House." Generally, the spectacle of the Upper Valley was one of the backwoods and powerful hillbillies, of logs and heavy timbers and leather, bearing on its surface a froth of delicate, graceful building and luxurious living and silk. It was a fine region in which to breed violent democrats, and the followers of Allen and Shays were already running wild among the critters of the mountains.

Down through northern Connecticut pioneer crudity was also in evidence until, beginning in Litchfield and New Milford, it faded into a maturer landscape where man, having first laid nature waste, had let her return on terms, to the beautification of the works of both. Here the primeval forest was shrunken back into well-defined woodlots, and many of these were already of second- and third-growth trees. The wide, always sloping, cleared fields and pastures had not only been stumped, but most of them had been stoned as well, and for a checkerboard of boundaries of fields, farms and highways the oxpower and sonpower of the big families had replaced most of the pioneer snake fences with the walls of New England. Along these same boundaries, especially along the walls of the undulating highways, and particularly in front of the farmhouses, the latest seedlings and saplings were being encouraged to form windbreaks for winter and to arch over-head into shade for summer. It was along the roads in the open country, rather than round the commons and the training grounds of the centers, that the planned arcades of New England were first encouraged to grow.

Between the highway walls there was still little care of any roadway, except as an individual might choose to crowbar out a stone or hammer off a ledge that had lamed his horse or upset his cart. The town roads, which were most of the roads, were surveyed, and local politics might occasionally work an improvement; but the towns were not legally responsible for injury due to road conditions as they are today. The highways were still simply wide strips which were kept reasonably clear of brush by everybody's cattle that grazed there, and within which you could proceed without committing trespass, at your own risk. They were navigable in fair weather for the frequent travelers on foot or horseback, and in 1761 there was almost no wheeled traffic in New England, except solid-wheeled farm carts. Those first town highways are now all gone, survived only by their crumbled and buried boundary walls running through stretches of returned forest. They were disregarded by later road builders because of their uncompromising directness. When the early Yankees wished to proceed from one point to another they followed crow flight, the amount of vertical distance they might have to travel being disregarded. Modern engineers have learned that it is often no farther around a hill than it is straight up one side and straight down the other.

Besides the town roads there were the colony highways, the forerunners of turnpikes and modern trunk roads, running approximately east and west by the most direct route between major centers, such as Hartford and Albany, without much regard for the interests or convenience of the intervening towns. Although these were laid out by the colonial governments, their maintenance was not much better than that of town roads. There were three of them crossing the southerly, longer settled part of the Valley: the King's Highway—afterwards called the Boston Post Road—crossing the river by the Stratford Ferry near its mouth; the Hartford-Woodbury-Danbury road, crossing the river by the Southbury Ferry; and the Hartford-Litchfield-Poughkeepsie road, crossing the river on the long, covered bridge at New Milford. Crosing the northern, younger half of the valley there were the Hartford-Albany road, passing through Goshen, Cornwall, Canaan and crossing into Salisbury by a ferry approximately where Route 44 crosses the river today: and there was the Great Road from Boston to Albany, crossing the river by the Great Bridge in Great Barrington. Direct north-and-south communication comparable to these east-west roads did not exist.

In 1761 the Connecticut Assembly appropriated money for a cartway from Canaan on the Massachusetts border to tidewater at Derby, and there was perennial agitation for clearing out obstructions in the river to facilitate the floating down of logs and spars from Cornwall's Mast Swamp and other parts of the old Greenwoods or Western Lands. But none of these proposals came to anything until much later. The towns maintained up- and downriver communication with each other by means of local roads zigzagging from center to center, not calculated to expedite the export of the little they needed to sell to raise cash for the molasses, glass, salt, tea and other luxuries they needed or wanted to buy. Much of the commerce of the Lower Valley and all of it of the Upper Valley was eastward and westward over the mountains.

Pointing this mosaic of crude highways, the farm buildings in the older, southerly part of the valley generally stood in a close of stone walls, with gates hung either from loftly, split-stone gateposts, or from heavy, horizontal, cut stones on the wall ends and framing the openings. Within the closes almost none of the pioneer huts remained. The common frame house varied from two rooms and a tiny loft to the substantial, two-story-and-a-half, ten-room, one-chimney, either clapboarded or shingled, unpainted, salt-box or equal-gabled structure which we think of today as the typical colonial Yankee dwelling. There were also plenty of the mansion type of houses, with two chimneys in the main body of the structure and a central hallway with wide stairs. There were indeed more of these than there were in the Upper Valley, only they were less pretentious, not necessarily any better decorated than the commoner one-chimney houses. In the Lower Valley democracy was already a fact taken for granted.

Outside of the house, the barn, the tool-shed with its

big carts, plows and other heavy implements, the cowshed,
the sheepcote, the corncrib and the rest were small and still
often of logs. A prominent feature within the close was the
well sweep. Within or without were the thatched haystacks.
And outside were the orchards. Altogether, the marked difference from the modern farm group was the presence of
the stone-wall close, the almost universal absence of paint,
and the dominance of the house over the other buildings.
And yet large families lived in gastronomic luxury on those
little farms, without the help of huge barns and silos with
which their descendants are not quite able to survive in an
industrialized world. The original farms were shelters where
men lived, with no responsibility except to God, instead of
being factories where man's function is to feed a remote
machine.

In addition to the two or more churches and sabbaday
houses, the town hall, the school and tavern usually found
near the center, the open countryside would display at some
of its secondary crossroads another church or two, five to
ten additional elementary schools, in the county towns and
in most of the others a grammar—what we would call a
"high"—school. Along the numerous streams that threaded
every town, big mill wheels sloshed their slow revolutions,
turning stones or saws. Already most of the dams were ro-
mantically dressed in moss and vines, and the ponds above
were the recognized swimming academies of the youth of
the neighborhood. In the summer the people congregated at
meetings, dances, bees and fairs, coming afoot, on horseback, in carts, and beginning at about this time, in four-
wheeled vehicles. In the winter they did the same in big
bobsleighs and latterly in smaller, trimmer sleighs and cutters
musical with bells. A way of life was established that remembered little of the Puritans, and nothing of the old
country whence they came.

With the swift increase of population following the end
of the French War and the elimination of the military significance of the northern towns as outposts, the commercial
activity, especially the traffic on the highways of the valley,

quickened and increased in volume. Single riders galloped the roads on their separate enterprises: the sale of luxuries to settlers who were beginning to be able to afford them, or the purchase of local lumber, lime or agricultural produce needed in the more thickly populated and less prolific regions. After the single riders plodded the ox-drawn carts and wagons, bearing the merchandise both ways to make good the exchanges. And, adding color to the scene and the promise of better roads, an occasional chaise trotted past. Or the coach of a rich man or royal representative jounced among the rocks and sinkholes of the highways or jangled up to a tavern, scattering a spume of hogs and chickens out of a wake of dust, children and dogs. New wealth, new people, and above all new ideas were crowding in. The simple, colonial period, when the battle was between Puritan religious idealism and Puritan greed, was now over.

In the main, idealistic motives in the period now past had triumphed over materialistic ones. Although ideas were taking new forms in 1761, the people of the valley were still a people who, like their Puritan ancestors, were dominated primarily by ideas of some kind rather than by material ambitions. They were still a people who were willing to risk their lives for their notions, but few of them were willing to risk either their lives or their notions for the hope of gain beyond a basic, sufficient living. The names and deeds that survive from the period are not those which were associated with gain. The names of the early traders and land profiteers are lost to all but the closest historical research; but the names of Samuel Johnson, Samuel Hopkins and Joseph Bellamy will be part of the history of the nation forever. Ephraim Williams, Sr., is absolutely forgotten, but the name of his son will survive while there are institutions of high learning in the world. The rich River Gods are gone, but Jonathan Edwards about whom they squabbled stands as the theological giant of pre-Revolutionary America.

In Edwards's life and works there is summed up the age that was past, and it was appropriate that his death was almost contemporary with the end of the Old French War. From that time the Puritan idealism, which in psychic terms was as live as ever in the Yankees, turned from religious to political objectives. For a long time "reason" and individual human rights in this world had been in the air. Now they began to crystallize into definite slogans and beliefs. The military experience gained in seven years of war by almost the whole male population, coupled with the habitual failure of the mother country to fulfill either her military or her financial engagements, had given the Yankees a sense of self-sufficiency and an impatience with British patronizing. New England as a whole was ripe for independence, and nowhere more so than along the mountains of the western fringe.

Between 1761 and the Revolution the numerous anecdotes expressive of the new age of political democracy and freedom belong in a later chapter. More appropriately here may be given two anecdotes that look back to the religious, colonial period. The first is an anecdote of piety, the second a tale of success in terms that were no longer typically American.

In the great drought of 1762 the Reverend Nathan Birdseye of Stratford—mentioned above as the father of a hundred and sixty-three great-grandchildren living at his death—found himself in a sorry case. He, his family, his servants, and a considerable number of his cattle were about to die from the failure of all the springs around—the river water being brackish. On the final morning when there was no water to be had from their own or the neighbors' springs, he gathered the household together and prayed a long time, while all present lamented to the Lord with loud cries. Then Mr. Birdseye took his customary walk, and as he crossed the parched fields his eyes fell on a dark spot, which proved to be moist. He called his men and they opened a spring which has not failed to this day.

More anachronistic than the Reverend Mr. Birdseye's faith and miracle was a story that began in 1770 and, in its theme of affection between Old and New England, might serve as a curtain on the first, or colonial, act of the drama of America. In the fall of 1770 there arrived in Stratford a handsome, dark-eyed young man who registered at Benjamin's Tavern as John Stirling, son of the Scottish Lord Stirling. Captain Benjamin, the tavernkeeper, was at the time doing some repairs on the golden rooster weathervane of Christ's Church. His friend and neighbor was the blacksmith Samuel Folsom who had come to Stratford to do the ironwork of the church, had settled there, and whose eighth child was seventeen-year-old Glorianna, the dimpled, blue-eyed, chestnut-haired, lively belle of the village. The cause of the young nobleman's arrival was never known, but the cause of his delaying there through the winter was Glorianna, whom he married in the spring. The baron, being distressed by his son's common taste, stopped sending him money, and young John went to work. When they had a child born in December he appealed to his father by letter and was peremptorily ordered home. He left, and it was presumed that Glorianna had seen the last of her nobleman. But not long after, a special ship arrived, with maids and nurses for the babies—a second having been born after young John left—and with fabulous gifts and bolts of Parisian materials for dresses, and a letter from the husband, saying that all was well and that she was to come to him. In due course the daughter of the colonial blacksmith became a baroness of the mother country, and herself the mother of seventeen noble little children. Meanwhile, her native land had lost interest in noblemen and their remote country, and its leaders would look on her story less with admiration than with contempt.

PART II

Liberty (1760-1820)

Independence

IN THE 1760's the rural population of the valley—which was almost all of it—was about what it is today. Life was still mostly conducted in terms of pewter, wood, homespun, oxen and ideas. But the content of the ideas was undergoing change, a shift of interest from religion to social rights, from theology to liberty, from God to man, from heaven to earth.

In theological terms the Great Awakening had been a revival of orthodox Calvinism, but it was the resultant individualism that really took with the people and held them after the religious background was forgotten. In the valley the great divines of New England, Bellamy and Hopkins—presently abetted by Dwight and Jonathan Edwards, Jr., Stephen West and others—were trying to save pure religion from political pollution. But the attention and passions of the people moved in the new direction, and the more numerous and lesser clergy were already thundering the popular doctrine that religion was synonymous with the love of liberty and country and the hatred of tyrants. And nowhere was there more open truculence and defiance than in the Place-beyond-the-Mountains where the people were not at all afraid of an authority a long way off that had nothing to do with their free daily lives.

The Stamp Act, which went into effect on November 1, 1765, caused riots in Boston and memorials and addresses to the king everywhere. Possibly the first act of open and organized defiance of Parliament's attempted tyranny was that of a Litchfield County convention which in February, 1766, resolved "that the Stamp Act was unconstitutional, null and void, and that business of all kinds should go on as usual"— that is, the British law requiring the use of stamps should be disobeyed. Following the Boston Massacre in 1770 two regiments of militia were immediately raised and equipped in Berkshire County, and at least one in Litchfield County. Home manufactures were encouraged, and all up and down the valley there were famous spinning matches from which the ladies emerged with "bloodie fingers." Major Thomas Melville of Pittsfield happened to be in Boston in December of '73 and took part in the Tea Party. When he came home his stately wife, knowing nothing of the affair, found some tea leaves in his boots, shook the unobtainable morsels into a paper and secreted it in her lavender drawer.

In 1774 the port of Boston was closed, the Massachusetts charter was revoked, and the war virtually began. Almost every town in the valley sent resolutions of support and supplies to the besieged and starving Bostonese, and appointed those committees of correspondence which, more than any other force, cemented America together. Most of the members of the militia became minutemen. A system of express riders was established for the rapid transmission of information. In July a Berkshire County convention assembled at the then year-old Red Lion Inn in Stockbridge. Promptly the convention adopted, and the towns enforced, America's first unconditional act of nonintercourse with Great Britain, sometimes referred to as the "First Declaration of Independence."

In August the same county, assisted by its neighbor downriver, further distinguished itself by the first complete defiance of Britsh authority. Nine years before, the county courthouse had been erected in Great Barrington as the shire town, standing squarely out in the middle of the rocky and muddy Main Street in what is still the central four corners of the village. It was a forty by thirty, story-and-a-half frame building, looking eastward down over the river, and was unadorned but for a fanlight in the eastern gable and some fancy paneling of the big double front doors. Here on August 16, 1774, the Court of Common Pleas was to sit, its judges under the new despotism being paid by the crown. The county sent a petition to Governor Gage in Boston, asking "that the courts of justice immediately cease, and that the people of this Province fall into a state of nature" until the present grievances be redressed. Gage disregarded the petition. Early in the morning of the 16th over a thousand men from Berkshire and five hundred from Litchfield County quietly congregated around the courthouse, solidly occupied it and refused to let Sheriff Elijah Williams of Stockbridge make a passage through them for the gorgeously accoutered judges who, at the suggestion of the leaders, presently left town. General Gage wrote to England: "A flame sprang up at the extremity of the Province. The popular rage is very high in Berkshire and makes its way rapidly to the East."

The following December, John Brown of Pittsfield was sent by the Provincial Congress to Montreal on the ticklish errand of feeling out the attitude of the Canadians. Meanwhile, the First Continental Congress had assembled. Of Connecticut's three delegates, Roger Sherman was from New Milford and Silas Deane had a farm in Salisbury and was a frequent visitor there. On the 17th of the following March, 1775, Stockbridge by a vote of 40 to 1 recommended autonomy, and the one man who voted in the negative had to flee for his life to the mountains where his family fed him secretly.

A month later, on the night of April 18th, a British detachment left Boston for the purpose of destroying certain stores and capturing John Hancock and Sam Adams in the vicinity of Concord. The alarm system in which Paul Revere was one of the first links continued across the province. At dawn on the 21st two fully equipped regiments of minutemen marched from Berkshire County, commanded respectively by Colonels Patterson of Lenox and Fellows of Sheffield, both later promoted to general. Litchfield County's regiment marched a few days later. About this time Great Barrington hoisted what was probably the first Union flag in the valley, though no description of it is given. To protect it from Tories, the staff was attached to a treetop, the trunk of the tree being thickly armed with iron spikes.

Toward the end of April ten leaders of Connecticut, mostly members of the Assembly and including General David Wooster of Stratford, devised a bold scheme, and to carry it out borrowed £810 from the colony treasury on their personal credit. Sixteen volunteers were obtained in Litchfield County, about fifty in Berkshire County, and the detachment marched up to Bennington and reported to the already famous Ethan Allen of Cornwall and Salisbury who was in command of about a hundred roughnecks, many of them from the valley, calling themselves Green Mountain Boys. Their chief occupation at the moment was fighting New Yorkers' claims in that country, but any kind of fight appealed to them. Besides Colonel Ethan, there were four other Allens from Cornwall in the outfit. Their cousin Seth Warner of Roxbury was third in command, and Remember Baker, another Roxbury cousin, was one of the officers. Second in command was Colonel James Easton of Pittsfield. On May 10th they took Fort Ticonderoga with disappointing ease, Colonel Allen demanding and receiving the British commander's surrender "in the name of the great Jehovah and the Continental Congress." The next day Crown Point capitulated to Seth Warner, after which he was given a colonelcy and served with distinction in the subsequent northern campaigns, especially in saving the day at the Battle of Bennington. Connecticut sent a thousand men under Colonel Hinman of Woodbury, for the permanent garrison of Ticonderoga and Crown Point.

On June 17th several of the river towns reported the sound of cannonading to the east. Presently it was learned that Bunker Hill was being fought at that time—some two hundred and fifty miles away! When one Walker of Lenox heard the news, he was shingling his house. Without ado, he dropped his hammer and started for Boston. On June 28th, General Washington crossed the river on the Stratford Ferry, on his way to take command of the Continental Army besieging Boston. A few months later Mrs. Washington followed him in a "chariot drawn by four white horses ridden by black postillions in scarlet and white livery and white cockades." In that year of '74 young Aaron Burr, grandson of Jonathan Edwards, was studying law with his brother-in-law, Tapping Reeve of Litchfield. In September he enlisted, went with Arnold to Canada and spectacularly carried a message, disguised as a priest.

On his way up to the Green Mountain country, Ethan Allen had paused long enough to nourish the infancy of the biggest industry the Valley was to have in its first three centuries. Just when he went to Salisbury from Cornwall does not appear, but in 1762, when he was twenty-four, he, with the Forbes brothers from Canaan and John Hazeltine of Uxbridge, Massachusetts, bought the water power at the outlet of Lake Wonoscopomuc in Lakeville, in Salisbury, and there built the first blast furnace in the valley and the only one in Connecticut that stayed in blast throughout the Revolution. Three years later Allen sold out and went on North to take command of the defense of the New Hampshire Grants against the claims of New York. Early in 1776 the Lakeville furnace, having passed into the hands of Richard Smith, an Englishman who had just found it prudent to return to his native land, was taken over by the Connecticut government and expanded into one of the two or three foundries in the young nation where mortars, cannon, shot, grenades and numerous military utensils were cast in numbers sufficient to be an important factor in the war. Later, back in private hands, this ironworks manufactured the guns of the frigates *Constitution* and *Constellation* and of the Battery at New York.

In May, 1776, Connecticut declared its independence without waiting for company. Massachusetts, though not doing it expressly, had already implied the same intention by substituting "The people of the Commonwealth of Massachu-

setts" for "His Majesty George the Third" on legal documents, including officers' commissions. At the Philadelphia
convention in July, two of Connecticut's four delegates,
Roger Sherman and General Oliver Wolcott, were from the
valley—incidentally, a third, William Williams, was a son
of that Reverend Solomon who had been one of the chief
persecutors of Jonathan Edwards. Five days after the Declaration of July 4th, His Majesty George III, as reproduced in a
gilded statue of lead erected in New York after the repeal
of the Stamp Act, was unseated from his pedestal, dismem-
bered and scattered. The slab on which the horse stood served
first as a gravestone, afterward as a steppingstone, and is now
in the Museum of the City of New York. The royal head,
after having its nose broken off, was rescued by a British
officer and sent to England. The bulk of the statue, being cut
into convenient segments, was secretly carried out of the city
on oxcarts. A century later, the tail of the horse and a chunk
of saddle were dug up in Wilton, Connecticut, where they
had either fallen off their cart or been stolen. The rest proceeded to Litchfield according to plan, and was housed in
a shed in the orchard of General Wolcott. The general personally chopped up the king further with an ax, whereafter
he was melted down and cast into 42,088 bullets by the
Wolcott daughters, Laura and Mary Ann, who made a gala
occasion of it, assisted by ten-year-old Frederick, and the
neighbors "Mrs. Marvin" and "Ruth Marvin."

One of the famous houses on the lower, tidal reaches
of the river, between Stratford and Ripton, was that of the
Wooster family, the descendants of Edward Wooster the
"wolf-killer" of Derby. The mansion had a secret, underground passage that led to the shore and was associated with
Indians, Negroes, smugglers and stores for the Continental
Army. In 1775 David Wooster was sixty-five years old and
the senior soldier in Connecticut, having been a brigadier in
the old French War. He was one of the eight original briga-
diers created by the Continental Congress, and succeeded
General Montgomery in command of the expedition against
Canada. After that expedition he retired from the national

service and took command of the Connecticut militia, with the rank of major general. He was at his home in New Haven on the evening of April 25, 1777, when he was notified of General Tryon's having landed at Norwalk and set out northward toward Danbury, with the obvious intention of destroying the considerable stores there. General Benedict Arnold happened at the time to be on leave in New Haven and volunteered his services. During the next eighteen hours, while Tryon was marching his twenty-five hundred British and Hessians northward, Wooster and Arnold succeeded in scraping together about a hundred Continental soldiers, four hundred militia and two hundred civilians who took down their muskets from their mantelpieces. Litchfield sent the "last fourteen men in town" between fifteen and seventy-six. They arrived too late for the battle, but took part in the pursuit.

During the afternoon of Saturday the 26th, Tryon reached Danbury unopposed and performed his mission, the inventory of stores destroyed including, among much else, 4,000 bbls. beef and pork, 1,000 bbls. flour, 5,000 pairs shoes and stockings, 1,020 tents and marquees, and 120 puncheons of rum. The method of destruction was by fire or breakage, except in the case of the rum which was consumed, leaving the army in an unusually riotous condition, even for a plundering expedition.

When Tryon learned about midnight that Wooster was in Bethel, six miles away, and decided to move out, his major achievement was the formation of his drunken command. Before the departure, nineteen houses were burned, besides numerous shops and stores, altogether about half the village which at that time was strung out along Main Street between South and West streets. The numerous properties of Tories had already been marked with lime crosses to be spared. This wanton destruction, though systematic, was hasty and need not have been effectual but for the terror of the women and children who cowered in their houses while the soldiers roared about the streets. It had rained through the evening and the clapboards were damp. The method of ignition was to lean a flaming pine torch against the house. The mistress of the house at the corner of South and Main said she could easily have put out the torch with a pitcher of water, but she was afraid to open the window and show herself. In the fire all the town records were destroyed, which has left Danbury with meager sources for the story of its beginnings.

It was faint dawn before the last of the column of raiders cleared the smoking village. Meanwhile Wooster, learning that Tryon was about to evacuate, had dispatched Arnold across country in the dark with their main force of five hundred men, to intercept the enemy at Ridgefield. With the remaining two hundred Wooster himself would march to Danbury to attack the rear of the column. He overtook it near Ridgebury at eight o'clock when the enemy was at breakfast, and so impetuous was the attack that the Americans got off with forty prisoners without any but the lightest casualties. At the next attack the British had their artillery ready. As the grapeshot ripped Wooster's line it wavered. Being out in front on his horse, the sixty-seven-year-old general turned in the saddle, laughing, and shouted, "Come on, boys! Never mind such random shots!" At that moment a musket ball, supposed to have been fired by a Tory, severed his spinal cord, lodged in his stomach, and he fell from his horse. He was carried unconscious from the field and to Danbury on his unfolded, wide, red, general's sash, while his aide re-formed the line and marched it off in good order.

In Ridgefield Arnold's 500 held up five times their number all day before they were flanked and retired to harry the flank of the bigger force. In one charge of the enemy Arnold had his horse shot under him with nine musket balls, according to the farmer who skinned the animal the next day. During the pursuit Paul Peck, seventy-five years old and the acknowledged leading hunter of Litchfield County, got a good rest on a wall and killed an enemy every shot till a squad rushed him from behind, grabbed his gun and beat his brains out with it.

In Danbury, General Wooster was taken to the house of Nehemiah Dibble, which had been spared. This hospitality, however, did not save Dibble from the consequences of being a Tory, for a gang of small boys captured him, forced him to the Still River and gave him a series of vicious duckings. Wooster lingered four days. Congress appropriated $500 for a monument to him, which was never built. Much later the city of Danbury tended to the matter.

At the time of Tryon's raid Danbury's famous spy Enoch Crosby was at the height of his spectacular career in New York State, joining Tory companies and having them captured, himself in every case risking and once or twice narrowly escaping death at the hands of the capturing detachment which never knew who he was.

The alarming advance of Burgoyne in the summer of '77 so thoroughly emptied the valley towns in response to calls for short-term volunteers that there were rarely enough voters to hold town meetings. The Reverend Thomas Allen, the fighting parson of Pittsfield, was chaplain of a Continental regiment during the retreat before Burgoyne, and some of his stirring sermons to the men are preserved. An entry in his always graphic diary for June 26th tells the adventures of two soldiers from home who fell in with too many of Burgoyne's Indians:

> This day, as John Whiting and John Batty were returning from Lake-George-Landing, they were fired upon by a number of Indians; the former of whom was shot through the head, and then stabbed in his throat, breast and belly, and, in addition to all was scalped. He was a likely lad of about eighteen years of age, and belonged to Lanesborough.
>
> The other, John Batty, had two balls pass through his thigh, one through the small of his back, and one obliquely through his breast, and his scalp taken off during all of which he was quite sensible, and was obliged to feign himself dead during the stripping him of his armor, and taking off his scalp, which caused great pain. After the Indians retired, he got up, and ran and called for help, and was soon carried in. He was living the day before the retreat, and, it was said, was left behind.

During the Bennington foray in force in August, the Stockbridge Indian Company, under Captain King Solomon, was on scout duty with General Stark, which, as always when there were Indians with the enemy, involved their risking their lives every time they returned to their own lines where they were certain to be fired on by the pickets. At this time the Reverend Mr. Allen was back with his civilian flock in Pittsfield. When, on Friday, August 15th, the appeal for more militia arrived, he first assembled and blessed his congregation, his musket already in his hand, then set out in the rain for the front in his pastoral sulky for war chariot, and was among the first to cover the twenty-five miles to Bennington and report for duty. Before dawn on the 16th he informed General Stark that the Berkshire militia had had too many cries of "Wolf," and that if he didn't give them some fighting that day they would never report again. Advancing to the battle, Mr. Allen, being with the center and realizing that some of his old parishioners were with the Tories in the outpost trenches of the enemy, failed to obey a command to halt, proceeded close to the hostile lines, mounted a fallen tree in full view and harangued them. In reply he got a volley of musket balls, riddling the tree under him, which so annoyed him that he turned back to his young brother, Lieutenant Joseph Allen, who had followed him up, took his musket and fired back what legend says was the first Yankee shot of the battle.

During the pursuit of the enemy Mr. Allen succeeded in capturing a Hessian surgeon's horse, loaded with panniers of wine. The good minister began at once to administer the wine to the wounded, but he managed to save for himself two bottles which descended in his family. His war chariot came in handy, for in his expense account for the day he entered, "Received, for use of my cart, and damage by prisoners, one pound, one shilling." When asked later whether he killed anyone at Bennington, Mr. Allen said he did not know, but that, observing a flash often repeated from a certain bush, and that it was generally followed by the fall of one of Stark's men, he fired that way, and "put the flash out."

All the detachments of militia from south of Pittsfield

arrived too late for the battle. Somewhat more credibly than in the case of Bunker Hill, the sound of the cannon was reported as far south as Stockbridge. Dr. Partridge of that town reached Bennington that evening in time to attend the wounds of Colonel Baum who had commanded the British forces and died two days later. With the close of hostilities, Parson Allen acted as abruptly as he had done at their beginning. The battle having ended with darkness Saturday, August 16th, he was back in his pulpit and preached as usual the next morning.

Following the surrender in October, Burgoyne's large, captured army was marched eastward across the Valley, and many of the towns to this day preserve legends of the red-coats passing through on certain roads. One of the biggest detachments went through Great Barrington, the weary and fever-ridden captives being divided between two encampments on the borders of the village. The "finest park of artillery which had then ever accompanied any army" was strung along the Main Street, and the children had a field day crawling into the maws of the big brass cannon. Burgoyne himself was entertained in the Dwight mansion by Colonel Elijah, the son of General Joseph who had died a dozen years before. The house then stood on the Main Street, on about the line of the Berkshire Inn, to make room for which it was later moved back to its now hidden position. For profuseness and delicacy of paneling, moldings and wood carving it would be hard to beat it anywhere in New England. Colonel Dwight gave a reception for captured General Burgoyne in the more modest of the two parlors flanking the entrance into the big hall. Legend has retained the report of the colorfulness of the occasion, which was doubtless as anomalous in that world of buckskin and homespun as was the mansion itself, looking down on the stinking pesthole of Main Street, and half a mile across Ash Swamp to the river.

One advantage of Burgoyne's surrender was the fact that the prisoners—many of whom, both English and German, settled in the valley—included some skilled artisans. Many of the moldings and fireplaces of the late eighteenth.

century were the work of the Hessians. An English officer under Burgoyne was the architect of the beautiful Senator Elijah Boardman house built in 1790 in New Milford.

The valley's most versatile Revolutionary personage was David Humphreys of Derby who, beginning as a young line captain, rose to General Putnam's staff in 1778, and to be a colonel and Washington's aide in 1780. Throughout the war he and Joel Barlow and Timothy Dwight wrote militant verse to stimulate the soldiers. At Yorktown he performed gallant line service, for which Congress voted him a sword. After the war he lived with Washington at Mount Vernon for a year, whence he went abroad as secretary to the commercial mission of John Adams, Franklin and Jefferson. When the mission ended, he returned to Derby, served in the Assembly and became one of the leading Hartford wits, his verse having much contemporary popularity. In the 1790's he was minister successively to Portugal and Spain, and married a rich English lady. In 1812 he was put in command of two regiments of Connecticut militia. He ended his days in Derby raising merino sheep which he had imported from Spain, at the same time founding the first textile mills there for its processing.

Colonel Elisha Bostwick of New Milford was also an aide of Washington's and crossed the Delaware with him.

General John Patterson of Lenox, after reporting his regiment with phenomenal speed following Lexington, dug the first redoubts in Charles Town in which he successfully defended the American rear during Bunker Hill. Afterwards he was with Arnold in Canada, where he lost all but 220 of his original 600; fought with Washington at Princeton and Trenton; was promoted brigadier; fought in the Burgoyne campaign, and at Monmouth; was promoted major general at the end of the war and commanded the Berkshire militia in the postwar difficulties. Later he moved to New York State and served in Congress.

General Heman Swift of Cornwall was at first colonel of the 2d Connecticut Line, which Washington is said to have called the best regiment in the army, commending it in orders for discipline. Promoted to brigadier, General Swift became part of Washington's staff and commanded Lafayette's first bodyguard. After the war he commanded the militia of Litchfield County.

General John Fellows of Sheffield, who with General Patterson—both then colonels—was prompt in reporting his regiment to Boston after Lexington, commanded a brigade at Brooklyn and White Plains, and in the Burgoyne campaign.

General Oliver Wolcott, signer of the Declaration, member of the Continental Congress, holder of many offices during the war, saw to the melting of George III in his orchard; as a general of militia organized and sent to the front many regiments; commanded a brigade at Saratoga; afterwards was secretary of the treasury in the federal government, lieutenant governor and governor of Connecticut.

Other militia generals from the valley included John Ashley of Sheffield, Thomas Ives and John Whiting of Great Barrington, and General John Sedgwick of Cornwall, elder brother of Theodore Sedgwick of Sheffield. Upon one of General Sedgwick's departures from his home in Cornwall Hollow, the Tories burned his house so promptly that it was possible to pursue him and get him back, and while the fire was still raging he gave orders for the reconstruction, which was completed while he was away in action.

Colonel Elisha Sheldon raised in Litchfield County the first cavalry regiment in the Continental Army, which acted throughout the war as Washington's bodyguard, providing messengers and detachments for all manner of special duties. Major Tallmadge of that regiment, who settled in Litchfield after the war, performed many confidential missions for Washington. He was in charge of Major André from the night of his capture until his execution, saw Arnold's implication from the beginning and made recommendations which, if they had been carried out promptly, would have led to the capture of the traitor. That night Washington was stopping with General Wolcott in Litchfield. On his arrival at West Point the next morning, there occurred the breakfast at which the treachery of Arnold was discovered. But Arnold had already fled to New York and before he could be caught was aboard a British warship.

The Tory minority is variously estimated at a third to a tenth of the population. It was organized into companies that usually operated as guerrillas. Under orders from the state legislatures the Committees of Inspection and Safety in the towns took over the property of Tories who operated with the enemy, and the names of all Tories were published prominently in the papers. A group of militia in Newtown, calling on Mr. Glover the Tory, found him in bed and amused themselves rousing him with pricks of their bayonets. They also helped themselves to a batch of pies from Mrs. Glover's oven. When one of them threw a piece to the dog Mrs. Glover asked them not to do that because the pie, though good enough for them, was not good enough for the dog.

Most Tories had hiding places in or near their houses, the empty space between chimney and wall being a favorite hide-out. Besides, there were large Tory caves, where their bands congregated in force and kept their plunder. One of these was near Gaylordsville in New Milford, and others were in Great Barrington and Lenox. Legend has it that upon entering the Lenox cave the Tories reversed their boots, so that the tracks were always leaving the cave but never entering. The rich and educated were all suspected of being Tories and were often mistreated. Timothy Edwards, son of Jonathan, in effect gave everything he possessed—about £1,000— for the support of the army; yet he was afterwards waylaid by five thugs and beaten for a Tory. Elijah Williams, who actually was too selfish to be identified with any cause, British or American, was several times imprisoned and examined for alleged Tory sympathies.

Of the three peace commissioners who went to Paris in 1782, Silas Deane and Roger Sherman made two—Sherman was now ex- the valley, having moved from New Milford to New Haven. Of Connecticut's three delegates to the Constitutional Convention of 1787, William Samuel Johnson of Stratford was from the valley, Roger Sherman was formerly of the valley, and Oliver Ellsworth of Windsor, future chief justice of the United States, was to give his name to an independent parish in the town of Sharon. Sherman, by the way, was the only man to sign the four definitive documents: the Articles of Association, the Declaration of Independence, the Articles of Confederation, and the Constitution. He was on the respective committees that drafted the Declaration and the Articles of Confederation.

Theodore Sedgwick of Great Barrington, Sheffield and Stockbridge, brother of General John of Cornwall, was a colonel in the army, a member of the Continental Congress of 1785-1787, the first federal House of Representatives in '89, the federal Senate in '96, apparently not completing his term, for he became speaker of the House in '99; in 1802 he was appointed to the Massachusetts Supreme Court.

Ezra Stiles, president of Yale, who owned properties in Cornwall and elsewhere in the valley and spent much time there, concluded in his diary concerning the Constitution of 1787:

1. That it is not the most perfect constitution, yet
2. That it is a very good one, and that it is advisable to adopt it.
3. That though much of it will be permanent and lasting, yet much of it will be altered hereafter by future revisions. And
4. That the best one remains yet to be investigated.

The valley's chief contributions to the Second War for Independence (1812) were those of the two Hulls of Derby, General William who surrendered Detroit, was court-martialed, convicted, reprieved, and is whitewashed by modern history, and Captain Isaac, whose destruction of the *Guerriere* with the *Constitution* was the bright feature in the first year of the war and caused the composition of America's best contradance, *Hull's Victory*. General Peter B. Porter, who declined the command of the army, was a product of Salisbury, though he was living in Buffalo when hostilities broke out. Throughout the war John Cotton Smith, son of Cotton

Mather Smith the minister of Sharon, was governor of Connecticut.

Although the valley was the scene of no major engagement during the Revolutionary period, the towns consistently exceeded the levies of troops asked of them. Of the two motives behind the Revolution—the desire of the mercantile plutocracy to get rid of British control and the broader political idea of individual freedom—the valley was impelled almost exclusively by the latter. The significant incidents for this region were not the military ones, nor even the major political events in Hartford or Boston or the successive federal capitals. The significant events were those of aspiration on the part of the little people, the propertyless who took the idea of freedom quite literally, the poor farmers who, having fought and won the war at great cost, fondly expected some amelioration of their lot. In the valley the purpose of the war was not for the rich to get richer. It was to pursue an idea about liberty whose complete application would probably have been impossible. Of the big names, Ethan Allen, the champion of the poor, was the typical man from the Valley. In a changed form, the tradition was continuing, the ascendancy of ideas over material things.

Born Free and Equal

IN SPITE of numerous pious resolutions, and even prohibitory laws, Massachusetts and Connecticut had during the Revolution about 5,000 Negro slaves apiece. In the larger settlements of Connecticut the Negro population had a colorful social life of its own, including frequent balls. In Hartford the great event of the year was the election of the colored governor, whose inauguration consisted of a parade of great pomp in the most pretentious gear and on the borrowed horses of the slaves' masters, the "governor" riding on a white horse and attended by obsequious aides, the whole accompanied by a bedlam of brass horns, fifes, drums, fiddles and shouting, and ending with a drunken banquet. In 1800 the annual election and inauguration were transferred to Derby, the flourishing mercantile and manufacturing village in the valley, the town where the Devil had been the dominant influence on life from the start. Meanwhile, Connecticut in 1774 had prohibited the slave trade, and in 1797 had enacted that slaves born after that year should be manumitted at twenty-one. In 1800 there were in fact only 931 slaves left in the state. In 1840 there were seventeen. In 1848, when unconditional emancipation was passed, there were still six.

Meanwhile, through the genius of a slave a hundred and fifty miles up the Valley from the fake African pomp of Derby, Massachusetts had accomplished emancipation in a more graceful and effective fashion. Born of slave parents in New York, Elizabeth Freeman—called "Bett"—and her sister were bought as children by Colonel John Ashley of Sheffield.

Colonel Ashley was the richest landowner and leading squire of that town, and had been one of its first settlers in the 1720's. In 1737 he had built his mansion at the southern limit of the township, just above the Connecticut border, and about four miles from the Center. It stood on the bank of the river where it winds so indolently through the plain as several times to return upon itself and create a series of shallow lakes. Just before the Revolution Colonel Ashley's son, also named John and a general of militia, had built another mansion about a quarter of a mile downstream from his father's.

Recently Colonel Ashley's house has been moved a little way inland, but when Bett was waitress there it still stood on the river. And when Bett was waitress there the old colonel habitually entertained the highly educated oligarchy of Berkshire and Litchfield counties, including Colonel Theodore Sedgwick, already the leader of the Berkshire bar, and Tapping Reeve who was about ready to found in Litchfield the first law school in America. There in the unique upstairs study, with its shell cabinet for bottles and decanters like a dining room, the gentlemen would retire after dinner and the best talk in the valley would be exchanged. And there, all through the great years of the sixties and seventies, Bett served the gentlemen their port and tobacco and grog, heard everything they had to say about liberty and the rights of the individual, and indulged her principle of "keepin' still and mindin' things." Finally, in 1780 she heard the minutest discussion of the new constitution Massachusetts was in process of adopting, its first constitution as an independent state, a constitution which many of the gentlemen there were having a hand in shaping. She noted the Bill of Rights, which Berkshire County had taken the lead in demanding, and she noted especially the preamble to the Bill of Rights, which stated that all "men" were "born free and equal." Though she could neither read nor write, Bett began to reason like a lawyer. Though the idea of being born free was new to her, she began to grasp it.

Meanwhile Bett's younger sister was a kitchen servant

downstairs, and there were other slaves about the place, including a man called Brown. One day shortly after the adoption of the Massachusetts constitution, Mistress Ashley was moved to make a pass at Bett's sister with hot fire tongs, and Bett, interposing her arm, got a scar which she carried for life. With the lofty pride that marked her always, she left the house, walked the four miles up to the Center and appeared at the house of Theodore Sedgwick.

Colonel Sedgwick was at first not impressed by her inquiry whether she could not obtain her freedom under the new constitution. But the more closely he listened to her argument that, since she was not a dumb beast, she must be a "man" within the meaning of the Bill of Rights, the more seriously he began to consider the question. He was a friend of Colonel Ashley and the contemporary of his son General Ashley. But first of all he was an honest lawyer. He knew that the framers of the Bill of Rights had not intended thereby to free the slaves in the state, but he finally concluded that the language they had used unquestionably had that effect. He told Bett he would take her case.

On Colonel Ashley's complaint, the sheriff led his property back into bondage, and Sedgwick did nothing to prevent it. He rode down to Litchfield to talk the thing over with his friend Tapping Reeve, who agreed with him and consented to act as associate counsel. At some time before they filed their bill, the slave Brown joined in the action as co-plaintiff. In the case of *Brown and Bett v. Ashley* the plaintiffs had as distinguished counsel as New England could offer in that age of distinguished lawyers. Colonel Ashley employed Davis Noble of Williamstown and Jonathan Canfield of Sharon, who at that time were stars in their respective states only a little lower than Sedgwick and Reeve.

The case was tried in Great Barrington in 1781, a month before the surrender at Yorktown, which occurred between the trial and the appeal. It was recognized as a test case involving, on one side, the actual application of one of the leading principles for which the Revolution was fought and, on the other side, over a million dollars' worth of property. In the trial the jury not only granted the plaintiffs their freedom but awarded them wages from the time they had been twenty-one; and the Supreme Court affirmed the judgment. When Colonel Sedgwick asked Bett what she wanted him to do with the money, she told him first to pay all the lawyers well, and to hold the rest till she needed it.

Although offered handsome wages at the Ashleys', Bett refused to return, and entered the service of the Sedgwicks, who shortly thereafter moved up to Stockbridge. In the mansion which Theodore Sedgwick built there, she lived for twenty years, beloved by the family over all of whose members she tyrannized. The Sedgwick children called her Mum Bett, and it is by that name, with its implication of humble status, that she is usually known. Her case legally abolished slavery in Massachusetts, the first abolition in America, and in the census of 1790 the state reported no slaves. After 1781 anyone was free to walk out if he wished, though until about 1800 a decreasing number of former slaves preferred to remain in their old state of dependence. Early in the nineteenth century Mum Bett and her husband moved into a house of their own. But she remained for practical purposes a part of the Sedgwick family, and she is buried in their lot in the Stockbridge Cemetery. On the epitaph on her monument, written by Theodore Sedgwick's famous daughter Catherine, she is curiously not celebrated for her major part in emancipation; though otherwise she is given full honor:

ELIZABETH FREEMAN
Known by the name of
MUM BETT

Died December 28, 1829. Her supposed age was 85 years.
She was born a slave, and remained a slave for nearly thirty years:
She could neither read nor write, yet in her own sphere she
had no superior or equal; she neither wasted time nor
property: she never violated a trust, nor failed to
perform a duty. In every situation of domestic
trial, she was the most efficient helper
and the tenderest friend.
GOOD MOTHER FAREWELL

In contrast to the emergence of the slaves from bondage was the decline of the Stockbridge Indians, the wards of the state. With the departure of Jonathan Edwards in 1758 and his replacement by the Reverend Stephen West, the primacy of the interests of the mission in Stockbridge came to an end. Mr. West—later Dr. West—was a dapper little man with a good leg, and popular with all the right people. He was what is called "deeply pious," which meant that he was on the side of the strongest angels; and his wife was a Williams. Under his leadership the Indians, being now thoroughly civilized and pacified, emerged from ministerial and official protection against their own weaknesses and those of the whites, took their chances in the rough-and-tumble scramble for the frontier, and in consequence promptly lost the head start they had had in the ownership of most of the land. Almost as fast as the Indians took up the outlying lands of the town, the holdings passed into white hands. Since it was still illegal to sell an Indian's land for debt, the methods used were ingenious, payment for the doctor's bill, compensation for accidentally killing an ox, consideration for a white man paying an Indian's fine and so letting him out of prison.

In 1762 the Indians memorialized the General Court, reciting that they had always lived at peace with the English, had fought for them against the French in the recent war and lost many killed. They claimed that, nevertheless, much of their outlying lands had already been disposed of by the province at public sale, and the previous Assembly had voted to sell all the rest. The two houses of the General Court gravely appointed a joint committee to examine further into the claims of the Indians. Exactly what was done it is difficult to ascertain, but the fact was that their debts were already nearly as great as the value of the undivided land in the town. In 1765 the General Court at last voted that the Indians' land could be sold for debt, the same as any white man's. This was tantamount to dispossessing them.

Stockbridge's principal land speculator and trader during the Revolutionary period was Elijah Williams, son of old Ephraim and owner of the castle on the Hill. While his purposes were as ruthless as his father's, his methods were less crude, for he enjoyed a qualified popularity and many elective offices, including sheriff and member of the House of Representatives. Furthermore, his life was picturesque for its wide variety of interests, voluminous notes for histories of Rome and ancient England being interspersed among his papers with recipes, bills of sale and receipts for iron, buttons, land, wheat, gold vellum, lace, scarlet cloth, slaves, and legal evidence of many lawsuits in which he was more often defendant than plaintiff. In 1762 he bought an £18 necklace from the silversmith Paul Revere, and two years later was sued by Mary Wilson for the support of a bastard of which she was delivered. It does not appear what came of this action, but in the same year David Crocker was fined for "unnecessary travelling on the Lord's Day," and Elijah himself as sheriff once served a warrant for "hitching up a horse on the Sabbath." By whatever means, he came into the possession of more land than anybody else, including a good part of the neighborhood of Queensborough over the mountain in the west of the township. There he showed himself more than a common speculator, for he financed and operated iron furnaces, foundries and a local store, saw to the construction of good roads, the establishment of a separate parish and the employment of a minister. Thus through his enterprise he was the real founder of the new town which in 1774 was incorporated as West Stockbridge. If the work of the Lord in Stockbridge was still the protection of the Indians against their own weaknesses, then Elijah Williams was as much on the Devil's side as was his less picturesque father. Actually, in the period between 1758 and 1775 it would seem that the Lord had abandoned this project and turned His attention to the rising tide of liberty in a non-Indian sense, for during this time no champion of any kind seems to have taken the part of the natives.

From the beginning of the mission the Indians, having the preponderance of the population, had a majority of the town officials, almost always including the two selectmen. But in 1774, the critical year in the relations with England, there appears the anomaly of two sets of selectmen, one for the Indians and one for the whites, the whites having three against the Indians' two. Already the town had a population of about 900, of which not over 400 were Indians. Already the whites had their separate school and a better one than the natives. Already the economic power, the possession of land, had passed from the Indians. Henceforth their political power was only a form. King Solomon, successor to King Ben as sachem and perennial selectman, continued to hold office a little while longer. But his presence, and that of his colleague, at the selectmen's meetings no longer carried weight. For a little while longer, also, the Indians occupied some of the minor town offices, such as those of constable and tithingman. In 1775 Dr. West turned over the Indian congregation to young John Sergeant, son of the original missionary. From that time they resumed integrity as a church, but it was an integrity entirely separate from that of the town, which was now controlled by the whites. The sham of the half-white, half-Indian government lasted till 1779 when the Indians held office for the last time. Appropriately, Abraham Konkapot, son of the original Captain John, the leader in founding the mission, was the last Indian constable.

Although Dr. West was singularly indifferent to the welfare of his Stockbridge Indians, there lived in the village a Reverend Mr. Kirkland who, keeping his family there, spent part of each year in New York State as missionary to the Oneidas. During the Revolutionary nonintercourse with Great Britain someone bootlegged some tea to Mr. Kirkland and he invited his reverend colleague to share the sin with him. As they were sitting over the pot there was a knock on the door, and in his haste to secrete the *corpus delicti* the Reverend Mr. Kirkland spilled it in his lap, badly scalding himself through his proper, tight-fitting breeches. It was one of his Oneidas at the door, come with a message for him. The Indian neither understood nor resented the long delay before the minister appeared.

Meanwhile, as in the Old French War, the Stockbridges were doing their bit, many of them having enlisted in 1774 as minutemen under their Jehoiakim Metoxin. Shortly before Lexington their chief sachem, King Solomon Unhaumhauwaumut, delivered a notable oration before the provincial Congress of Massachusetts in which he requested, among other things, that his men be allowed to fight in their "own Indian way. Only point out to me where your enemies keep, and that is all I shall want to know."

Great care was taken to explain the quarrel with England to the Indians, and the upshot was that they supplied a full company—virtually all the braves in the tribe—under their Captain Abraham Nimham in Colonel Patterson's regiment. Fighting in their "own Indian way," they traveled to Boston after Lexington, complete with wigwams, squaws and papooses, and their village became a permanent part of the circle round the city during the siege. They served through the war, experiencing horrible sufferings though perhaps no more than many of the white units. Captain Nimham and many others were killed. After the surrender at Yorktown Washington, in recognition, presented to the tribe an ox for a barbecue and a "supply" of whiskey. At the ensuing banquet and dance on Laurel Hill in Stockbridge an effigy of Benedict Arnold was shot, scalped and burned, and afterwards the tomahawk of war was ceremoniously buried. Some doubt is thrown upon the extremity of this orgy when it is learned that the young missionary John Sergeant, Jr., presided at the festivities. In 1792 Congress voted an annual income of $1,500 to the Stockbridge Indians, which proved valuable to them in the care of their poor.

The final, pathetic surrender of the Indians, voluntary as always and yet as always inevitable, is contained in their petition of September 21, 1783:

To the Senators and Wisemen of the Commonwealth of the Massachusetts who are about to smoke their Pipe together in doing the Great Business of the State.

We, the Chiefs of the Moheakonuuk Tribe of Indians [that is, Mohican, the generic tribe of all the River Indians] residing in Stockbridge, this day met together to beg you to listen to us for a few words.

Brothers! We remember we were once great, and you were small when you first came on this Island but afterwards we became small as you became great, and now we are very small and you are very great. We also remember that our Forefathers have often looked to you for Protection, advice and assistance. We with Pleasure look back and consider you have always heard us, when we have spoken to you. Now, Brothers, since we are small we look to you as children to their Fathers. We wish you would always remember as parents do their children. Brothers! We will put you in mind that ever since we first saw you, we were always true friends to you in all the Wars, until this present day. In this late war we have suffered much, our blood has been spilled with yours and many of our young men have fallen by the side of your warriors, almost all those places where your warriors have left their bones, there our bones are seen also. Now we who remain are become very poor. Now Brothers, we will let you know we have been invited by our Brothers, the Oniadas, to go and live with them. We have accepted their invitation.

Brothers! We will now tell you what we desire of you. We wish you in your wisdom to make some laws that will protect and guard us while we may remain or hereafter have occasion to come into your Government. We wish you to appoint a few of our neighbors, whom we believe to be our friends, to take care of the little interest of land we have in this Town, . . . either to sell or lease it out for us. . . . We wish to have them directed, carefully to examine into all our bargains for land that the White People have made with us and see that we hant been cheated and endeavor to do justly by us and by those who have bought of us and have not as yet had their land confirmed to them, that when we are ready to remove, we may feel well toward all our neighbors. . . .

Brothers! We will only ask one thing more, that we might not be sued in the laws for any future debt we may hereafter contract.

In that last sentence is the wince of the humbled but incorrigible child, asking only that he be relieved from further responsibility for the fault that he knows he will never correct.

On their large reservation in Madison County, New York, the Oneidas eventually gathered about a thousand Indians, and the Stockbridges who removed there named the section allotted to them New Stockbridge. More than two hundred emigrated thither in 1784 and 1785, the last to leave being Abraham Konkapot and Hannah his wife. Only the senile remained in Stockbridge, preferring to die in their old home, and becoming for the most part objects of charity, characters of combined humor and sadness like the other relics all down the valley who had remained to be absorbed in the white tide. John Schebuck was one of those who remained and lived by begging. When he was turned from her

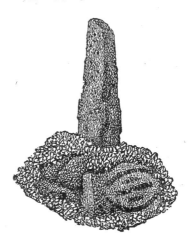

door by a bride who had just arrived from Cape Cod, he asked in mock indignation if a "Scape Scodder" thought to come here, turning out "old 'habitants."

So ended the only attempt in the valley to solve the Indian problem by completely and systematically absorbing a whole tribe into white civilization. If the experiment had been started a century earlier than it was, and could have been carried through four or five generations while truth in the valley was generally envisaged in religious dress, it might have succeeded. But in 1734, when the mission was founded, idealism was already following a new political light, the notion that politically all men were born free and equal.

Under this ideal the slave could rise into enfranchisement and success. But the Stockbridge Indians had been enfranchised from the beginning. Politically, nothing more need be done for them. Wherefore, little was done for them, and, after the start given them by a few consecrated men, they were permitted to slide back into degeneracy. The notion that "free and equal" might have more than a political application was one which would not take form for a long time.

Liberty and the Land

I T IS STRANGE that men of the undoubted social idealism of Colonel Theodore Sedgwick, Generals John Sedgwick, Heman Swift and many others should have been blind to any economic aspect of liberty. These leaders of the Revolution were perfectly willing to fight alongside the small farmers for their right not to be taxed without representation, their right to trial by jury, to free speech, free press, free assembly and the rest. But when these same farmers, comprising a large minority of the population of Massachusetts, had mortgaged their farms or otherwise borrowed ruinously to support their families while they were fighting for liberty, and then, in the chaotic economy after the war, were unable by the utmost of energy and economy to pay their debts and taxes, the leaders who had fully grasped the meaning of liberty in political terms saw no violation of it when these men were sold out of house, home and tools to meet their obligations.

Privately, such men as Theodore Sedgwick pitied and aided their neighbors who had come to this pass. Indeed, the humane principle of pity—combined with the political pressure of a strong minority—considerably softened the harshness of the law toward those who rose in Shays' Rebellion to defend against the state what they took to be the same rights they had just won from Great Britain. Vaguely, humanely, everyone knew that the grievance of the rebels was just. Yet no one, not even the organizers of their rebellion, saw any great principle of jurisprudence involved. Under their third-rate leadership, the Shaysites were a disorderly mob whose only accomplishment was to lose the sympathy of the public which they had enjoyed in the beginning. But if they had been led by a Sam Adams or a Paine or a Jefferson, they might have written into federal and state Bills of Rights one or two provisions the lack of which has already cost much blood, and is liable to cost a great deal more before they are achieved.

The fact that no first-rate leader arose to integrate the cause of Shays' Rebellion showed that people were not yet ready to recognize the principle of economic democracy—as they are still unready a hundred and sixty years later. Jefferson saw the importance of it, the necessary dependence of a democratic state on a foundation of small farmers who owned their land. But he saw it as a matter of political policy to be advocated, not as a principle of constitutional law to be fought for without compromise. Being in France during the uprising, he expressed himself sympathetically with the rebels, but in political terms only. He was less concerned with their grievance than with the fact that they could find a not too costly way of expressing it. Writing to President Ezra Stiles of Yale—who was a large property owner in the valley—Jefferson said: "The commotions which have taken place in America, as far as they are yet known to me, offer nothing threatening. They are proof that the people have liberty enough, and I would not wish them less than they have. If the happiness of the mass of the people can be secured at the expense of a little tempest now and then, or even of a little blood, it will be a precious purchase. *Malo libertatem periculosam quam quietatem servitutem.*"

In the background of Berkshire's considerable participation in Shays' Rebellion was a chronic resentment of authority, which had shown itself in the earliest resistance to the crown and, at the very time that the county was heavily supporting the Revolution with both troops and money, an equivalent resistance to the new state government under a charter from the Continental Congress which was thought to establish a too centralized government. Although the leader of this resistance to state authority, Pittsfield's famous fighting parson, Thomas Allen, violently opposed the Shays movement, his initial radicalism, which he preached throughout the county during the Revolution, was certainly a bridge between the periods of discontent that produced the two rebellions.

The fundamental causes of the Shays uprising of 1786-1787 were: enormous public and private debts incurred during the Revolution; enormous taxes to meet the principal and interest of the public debt; the virtual absence of specie from circulation, which was only in terms of various debased currencies, including the "continentals" in which most of the soldiers had been paid; the consequent inability of thousands of small farmers and merchants to pay their debts and taxes without losing their properties; $1,250,000 still owing the soldiers in Massachusetts. The uprising was essentially one of debtors, but their complaint was strengthened by the fact that the reason for the impoverishment of most of them was their having fought in the war, neglecting their own affairs, and in the end getting paid not at all or in worthless currency.

The immediate precipitating causes were: the Massachusetts Constitution of 1780—the same one which inadvertently had freed the slaves—which favored the rich in the suffrage, in the state Senate, and in qualification for office, representing as it did an effort on the part of the conservatives to order the economic chaos and get the state finances on a sound basis; the postwar luxuriousness of the rich who had hoarded specie, especially the purchase of manufactured goods and luxuries from Great Britain, which could be paid for only in specie, thereby further paralyzing the local market (in 1784 and 1785 the United States imported $30,000,000 worth of goods from Great Britain and exported $9,000,000 worth, the unfavorable balance being represented by export of specie); the incarceration for debt of many propertyless debtors under the old statutes still permitting it; most of all, the suits, attachments and executions for debt of which there were 3,700 in one county in Massachusetts in the two years 1784-1785; as a result of these suits, the inordinate increase in the number of lawyers, with their large fees; as a final aggravant, in the summer of 1786, wide publicity of the news of the arrival in London of the ship *Mary Barnard* carrying about $60,000 in specie from Boston.

By that time the revolt was already organized, though violence had not broken out. At various times and places during the next six months the rebels may have had as many as 10,000 men under arms; but they never had more than about 3,200 in one vicinity at the same time, and in that instance only 1,800 acted in concert. In Berkshire County there may have been as many as 2,000 who at one time or another wore the hemlock, with the addition of a few hundred sympathizers from Litchfield County. But with the exception of the early courthouse mob, nothing approaching that number was ever in the field at one time. Behind the openly disaffected in Berkshire, the number of sympathizers was large and unknown, creating a tension of suspicion in each town where neighbor was turned against neighbor and relative against relative. In Great Barrington several town votes indicated that the Shaysites were just short of a majority.

It was this quality of a neighbors' quarrel which made both sides reluctant to fire when they faced each other, and contributed to the ascription of cowardliness to the Shaysites. They were, to be sure, a ragged mob, containing a large fringe of drunken, loud-mouthed, undoubtedly cowardly wastrels. Yet their nucleus was of high-minded, angry, dispossessed farmers, who had many times faced the professional soldiers of Great Britain. The distinguished badge of the Shaysites, or "Regulators" as they called themselves, was a sprig of hemlock stuck in their hats, while the government forces—where they were not uniformed militia—stuck wisps of white paper in theirs.

The Regulators accepted but little discipline from their leaders, who were mostly Revolutionary ex-officers, and the leaders recognized no seniority among themselves. The name of ex-Captain Daniel Shays is identified with the uprising because he was one of the first in the field, having for months drilled his "troops," and was in command at the critical collision. But nobody else took orders from Shays if he was not minded to. The leader in Berkshire County was Eli Parsons of Lebanon, New York, just over the border.

The anger of the rebels concentrated most naturally upon the courts and the lawyers who were visibly taking their property and imprisoning their persons. Also, they remembered that the first resistance to Great Britain had taken the form of obstructing the crown courts, and they deduced that similar action in the present crisis would win equally effective results. During the summer of 1786, each of the western counties of Massachusetts had conventions of Regulators, passing miscellaneous resolutions condemning the courts and the Senate, demanding moratoriums, further issues of paper money, embargoes on British imports, and similar measures. Berkshire County's convention at the end of August was the mildest of these, possibly because it met at Lenox where the disaffection was the least among the Berkshire towns. Being dominated by the conservatives, it was hardly a convention of Regulators at all.

Less than two weeks later they showed their real power in Great Barrington where the Court of Common Pleas was to sit on September 12th. During the night before and the morning of that day, an armed mob of about two thousand assembled in the street surrounding the court house, and threatened to demolish it. The local militia had been called out to protect the court, but since it numbered about forty men, it did not venture to do its duty. When the court officers and the judges appeared they were blocked from entering the courthouse. They retreated to a private house and adjourned *sine die*. Then the four judges were taken into custody by the rebels, led to the house of one of them, a Dr. Whiting who, in fact, was considerably in sympathy with the insurgents, and there compelled to sign a pledge that they "would not act under their commissions until grievances were redressed." Although surrounded with angry and drunken bayonets, Colonel Elijah Dwight, one of the judges, stoutly refused to sign the paper. Having bullied three out of four judges, the mob proceeded to the jail, broke it open, released all who were imprisoned for debt and forced off the prison limits those who had given bail for the liberty of the limits.

A few weeks later the Supreme Court was scheduled to sit in Great Barrington. Notice was published that the session would be postponed, but the rebels, proclaiming this announcement to be a ruse, assembled in force as before. Being disappointed in their hope of baiting the judges, much of the mob got drunk and set out to impress the town, swaggering about, cursing, firing their guns through signs and the walls of houses, searching for the local deputy sheriff and threatening his wife with bayonets at her breast when she refused to tell where he had hidden. Thus the rebels began to exhibit the offensive braggadocio which characterizes uprisings of persons who believe themselves inferior to those they are attacking. And thus the mob began to lose the public sympathy its cause and individuals had enjoyed before.

During the remaining three months of 1786 the major demonstrations of the rebels were outside of the valley, Eli Parsons and his men limiting their activities to proselyting, swaggering, threatening the lives of prominent citizens such as Theodore Sedgwick, collecting provisions, and leading forces out of the county to join in demonstrations elsewhere.

The turning point of the rebellion occurred on January 25, 1787, when Shays with 1,800 men besieged the Springfield Arsenal, which was occupied by General Shepard with about 1,100 state troops. Both Parsons with 400 Berkshire men and Luke Day, the most talented of the leaders, with a larger force were within easy distance but refused to respond to Shays' appeal for help. After firing one of his artillery pieces over the heads of the Regulators, General Shepard ordered it trained at the center of their line. When the smoke cleared four lay dead in the snow and a fifth was in his last agony. Shays was brave enough, but he could not check the panic that ensued and eventually joined it. Two days later General Lincoln arrived with the main state force of 4,400, and in spectacular fashion pursued Shays' scattering heroes over the northern and western part of the state, through deep snow and increasing blizzards and cold. Shays himself escaped into New Hampshire. For the first time Governor Bowdoin of Massachusetts appealed to neighboring governors for help. The replies from Connecticut and New York were prompt and effective.

The scattering of a guerrilla force such as that of Shays did not mean its destruction, and Parsons in Berkshire was no whit cowed. General Patterson, commanding the small state force in the county, appealed to General Lincoln for aid, and Lincoln responded by himself marching to Pittsfield. On February 15th Parsons, lurking beyond the border in New York State, which was presently to be made untenable for him, issued a famous, rhetorical letter, in which the phrase "fire, blood and carnage" figured prominently, and in which he also promised his fellow citizens that he was going to "Burgoyne Lincoln."

The irony is that at that moment Parsons, with his possibly a thousand men, divided between Lebanon, New York, and Pownal, Vermont, could have carried out his threat. The enlistment period of Lincoln's force ran out shortly before his replacements arrived, and for a few days following Parsons' fierce proclamation, the entire government force in Berkshire County was thirty men. New levies were being recruited, but they were not yet organized. Hastily a Home Guard of forty or fifty was raised in each town, with general headquarters at Stockbridge. The situation was still serious, but the rebel leader had failed to grasp his best opportunity.

Having dispatched his fiery letter, Parsons sent a force of two hundred men under one Hubbard into West Stockbridge to recruit. In order to check this process, three columns of the Home Guard marched on West Stockbrige by the three possible roads. The central column, commanded by Colonel Theodore Sedgwick, put out an advance party of thirty-seven infantry and seven horse. Reaching West Stockbridge first, this detachment was fired on by the outposts of the Regulators, who then retired into their main body, which was already formed. This proved to be one of those cases where most of the men wearing the hemlock boughs were intimately acquainted with most of the government men with their patches of paper, in consequence of which the rebels, when they were commanded to fire, failed to obey. Colonel Sedgwick, coming up at this opportune pause, rode out between the lines and ordered the rebels to lay down their arms. Some obeyed; others fled; there was a scattering fire for a few minutes in which a few Regulators were wounded; then, the two flanking columns closing in from the north and the south, eighty-four prisoners were taken, with a few more added during the ensuing pursuit.

About the same time a comic-opera event happened in Lee, whither two hundred and fifty of the Home Guard went out after three hundred Regulators. The latter, stealing the yarn-beam from the loom of a lady, mounted it in the guise of a cannon, and when the government force appeared they were sufficiently impressed to make lenient terms with the rebels, who promptly surrendered.

On February 26th, southern Berkshire's levy for Lincoln's force assembled at Sheffield and marched up to Pittsfield, leaving the southern part of the county less protected than ever. Whether by luck or by design, the following morning just before dawn a force of about one hundred Regulators under ex-Captain Perez Hamlin of Lenox rode into Stockbridge in sleighs and did a very thorough job of plundering, drinking, and taking prominent men prisoners. From every family came the same story of being awakened in the dark to a vision of tall soldiers with their green boughs and gleaming arms in the candle- or firelight. One of the Regulators, who was an ex-Hessian trooper from West Stockbridge, felt he had sufficiently served the cause when he stole a fine horse on which he forthwith disappeared in the direction of Canada and was not heard from for twenty years.

Theodore Sedgwick, having long secreted his papers, had left town, and the visiting rebels were confronted at his mansion by the redoubtable Mum Bett. In an iron chest in her room in the attic was all of the family silver and much jewelry from neighbors. Mrs. Sedgwick was sick in bed. When Bett came to her in the twilight of that February 27th dawn, saying the Shaysites were at the door, that she had two pistols loaded and believed a shot over their heads would disperse them, Mrs. Sedgwick insisted that she admit them. Bett opened the door to them, holding a candle in one hand a heavy shovel in the other, and assured them that they would find neither Colonel Sedgwick, arms nor ammunition. The men swaggered in all the same, said they would first search the cellar, and someone reached for a light. Bett informed them with an air that she would be delighted to light "the gentlemen" to the cellar or anywhere else, but that she would not give them the light to burn down the house over the head of her sick mistress.

Bett had long foreseen this ordeal, and in the cellar had hidden the wine and spirits, while displaying beer prominently in the wine closet, beer in bottles whose corks she had drawn to flatten it and had afterwards replaced them. Once in the wine closet, one of the ruffians picked up a bottle of the beer and broke off the neck, whereat Bett rebuked him, saying that if they wished to drink like gentlemen she would be happy to fetch the corkscrew and draw the corks for them. Several of the party having tasted the flat beer from the broken bottle, they agreed loudly that if that was the sort of bitter stuff gentlemen drank they would have none of it. Then they started helping themselves out of a barrel of pickled pork, till Bett shamed them by saying that she saw now what they came for instead of ammunition and prisoners. Then she led them through the bedrooms, where in their usual fashion they poked their bayonets under beds and into closets, lest Colonel Sedgwick be concealed there.

At last, to Bett's chagrin, they went to the attic, presently entered her room and demanded that she open the iron chest. At that she knelt on the chest and brandished her shovel. "Oh, you had better search this!" she shouted. "An old nigger's chest! You are such gentlemen!" So she shamed them out of finding the valuables, and they were just leaving the house when a young niece of the Sedgwicks' appeared and asked courteously if they would care to see the stables. They allowed they would. One of the two horses they stole was one which Bett herself rode. It threw its captor beside the house, and Bett, running out, took it by the halter to the meadow gate and gave it a slap to send it galloping. Before they left town the Regulators caught the horse again and he was never returned. The other horse they took was broken by hard riding.

Meanwhile voluntary couriers had scattered in all directions to give warning of the raid, especially northward to Lenox, Pittsfield and to General Lincoln, and southward to Great Barrington and Sheffield. When it was plain that the Regulators were bound in the latter direction, a former member of their party but now reclaimed by law and order rode through their column, being permitted to pass because they thought he was still with them. On the way down to Great Barrington he wore out his whip on his poor horse's flank and afterwards shattered his ramroad in the same way. Meanwhile, the rebel column in their sleighs cleared Stockbridge with a considerable body of prisoners, including one Solomon Gleazen, the village schoolmaster, marching in front of them on foot and slowing their progress. Behind them they left a number of casualties to rum in the snowbanks of the village. The party was uproarious and dangerous, having met with plenty of liquor and no opposition.

Because of the slow march of the Regulators, Great Barrington had sufficient warning. It was ten o'clock when its women, children and old mean heard the ring of the approaching sleigh runners and the shouts of the drunkards through the cold air. Most of the valuables in the village had been hidden before, but in the last two hours all the rest had disappeared, especially the pewter which was much coveted by the rebels for bullets. The forty able-bodied men remaining in the village, under the command of Captain Thomas Ingersoll, had taken sleighs in a tactical retreat to Sheffield, being themselves short of bullets and taking along what lead they had to cut into slugs. On their arrival in Sheffield the Home Guard there was routed out and formed under Captain Goodrich; General Ashley came up to the Center to take command of the entire force of about eighty men; and sufficient sleighs for the total detachment were harnessed and lined up in the street, facing northward.

Meanwhile in Great Barrington the Regulators did their pillaging in more haste than they had shown in Stockbridge, being doubtless apprised that the forces of order were organizing. As usual, they visited the jail and, the jailer Ebenezer Bement having gone off with the Home Guard, they demanded the keys from his wife, "a bright, black-eyed little woman." She unlocked the door herself, and as the Regulators entered to release the prisoners she sang to them a sad song then current:

> Hark, from the tombs a doleful sound,
> My ears attend the cry.
> Ye living men, come view the ground
> Where you must shortly lie.

The wife of General Thomas Ives, like Mrs. Sedgwick in Stockbridge, was conveniently ill and a neighbor woman was doing the housekeeping. Before he went off with the men, General Ives instructed her to admit the Shays men and treat them civilly, but especially to follow them around and ascertain as nearly as possible who they were. They did visit the house in large numbers and, being informed that Mrs. Ives was abed, behaved with exceptional moderation, merely stealing a few provisions and consuming a "large quantity" of General Ives's cider which came up from the cellar by the pailful. At the taverns they helped themselves to spirits in their usual loud fashion, and by one o'clock when their column, preceded as before by the prisoners, headed out of the Center southward toward Sheffield, they left another little squad of alcoholic casualties behind them. In fine the Regulator and home guard "armies" were of about eighty men each. Furthermore, though most of the Regulators were drunk, it must not be supposed that many in the forces of law and order had failed to take the usual means to fortify their courage and their resistance to the cold.

At almost the same moment Captain Perez Hamlin and General John Ashley respectively put their little columns of sleighs in motion southward and northward toward each other in the wide, flat, snow-buried valley between its distant mountain walls under a bright blue, winter sky. The direct road up to Great Barrington was the Meadow Road along the river, and this General Ashley intended to take. But just at the fork north of Sheffield Plain, where the river sweeps in close to the highway, he learned that the rebels had turned westward at the South Burying Ground of Great Barrington, taking the road toward Egremont and the New York State line.

Just what Hamlin's purpose was in doing this is not known, but Ashley thought he was making a break to get out of the state with his loot and his prisoners. He took the left, or westward, fork off the Meadow Road and ordered the sleighs into a "furious" gallop. This left fork was the Back Road to Great Barrington which, roughly paralleling the Meadow Road a mile west of it, eventually met the road the Regulators had taken from Great Barrington toward Egremont. But far short of that junction, indeed only about a mile above the fork, there was a turn and a short cut to Egremont by means of which General Ashley hoped that he could head off the Regulators, they being impeded by their prisoners marching on foot. Up the back road under long, cracking whips galumphed the heavy farm horses at full sweat and steam. Round Pitcher's Corner one by one slewed the heavy bobsleighs, geysering the snow, and straightened out westward. Past Asher Saxton's Tavern in Egremont. Presently the road bent to the right, where the same road joins the modern turnpike, and they poured out onto a little plain, on their left the icy magnificence of Mt. Everett, on their right over the near ridge the remoter horizon of East Mountain, to the north a shoulder of Monument, Tom Ball and Yokun, all enormous and glittering in their ice and snow. Across the plain they galloped a hundred rods to the bridge over Hubbard's Brook, where all around them under the snow lay the still unopened marble quarries that one day were going to make, not Sheffield, but Egremont famous. One by one the sleighs ground over the icy bridge. A single rider steamed up from the rear, won to the head of the column, and shouted to General Ashley that the enemy was behind him. Instead of continuing toward Egremont, they had turned down the back road, had reached Pitcher's Corner not long after the Home Guard, had turned there and, instead of being pursued, were now the pursuers.

This was one thing Ashley had not foreseen. He got the column halted, and there was a minute or two of great confusion while "the sleighs were thrown out of the way." Then Captain Goodrich of Sheffield deployed his company on the right of the road, and Captain Ingersoll of Great Barrington deployed his on the left. In a single battle line centered on the road they waded forward through the snow over the solid stream and up the gentle slope through the thin woods. But for the snow it was easy going, with cover offered by the trees as might be required. General Ashley was probably in the road between them, for his voice was audible to both companies. In this formation they had advanced about fifty rods when they heard the ring of runners approaching behind the turn around which they had recently come down into the plain.

It was a drunken, absurd and sad remnant that spilled out over that flat between the hills for what is called "the last battle of Shays' Rebellion." Actually, they represented the great principle that a man who is willing to work is entitled to own enough of the means of production to support himself and his family. But it is safe to say that there wasn't a man among all the Regulators who could have formulated the principle, beyond growling that he was sick of seeing the lawyers getting everybody's property. Actually they were right in their profession that they were fighting for liberty, but their definition of liberty would have identified it with that license which they themselves practiced and which had properly lost them the support they had at first enjoyed. Doubtless much of their swaggering was due to their too recent emergence from the English class system which left them uncertain, boastful and loud before their "betters." Add further an instinctive law-abidingness in most of them. Add, finally, the fact that many of this particular group were from Great Barrington and some from Sheffield, so that they knew many of the Home Guard they were supposed to destroy with "fire, blood and carnage." Out of these factors you get a sufficient explanation for their reticence to fight with the spirit many of them had shown against the British. It was the end of America's first populist movement, anarchical, boyish, pathetic, that swung round the turn on the road from Asher Saxton's Tavern to Francis Hare's, and saw facing them along the edge of the thin woods on both sides of the road about seventy-five rods in front of them a line of eighty men advancing to meet them. Out in front, in the road between the two companies, stood the well-known figure of General Ashley. Huge Everett near by, and far off Yokun and Monument, looked down their long, snow noses at the sad end of what might have been a powerful and dignified movement in American history.

When the Regulators first saw the Home Guard their prisoners were marching out in front as usual. Their first act was to jump out of the sleighs and run forward to the prisoners, behind the partial protection of whom they loaded their muskets. They seem never to have effected a proper deployment, but to have bunched in the road, exchanging a desultory fire with their attackers, whose ordered line came slowly on.

At about this time there occurred the burlesque act of Moses (Mut) Orcutt, a Revolutionary veteran and local poet who was in the Great Barrington Home Guard. Being drunk, he stepped forward out of his battle line, knelt in the snow, laid aside his musket and powder horn, tore back his shirt and called on the enemy with a mountain-shaking oath to "fire upon the body of Moses if they dared." One or two of the Regulators did fire on him and wounded him slightly, and this piece of genuine cowardice may have precipitated what followed.

The Home Guard heretofore had been firing at will and little and carefully, in order not to hit the prisoners who were in front of the bulk of the rebels. How much if any damage they had so far done does not appear. On their own part they had lost one killed and two wounded, including

Mut. Solomon Gleazen, the Stockbridge schoolmaster who was one of the prisoners, in attempting a break during the confusion, had been shot through the neck and killed. Now the two companies of the Home Guard, flanking the road, had advanced far enough so that one or both of them had a clear aim at the rebels behind the prisoners. The time had come for volley fire and General Ashley released it with his famous shout, "Pour in your fire, boys, and may God have mercy on their souls!" At the first volley thirty-two of the

Regulators fell, two of them dead, and the rest ran. At that moment a certain Captain Walker with the Home Guard from Lenox came on the double round the turn into the plain, just in time to take fifty prisoners which, with the thirty-two previous casualties, just about accounted for the rebel "army."

The triumphal procession of sleighs northward was over a mile long, and was hardly less noisy than the advance of the Regulators in the morning. The latter were deposited in the Great Barrington jail to its capacity, thus fulfilling the prophecy of Mistress Bement, the jailer's wife, a few hours before, and the overflow was marched on up to Lenox, which shortly was to succeed Great Barrington as the shire town.

In the Great Barrington jail some of the culprits now enjoyed some solace for their plight. General Ives, having got from his housekeeper an approximate list of those who had visited his house, came to the jail and demanded that those who had been there confess. Every Regulator denied it. General Ives said he was sorry to hear that none of them were guilty, because he wanted to thank those who had been there for their considerate behavior in view of his wife's illness, and to give them some special food he had brought. Every Regulator now pleaded guilty. The record is obscure as to whether the general treated all, or none, or only the deserving ones.

This was the last organized violence of the rebellion, although the disaffection and swaggering libertarianism of it has continued in various forms to this day. After the "Battle of Sheffield" the organization moved out of Massachusetts. As late as May, 1787, there was a fresh company of Shays' minutemen raised in Sharon, and when General Swift was ordered by Governor Huntington of Connecticut to break up the business, calling out the militia if necessary, he wrote that he must proceed secretly because of the great popularity of the movement, and that he was considered "a speckled bird" for opposing it.

In Massachusetts, the military in force was quartered on the people of Pittsfield throughout the summer. A squad was billeted in the tavern of Captain Jared Ingersoll on the corner of North and present Depot streets, the captain being a Regulator and languishing in jail in Northampton, while his wife ran the tavern. The resident squad of soldiers bought a barrel of cider, rolled it into the taproom, and began to dispense it to the public for their own profit. Mistress Ingersoll, entering the room, personally rolled the barrel into the street.

During that summer of 1789 most of the rank and file of the Regulators were pardoned, upon their taking the oath of allegiance, and under sundry temporary suspensions of their civil rights. Many prominent citizens who had supported the movement in various ways were subjected to formidable fines and prison terms, including, curiously enough, that Dr. William Whiting of Great Barrington who was one of the judges abused by the Regulators when they first obstructed justice in Berkshire County. Fourteen of the military leaders of the rebellion, including six from Berkshire County, were condemned to death for high treason and fled into Vermont and New Hampshire whence no serious effort was made to extradite them. Eventually, they were all pardoned. Eventually, also, under the new federal government, constituted this same year of 1787, all the veterans of the Revolution, including Shays himself, were properly compensated for their old services in the army and paid a pension besides, without inquiry into their behavior in the meantime.

In their opposition to centralized government and privileges for the rich, the Regulators of '86 and '87 became the Anti-Federalists of '88 and eventually the members of the original Democratic party, the supporters of true liberals like Jefferson and of mob organizers like Aaron Burr, the grandson of Jonathan Edwards. So close was the issue in Great Barrington in '88 that in the town meeting to choose a delegate to the convention to consider the new constitution, Colonel Dwight was not sure of his seat till a committee of the convention had considered his election. This was the Massachusetts convention which the town of Lanesboro claims the address of its illiterate delegate swung into the federal column.

The general opposition to plutocracy represented by the Regulators has taken many forms in our history, but it was never based on a more just principle than that implicitly represented by the farmers of Shays' Rebellion whose essential claim was that they should not because of patriotic debt be deprived of property essential to life. Here was an economic principle implementing the political principle that no man should be subjected to authority in which he had no voice. Ignorant, absurd, shabby, licentious and criminal as many of them were, they were yet on the side of ideas, the tradition of the valley, as against entrenched, material power, on the side of the Lord as against the Devil. In their crude way they continued the march of those ideas which were one of the motives in the Revolution, those ideas which, through varying degrees of victory and defeat, have continued to march through Jefferson, Jackson, Lincoln, Bryan, Henry George, both Roosevelts, and less convincingly through the sundry uprisings of industrial labor.

Contemporary with Shays' Rebellion, and likewise rooted economically in agrarian impoverishment and politically in the desire for liberty, was the surge of emigration northward and westward which began during the Revolution and "threatened to empty New England" until about 1800, when it abated for a dozen years of so. How effective a safety valve this was against a more powerful explosion than that of the Regulators is implicit in the fact that in the valley the deforestation of the hilltops had already let the weather sweep many farms of topsoil down into the valleys, where the number of farms thus made was fewer than the number lost on the newly "rocky hilltops of New England." In agrarian terms the valley was fully developed, partially ruined, and overpopulated. The average young man in the typical big family in the 1780's and nineties had no local prospect but to settle down as the hired man of his father or his older brother, a function reserved for the very young and the very old and contrary to the Yankee prejudice, already established, against working for anybody else. In contrast to this debasing prospect, he heard the siren voices of land companies and the true reports of neighbors who had gone before, calling him to the fabulous wonders of Vermont, of western New York, and presently of the Western Reserve and beyond. In the sweeping claims of New England that it was the unenterprising, the impoverished, and the criminals who went west and in the equally broad claims of the West that it was the enterprising ones who had the gumption to pull up stakes, both are happily right. Like all pioneer movements, this one included many who were fleeing from the law, and it included many more who were broke as a result of the war, either with or without their own fault. And it contained likewise a large proportion of the most ambitious youngsters from large families who were determined to hew out for themselves a place in the sun.

Organized emigration from the Lower Valley began as far back as 1667 when Robert Treat led an expedition which founded Newark, New Jersey. In 1753 began the settlement of the Wyoming Country, being the northern two-fifths of Pennsylvania which was claimed as a part of Connecticut's original grant. In 1774 this settlement along the Susquehanna had about 3,000 inhabitants, most of them from Connecticut, and was organized into a town called Westmoreland which was made part of Litchfield County. Two years later it became a separate county under the same name, and in 1778, when all of its able-bodied men were away in the army, it was wiped out by the notorious Wyoming Massacre carried out by Tories and Indians. In 1782 Congress took the already long-disputed territory away from Connecticut and gave it to Pennsylvania, compensating the former state by good title to an equivalent territory of 3,300,000 acres in future Ohio. This, being all that Connecticut retained out of its original claims to the Pacific, became known as the Western Reserve.

At the time of the settlement of the Western Reserve of Connecticut, it was still an uninviting wilderness occupied by dangerous Indians. Consequently the first wave of the post-Revolutionary emigration was northward into the New Hampshire Grants (later Vermont) and westward into central New York. When in 1777 "The Grants" declared statehood independent of both New Hampshire and New York, and were promptly acknowledged by the former, they took the name of New Connecticut, and the new commonwealth was particularly referred to as a "child of Litchfield County." Ethan Allen and his young brother Ira, Vermont's great philanthropist, promoter and profiteer, were from Cornwall. Seth Warner was from Roxbury. The first governor, Thomas Chittenden, was from Salisbury. Two other early governors were from Litchfield County, likewise three early United States senators and one early chief justice. A glance at the modern map of the state shows sixteen towns named after parent towns in the Connecticut part of the valley (including eleven from Litchfield County): Bethel, Bridgewater, Brookfield, Canaan, Cornwall (which, like Cornwall, Connecticut, contains a Cream Hill), Derby, Huntington, Milton, Orange, Roxbury, Salisbury, Sharon, Sherman, Warren, Washington and Woodbury. Against the sixteen named after river towns, there are twenty-four towns on the modern map derived from parent towns in the five-sixths of Connecticut which is outside the valley. From Massachusetts the relative representation of valley names is only slightly less impressive—Berkshire, Hancock, Pittsfield, Richmond, Sheffield and Stockbridge; and against these six, twelve from the thirteen other counties in the state. Gamaliel Painter of Salisbury founded Middlebury College. Typical of the organization of the Vermont towns was the first town meeting of Castleton which was held in the house of Amos Bird of Salisbury and adjourned to meet again in Castleton the following May. Hinesburgh was settled by people from Canaan, with a large increment from New Milford.

Contemporaneously with Vermont, central and western New York was being filled up from New England, especially Connecticut. No statistics exist, however, to indicate how large was the share of the valley in this wave of emigration, and since the New York towns were generally given either

Indian or classical names, the method used for inferring the origin of Vermont towns is not available.

Nor is there any way of gauging the valley's share in the settlement of Connecticut's Western Reserve which began in 1795, under a high-pressure committee appointed by the Assembly. In 1787 the Continental Congress had passed the Northwest Ordinance, providing government and protection in the whole Northwest Territory, but it was not until 1795 that the popular pressure for pioneering forced action by the state. Meanwhile, in 1791, Vermont had been admitted to the Union under its permanent name, and New Connecticut became for a time the name of the Western Reserve. A town name transplanted from the valley is Kent, while the Ohio towns of Boardman, Canfield, Tallmadge, Johnson and Hudson were settled by and named after Litchfield County men. Generally, as in New York, Western Reserve pioneers accepted Indian names or chose new ones, instead of transplanting the names of the towns whence they came.

The rush for new land after the War of 1812 carried past the Western Reserve and clean out to and beyond the Mississippi, skirting the southern strip along the Ohio where the slave people from Kentucky and Virginia were strong. Three Collins brothers from Litchfield founded Collinsville, Illinois. Amenia, South Dakota, was settled by Sharon people. By the early nineteenth century, Goshen was already a great cheese center, and in 1810 Lewis N. Norton there invented, and presently patented, pineapple cheese, through the chance expedient of pouring curd into a knitted sock in which it was twisted and hung to dry, the sock accounting for the traditional markings on the cheese. Mr. Norton did not emigrate to the fine lands of Wisconsin, but many of his townsmen did. They took with them their cheese hoops and founded the industry in which Wisconsin now leads the country; at this writing, leads the world.

In this, as in all the great westward movements in America, the motives of liberty and gain were mixed in what proportions it is impossible to say. All that is certain is that by about 1820 the second wave of emigration from the valley had spilled westward, and while it had swept many thousands away another wave from eastern New England had more than replaced them. The population of the valley had actually increased by about fifty per cent and for the next twenty or thirty years remained approximately stable. The flaming ideal of liberty, which had fought the Revolution and Shays' Rebellion, had contributed largely to the recent exodus. Now it hardened into the cranky independence of Yankee character. The old Puritan need for idealism began to look for new expression in terms of life in a settled, numerous population having an established relation to its land. And likewise the impulse for gain, the motive of the Devil, began to look, more sharply than before, for realization in new and nonagrarian terms.

Liberties with The Lord

BEGINNING with the opening wedge of the Halfway Covenant in 1657, increasingly deep cracks were pried in the armor of orthodoxy. One of the earliest founded, longest sustained and most absurd of church controversies was that in which freer souls gradually introduced real music into the Congregational churches in place of the original, lugubrious practice of "deaconing" the psalm or hymn, the deacon singing or intoning a line and the congregation repeating it after him in a bedlam of individual musical impulses. Under the "old way," also, the male congregation—the women kept meek silence—might sing the hymn right through without the help of the deacon and without reference to each other's time or pitch. The "new way" wished merely to introduce orderly singing, involving both men and women, a unanimous melody, and even harmony. This regularity smacked to the wary of "popery"—uniform praying would be next. The struggle was prolonged, bitter and in retrospect entertaining. As late as 1770 Lenox, in its first town vote setting up the church, found it necessary to duck the issue, enacting "that the singers agree among themselves who shall tune the psalm"—that is, lead the singing—whether the deacon or the selected choir with its leader.

Somewhat less grave, because not so easily associated with either doctrine or Biblical citation, was the matter of introducing heat into the "sacred refrigerator" wherein the valley shivered for at least four hours every Sabbath for about a century and a half. In other parts of New England there are much earlier references to the use of foot stoves by ladies and specifically permitted old men, but the first evidence I find of them in the valley is in December, 1768. At a town meeting in that month, the worthies of Sharon, clearly impatient with the use of the dangerous innovations

in the brand-new second meeting house just completed, solemnly enacted as follows:

It being represented to this meeting that stoves are frequently left in the meeting house with fire in them, whereby it is much exposed to be burnt; the town taking this matter into consideration, agree and vote that no stove shall be left in the meeting house, with or without a fire in it, and suffered to remain there after the meeting shall be dismissed at night, or through the night, on the penalty of ten shillings for a stove so left. . . .

The introduction of a single, central stove warming the whole building was everywhere stoutly resisted as a concession to carnality. Possibly the first victory for sinful comfort in New England occurred at Litchfield in 1816, in the famous second meeting house, built in 1762, where the great Lyman Beecher was already the minister. After a long battle a committee of seven young members of the congregation got permission to install in the central aisle a stove on trial. The Sunday of the trial was a balmy one in November. Several of the pro-stove members, on entering, walked ostentatiously to the sheet-iron monster and stood warming their hands. Members of the anti-stove party grumbled about the temperature and carefully held back their coat tails in passing the monster. In the midst of the sermon Mrs. Peck, overcome by the heat, rose and left the church in a fainting condition. The stove had not been lighted.

Of graver import was the gradual liberalizing of doctrine, from the Halfway Covenant down to the kindly God of Unitarian William Ellery Channing and his friend Judge Theodore Sedgwick in the second decade of the nineteenth century. I have already pointed out that the permanent effect of Edwards's insistence on individual experience in the Great Awakening was to strengthen the social and political libertarianism that was already finding its way into many pulpits. Not only did this rise of the ideal of liberty prostitute religion to political purposes, but it injected into religion itself an individualistic tendency which led to a scattering of doctrine, a religious anarchy which augured ill for any consistency of belief, and for organized religion in the future. In 1770 Whitefield was back for his last tour of America, preaching the theory of being privately born again, which by implication made every one of his hearers rather than their ministers or deacons the judges of their own religious state. He preached to enormous audiences in Great Barrington, Canaan, Salisbury and Sharon, the Salisbury meeting overflowing the meeting house and being held in the open air, and the larger Sharon meeting house being equipped with special bleachers for the occasion.

In 1782 Stockbridge completed its big, ugly, heavy-timbered second meeting house, and in the same period suffered a jar to the safe and sane reign of little Dr. Stephen West. A member of the congregation was the handsome widow Lavinia Deane who had a few small children and took into her house as a boarder a recent arrival in town, Mr. John Fisk. He was one of the schoolteachers, made no secret of the fact that he cared nothing for the church, its minister and officers, and made less secret of the fact that he proposed to marry Mrs. Deane. Having heard that Fisk had said "I swear" and "Damn it," the church elders appointed a committee to admonish Mrs. Deane not to marry him till they had considered his character further. Whereupon they heard that he had said, while driving, "God damn that whip" and "God damn your soul to hell," and promptly concluded that it would be "inconsistent with the rules of the Word of God for Mrs. Deane to" marry this "openly immoral and profane man." Mrs. Deane, who took the church seriously, both for herself and for her children, retorted that he had merely used "a few airy words," had done nothing wrong, and so married him. Instantly the church excommunicated her. To the annoyance of Dr. West, Mrs. Fisk, egged on by her energetic new husband, demanded her right of a church council.

The council was packed against the Fisks from the start. But during its deliberation the distinguished Dr. Joseph Huntington of Coventry happened by and took the occasion to liven Stockbridge with a little last-minute doctrine. Human marriage, he said, was not, as they assumed, a symbol of Christ's marriage to his church. Human marriage was a carnal, civil and social fact based on the human fact that two people were in love with each other. It was not necessary to a successful marriage that both or either party be in a State of Grace. And he went on to say that persons who were not saved often made the best rulers, husbands and wives. The council was shocked and the Fisks lost their case. But little Dr. West, whose aim was appeasement and peace, was troubled by the peculiar ideas he had heard. He remained troubled for the rest of his life, trying to understand this strange new world.

Best evidence of the scattering effect of libertarianism upon religion was the multiplication of sects following the Revolution. In 1780 and 1781 Mother Ann Lee in her tour of New England established Shaker communities at Hancock, West Pittsfield and Tyringham. While exciting the usual local gossip, they erected the usual substantial Shaker buildings, including the big, circular, communal barns. And they made their contribution to the unique Shaker music, dancing, crafts, inventions and industries.

Less reputable was Jemima Wilkinson, the "Universal Friend" who, having almost died of a fever, claimed upon her

recovery that she had indeed died but that Christ had re-entered her body which thereby became the second Incarnation, a view which she was able to impress upon numerous followers. In 1782 she appeared in New Milford, and in 1784 had a sufficient congregation—called irreverently "Jemimakins"—to build her a church in Northville in that town. On one occasion she held a meeting on the shore of the river, having previously announced that she would walk on the water. At the end of a long sermon, she asked if they all had faith that she could do this miracle. Being assured that they did, she personally inquired of each one if he had faith. Finally she announced that it was true that they all had faith that she could do it; wherefore, it was unnecessary to do it. In 1789 she disappeared, saying to her followers that she was "going to prepare a place for them" and that she would send for them. The place she prepared was 14,000 acres in Yates County, New York, with a settlement in it which she called Jerusalem. True to her word, she sent for her followers in New Milford, and a large, pioneer expedition went out to her, splitting many families. One of her hypocrisies was the pretense of poverty, though among her many talents was one for accumulating property which she always took in the name of some close follower. In Jerusalem she was sometimes visited in the evening by angels, one of whom was reported to have been a neighboring judge. She said that when she died her body would vanish in thin air. But after it was kept a few days in the cellar it was found necessary to bury it secretly in the garden.

The Episcopal Church, including many Tories, fell off during the Revolutionary period, but generally recovered and increased afterwards. An exception to the recovery was the parish in Goshen whose church had been built in 1767, a crude affair never painted, with slab seats and "something to serve as a pulpit." The congregration having evaporated, the building was sold in 1788 to the Congregational winter parish of North Goshen. Thither in '92 it was drawn in what, according to a local diarist, was "a great drawing as I can well remember." Being deposited at its new site, it remained without attention or repairs "until the great storm in March, 1796, when it was blow down and destroyed." In 1783 at a conclave at Woodbury of ministers of the late Church of England, the Reverend Samuel Seabury, previously an active Tory, was consecrated the first Protestant Episcopal bishop in America.

The Baptist and Methodist faiths appeared in the valley and grew rapidly between the Revolution and the end of the century, despite the sincere and vindictive efforts of many of the Congregational ministers to suppress both. In Danbury there occurred a typical budding and breaking off of sects. In 1771 a group of the local Congregationalists seceded and became Sandemanians. After the Revolution a

group of this same, meanwhile increased, Sandemanian congregation seceded to join a sect called Whitists. Later, in
1817, a group of the meanwhile increased Whitists broke
away and became the second congregation of the later large
sect, the Disciples of Christ. Actually, what was happening
was the rapid decline of the Congregational hegemony in the
valley and elsewhere in New England. Legally, the unorthodox sects had won the right to collect taxes for their own
purposes far back before the Great Awakening, but actually
the Congregational ministry had remained the dominant
force in all the communities. Now, on the wings of political
liberty, the people were throwing off this century-and-a-
half-old control and were thinking for themselves.

The plainest tendency everywhere in New England in
the postwar period was the decline of all religion, the debauch
of worldliness, cynicism and crime that follows war.
In the 1790's drunkenness seems to have been almost
the normal condition of mankind, including most of the
ministry, and gambling the daily occupation. How free sex-
ual relations were at the time—bundling between engaged
couples was no innovation—is hidden behind the Victorian
blushes of most of the town historians. Through the blushes,
however, there comes a pretty general agreement that in this
period the youngsters of the wealthier families frequently
held balls which lasted most of the night; to which the
young gentleman conducted the young lady sometimes five
or six miles on the pillion behind him, "her arms about his
waist"; at which "the ladies sipped their wine, and cider,
and did not disdain the more . . . seductive flip, or yet more
tempting cordial, while the gentlemen indulged in even more
fiery and exciting beverages"; after which the young blood
escorted his lady to her remote home, she again sitting on
the pillion behind him. In this dark cloud of sin the blushing
historian of Pittsfield is able to find a faint silver lining in
the fact that "happily, the floor was as yet innocent of waltz
or polka." For the "lower orders" of society there were held
in "the less respectable taverns" a "coarser class of dancing
parties" known as "Shake-down balls." "Chastity . . . was

hardly looked for or expected in the class which attended them."

In this same category of self-indulgence comes gluttony. On May 1, 1795, a church ordination supper was served for twenty-three saintly guests at the tavern in Lenox, the site of and ancestor of the Berkshire Coffee House and the present Curtis Hotel. The menu for the twenty-three visitors included: "2 roast pigs, 2 turkeys, 10 doz. eggs, 12 bottles of Madeira, 2 pints of brandy, four bowls of sling, 18 large glasses of punch, 8 bottles of sherry and 24 glasses of bitters better known as cocktails."

More significant than this fashion of sensuousness was the underlying wave of considered atheism and deliberate blasphemy, chiefly on the part of the young. "At the accession of Timothy Dwight to the presidency of Yale in 1795, unbelief dominated the college. There were societies whose members called one another by the names of noted infidels; the college church was almost extinct." "The means of grace were little valued; public peace was broken by disorderly and riotous conduct. Our midnight slumbers were disturbed by obscene songs and drunken revels. The laws were trampled on with seeming impunity. Magistrates were defied and abashed. The . . . Sabbath was violated palpably and openly. . . . The most solemn scenes were exhibited in mockery, and . . . the disciples of Jesus were all the while asleep."

In the valley towns a favorite pastime of youth seems to have been to ring the church's solemn bell at disturbing times. One Sabbath morning the orthodox congregation of Washington, Connecticut, assembled to find a wagon hanging from the peak of the church steeple. In Woodbury the Lord seems to have interposed a warning finger. On the Sunday following a particularly riotous and noisy party of young people in one of the taverns, the Reverend John Searle reproved the affair openly from the pulpit. During his remarks one of the young men involved rose with expressions of contempt and lounged out of the church. As he was going out the door the minister called, "Perhaps you may never have another opportunity to come to this place; but I leave it with the great God." The boy went home and took to bed with no recognizable ailment, languished a few days, and died "without any bodily pain."

Unedifying brawls between town and minister regarding the latter's compensation had been the rule rather than the exception in the valley from the beginning. One of the most picturesque of these reached its trying phase in this post-Revolutionary period. The Reverend Hezekiah Gold had been ordained in Cornwall in 1755. From early in his long ministry there was a valid disagreement about church membership, for Mr. Gold was a reactionary and persuaded a majority of the congregation to eschew the Halfway Covenant. Through the years, personal differences multiplied and' rankled, until during and after the Revolution the town found itself especially aroused in what was a frequent complaint everywhere, that the minister, being a wealthy man, was still exempt from taxes and so was bearing none of the heavy, common burden of the war. Mr. Gold offered to contribute the equivalent of a current tax upon his property but at his own appraisal. The town promptly voted his proffer not enough. The minister had with him a bare minority of the town and a bare majority of his congregation. In 1779 the town voted to call a council to consider his dismissal, and the church voted to disregard the town's action. One Sunday Mr. Gold was locked out of his church. On another occasion he entered just as one of the deacons, who was of the opposition, was taking advantage of his tardiness to start the meeting with a hymn, when a young woman of the minister's party picked up a footstool, knocked the hymnbook out of the deacon's hand and gave God's vicar his cue. Mr. Gold was fined by Justice Russell for assaulting James Sterling. On Thanksgiving Day he was ejected from the pulpit. The famous Dr. Bellamy of Bethlem was called in more than once to mediate. In 1780 most of the objectors withdrew to form a new congregation which later built the exquisite North Cornwall church. Mr. Gold resigned, and was duly dismissed, in 1786. Ezra Stiles, preceding Timothy Dwight as president of Yale, frequently visited Cornwall during Mr.

Gold's pastorate, and sometimes stayed with him. In his diary Dr. Stiles noted: "Wealthy ministers in Litchfield County—Mr. Gold, £3,000."

From credible records it appears that Great Barrington continued to distinguish itself as the garden of the Devil which its first minister, the Reverend Samuel Hopkins, had found it to be. In 1769 he was dismissed for no reason except that the town was unwilling to pay him enough to live on, and soon thereafter he entered upon his distinguished career at Newport. From that time until 1806 the Congregational church had no established minister except for the three years 1787-1790 when the Reverend Isaac Foster was the incumbent, sought and obtained dismissal for lack of support, "and as his predecessor had done, twenty-one years before, sued the town for arrearages of salary."

Theretofore and for a few years thereafter the town hired preaching, a volunteer committee of women taking it upon themselves to sweep out the meeting house whenever a minister had been obtained. In 1794 Samuel Hopkins paid a visit to his old parish in the company of the Reverend Dr. Patton, who made a record of the occasion: "The people were without a minister, nor was there any convenient place to assemble for public worship. Doctor Hopkins inquired if his former meeting house could not be fitted for the purpose for one Sabbath; but it was found to be impracticable, as the windows were broken, the door had fallen down, and the floor had been occupied by sheep, who resorted to it from the Common at night, and in storms. It was further said that if a meeting should be appointed anywhere else, there would be but little interest taken in it; but few would attend. It was common for those who regarded the Sabbath . . . to go to other towns to enjoy them; while others devoted the day to visiting, to sitting in taverns, to horse racing and other amusements; but Mr. Hopkins supposed they expended much more in these ways, and the consequent dissipation and extravagance, than would be necessary for the support of the gospel ministry among them."

In 1798, President Dwight of Yale set down his impressions of both Great Barrington and Sheffield:

It is probable that there has been more horse-racing in these two towns than in all the state of Massachusetts besides. . . . The soil is excellent, yet we saw very few marks of thrift or prosperity. The houses are in many instances decayed; the Episcopal church barely decent; the Congregational ruinous. . . . Religion has had here, generally, a doubtful existence, and during the little time in which they have had a minister of the Gospel, he has scarcely been able to find a subsistence.

(Here, it will be recalled, was the hotbed of disaffection in Berkshire County during Shays' Rebellion.)

Statistics are not available as to the probable increase in crime during the Revolutionary and post-Revolutionary periods. It may or may not be coincidence that most of the few foul crimes reported in the histories of the valley towns are concentrated in and closely around this period: an unusually bestial murder of a whole family in Woodbury by combined beating and burning; an extremely bold robbery in Bethlem from which one young man, escaping, "ran three miles to Bethlem Meeting House, without stopping to give an alarm"; two burglaries in Lanesboro (being in '87 and defended on the ground that the aim was to get supplies for the rebellion); three cases of rape, and one of incest. All these being capital crimes, the culprits were executed either in Litchfield or in Lenox, which latter had in 1788 succeeded Great Barrington as the shire town of Berkshire.

In Lenox the executions were staged as a colorful and impressive spectacle. From the jail to the gallows the condemned was conducted by a solemn parade. At the head rode the sheriff on horseback, wearing his official sash and bearing his official sword. Then came the fife and drum corps, playing a death march. Then the military escort surrounding the cart wherein rode the prisoner with his coffin. At the rear walked the assembled clergy of the county. When the prisoner was on the scaffold one of the ministers addressed to him a long and fiery harangue, prolonging the awful suspense sometimes to an hour while he terrified the condemned man—and the surrounding multitude—with assurances of the hell whose doors would shortly close on him forever, and sometimes at the close adding a perfunctory hope that the Lord might have mercy on him. During the same period Danbury, now the half-shire town of Fairfield County, had the only two executions of its history, the crimes being of such enormity that the historian has neglected to name them.

The postwar moral slump lasted for perhaps twenty years and was followed by one of America's great revival periods whose beginning may be placed, as accurately as anywhere, with a series of sermons which President Dwight preached to his Yale boys in 1797 and which seem to have impressed both them and New England. Within four or five years the dominant quality of society changed from moral cynicism to religious zeal. Except in the case of the Shakers, and of scattering instances everywhere, the violent and hysterical exhibitions that had marked the Great Awakening of sixty years before were not now found in New England. The former bedlam emanating from the horrors of perceived hell and the joys of convinced salvation, the old medley of groans, screams and prophesyings, all this moved westward to the camp meeting. But with an increased, or perhaps restored, dignity in expression, there were plenty of features that seemed to identify the new movement with the old-time Calvinism, whether of Edwards and the Great Awakening or of the earliest Puritans. There was everywhere the same torturing self-examination in order that the delusions of Satan might not be mistaken for the revelations of divine grace. The faith in and the study of the literal meaning of the Bible was everywhere revived, and it was in this period between 1800 and 1820 that the modern Sunday school was founded. The Sabbath, from sundown Saturday till sundown Sunday, was again deified, and in Connecticut a new spate of "blue" laws punished in effect all physical movements on that day except walking to and from meeting, getting the cows, walking to and from the graveyard, and attending the sick.

Even before 1800, Freeborn Garretson, the great Methodist revivalist, visiting Cornwall, recorded that he "found that the Lord had begun a blessed work in this town." Centering in Southbury, Moses Osborn led a tremendous revival in all the surrounding territory, his converts, significantly enough, being divided ad lib. between the Congregational, Episcopal and Methodist churches. The War of 1812 having been a small war, disrupting few homes and eventually strengthening rather than weakening the economy, the revivalism that preceded it seems to have picked up immediately in its wake, without an intervening debauch of materialism. In 1815 Joshua Bradley wrote that "In . . . New Marlborough, Goshen, Cornwall and Salisbury, sinners hastened to Christ as clouds, as doves fly to their windows. From the most current information received, I conclude that 700 were born again in these towns, in the course of the revival." (The towns he referred to included, besides the four named, three neighboring ones outside the valley.) At the beginning of the wave of revivals there were seventeen members of the Congregational church in Salisbury, and at its close there were two hundred. In 1806 President Dwight, visiting Great Barrington again, "observed with satisfaction that the people are beginning to exhibit more generous proofs of industrious exertions"; and he "learned with particular pleasure that the Presbyterian"—that is, the Congregational—"congregation had settled a regular and respectable minister, after a vacancy of thirty-four years. A spirit of improvement was visibly increasing." In Bridgewater Parish of New Milford the Reverend Reuben Taylor was minister from 1810 to 1815. He bought an orchard of young apple trees from Mr. Sturdevant of his congregation, the consideration to be a series of sermons on election. Mr. Taylor began payment with a powerful one the next Sunday, and following the service Mr. Sturdevant said, "Mr. Taylor, we will call the tree account square."

Meanwhile, Lyman Beecher, at once a prophet in his own right and "the father of more brains than any man in America," had in 1810 accepted the pastorate of the

Litchfield Congregational church the careful reproduction of whose big meeting house, built in 1762, stands today a little distance from the original site. His daughter Harriet, born in 1812, wrote later her childhood impression of her father's tabernacle: "To my childish eye, our old meeting house seemed an awe-inspiring thing. To me it seemed fashioned very nearly on the model of Noah's Ark and Solomon's Temple. . . . Its double row of windows; its doors, with great wooden quirls over them; its belfry . . .; its steeple and bell; all inspired as much sense of the sublime in me as Strasbourg Cathedral. . . . How magnificent, to my eye, seemed the turnip-like canopy that hung over the minister's head, hooked by a long iron rod to the wall above! And how apprehensively did I consider the question what would become of him if it should fall! How did I wonder at the panels on either side of the pulpit, in each of which was carved and painted a flaming red tulip, with its leaves projected out at right angles, and then at the grape-vine, in bas-relief, on the front, with exactly triangular bunches of grapes alternating at exact intervals with exactly triangular leaves. The area of the house was divided into large square pews, boxed up with a kind of baluster work, which I supposed to be provided for the special accommodation of us youngsters, being the loopholes of retreat through which we gazed on the remarkabilia of the scene. . . . But the glory of our meeting-house was its singers' seat, that empyrean of those who rejoiced in the mysterious art of fa-sol-la-ing. . . . There were usually seated the bloom of our young people, sparkling, blushing and modest girls on one side, with their ribbons and finery, making the place as blooming and lively as a flower-garden, and fiery, confident, forward young men on the other." (Mrs. Stowe seems not to have been impressed by the enormity of the stove which was introduced, as already described, in her fifth year!)

Of the anthology of anecdotes about the great Lyman Beecher, the section dealing with his absent-mindedness is perhaps the most hilarious. It seems that, among other omissions, he was forever forgetting his midweek prayer meet-

ing—which, incidentally, was, besides Sunday school, another
innovation of the period. On the affirmative side he was much
given to fishing on Little Pond, in his boat christened *Yellow
Perch*. On one occasion when he had to be sent for and
apprehended there, he hastened his nag to the meeting house
more vigorously than usual, and entered with more than
usual embarrassment and dignity. As he mounted the pulpit
a small, live fish fell out of one of his tail pockets and
flopped down the steps to the floor.

Dr. Beecher held his big family together in a fabulous
solidarity of love for him. Nevertheless, he had trouble getting his battalion of strong sons to pile the wood which
the parish supplied. At length he resorted to a low stratagem.
He had an annual, spring contest with a New Haven minister
as to who could produce the first cucumbers in his cold
frame. This was the sort of thing in which the family would
present an unbreakably united front to the enemy. Dr.
Beecher instructed those parishoners who drew in his wood
to dump it on top of the cold frames where the cucumbers
were to grow. Then, at cucumber planting time, he would
discover the location of the wood, to his dismay. Instantly
the whole family—including the girls, who were forbidden to
do it—flew at the wood and had it piled in a few hours.

In spite of the reactionary appearance of the Great Revival of 1800 and the years following, it represented in
actuality a new departure in religion so radical that by orthodox standards it might be called a departure from religion
altogether. In the new point of view there were two tendencies at work, both of which must have caused Jonathan
Edwards and Joseph Bellamy to blush in heaven. First, there
was the libertarianism that has been mentioned, the political
individualism of the Revolutionary period translated into the
right of every little group to run off and found no matter
how bizarre a new sect. One step beyond was the complete
anarchy wherein every little man could say, "Yes, I am a
religious man at heart, though I never go to church." The
emphasis was really on the freedom of every little man and
not on the will or plan of God. The ancient idealism re-

mained, but in each heart it went a private way which not even Edwards with his "heart religion" would have recognized.

Related to this human individualism, and perhaps even more significant of new directions, was the practical, earthy humanitarianism that now appeared in the cloak of religion. In spite of being called "the great gun of Calvinism," Lyman Beecher was actually one of the prophets, a "pioneer in a more genial theology," for which he later suffered a church trial on the part of a reactionary group of ministers in Ohio. Against the losing fight for total depravity and predestination on the part of Dwight, Hopkins, Jonathan Edwards, Jr., and West—all fighting in the tradition of Edwards and Bellamy and more or less connected with the valley—the original minds of the age were working on a scheme of salvation, a cosmic drama, run by a kindly God who wanted to forgive and to save. The sincere, unequivocal desire for eternal life, or simply the honest effort to live a good life on earth, would be sufficient to win forgiveness and salvation from a loving God. In Stockbridge, little Dr. West saw some of his leading parishioners come under the spell of the dangerous radical William Ellery Channing and his Unitarian doctrine. And chief among them was the great Theodore Sedgwick, now a judge of the state Supreme Court, Stockbridge's first citizen and the pride of Dr. West's respectable congregation. Undoubtedly the last to do so in the valley, the little minister discarded his knee breeches. His grip on life was gone, and not even his good leg had meaning any more.

Part of the humanizing of religion during this period was the birth and rapid growth of home missions, men taking into their hands the business of regeneration which originally was God's prerogative. Almost every town in the valley had its "Moral Society" or its "Missionary Society," organized between 1795 and 1800, and they did good work in introducing thousands to a religion they could understand and which comforted them. The dark continents of New York and Pennsylvania seem to have been selected for the special attentions of the early "foreign" missionaries.

Connecticut's Home Missionary Society—1798—was the first state home missionary society in the country. Three years later was organized the American Home Missionary Society which, between 1801 and 1850 increased church membership tenfold while the population was increasing fivefold.

Most significant of all was the appearance at this time, in the name of religion, of movements for social improvement. Samuel Hopkins and Lyman Beecher were not only temperance preachers but temperance organizers. Beecher would surely have been an abolitionist if there had been an abolition society at this time, for he presently got himself into trouble preaching against slavery in Ohio too close to the Ohio River. He and Hopkins were pioneers in a humanistic religion which the future would endorse. Beecher had two famous children whose names were Henry and Harriet. Just over the divide in the Naugatuck Valley, the new era was coming of age in a pair of promising youngsters. In 1820 Bronson Alcott was twenty-one and John Brown was twenty.

The new philanthropic approach to religion had in it not the revival but the death warrant of old-time Calvinism. This was the dawn of a wholly new age, an age of rationalism, or "realism," and applied Christianity. God still existed as the spirit of Good and it was man's duty to conform with the Spirit. But the earth was no longer the Lord's. It was man's, and it was up to man, not to prostrate himself in his depravity but to make the best of what he saw around him and to be the keeper of his millions of brothers. It was absurd and hypocritical to call yourself a Christian while you knew that a drunkard was beating his wife or an owner his slave. Best tend to such realities first, and let your State of Grace take care of itself. For a long time yet, philanthropists would continue to attack social problems in the name of religion. The change would not be complete until they attacked them simply in the name of society, the physical well-being of mankind here and now. Beecher and Hopkins—and for that matter John Brown—would still have been horrified by the thought that man lived by bread alone, that all you needed to perfect him was to fill his belly and minimize his bodily discomforts. But in attacking the human realities, observable to the senses and the earthly reason, they were moving in that materialistic direction. The scientific and industrial age was just around the corner.

Miscellanea and Portents

$\mathbb{A}$T THE END of the Revolutionary period, in 1820, the population of the valley had increased from the 47,-836 it had been in 1774 to 73,570. The increase was accounted for to a great extent in the villages, notably those of Derby, Danbury, Litchfield and Pittsfield. But the rural towns also had increased, reaching their highest level of population, which they held till after the Civil War. In the Lower Valley the new towns of Bethlehem, Brookfield, Oxford, Roxbury, Shelton, Sherman, Southbury, Warren and Washington had been carved out of the older ones; and in the Upper Valley, Lee, Mt. Washington and West Stockbridge—besides Dalton, Hinsdale and Washington, granted out of state lands. It was still a countryside of farms, averaging a hundred acres, checkerboarded in walls over the now generally grassy slopes of the wide hills. Almost all of the low-lying land had now been cleared and cultivated, while on the hilltops the older farms were being increasingly abandoned and the forest was returning.

In the farm closes, some of the houses were now painted red, and a few white, but the majority were still the old unpainted, weathered gray. In the centers of the townships and other crossroads tending to become villages, trees were increasingly permitted to grow, concealing under groves or parks all of the buildings except the church spires which now pointed toward Heaven in the glory of white paint. Chief among the new public buildings were Litchfield's impressively columned second courthouse, built in 1798, and that of Lenox built in 1816 which, with its delicate, floating

232

belfry, remains one of New England's most beautiful structures of the "classical," or Greek revival, period.

Between the villages still ran the town roads, most of which were still forbidding to any traffic but riders and ox-carts. But, crossing the valley, most of the old colony roads had now been leased to private companies which maintained them as hard-surfaced turnpikes supported by tolls. On these, coaches and horse-drawn wagons rolled freely, encouraging intellectual and commercial contacts with the outside world, both of which opportunities were being seized by the local Yankees. Stagecoaches ran on regular schedules to Hartford, New Haven, New York, Springfield and Albany. The first long-span covered bridge in Connecticut was built at Cornwall Bridge in 1806, and others followed immediately at West Cornwall, Kent and Gaylordsville. In spite of agitations for good north-and-south transportation, by either road or canal, along the river, this communication remained unestablished, and the farmers of the Upper Valley still had to haul their produce over the western mountains to tidewater on the Hudson.

Along the lines of improved transportation the valley maintained consistent contact with the rest of the nation. Litchfield in 1784 established the first newspaper, the *Monitor*. Pittsfield followed with the *American Sentinel* in '87 and the *Berkshire Chronicle* in '88; Stockbridge in the same year with the *Western Star;* Danbury in '90 with the *Farmers' Journal*. Litchfield, Pittsfield and Stockbridge were also the first to get United States post offices to replace the informal private ones that had been run before, the three centers being honored by the federal government in the same year of 1792. The philanthropic trend in religion was related to improved communication and the increased enlightenment that went along with it. Danbury had established the first public library in the valley in 1771, but it was destroyed in the British burning of 1777 and was replaced in 1793 by a better one. Meanwhile Stockbridge started a library in 1783, while Loring Andrews, who was about to be both postmaster there and editor of the *Western Star,* ran a good bookstore. Pittsfield got the next library in the valley in 1796, and after that they began to sprout everywhere.

The educational history of the period is mixed. In both Massachusetts and Connecticut the old public school system declined. Connecticut gave the proceeds of the sale of the Western Reserve to the towns for use in the schools, but the result was a glad desistance on the part of many of the towns from the local appropriations which were still necessary to keep the schools up to standard. At the same time the first private schools of consequence began to appear. In 1787 the Berkshire County Medical Association was formed, the purpose being to provide better instruction for apprentices. The heyday of America's first law school in Litchfield was under its founder Tapping Reeve who taught between 1784 and 1820. The two most distinguished of its thousand graduates in the period were John C. Calhoun and Horace Mann, besides three Supreme Court justices, seventeen United States senators, ten governors of states, and seven foreign ministers.

As a twin star in the Litchfield sky, Miss Sally Pierce opened her famous Female Academy in 1792, and its excellent building was completed in '98. Miss Pierce herself taught until 1832. By that time it had become the most celebrated school for females in the country. The students were required to attend church every Sabbath "except some unavoidable circumstance prevent, which you will dare to present as a sufficient apology at the day of judgment." There was a severe rivalry between the Academy girls and the local girls for the attentions of the students at the Law School. Both Academy and Law School gave large balls annually at Phelps Tavern on the Green, the Academy girls under sixteen not being permitted to attend. Judge Reeve was the first man in America to advocate equal education and full legal equality for women, wherefore he gave Miss Pierce every assistance with her school.

In 1795 Mrs. Mary Northrup left to the town of Brookfield—cut out of southern New Milford and incorporated in 1788—a fund of £147 4s. 6d. for educational purposes. To this day the interest of the fund is known as "Molly Money," and is divided among the school districts each year.

A favorite resort of Tapping Reeve's Law School boys was the house of the wealthy Captain Joseph Ruggles of Brookfield. Besides harboring several eligible young ladies, the house was architecturally unique. One whole end of the living room was of uncovered masonry, with an enormous, semi-circular hearth bowed out into the room and many mirrors above the long mantel. At least one of the Ruggles girls, Lucia, escaped the legal clutches of Litchfield, for she married a Dr. Holman and, with her brother, they became medical missionaries in the Sandwich Islands. Completing the circuit of the world on their return, Mrs. Holman brought back from Hawaii a still exciting cape of a thousand feathers, each feather from a different bird.

Another romance neighborly to the Ruggleses was that of Phebe Marietta Noble whose father Sylvanus owned a lot of ancestral land in south New Milford on the Brookfield line. In the late teens of the nineteenth century Miss Phebe became engaged to David Adams Foster, a great blood of Brookfield, and they were married in 1820. Meanwhile Sylvanus built the beautiful house that still stands on Route 7 just above Brookfield Junction, and gave it to his little daughter. Since then it has figured in local annals as the "Dower House." Edna Ferber built around it the story of *American Beauty*, which is fictional but for its celebration of the beauty of the mansion.

Something of the farming methods of the period is recorded in the diary of Ezra Stiles, whose father died in 1760, leaving him divers tracts of land, including about four hundred acres in Cornwall. Dr. Stiles quotes a verse of his father's about Cornwall:

> Nature out of her boundless store
> Threw rocks together, and did no more.

In 1762 the young man, then established in Newport, began to make annual pilgrimages on horseback to view his various lands in his native Connecticut. In 1774, after a week's journey, including a day's delay in Hartford to hear the local reaction to Gage's arrival in Boston, he at last reached Litchfield:

May 31   at Litchfield. For washing a shirt, 1/. Oats 4d. Rode to Mr. Gold's [that is, to Cornwall].

June 1   Yesterday visited my lands and found about 30 acres under improvement. Can cut 6 loads hay at least. Some sowed with wheat, some with flax. Orchard 65 apples trees, out of 100 set out in 1764 and 1765, a fire having broke in . . . To Mr. Gold for trouble and drawing leases, 6/, children 3/9. . . . After breakfast set out on return. Dined at Mr. Heaton's in Goshen. Lodged at Cousin Bissell's in Torringford.

October 4, 1778   [the year he became President of Yale] Viewed my farm in Cornwall, . . . Orchard 60 trees aet 15. Cut 12 T hay this summer; may cut 20. . . .

In 1784 Dr. Stiles, "set out with my wife for the election at Hartford, where he "dined with the clergy (Trees in bloom)," listened to sundry "accusations and aspersions and injurious reflections" on Yale contained in certain memorials to be presented to the Assembly, proceeded to Norfolk "thru the Greenwoods," where he counted 400 rings in one freshly cut pine, and so proceeded toward Canaan ("Cherry trees in blossom in Norfolk").

May 19   Sixteen thousand pounds of Maple Sugar made at Norfolk in—1774. This year 1784 about one third more. Sell at 6d per pound, or 50/ per cwt., made by 180 families. . . . Sugar works in Goshen have lasted about 40 years and are still good. . . .

May 20   Viewing the College Farms in Norfolk and Canaan on which the Tenants had this winter past 11 sugar works and maple orchards, 150 to 250 and 300 trees each. One of seven acres I counted about 300 maple trees or perhaps 100 and 150 years old yielding 2 to 4 lbs. sugar each.

May 24 Litchfield. Examined Benj. Hanks' air clock. It will go 8 days without winding up; a ventilator moves with every breeze. 2 hrs. ordin'y breeze will wind up the whole 8 days.

May 31 Lodged at Mr. Farrand's in Canaan—where we saw a large quantity of marble, a continued rock or mountain of marble, perhaps two miles in length. [Still worked profitably for lime.] . . . Rode to Rev. Mr. Lee's of Salisbury, dined and went to view college farm there, and found it in good cultivation. . . . Rode to Cornwall, viewed my own farm there and lodged at Rev. Mr. Gold's.

1788 Rent from Cornwall farm £8/10

1789

July 23 To Cornwall. Beginning my harvest there. Visited my farms. Lodged at Mr. Mallery's, my Tenant, who has sowed me a nursery of mulberry this spring, about 4 or 5,000 seeds.

1794

February 26 Mr. Hart from Cornwall came here and brought me butter and cheese as part of the rent of my farm there. I let it to him for another year.

1795

January This day I received £12 rent of my Cornwall farm.

An expense account from a later period gives some idea of current values. In 1819 one William Jones of Newtown became a town charge and was cared for by Philo N. Platt until his death in December of that year, on which occasion Mr. Jones submitted the following, itemized bill to the selectmen of the town:

Town of Newtown to Philo N. Platt, Dr. To going to Redding after a physician, four miles, .33. Paid Philo Gilbert 20¢ for the use of his horses for the same, .25¢. Going to Redding after bark tea for him, .16. Going same, .35. Going after watchers, going after medicine, going to Umpawaug after shirts for him, seven miles; paid Philo Gilbert 28¢ for his horse for the same, .50. A pint of rum for medicines for him and going to Redding, two and a half for the same, .26. By going to Taunton to notify the selectment of his sickness, 4 miles, paid Eli Platt 16¢ for his horse to ride for the same, 25. Going to Redding after bark tea for him, .46. Going to Taunton to notify selectmen of his death, paid 16¢ for use of horse for the same, .25.

Funeral charges:

To one quart of rum for attendants at his burial and going after same .33. To one white handkerchief, .33. Paid one dollar to Mrs. Olmstead for cleaning his bed, washing shirts & other clothes for him, 1.00. A winding sheet, 2.25. Preparation for burial, .25. For my trouble in watching and continued attendance from the first day of his sickness to his death, $15.00.

The physician's bill was: "Six visits, advice; attendance and medicines, $5.80."

Besides there was "Philo Gilbert's bill for watching one night and assisting at the burial, .75"; and, "Ichabod Gilbert's bill for making coffin and assisting at the burial, $3.00"; and a bill of $1.50 due some unnamed person for "digging grave." Upon these total claims of $32.50, the selectmen acted on March 15, 1820:

Thirty dollars allowed on the above bill by us.
Abijah Merritt,
Clement Fairchild
Selectmen

The events of the year 1800 were appropriate to the turning of a century. In Congress the great Federalist Theodore Sedgwick of Stockbridge suffered as speaker of the House the ignominy of announcing the election as president of the great Democrat Thomas Jefferson. Shortly thereafter Jefferson, the philosopher of the little man, bought a quarter of a continent from France, and the eyes of America turned westward more hungrily than ever. Steamboats began to paddle up and down bays and tidal rivers. There was wild talk of steam railroads that would carry freight faster than a gallop. America began to think in titanic terms.

Besides the shift of the center of Yankee ideation during the Revolutionary period from the Power of God to the Rights of Man, there was beginning at the end of the age a shift in the common application of Yankee shrewdness from simple swapping to speculation and industry, from land to manufacturing. A forerunner of the purely mercantile aspect of Big Business was Peter Pond of Milford, born in 1740, who, after a spectacular career as a soldier, traveler and trader in remote parts, was one of the organizers, in 1783, of the Northwest Fur Company, the equal in resources and power at that time of the East India Company.

More closely associated with the valley was its richest citizen during the Revolutionary period, Jabez Bacon of Woodbury, who, like Pond, had what a later age would call "vision." Bacon never troubled himself about pennies or other details, but, entering the store of a rival, would give a slow glance around and thereupon make a generous bid for the entire stock from floor to ceiling. The stock in his own general store in Woodbury became so large that he undersold all the surrounding merchants, many of them coming from New Haven and Hartford to buy at his retail prices, after which they would be able to sell at current prices and make a good profit. By his grandiose methods Bacon made and lost, not dollars but fortunes. His biggest deal was in New York in the late 1780's, when he was almost sixty and at a low financial ebb. He sent a shipload of fine pork to Manhattan, but on arriving found that the merchants were expecting that day two shiploads from Maine which they hoped to get at a lower figure. Bacon rented a horse and galloped up alongside the East River till he was in the open country opposite Blackwell's Island. There he hired a farmer to row him, and waited. The two freighters hove in sight through Hell Gate and squared away down the East River on the light breeze. Bacon's farmer rowed him out and, quite unannounced, he boarded the first of the vessels with his one-man piratical intentions. In the next ten minutes he bought the complete cargoes of both vessels, which required the pledge of his then entire fortune. He cleared $40,000 on the deal, which set him again on the upward trend, so that he was able to die in 1806 at one of his high points, $450,000.

It was Bacon, incidentally, who in 1760 bought the in-
dentured Irish boy Mathew Lyon who later in Vermont and
Kentucky became one of the finest democrats of the Revolutionary and post-Revolutionary periods. When there were
only a few more years of Lyon's bond to run, Bacon sold
him to Hugh Hanna of Litchfield for a yoke of oxen, giving
rise to Lyon's later, favorite oath, "By the bulls that bought
me."

If the Yankees whose libertarian instincts took the form
of gambling had confined their efforts to the distribution
of local agricultural produce, they would have had little evil
effect on the valley and the nation. In Lenox, shire town of
Berkshire, the farmers assembled on market days and took
their positions in the street, but no one must begin bargain-
ing until after the courthouse bell rang like the starting gun
of a race. The Berkshire Agricultural Society was formed
in 1807, and the first fair was held in Pittsfield in 1811,
when the feature of the parade was sixty yoke of oxen drawing a plow. These activities, and even the more spectacular
ones of Jabez Bacon, represented no shift from the agrarian
basis of life on which the idealisms of almost two centuries
had their economic foundation. But at the same time there
were other tendencies afoot which, coupled with the Yankee
big-scale gambling talent exhibited by Pond and Bacon, had
in them the potential victory of the Devil over most of
America and some of the valley.

In 1780 Zadoc Benedict, who lived on properly named
Beaver Brook north of the village of Danbury, began, in a
little outbuilding which he painted red, making beaver hats
from the fur of the trapped animals. Presently others began
to sell Mr. Benedict the pelts of beaver, muskrat, rabbit and
all small, fur-bearing animals which abounded in the woods
and streams of the town. Benedict got a journeyman to
help him and two apprentices. Other local men of enterprise
learned the hat trade and set up rival "factories." At the
beginning it was a healthy business, based in an honest pride
in craftsmanship. If you wanted a hat you went and had it
made to your order. But it wasn't long before the notions

and talents of Pond and Bacon began to appear. By 1800 Danbury, a village of about 2,500, was producing 20,000 hats a year and easily led the nation in the industry. The chief market was New York, but in 1816 there were two stores in Charleston, South Carolina, that sold nothing but Danbury hats.

In 1802 Derby lost a fight that was already generations old. Where the ferry had plied between Stratford and Milford since 1648, conveying across the river Washington, Lafayette and everybody else who traveled, there was built in 1802 a drawbridge, appropriately christened the George Washington Bridge. Shortly, ice carried it away, and Derby gave thanks to God. In 1813 a better bridge was constructed, with a bigger draw, and survived fifty-five years. At about the same time Derby moved slightly in the new manufacturing direction with the erection of David Humphreys's woolen mill in later Seymour and of a tool mill. In 1807, Abijah Smith, a famous peddler, returned from Pennsylvania with samples of "black stone" which generated more and longer heat than charcoal. The Tontine Hotel in New Haven ordered some and burned out all its grates. The Collins brothers of Collinsville found it invaluable in forging their steel tools.

Pittsfield, having a large cantonment of soldiers, a depot for prisoners, and a commissary station during the War of 1812, was one of the few spots in New England that profited directly from that conflict. Its little local mills, where the farmers brought their grain, lumber, flax and wool, and its small forge, where iron was hammered out for local uses, were overshadowed by factories many of which captured and kept outside markets. By 1820 Pittsfield, with a population about equal to Danbury's 2,500, was manufacturing for export about 2,000 muskets a year, both wrought and cut nails, marble monuments, Rumford fireplaces, linseed oil, carding and other textile machines, rope, canvas, potash, leather, packed beef and pork, and it had its own bank and insurance company. All this directed the major preoccupation of an increasing number of people away from ideas

and into channels of gambling at best, and at worst of un-
spiced greed.

In spite of these new threats of the Devil, the bulk of
the Yankees in the valley in 1820 retained at the center their
essential Puritan quality, the quality of life organized around
some kind of idea. Only in most of the people this idea
was no longer an image of an inscrutable God with an irresistible and slightly sinister will. More typically now, it had to do
with human rights in political and earthy terms; or with a
kindly God of many sects, even a God of individuals whose
religion was private and secret; or the idea might have nothing to do with God, liberty or even morals, might have to
do with panaceas, gadgets and formulas, might be crackpot
in a fashion that would have invited the witch-conscious,
public eye of a century and a half earlier. Anybody had a
right to be a "character," and it was probably about this
time that Yankee communities began to produce and to tolerate them.

And likewise by this time, if not earlier, we can assume
that Yankee character is complete with its idealism, its can-
tankerousness, its shrewdness and, softening and uniting the
others, its humor. The Yankee knows now that the new
Jerusalem is not going to descend, that his own private idea
will fail at last, that not even wars of liberty eliminate poverty and privilege, that in the long run not the wealth of
Croesus will bring him contentment. Yet, knowing these
things, he knows also that he must live as if his idea were
going to triumph, as if liberty were any moment worth
dying for, as if the salvation of his soul depended on prudence
and industry. And thus living always in the clear understanding of life's deepest paradoxes, he knows how to laugh
and to enjoy.

In the conflict between the Lord and the Devil in the
valley, the Lord of ideas still has the upper hand. The majority of the people are still motivated in their choices by something they must believe for their soul's peace. Yet there is
an ominous element in the heterogeneousness of the new
faiths, in the decline of the old Congregational orthodoxy.

When the whole community was aligned behind a single idea, not all the devils in hell could shake it. But now, with every little man holding his own, independent view of things, Satan is given the chance to divide and conquer. The Presbyterians will look on impassively at the destruction of the Sandemanians who have left their fold, and it is hardly to be expected that the Shakers and Episcopalians in the hour of trial will fly to each other's support. There is no common strength in the preoccupation of leading ministers, each with his own pet hopes for men's physical and social comfort rather than with their immortal souls. Even in the common patriotism and the general idea of liberty there is no longer any integrating force. Political notions are as controversial and the cause of schisms as bitter as those of religion. Indeed, it is in the very idea of liberty that a new danger lies, in the economic interpretation of it as the right to get the better of the other fellow by any means, in a concept of society as a battle royal, a concept under which, when it is further developed, man will be likened to the supposedly predatory beasts of the jungle. At the end of the Revolutionary period the Lord of ideas is still on his throne in the center of the stage. But we are uncomfortably aware that the Devil is close by in the wings, that he has yet to come on the stage and issue his major challenge. The scene in the valley was never more peaceful, the prospects of the Yankees in their villages and farms never more promising. The air in the valley is quiet. But it is an ominous quiet, with a denseness in it, as before a hurricane.

PART III

Strange Gods (1820-1870)

Of Stone and Iron

IT IS UNLIKELY that many Yankees foresaw, or would have desired if they had foreseen, the fabulous wealth with which the continent was going to reward their canniness, their industriousness and their daring. All they really foresaw and determined to carry out—those of them who were still in New England—was to improve their circumstances above that of farmers on a generally wasted and partially impoverished soil. To their long-established shrewdness in swapping and selling their domestic produce, science was now adding the possibility of mass production. In the wake of numerous inventions—and even before the high development of steam —anyone who could get water rights on a river could start manufacturing any of scores of articles in a big plant called a factory, and could do it on a scale that permitted sale at prices at once discouraging to old-fashioned home manufacture and ruinous to the little old mills that served only local markets. The spectacular horizons of the industrial age were opening. The Yankee idealism that first had attached to the glory of God, and secondly had identified itself with the idea of liberty, was increasingly dazzled and invited by the Devil's proposal of worldly gain.

In spite of the construction in 1813 of the second, and successful, drawbridge across the mouth of the river between

Stratford and Milford, the chief business of Derby, thirteen miles upstream at the head of tidewater, remained for another quarter of a century that of a port—shipping and fishing. But at the same time, beginning with Humphreys's woolen mill in the first decade of the nineteenth century, a slow shift to manufacturing was going on. An event ominous for the old shipbuilders was the appearance on the river in 1824 of the steamboat *General Lafayette* from New York, comfortably paddling its way up to Derby before a holiday crowd along the banks. By the time the draw of the Stratford-Milford bridge fell in the river in '68 and stayed there four years, blocking traffic, manufacturing already represented the real interest of the town.

In 1830 the first factory for hoop skirts in America was set up and flourished in Derby; five years later the first factory for machine-made pins; in 1836 the first factory for machine-made tacks; in 1837 the first American manufacture of paper from straw. By the last year there were also in Derby Township a sheet-copper and copper-wire factory, an auger factory, one for making carriage axles and springs, another turning out nails, another making flannels and satinets. The power for these was furnished by a canal from the Naugatuck. The Housatonic still flowed undammed between the bluffs of Derby and Shelton. Factories increased at a geometric rate. In 1865 there were thirteen hoop-skirt plants alone, and a number of them were boldly exploring farther into corsets.

Danbury's continuing advance in the leadership of America's hat industry was even more spectacular. By 1835 the supply of beaver and other small fur-bearing animals was getting low, so Danbury decreed the silk hat for the continent. By the close of the Civil War, the interchanges of ownerships, partnerships and firm names made it difficult to state precisely how many Danbury factories were then selling hats to America. Twenty is a conservative figure, and the output was about two million hats a year. By then Danbury was also making paper, oil, nails, combs, and numerous types of tools and small machinery.

With the commitment of Derby at the head of tide-water and Danbury on the tributary Still to what proved to be a permanently industrial basis, we may bid farewell to them as part of the Puritan tradition of the valley. At the mouth of the river, Stratford and Milford held on a little longer. But from now on the domination of life by some kind of idealism is to survive, if it is to survive at all, in the ninety-mile sweep of the valley from Derby up to Pittsfield. As already pointed out, Pittsfield at the end of the Revolutionary period was showing signs of becoming an industrial city. Most of the industries operating in 1820 increased between that time and the Civil War, and a few new factories, especially woolen mills, were added.

But the big and ominous growth in Pittsfield, or rather in the Pittsfield region from Dalton above it down through Stockbridge below, was in papermaking. On the other hand, the manufacture of paper is special in that relatively few employees are required for relatively large production. In this fact there was, and for much of the region there remains, the hope that the industry will not spawn around it a series of cities devoted to the making of profits and slums.

Though there were isolated paper mills in New England before Wiswall, Crane and Willard started theirs in Dalton in 1801, the Pittsfield region was the first large area in America to go into papermaking, and it has retained its importance in the industry through the nineteenth century and down to date. Though Dalton had the first mill, Lee took up the business more comprehensively, and by 1840 this one town was producing a fifth of the paper used in the country. One of the smart manufacturers there perpetrated supposedly Leghorn straw hats of paper, and made hundreds of thousands of sales before the fraud was discovered. Another of the big mills at Lee eventually swung into the production of 100,-000 paper collars a day. The New York *Herald* was printed on Lee paper, and it is said that Horace Greeley's friendship for one of the Lee manufacturers got him the credit to buy the paper to start the *Tribune*. Mr. Greeley's other connection with the valley was in marrying a wife from the then distinguished and now ghostly heights of Dudleytown in Cornwall.

During the Civil War a Lee papermaker was caught making banknote paper with a water mark "C.S.A." He was able to convince a federal court that the firm which ordered the paper had supplied the molds that made the watermark, and that he had no notion what the paper was intended for. At the end of the war there were twenty-eight paper mills in Berkshire County strung along the river between Dalton and Great Barrington, seventeen of them in Lee. Yet, because of the small force required in a single paper mill, the two or three each in Lenox, Stockbridge and Great Barrington had but slight tendency to urbanize those communities, except in so far as they were mild eyesores on the scenic glory of the valley; and even Pittsfield remained in aspect a sprawling country village, without the urban congestion and filth of Danbury and Derby.

In that rapid dawn of the industrial age between the twenties and the seventies, every town in the valley that had water power to turn a factory wheel was threatened with the new light. In 1834 Newtown Center, a village of fifty families, had—besides the usual old local grist-, saw- and cider mills, and tanneries—a cotton mill, a hat factory, a comb factory, a woolen mill and a brassworks. In '39 in Sandy Hook an impoverished crank named Charles Goodyear, fascinated by India rubber, with which he had been experimenting for years, by mistake dropped some, mixed with sulphur, on the hot stove, and so discovered the process of vulcanizing. Southbury, across the river, had in 1835 a paper, a tool, a hat, a satinet, a shears and a tinware factory. Woodbury in '54 had three shoe, one tin, one silver spoon, one spectacle, two carriage, one button, one powder flask, one felt, two cassimere, one shears, one thimble, one shawl, one carpet tack "leathering," and one suspender buckle factory. Most of these plants were, of course, small in output and crudely housed. But the point about them was that they were manufacturing by machine methods for sale to foreign markets. Life was no longer a local affair in which you worked hard for the basic comforts. Life was a scramble in which the aim was to get rich.

Every town up the river had its little factories. In Cornwall there were two prosperous shears works. In Sharon there were, among others, the Macedonia Wagon Shop and the remarkable factory of Hotchkiss and Sons which seems to have turned out all kinds of forgings, castings and machinery, including monkey wrenches, saddlery, hardware specialties, special snaps and buckles, special currycombs, special garden tools and trunk hardware, besides plows, cultivator teeth, mowing-machine fingers, shaft couplings, and eventually munitions for the Civil War. At least the first six items named above were invented by the crippled brother, Andrew Hotchkiss, whom the family educated in mechanical engineering for the purpose and who maintained a laboratory in the factory. His first invention was a handcar to get himself around the plant. Another Sharon inventor was Joseph Bostwick, who contrived a mousetrap which became so nationally popular that Sharon was known as Mousetrap Headquarters. Though Bostwick was a big-time operator, his mousetrap was mostly hand work and he let it out instead of maintaining a factory.

In Canaan Township there were always three or four factories at the Great Falls in what is now Falls Village, where paper was manufactured in 1787, and where what is said to have been the first carding machine in Connecticut was built in 1802. The industrial fame of Salisbury and Mt. Riga is not in terms of small factories, but a series of these, including a scythe, bicycle and a trip-hammer shop, made, with their dams and ponds, a flight of steps out of the little stream running down the mountain. In the year 1830 the Harris Scythe Works turned out over 10,000 scythes.

The industries of Great Barrington have been unique in that all of the best water power, just below the Great Bridge, was granted early as a monopoly and has remained so, a single interest erecting and running several mills of different kinds. In 1836 the Berkshire Woolen Company came into ownership, and in '58 and '59 built the big stone factory which remains. Housatonic, on the Stockbridge boundary, has been one of the paper towns from the beginning. A little south of it the Rising Paper Company presents a fine example of Victorian factory architecture, the tradition of the medieval castle, defiant with crenelations and towers.

Because of the gentleness of the current in and around Stockbridge village, it has never had a factory but, before the Civil War, Glendale was making cottons and woolens, wagons and sleighs, boots and shoes, and fine furniture, and Curtisville had factories making woolens, chairs and paper pulp—said to have been the first wood-pulp mill in the region—besides a foundry and a machine shop. In 1853 at Lenox Furnace—now Lenoxdale—there was built the famous Lenox Glass Works which ten years later was said to cover more area under one roof than any other building in the world. Besides its dominant paper business, Lee manufactured woolens, chairs, carriages, carding machines and gunpowder. Lee's magazine claimed the distinction of being the only one in the United States that never blew up; certainly Pittsfield's went off in 1838 with seven hundred resounding pounds.

Parallel with the rise of factories, factory or commercial methods came more and more to replace the old subsistence idea in farming. Goshen in this half century became the leading cheese market in the country. In the valley of the Still River, the richest part of the whole Housatonic Valley, production of tobacco began in the fifties, though it did not reach appreciable proportions till later. Stock raising became a real industry in many towns, including the fattening of beef brought in from the West on the hoof. Even for the farmer the dream of liberty became synonymous with the dream of the dollar sign in the sky.

Exceptional in the general trend were the Shakers, with their colonies at West Pittsfield and Tyringham. Though they went in for cash crops as vigorously as any, their cash was for the common good and was not individually enjoyed. In this early industrial period a formidable list of inventions is claimed for them, mostly of a laborsaving nature, of which

the following twenty-five are the principal ones: the screw
propeller; Babbitt metal; the rotary harrow; the automatic
spring; the sash balance; the governor of an overshot water
wheel; the turbine water wheel; the threshing machine
(1815); the tongue and groove machine; the planing machine; the fertilizing machine; a machine for splint making,
basket working, and box cutting; cut nails; the circular saw;
a washing machine; an improved windmill; a summer covering for a flatiron stove; the stove-cover lifter; the Shaker
wood stove; a machine for twisting whip handles; a pipe
machine; a pea sheller; a batter worker; a "self-acting" cheese
press; the first one-horse wagon in America.

In the Main Valley from Pittsfield to Derby lay the
most serious threat of the commercial age, not so much in the
miscellaneous little factories as in the big industries that characterized the whole region, industries inviting local specializa-
tion and leadership in the nation, as hats already did in
Danbury and paper in Lee. In the things that could be
produced all along the Housatonic more profitably than elsewhere lay the real hope of great cities, great wealth, great
poverty, and the loss of great idealism.

There, to begin with, ran the river in its "marble bed,"
from its central sources down as far as Newtown, most of the
rock outcrops in this long belt being of a statuesque whiteness. By 1800 Philo Tomlinson, a native of Derby, was
quarrying and sawing marble into slabs in Marbledale in
Washington Township—incorporated in 1779 out of a

combination of old Judea Parish of Woodbury and a slice of New Milford, and being the first town in the country to be named for the commander in chief. For power Tomlinson used the East Aspetuck River. While most of the devices he introduced were long known, his combination of them was his own, and he was in effect the inventor of modern marble quarrying and sawing, using a water-driven, toothless gang saw of soft iron fed with water and sand.

By 1830 there were fifteen quarries on the East Aspetuck within a distance of three miles, and there were about twenty mills processing the marble and shipping it all over

the country. About this time the big quarry in East Canaan was opened, using the unique feature of saws toothed with diamonds brazed into the blade. Already the famous quarries adjoining on either side of the Sheffield-Egremont line were in operation, and in 1838 the Sheffield one supplied the big columns for Girard College in Philadelphia. Solid blocks fifty feet long were taken from this quarry, with the help— always precarious—of a little gunpowder. There were smaller quarries in upper Egremont and in Alford. In Great Barrington there was a clouded marble quarry and several quarries of "blue stone," excellent for building and peculiar to that town.

Northward, Stockbridge, West Stockbridge, Lee and

Lenox all had their marble quarries and works. The industry at West Stockbridge had begun in 1802, only two years later than that at Marbledale. In 1803 the firm there signed a contract to furnish the marble front of the New York City Hall, begun in 1803 and finished in 1811, the price being $1.06 a foot for the 33,000 cubic feet that were furnished. Whatever may have been the difficulties elsewhere, the marble delivered in this contract proved to have a resistance to weather exceeded by no other marble in the world. West Stockbridge marble was much in demand, causing the quarry owners to try sawing by steam instead of by water power. The steam method, however, proved too expensive and it was abandoned. Charles B. Boynton, the owner of the principal quarry, invented a machine for planing marble. At one time seven sawmills were busy at West Stockbridge.

Only one quarry in Lee is mentioned, but it did a prodigious business, supplying the marble for the extension of the Capitol in Washington, as well as most of the requirements of Philadelphia, where marble building was fashionable in this period. There were quarries also in Pittsfield and Lanesboro, the latter one getting the contract for the old Capitol in Albany. In 1850 at least twelve towns in the valley were daily, and often nightly, troubled by the slash of the saw, the stroke of the drill, the stamp of the channeling machine, the detonation of light charges of explosive to loosen the huge blocks. And a dozen more towns had equal resources not yet opened. What was available was the whole marble, western wall of New England from Danbury to Canada. There was enough for everybody to take what he wanted and still leave the surface of the wall intact, looking defiantly westward. Here surely, with the help of better north-and-south transportation, was an opportunity that was going to enrich every Yankee in the valley.

But the prospect for marble dukes was unimpressive compared to that for iron princes. The tradition of Salisbury iron—the name commonly given to all the ore of the Housatonic region—is older by ten years than the official settlement of the town that was to become the first center of the industry in America. Among the half dozen or so Dutch and Yankee pioneers who were building cabins in the Salisbury region in the 1730's was one Daniel Bissell of Windsor, Connecticut, who almost got away with a major killing. About a mile east of what was shortly to be settled as the New York boundary, and about three miles west of a lake at whose outlet there was soon to be a village, he got in 1731 a grant from Connecticut of a good-sized hill whose surface was estimated as comprising a hundred acres more or less. Its base was about half a mile long by a quarter of a mile wide. Besides the area of the hill, it is possible to estimate its weight. Beginning in the 1730's, mankind, helped by beasts and machines, turned it inside out, changing it from a hill to an enormous hollow which in turn was leveled up by water into an unattractive lake in the shape of a huge dead starfish, still patent beside the highway between Lakeville and Millerton, New York. In order to effect this transformation mankind removed, or caused to be removed, during a century and three-quarters, more or less, some 1,500,000 tons of material; and if we presume that the hole is as big as the hill was, then the hill weighed some three-quarters of a million tons, rather more than less. The reason that man so ravenously ate up this hill was that the material removed contained the best grade of iron ore yet—to this day—discovered anywhere in the earth except in Sweden.

Mr. Bissell's hill was very early christened Ore Hill, and it remained his until 1734. In that year a group of seven highjackers persuaded the Connecticut Assembly that Bissell's deed was faulty and that they should be given title. In this group there were three names already noteworthy for a tender concern for any commercial possibilities in western New England. There was Philip Livingston of New York, John Ashley of Sheffield, and Dr. Elisha Williams, at this time rector of Yale.

Another pioneer, and one who fought off the wolves longer than Bissell did, was Thomas Lamb, who is said to have been the first white man in Salisbury—at an unknown date—and who at least is there when first heard from and long enough there to speak Indian naturally. Some time before 1734 he, like Bissell, got a grant to a hill where now is a lake between Lakeville and Salisbury village, a lake which latterly filled in a hollow for some two centuries known as the Davis Mine, a hollow of approximately the size of that of Ore Hill. The Davis Mine Lake has less mutilated shores than those of Ore Hill, and a boys' summer camp flourishes beside it, swimming and paddling above the ghosts of millions of dollars.

Lamb started the golden flow in 1734, when he set up and began to operate a forge for wrought iron at Lime Rock, the first in the Salisbury region. He seems to have been a man of larger "vision" than Bissell, for he also bought the water rights of the outlet of the neighboring lake called by his Indian friends Wonunkipang-okhe, now spelled Wonoscopomuc. In 1748 he sold these rights to three men—the names of two of them were Williams and Stoddard—who, though they smell like speculators, at least made the honest gesture of setting up a forge to run with their water power. Shortly they sold the rights and the forge to one Owen whose only place in the story is that of a channel through which the Lakeville site reached its first highly productive ownership.

There now comes into the scene one of the three most picturesque characters in the history of Salisbury iron—the second being the man who for three years was his partner. Samuel Forbes is variously referred to as "Captain" Forbes—though I find no record of any commission or military service —and, more generally, "Esquire" Forbes. As befits a mythological demigod, the facts about him are both vague and embroidered by the affection and wonder of succeeding generations. One thing about him seems certain, his surviving portrait. By its evidence he surely wore the ugliest face that ever covered a human soul. Legend says that he was of a size, a power of muscle and a power of will to match his dreadful face, everything that could be expected of a classic ironmaster, a man who not only could bend the great bar when it was cold but who doubtless would wash his hands in the molten flood as it poured red from the hearth into the "breast," and whose own vocal outpourings were beyond question as red and as hot.

At an unknown time previous to 1762 Samuel and his brother Elisha appeared in Canaan. In 1770 Samuel built a house on the Blackberry River near the modern Samuel Forbes Bridge on the Lower Road to East Canaan. At an unknown time, possibly before he built his house, he became smitten of Lucy, daughter of Amos Peirce, a young lady who is said to have been his equal in physiognomy, physique and strength of will. On one point they seem to have agreed from the start, the desirability of getting married. Since Papa Peirce held a different view, an elopement was arranged, and the two coy titans rode off on the same unhappy horse into New York State where they were duly hitched. On returning to the homestead, Samuel pitched a rope over his new barn. "Now, my sweet," said he, "do you draw down on your end and I will draw on mine, and whichever draws the other over the roof is to rule this roost." They both pulled with no effect. "Now, my sweet," proposed Samuel, "do you come around on this side, and let us draw together." The sweet Lucy complied, and together they pulled the rope over the barn. "Let that be the way this house will be run," quoth Samuel.

One of the refreshing things about Esquire Forbes is that, while remaining always a master workman, he yet had a powerful finger in the capitalization too, met the ruffle-shirted elegants on their own ground and came out with as many plums as the best of them. By 1762 he and his brother had somehow muscled in among the seven other proprietors of Ore Hill, and in that year they sold five-eighths of their eighth share to a certain Colonel John Hazeltine from Uxbridge, Massachusetts, and a young giant from downriver in Cornwall called Ethan Allen. In the same year the Forbes brothers, Colonel Hazeltine and the Allen brothers—Ethan got his brother Heman into the partnership—bought from Owen the water rights and forge at the outlet of Wonoscopomuc Lake. There, on a site now covered by the Holley

Manufacturing Company, they forthwith built, not the first blast furnace in New England by a half dozen or more, but the first one in the valley, the first real furnace, as distinguished from a forge, built for the smelting of Salisbury ore, the initial furnace of a great industry and one which shortly was to make a major contribution to the independence of the United States.

It was a large furnace for the time, its typical egg-shaped body about twenty-four feet high by ten at the widest diameter, the whole enclosed in a twenty-four-foot cube of solid masonary, taking the bigger than usual quantities of three tons of ore, 250 bushels of characoal and half a ton of limestone, or "flux," at one "charge." The product of such a charge was about two tons of iron. The forced draft was supplied by huge leather bellows powered by the water wheel at the outlet of the lake. As the iron melted it flowed down on the hearth, along with the floating slag, and out into the breast, or pond, where, when enough had accumulated, a clay plug at the bottom of the dam was knocked out and the molten iron flowed down through clay channels to the waiting molds. Like all early furnaces, this one stood on the approximate level of the stream that ran the bellows, yet near enough to the higher bank for a plank bridge to be laid across to the furnace top where its mouth was fed from the continuous procession of charcoal carts and horses carrying ore in big saddlebags. Quick death was perpetually offered both at the top and at the bottom of the furnace, while life at both volcanic ends was continually precarious with explosions of inner gases belching out jets of fire. Deep inside the charge there were occasional blocks, or "bridges," due to uneven combustion, to be broken down by any of the several life-risking methods, the price of failure being the "freezing" and ruin of the furnace. Over all of this the iron-master presided, a man who must be an artist dealing not only with chemical and physical elements, whose produce depended on perfect combination, but with elements which at the same time were measured in tons and vast degrees of heat and whose mishandling might involve the horrid death

of dozens of men. Forbes, Hazeltine and Allen employed
fifty-nine men at their peak. Later furnaces employed up to
two hundred.

For two years the new furnace in what henceforth was
called for many years Furnace Village poured out it pots,
kettles and other common utensils, Ethan Allen the while
living in a house near the present Lakeville station which,
like the rest of his houses, has disappeared without trace. By
'65 he had stayed long enough in one place, and he and
Hazeltine sold out to a new pair of brothers, Charles and
George Caldwell of Hartford. Following the closing of the
deal, the principals, or some of them, seem to have had a
friendly party as was appropriate. Allen, who was never
celebrated for restraint, had several times before appeared
on the Salisbury court calendars. Following this particular
celebration he was dully summoned "For that the said Ethan
Allen did, in a tumultuous and offensive manner, with threatening words and angry looks, strip himself even to his naked
body, and with force and arms, without law or right, did
assail and actually strike the person of George Caldwell of
Salisbury, aforesaid, in the presence and to the disturbance of
His Majesty's good subjects." This was the same Ethan Allen
who, a few years later, when New York had put a price on
him dead or alive as leader of the Green Mountain Boys, rode
into Albany alone, entered the tavern frequented by the
politicans, ordered a bowl of punch, drank it all, set it down,
faced the room, put his fists on his hips and said, "Now then,
my name is Allen. Who wants that reward?" History is anti-
climactic in that it does not appear that Giant Allen and his
partner Giant Forbes the ironmaster ever suffered any misunderstanding.

Despite claims to the contrary, it seems certain that the
Lakeville furnace was the only one in blast in the Housatonic
Valley before the Revolution. In 1768 the Caldwells sold it
to Richard Smith of Boston and Salisbury, and in the ensuing
difficulties Mr. Smith found it necessary to abandon his property and hasten to England. Connecticut's war governor,
Trumbull, had the property inspected, took it over for use

by the state a few months before it was a state, put it under a competent personnel and commanded them to set to work turning out ordnance. Esquire Forbes, who had served through the Caldwell period, resumed as ironmaster. Dr. Joshua Porter of Salisbury, an assemblyman and a colonel of militia, was appointed "chief provider and overseer of the works"—later he was called into military service as a physician, and in a crisis he led a regiment at Saratoga. There was also a special cannon founder and three cannon molders.

The making of cannon was a special art. They were cast solid in molds buried muzzle-end-up in sand, to which channels from the furnace carried the molten metal. When a piece had cooled, the "sprue"—that is, the iron left in the channel from the furnace—was filed off and the gun was hoisted breech up in a boring machine that let the muzzle down over the boring drill which was turned by a long arm drawn round and round by a horse. It was unusual to get the bore perfectly true, wherefore it was one of the duties of an artilleryman to know by how much—frequently as much as a quarter of an inch—"lieth the Bore to the right or left, and in shooting the piece, must be ordered accordingly."

The only accurate account of the output of the Salisbury forge during the Revolution is that of Colonel Porter for the first seven months of blast, ending on December 31, 1776. During this seven months there were produced: 117 tons of 9-pounders, 12-pounders and 18-pounders, making about eighty-five of these heavy cannon; 92 tons of 3-, 4- and 6-pounders with swivels, making about 97 of these light pieces; 38 tons of shot and ball; 15 cwt. of grapeshot; 3 cwt. of hand grenades; 3 cwt. of post; about 95 tons of pig iron and miscellaneous castings; some seven tons of rejected material. This was for the first seven months, through '76. As the furnace remained in blast all through the war, and was increasingly under pressure both from the army and from the navy of privateers, it is a fair guess that it turned out close to a thousand each of heavy and light cannon, besides ammunition and miscellanies.

Throughout the Revolution Esquire Forbes, while doing

a competent job as ironmaster in Salisbury, was running a forge of his own in Canaan, sending the ore over from Ore Hill on horses' backs and specializing in anchors—one-half to two-and-a-half ton jobs—which he shipped off to the coast, each with its own ox team of two to six yoke. Not feeling his time sufficiently occupied, he dreamed of starting a nail factory, the nails to be made out of slit rods instead of being hammered out of bar iron in the tedious, old-fashioned way. The difficulty was that there was a secret about slitting the iron rods and it was closely held by the one or two slitting mills in the country. Just how Esquire Forbes overcame this difficulty supplies the material for two, slightly conflicting stories. The popular version finds the answer in the now happily fused loves of Samuel and his Lucy. According to this account, there were two factories which held the coveted slitting secret, one in Boston, one somewhere in Maryland. The now devoted Lucy went to Boston and by some ruse not stated got into the holy region where the mystery was practiced, observed and brought home the secret. The more pedestrian version says that Forbes hired one Isaac Benton, a mechanic and millwright of Salisbury, to do the dirty work. In this version the sole slitting factory was in New Jersey, and Benton visited it and hung around some time, posing as a mendicant and passing in and out of the mill freely to beg. Either version of the tale is credible, if it is understood that these were the primitive days of factories, when machinery of all kinds was, so far as possible, operated outdoors, the building around it being made of crude boards, limited to a roof and, where necessary to fend the weather from a machine, a screen of siding. It was common practice for any passer-by to lounge in, put his foot upon a nail keg, gape at the wonderful machinery, and pass the time of day for as long as he was o' mind to. Anyway Esquire Forbes made his really great fortune out of nails, and this was the way it began.

After the war Richard Smith reported from London, saluted the new flag, and got back his Lakeville furnace and his share in Ore Hill. However, in a year or two he returned to London for good. After going through several hands the furnace, water rights and a big share in Ore Hill came, in 1799, into the hands of Luther Holley, not himself a big operator, but the father of America's greatest iron dynasty. In 1810 title in the furnace and appurtenant interests passed to Holley and Coffing, the original Holley in this partnership being John Milton Holley, son of Luther. Soon after the formation of the partnership he built the beautiful, delicately proportioned house, now on the hill opposite Lakeville's line of wooden business blocks, that was copied at the 1932-1933 Chicago World's Fair as "The Connecticut House."

A Salisbury legend has it that Alexander Hamilton came to the town at an unspecified date to study surveying with Samuel Moore, who published America's first textbook on the subject. Since this legend is without support, it cannot be stated with conviction that Holley and Hamilton were acquainted. At least the former was a great admirer of the latter, for when in 1804 he had a son born immediately after the great Federalist had been dispatched by Burr— Burr the grandson of Berkshire and the student and brother-in-law of Litchfield—Holley named the boy after the fallen statesman. Alexander Hamilton Holley became the heir apparent of the royal line. His mother was Jane Lyman of Goshen.

In the meantime, between 1777 and 1781, one Captain Ball had built a dam across the outlet of a pond on a bleak summit a thousand feet above Salisbury Center and reached by a two-and-a-half mile climb up a wild and picturesque ravine. A little way below the dam he built a forge and a millrace to serve it. Probably he built better than he knew. The location was five and a half miles and a thousand vertical feet from Ore Hill, and almost as far from the Davis and other mines now opened in Salisbury. But the water power was excellent, the supply of fuel in the hardwood forest seemed limitless, and, most important, the finished iron could be delivered downhill all the way to water transport on the Hudson. Sometime in the nineties a partnership of Kelsey and

King bought out Ball, improved the dam, and in 1806 started to build a furnace.

Already the Holley and Coffing interests were considerable in the iron picture, either Luther Holley or the partnership having got hold of the Lakeville furnace with all its rights, a large interest in Ore Hill, all the original rights of Lamb at Lime Rock and the Davis Mine, besides big interests elsewhere in Connecticut and in the Western Reserve. In 1808 the partnership bought the water rights, dam, forge and half-finished furnace on the mountain from Kelsey and King, and by 1810 had the furnace in operation. Either at the mountain or the Lakeville Furnace, or at both, they cast the anchors and anchor chains for the frigates *Constitution* and *Constellation*, the former of which was presently to be commanded by Isaac Hull of Derby. Its anchor was surely cast on the mountain, and the wheels of the cart that carried its three tons to the Hudson behind a six-yoke ox team had to be chained against skidding down the steep and rocky way.

Meanwhile Holley and Coffing had not been able to hire enough local labor to run their interests, for the Yankees, though glad to burn charcoal and sell it to them, had libertarian prejudices against working for wages. So they imported a few hundred Swiss and Lithuanian colliers who between them gave a name to the mountain and to the gay village that presently grew up around the furnace there. Because of its romantic location and history, Mt. Riga became the heart of the epic of Salisbury iron. By a dramatic coincidence, there occurred in the same year that Kelsey and King started to build the famous furnace an obscure and unnoticed event. Far down the river in Roxbury one Pettibone took out the first American patent for making steel.

For a triumphant age after 1810, Mt. Riga furnace glowed, rumbled and flared, its huge bellows groaning night and day, while scores of so-called charcoal pits—they were really piles, sometimes forty feet high—smoked on the surrounding mountains and up the backbone of the Taconics into Massachusetts. The village on the mountain boomed beyond the one below at the Center and the one on the lake where the other Holley and Coffing furnace was just as busy. As befitted a boom town, the population was fluid, but a notion of the numbers permanently there is gained from the fact that the normal annual payroll on the mountain in these years was close to $150,000. In 1821 there were 71 pupils in the village school, which stood on the highest and bleakest hill on the summit, at 1,800 feet above sea level the highest school in Connecticut. At one end of the long dam by the lake in the middle of the sprawling village was a general store so large that it had four regular clerks, was properly a department store, and kept in stock the finest imported silks in Connecticut. At the other end of the dam was the yet standing mansion of Joseph Pettee, the ironmaster, in whose ballroom there were frequent gay parties with a diplomatic flavor, there usually being a few foreign officers in the village letting contracts for Salisbury iron.

During the heyday in the teens and twenties, the Salisbury furnaces supplied most of the musket barrels for the Springfield and Harpers Ferry arsenals, and generally a large share of the ordnance for the army and navy. They also sent muskets to the Greeks in their revolt against Turkey, and cast the anchors and keels for two frigates presented to the Greeks in New York.

In spite of Mr. Pettee being engaged in an enterprise of the Devil, and in spite of Mistress Pettee being the leader in an extravagant little society, they both seem to have been mystics of the old Calvinist, or Puritan, sort. They had been married in 1806, the crucial year when the Riga furnace was started. According to their joint monument in the Mt. Riga cemetery—today the most living thing on the mountain— "Soon after the marriage of the deceased they both as they hoped; and within a short time of each other; became the subjects of divine grace, and since that period strove to live in the faith of the gospel, trusting wholly in the atonement of Christ as a ground of acceptance with their Maker. Rejoicing in this they died." This was in 1845, and the shadow of death that had fallen on Mr. Pettee was already approaching the furnace he had run.

Encouraged by the success in Salisbury, the whole valley enjoyed a mining craze in the first half of the nineteenth century, a craze that was quite justified because, like marble and related forms of lime, ore approximating that of Salisbury was to be found in almost anybody's back yard. There were a half dozen back-yard mines in Salisbury and one or more in most of the towns. Of mines intelligently and profitably worked, there were at least six in Salisbury, one in Sharon, two in Kent, one in North Canaan, three in West Stockbridge, two in Lenox, six in Richmond, and two in Lanesboro. In New York State, within the Housatonic watershed, there were mines at Millerton, Amenia and South Dover; while numerous mines of Salisbury ore operated in near-by Hillsdale, Copake, Ancram, Beekman and Pawling, towns that drain into either the Hudson or the Harlem River.

Furnaces likewise grew like great stone mushrooms: five in Salisbury, including the one at Lime Rock; two in Sharon; three in Kent, including the one at Bull's Bridge; one at New Preston; two in Cornwall; three in Canaan, including the one at Falls Village; three in North Canaan; one or more each in Great Barrington, Stockbridge, West Stockbridge, Lenox, Richmond and Lanesboro; six furnaces in New York in the Housatonic watershed, and five in other contiguous watersheds.

The famous Roxbury mine is in a class by itself, for its iron is of a quality quite different from that of the Salisbury type, and besides it contains or has been supposed to contain at various times most of the galaxy of precious metals and stones. High up on Mine Hill, which rises precipitously 550 feet above the Shepaug River, it was first opened in 1724. Beginning in 1760, it was worked by a company under the supervision of a German goldsmith named Feuchter who did his work in secret and kept his job by exhibiting flashes of silver to his employers from time to time. After his fraud was discovered, and while he was making his departure, one of his chests fell open, revealing some heavy bars of silver. It is supposed that the German arranged this accident in order to save his reputation as a metallurgist at the cost of appearing to be a thief.

Thereafter the quest for silver continued through the hands of several successive companies, the delusion being due to bright, silverlike flakes scattered through the iron ore. Early in the nineteenth century the last of these companies abandoned its long-term lease. The mine was not worked again till 1837, when it was discovered that the real treasure in the hill was iron. Two excellent furnaces were built by the owner and, after a few fatal explosions and the construction of two auxiliary furnaces to cook out the dangerous gases before smelting, the works settled down to steady production. A very high grade of ore was produced, subsequently used to make steel surgical instruments by the Bridgeport Silver Steel Company.

It is plain that Litchfield from an early day ardently desired to be in on the mining boom, as several unexplained holes in the town testify. The first investment to be lost of record was $10,000 on the part of P. T. Barnum, the showman of Bethel. Subsequently four companies with handsome prospectuses, one of which compared its concession to "Aladdin and his Wonderful Lamp," were formed with total allowed capitalizations of $1,400,000. Nothing was ever found but some beautiful quartz, a little copper ore, some nickel and quite a number of pure and small garnets.

But with some forty furnaces in successful blast in the sixty miles between Lanesboro and Kent, the industry was in general a success from the early nineteenth century to the Civil War, and it was plain that the valley, where tiny mills used to serve the local needs, had come into a new age. As if to make it clear that Iron was now King, the Iron Bank started business in Falls Village in 1845. And in 1854 Alexander H. Holley, head of the third generation in the royal dynasty of Salisbury, was elected lieutenant governor of Connecticut, succeeding to the governorship three years later. It was whispered irreverently that he got the nomination because there was a blizzard the day of the convention and he was the only candidate who showed up. Like all the Holleys, he was a man of striking features, implying at once great sensitiveness and great power. On the shore of Lake Wonoscopomuc, half a mile from his father's beautiful house, he built the Victorian mansion "Hollywood" which still stands under the big pines with its octagonal tower. Other Holleys built other mansions along the highway. The glory of iron was now complete. But something yet must be added in the

valley before it would be delivered without reservation to the Devil.

From the middle of the eighteenth century, when a cartway from Canaan to Derby was projected, and from the end of the eighteenth century, when an effort was made to clear the obstructions in the Housatonic, the industry of the valley was handicapped by the trouble and expense of getting its products out to tidewater. In 1808 Berkshire County agitated for a canal from Boston to Albany, but the Massachusetts Assembly voted it down. Then, in April, 1822, a bill that looked promising got past the Connecticut Assembly and resulted in the issuance that June of a memorable pamphlet, *Proposals for the Stock of the Ousatonic Canal Company:*

Books for subscriptions to the Stock of the Ousatonic Canal Company, to an amount not exceeding $500,000, will be opened in the following times and places, viz:—At Ensign's Tavern, at Canaan Falls, on the first Day of July next, at 10 o'clock forenoon, and on the 2d till 12 o'clock at noon: At Mills' Tavern in Kent, on the 2d of July, from 10 A.M. to 9 P.M.: at Booth's Tavern in New Milford, on the 3d of July, from 10 A.M. to 9 P.M.: At Warner's Tavern in Southbury, on the 3d of July, from 10 A.M. to 9 P.M.: At Keeney's Tavern, at Derby Landing, on the 4th of July, from 10 A.M. to 9 P.M.

These proposals were accompanied by recommendations of five commissioners appointed by the Assembly to oversee the business, and their report on the desirability of good north-and-south transportation in the valley is more candid in its language, and lists more clearly the actual resources of the region than any of the comparable prospectuses that followed. The proposals stated that Massachusetts would continue the canal north from Canaan at least as far as Stockbridge Center; and the Massachusetts Assembly did in fact charter a company to do this work, on condition that the Connecticut end of the project be completed. Altogether, it was a proposal to tap with cheap transportation the part of New England richest in natural resources most of which were still inaccessible. Never in the history of industry was there a sounder proposition.

And nothing came of it. There is faint evidence of continuing interest for three years. After that there is silence. No meeting of stockholders was ever held, nor a spadeful of earth turned. It is the first major instance of the mysterious failure of the Yankees of the valley to bestir themselves in their own financial interest. For, unlike quarries, mines, furnaces and factories, this proposal needed investment and support on the part of the general public. And the general public didn't care. It was content to stay at home on its subsistence farms and read its Bible, its *Federalist*, its Paine, and generally to tend to similar matters of importance. The charter of the canal expired under its ten-year limitation. So did similar charters for less valid canals from Sharon down the Harlem Valley in New York, and from New Milford to Danbury and down the Saugatuck Valley.

From the beginning of railroad building, Theodore Sedgwick, Jr., at Stockbridge, agitated for a line from Boston to his home town. In 1826 a petition for the road went to the Assembly, and there were mass meetings and demonstrations in the Berkshire towns and in at least Canaan in Connecticut. But nothing happened until '31, when New York State had chartered a railroad to run the thirty-one miles from the port of Hudson on the Hudson to the village of State Line. Then Massachusetts acted, chartering the same railroad to continue the three miles from State Line to West Stockbridge village. Work was begun in 1835 on this, the Hudson & Berkshire Railroad, and on a September day three years later the little steam engine *Greyhound* with its tiny boiler and lofty stack, dragging three flimsy stagecoaches on flanged wheels, snorted out of Hudson for its trial run of thirty-five miles on oaken rails. A half mile short of West Stockbridge it tooted to its brakemen, and those responsible functionaries bore down on the levers. With sundry yanks and jolts of disagreement between the coaches as to the proper rate of deceleration, the top speed of twenty-five miles an hour was checked, diminished, and brought down to a controlled crawl. To the cheers of a holiday crowd, the first train in the Housatonic Valley eased hissing into West Stockbridge and crashed to a stop without mishap.

But a few days thereafter the troubles of railroading began. This same *Greyhound* collided with a cow and was derailed. At the investigation the cause given was excessive speed, eighteen miles an hour. By that time Jason Clapp of Pittsfield had established a line of five luxurious horse coaches to West Stockbridge, and the passengers, changing from the mature, old-time vehicles swaying easily in their straps, to the infantile railroad cars, jolting, crashing and squealing, had reason to lean back on the conservative side and to express their regret of the arrival of these wild and newfangled days.

But the spirit of modernism was now at large and would not be confined. Already the Berkshire Railroad had been chartered and its line, extending that of the Hudson & Berkshire, was under construction from West Stockbridge down through Great Barrington to Ashley's Mills—now Ashley Falls. The reason for this was that in '36, a year after work was started on the Hudson & Berkshire line, the most pretentious railroad yet attempted in America had been chartered by Connecticut, and it would get traffic from New York up as far as Canaan which adjoined Ashley's Mills across the state line. By means of this intermediate road from Ashley's to West Stockbridge, the first railroad connection between New York and Albany would be effected, with the help of a little water trip at each end.

The Housatonic Railroad was chartered in 1836 to build a line for the sixty river miles—the line approximately followed the river—from Canaan down to Brookfield and thence, in the option of the incorporators, either to the Sound at Bridgeport or through Danbury and Ridgefield to connect with a proposed line from New York City. Previous to the application for charter a committee from the valley towns had hired engineers to survey the route, and their report, while more pretentious than that of the canal commissioners, is still reasonable in its recital of the great commercial possibilities of the region, once proper communication is established with the outside world. Here is a passage from the report dealing with the prospects at Bull's Bridge in southern Kent:

> The fall above-mentioned is capable of doing almost any amount of business; the whole fall . . . being 80 feet in the distance of half a mile, and as the banks upon both sides of the river are of a uniform character, the water may be taken along them at a moderate expense and used as often as may be required.
>
> There is a sufficient quantity of water flowing in this stream, at all seasons of the year, to impel almost any amount of machinery; a considerable portion of which is at the present *unoccupied*, and must doubtless remain so for some time, unless a different mode of transportation than the present is afforded; and which would be brought into immediate use were a railroad to be constructed in this region, and the place ere long become another Lowell.

Having got their charter, the promoters issued a flamboyant prospectus—though sticking close to the probabilities in comparison with modern publicity—in which it was pointed out once more that with the outlet of the railroad, Canaan Falls—that is, Falls Village, Bull's Falls, New Milford Falls and several points on the Still River would undoubtedly do the business of a Paterson or a Lowell, these being the two towns already far gone in the glories of factory production.

For two good reasons, the directors of the road made the bad mistake of electing the route to Bridgeport, instead of building for the direct connection with New York. One good reason was that the city of Bridgeport made the whole venture possible by subscribing $150,000 as a bid for the line. The other good reason was that, since a line to connect New York and Albany by way of the Harlem Valley was already projected, there was no assurance that if the Housatonic road was built to the New York border it might not be left there without connection.

In spite of the panic of '37, work was begun in that year. The following year the first *Annual Report*, while dignified, was yet a little shrill in its celebration of the profits the road was to enjoy. More financing was obviously required. Incidentally, it is interesting that in this report in 1838 it is mentioned that the railroad would carry mineral coal to the northern mines, thus showing that up in Litchfield and Berkshire Counties the supply of charcoal—that is, of forests—for smelting was already low. In this same year the railroad had its engineers report on the feasibility of connecting Bridgeport with New York. It is plain that all is not well. The original plan is impractical, the original investment inadequate, or both.

In 1840 an appeal was addressed by a committee of Bridgeport stockholders to the Common Council of New York, making the remarkable request that that body advise its citizens to subscribe a fresh $150,000 needed to finish the Housatonic Railroad, in spite of the fact that the all-New York line up the Harlem Valley was already under construction. The argument was that the Housatonic line was farther advanced than the Harlem one, which was true; that the Western Railroad of Massachusetts—the western third of the future Boston & Albany—was pushing its construction out of Springfield toward Albany, and that unless the Housatonic—via the short lines already operating in Berkshire County—reached Albany before the Western, Boston would steal a lot of western trade from New York. Somewhat halfheartedly the Common Council recommended the venture to New York "capitalists," not on the argument of beating the Western to Albany, but on the sounder ground that the Housatonic Railroad would benefit New York by making formidable contributions of mineral and agricultural products to its markets, and that, for the same reason, it was a good investment.

This was in July, 1840, and in the three years since construction northward from Bridgeport had begun, appreciable progress had been made. The first point in the valley to be reached was Newtown, and after the wooden tracks were laid in December, 1839, there were days of nervous tension in the knowledge that at any moment the first work train would come by. Concentration in school was lower than usual, for all were watching out the windows. At a shout from one of the big boys everybody piled out in the cold without permission and lined up on the stone wall as the monster clanked past, panting smoke and hissing steam. There was great to-do among the chickens and pigs of the village. An unbroken colt in a barnyard sailed over an eightboard fence, and throughout his long life was known as Gabriel. This was the second great event of that year in Newtown, though Charles Goodyear's earlier discovery of the method of vulcanization had passed without local notice.

A few weeks later the railroad was completed to New Milford, and on St. Valentine's Day, 1840, the first bona fide passenger train, an excursion train from Bridgeport, went through to that village. At that time there was a cliff dropping sheer from the New Milford green at the head of what has since been filled and called Bank Street, a cliff perhaps fifteen feet high and two hundred feet from the tracks. On the day the excursion train was expected, virtually the whole township gathered in the village and waited through the cold day until almost dark for the great sight. One of the leading citizens took it on himself to advise all and sundry that they should go no nearer the tracks than the cliff at the edge of the green, but that they might safely stand there "to watch the thing explode." When at last the whistle was heard all the church bells began to ring, and as the train screeched to a stop the old Revolutionary cannon south of the green spoke its welcome.

· Although work was pressed in the heavy snow of that winter, it was not until twenty-two months later, in December, '42, that the first train pulled into Canaan, and not until the following September that service reached Great Barrington. A few months thereafter the Housatonic leased the half-finished Berkshire Railroad, and in April, '44, the line was completed to West Stockbridge and the promised New York-to-Albany service was established. Unhappily, Massachusetts' Western Railroad had got through to Pittsfield and Albany some two and a half years earlier. The Housatonic line, however, was comfortably ahead of the Harlem line, which was not completed through to junction with Massachusetts' Western until '52.

Here is the timetable for that first year of the Housatonic Railroad's hundred-mile run:

Northbound Leave	Passenger	Freight
Bridgeport	12:15 P.M.	6:30 A.M.
Newtown	1:25 P.M.	8:25 A.M.
Hawleyville	1:45 P.M.	9:00 A.M.
New Milford	2:30 P.M.	10:15 A.M.
Kent	3:30 P.M.	11:15 A.M.
West Cornwall	' 4:20 P.M.	12:10 P.M.
North Canaan	5:15 P.M.	1:05 P.M.
Great Barrington	6:00 P.M.	2:15 P.M.
West Stockbridge	6:45 P.M.	3:15 P.M.

Southbound Leave	Passenger	Freight
West Stockbridge	11:30 A.M.	5:00 A.M.
Great Barrington	12:15 P.M.	6:00 A.M.
North Canaan	1:05 P.M.	7:00 A.M.
West Cornwall	1:54 P.M.	8:00 A.M.
Kent	2:35 P.M.	9:00 A.M.
New Milford	3:35 P.M.	10:15 A.M.
Hawleyville	4:30 P.M.	11:15 A.M.
Newtown	4:50 P.M.	11:50 A.M.
Bridgeport	6:00 P.M.	1:50 P.M.

In '47 the Stockbridge & Pittsfield Railroad was chartered, to run from Pittsfield down through Lenox, Lee and Stockbridge to a junction with the Housatonic line in Vandeusenville in northern Great Barrington. The bigger company promoted the Pittsfield extension from the beginning, and immediately upon its completion in '49 leased it for a figure which meant a seven per cent return to its investors. Thus the railroad in the valley was completed, on the route it follows today. From now on the promised returns would begin to pour in.

At about this time a citizen of Woodbury suffered a sad and costly disagreement with the Naugatuck Railroad, which had just opened and passed through Waterbury. Having spent the day in that booming brass town, the unfortunate rustic, being, as reported, "in a fog," mistook the railway for the highway to Woodbury and duly set out along it. Hearing the train approaching he properly pulled over to the right and so suffered the demolition of his horse and buggy, while himself escaping uninjured. He sued the railroad on the ground that he had given the engine half the way.

The operators of the Lime Rock Furnace were among the early manufacturers of iron strips to cap the wooden rails. It was soon country-wide practice, and dreaded "snakeheads"—resulting when an iron strip sprang loose from its spikes and was curled upward by the wheel through the floor of the car—were added to the other perils of lightning-

like transport. From this and other causes derailments were
frequent, but they were seldom serious because the passengers were able to pick up the flimsy coaches and set them
back on the rails. The only signal system was an official staff
which the train with the right of way carried along the
single track and passed to the other train waiting for it on
a siding. Firewood for the locomotives was provided under
contracts by farmers who kept it piled at stated places along
the right of way.

Now, with its industries booming and its railroad rat-
tling, the valley looked to the panoramic eye like a country
finally and completely delivered over to the Devil of commerce. In every town the little factories clanked and rumbled, and carts carried the products to the little railroad stations where the little engines, looking like the "stationary"
engines that later ran threshing machines, passed twice daily
in each direction, dragging the little three-coach passenger
or eight-car freight trains up and down beside the river.
From their lofty stovepipe stacks the locomotives spewed
continuous cinders and flame, keeping the grass and trees
of some parts of the right of way at all times afire.

In Washington, Connecticut, in Canaan, Sheffield, Egremont, West Stockbridge, Lee and Richmond, the marble
quarries kept parts of the towns mantled under white dust,
while the racket of sawing and blasting mingled with that
of the trains to whose sidings the carts creaked with the big
slabs.

To every station except Hawleyville and New Milford,
the little "pigs" and bigger "sows" of iron were likewise
hauled for loading from forty furnaces, of which a dozen
were along the river and a dozen more within a mile of it,
while all manner of wrought iron came from the forges that
were numerous in every town. Though the furnaces were
partially housed, still the great stone stacks gave up to the
sky an occasional burst of glow, and the breasts of molten
metal a sharper glare, while the leather bellows on beam
frames violated the echoes twenty-four hours a day with
animallike growls and groans audible up to five miles. To

serve the furnaces and the forges, virtually every mountain of the Berkshires and the Litchfield Hills smoked with charcoal piles, and through the years the shorn wastes where the forest had been grew up their sides to the summits. As from the original hilltop farms, the uncovered soil ran off the rocks, leaving the granite hills of New England more naked than ever.

At night the prospect was awesome, when the charcoal burnings on the hills were red dots like the stars of industry, when every furnace was a sky-filling glow, and the glare when it poured was the opening of the doors of hell in the darkness, while connecting these big fires, the burning grass and trees along the railroads made a chain of eerie flame. The whole valley was become an inferno, a devil's precinct horrid with groans and explosions and speckled with hectic fires where witches crouched and Macbeths hungry for power could get what prophecies they desired. Man had shown before that he could destroy the forest. Now he was going further and showing that he could replace nature and preempt the landscape with horrid growths of his own seeding.

It was the crude infancy, the stone age of industry. But it was already a powerful infancy, and the prospect of the valley disappearing under continuous cities and trembling to enormous modern railways and factories was yearly more promising. Almost yearly in the thirties, forties and fifties more furnaces were coming into blast. In '48 Ezra Cornell personally supervised the running of a telegraph line up the valley, four years after he had run the first one for Morse from Washington to Baltimore. In the fifties the baby coaches and carts on the rails gave way to cars prophetic of modern ones; the locomotives were enlarged, streamlined and equipped with the enormous funnel stacks, making them look like otherwise handsome men with monstrous noses. Now, also, they ran on all-iron rails; there were no more snakeheads; derailings were rarer, and more serious when they did occur. In the valley, industry and transportation were shaping toward modern form.

Yet beneath the smoky panorama that troubled the

blackbirds and the meadow larks working up the valley in the spring, there were hidden facts that might have given the blackbirds and the meadow larks some reassurance. The plainest of these was in the report of the Housatonic Railroad for 1843, which showed it $370,000 in the red. A year later the road was being run by trustees for the noteholders, and at the same time was giving notice of forthcoming application for permission to build a line from Bridgeport to New York. In '44 the New Haven & Hartford line—in operation since '39—completed its extension from Hartford to Springfield, where it connected with older lines for Worcester and Boston; thus the Housatonic lost its hope of the New York-Boston traffic. In '48 the New Haven & Hartford opened the all-important line to New York, which the Housatonic had wanted. In '52 the Harlem line opened, ending the Housatonic's monopoly of the New York-Albany traffic. For better or for worse, the railroad in the valley was reduced to dependence on the output of the region through which it ran, on the hope—still formidable—of Bull's Bridge becoming a bigger and better Lowell, Falls Village a Paterson, West Stockbridge to be in marble what Rutland was not yet, and—greatest hope of all—Salisbury to sprawl into an as yet undeveloped Pittsburg, and Canaan into a Youngstown. There was still every reason to hope that these lofty consummations would take place. Indeed, Falls Village seemed to be approaching its destiny when the big Ames Iron Works were built and went into operation across the river at Amesville.

On the other hand, the difficulties of the railroad were not the only dark straws in the wind. Some citizens of the valley were openly lacking in reverence for the vast possibilities that the railroad had opened. In 1859 Woodbury refused to let the important Poughkeepsie-to-Waterbury line cross its territory, for no reason except that it didn't see the value of the thing and didn't want to be bothered. In the meantime a curious decay had set in at the oldest roots of the principal industries. During the forties the twenty-odd marble quarries in Marbledale in Washington, Connecti-

cut, were one by one closing down for what specific reason
it is very difficult to discover, till in '50, with the closing of
the Goodsell quarry—one of the biggest—the industry there
ended. While there were fifteen new iron furnaces put into
blast in the forties and fifties, there were ten that went out
of blast and were abandoned in the latter decade. Among the
last were two whose death could not but be ominous.

In '36, John Milton Holley had died, and either then

or soon thereafter his son Alexander H., the future governor, got exclusive proprietorship of the Lakeville furnace,
the granddaddy of the whole industry and the nearest of
all the furnaces to the two leading mines, the Ore Hill and
the Davis. In '43 Mr. Holley tore down the furnace and
built on its bones the Holley Manufacturing Company, the
first cutlery works in America—the factory running today,
though at different work.

Already, up on Mt. Riga, the advantage of a near-by
fuel supply was burned out, and the charcoal was being
drawn from great distances up the mountain at proportionate

expense. One day in '47 the breast was filling with molten iron as thousands of times before, and the man with the sledge hammer was standing by to knock out the clay plug and let the "heat" pour out into the channels for the big sow and the little pigs. Then the red flow from the base of the great stack dribbled and stopped. In its volcanic interior iron and slag in combination had plugged the inlet for the air from the bellows that kept up the heat. What heroic efforts were made to prevent the threatened "freezing" are not in the record. Presently it occurred, the dreaded "salamander" solidified at the bottom of the furnace. The only cure was to tear the furnace apart, remove the cast stopper, and rebuild. For miles around lay the bushy desert where the forest had been. Pettee, the great ironmaster, was dead. In the surrounding village there were thirty or forty families whose livelihood was exclusively the furnace. Messrs. Holley and Coffing decided that the cost of the repairs was not justified. For the first time in seventy years the water of Riga Lake spilled over the big dam to no iron purpose, as it has done for a century since. But the people in the thirty or forty families did not recognize the end. In thinning rags and in tightening cold and hunger they clung to their Riga, their mountain desert, knowing that any day would come the word to rebuild.

Their Brothers' Keepers

BUT WHILE some of the energetic minds in the valley were concerning themselves with improving their own financial condition, other and equally energetic minds were concerning themselves with the general condition of mankind. The Puritan idealism that originally had followed a half-moral, half-aesthetic idea portrayed in the Drama of Redemption, and afterwards had followed a political idea called Freedom, now, in attempting to apply that freedom, began to construct a new idea of health and happiness in the world that in philosophical terms was just as materialistic as the industrialists' dream of stone and iron and gold. Almost everywhere this new form of the old idealism looked, it found something that ought to be improved, and as fast as the mine and railroad and factory builders were destroying men's souls, the educators and philanthropists, along with a sudden bloom of writers, were hastening to reclaim their bodies and their minds. The age of science, of observation and deduction, was in full bloom. Benjamin Silliman, who had been born in Trumbull in 1779 while his father was a prisoner on Long Island and his mother a refugee from burning Fairfield, was the valley's chief contribution to the nation's early list of distinguished scientists. On one point the legions of the Lord and those of the Devil were at last agreed. Life was an actual, physical business, here and now.

In 1791, and again in 1795, the Connecticut clergy had lost their fight for the proceeds of the sale of the Western Reserve land to be given to the churches, and instead it was given to the schools, the "school societies"—virtually districts—into which the towns were divided. In spite of this victory for the schools of Connecticut, elementary education in the state slid off disgracefully until the late 1830's; and the experience in Massachusetts in the same period is parallel. In the want of specific reports from the valley, we may presume that it shared the general degeneration of the two states it formed a part of. During the forty years prior to 1835, both relaxed the requirements on the towns for maintaining schools. By the latter date the older school buildings, usually nicely built of brick, were in ruins, and the new ones were filthy shacks. The teachers were incompetent and underpaid. No consistent course of study existed. In Connecticut six thousand children were out of school.

Abysmal as was this fall, the recovery was correspondingly meteoric. Almost exact contemporaries, the two states produced at the right moment two of the greatest figures in the history of elementary education, Horace Mann and Henry Barnard. Both did a long apprenticeship in regular politics, which was fortunate. In '38 and '39, respectively, each accepted the secretaryship of his own state's new board or commission, for whose creation he had been responsible. This represented the first strong, central control of education in either state. From that time forward each gave his entire devotion, with something close to saintliness, to his task and, after many reversals, each within the next twenty years was successful in his major reforms—standard curriculum, state normal schools and resulting improvement in the quality of teachers, better buildings and equipment, compulsory education between the years of eight and fifteen that was really enforced. Above all, Mann and Barnard reawakened public interest and pride in education, and put New England back on the track of its intellectual tradition.

Except for the fact that Mann was a graduate of Litchfield Law School, neither he nor Barnard had any particular connection with the valley. The Housatonic region's only special contribution to the general reforms was through Seth P. Beers of Litchfield. Between 1844 and 1849, when Barnard was absent setting up the educational system of Rhode Island,

Mr. Beers was superintendent of schools in Connecticut, a new office created at that time and held by Barnard after '49.

Even after the renaissance of public elementary education began in the thirties, public secondary education still lagged, and it was not until after the Civil War that the high schools, the heirs of the old grammar schools, were numerous enough to take care of the promising children— let alone all the children—of the towns. In the meantime, and beginning immediately after the Revolution, the semi-private "academies" took care of secondary education, and they are the first institutions of learning on that intermediate level to have left immortal and deservedly immortal reputations.

The academies, almost without exception, were run by highly educated men—usually ministers—and idealists whose only interest was to give the best possible training, preparatory for the service of either church or state, to every boy or girl whose talents deserved it. They were private in that they were privately endowed and managed, either by the master himself or by a board of trustees. A tiny tuition fee was charged and, though there were plenty of cases where the fee was remitted to the poor and worthy—for the academies were highly competitive in their quest for the most promising students—there is some evidence that this was not considered cricket. The master of Parker's Academy in Woodbury would never remit a penny because it would be unfair to his rival academies. On the other hand, when he particularly wanted a penniless boy or girl, he would exert the utmost efforts to induce others to finance the student.

Although these schools were legally private, they were not run for profit but in the interest of the communities that supported them. It was everywhere traditional that all the brightest children—and only the brightest—should attend them, and the boys at least must be prepared for college. The fees were hardly more than nominal, for the expenses of administration were trifling. Those were still the days when a minister or teacher, like everyone else, expected to do a little subsistence farming, was not interested in money for its own sake, and asked of his salary only that it take care of a few extras. Lenox Academy, one of the more expensive, cost $7 a term of 14 weeks, and the out-of-town students paid either $1.25 or $1.50 a week for board and room.

If a boy or girl who was recommended by his elementary school teacher, or was otherwise thought desirable, could not raise or borrow the little tuition involved, it was almost certain that the wealthier members of the community would tend to it for him, as either a gift or a loan. Responsible citizens were on the lookout for just such promising boys. The masters of the academies were competitively scouting for them all over the countryside, and indeed in distant parts. But for the margin of error and misfortune that fringes all human endeavor, and excepting the rare cases where a father positively forbade it, it can be said that every deserving child got an academy education. Conversely, the masters, being their own bosses and having high educational standards and small facilities, wasted no time on children simply because they could pay the few dollars tuition fee.

The result was that the academies undoubtedly represented the high point of American secondary education, from both the academic and the social point of view. On the one hand, they were not burdened with sixty to seventy-five per cent of deadwood that neither merited nor desired academic training beyond the three R's. On the other hand, they had the highest standards, and those highest standards were available to all who could qualify. A bright boy who deserved real mental training was not in the position he is in today where, if he cannot afford the high fees of the modern private schools, he must go to the public high schools where the equipment is kept polished and the standards are kept low in order that all the children may have a good time and all the parents vote for the boss of the commissioner of education. In the days of the academies you got the best education there was if you could take it. And if you couldn't take it, you went back to the plow where you belonged. In the one case, poverty would not handicap you and, in the other case, wealth was no help.

This was America's golden age, when the aristocratic tradition remained, but attached no longer to birth and not yet to wealth. It was recognized that the best should rule, and the job of society was to find out who were the best. The academies offered the way to find out, and were therefore at the heart of the machine. It is probably no great exaggeration to say that every man and woman of distinction in the valley, or in New England, who came to maturity between 1820 and the Civil War was graduated from one of the academies. The more famous schools collected boarding students from all over the nation. It is interesting to find that the historian of every town that had an academy always speaks of it as *the famous* So-and-so Academy, assuming with something deeper than home-town boosting that this particular one was really the greatest school that ever existed. From a detached viewpoint it is difficult to choose between them, to say that any one of them was better than the others, though naturally they must have varied widely in quality. Some indication of excellence is the list of graduates, but these lists are difficult to come by, and in some cases do not exist.

Because of its several associations with Tapping Reeve's Law School, Miss Sally Pierce's Litchfield Female Academy has already been mentioned. While Miss Pierce herself taught there, from 1792 to 1832, it seems to have had a fair claim to being the most celebrated girls' school in America. Meanwhile other academies were sprouting rapidly. Derby Academy had been founded in 1786. In 1790 the wealthy James Morris established in Litchfield South Farms, against fierce local opposition, his Morris Academy, which was the first coeducational boarding school in America. Of his acquisition of the independent means that made it possible for him to found the school, Morris left a naïve account: "A kind of providence had always found a way of escape for me. . . . In June 1789 God was pleased to remove my dear father by death . . . and a considerable sum of money and cattle were placed in my possession." During the early period of the school, one of the local churches formally charged Morris with breaking the peace because he customarily took his girl pupils home at night. But by 1803 his work had won so much approval that his friends built him the big academy building that functioned as a boarding school until the middle eighties, was then used as a barn for a few years, and in 1892 was torn down. Meanwhile Morris had become the great man of southern Litchfield, and when in '59 the South Farms were cut off and separately incorporated, the new town took his name.

Another early secondary school was Milford Academy, founded in 1797, the neat little cupolaed building which it occupied after about 1810 now standing in boarded-up and half-ruined dignity between the First and the Second Church of Christ at the head of the historic pond in the center of the village. In this school the teacher sat in the center of the room, the younger children in a circle round him, the older ones in the wider circles back toward the walls. It is difficult to see how the little building could have housed enough students to graduate about twenty a year, which it is supposed to have done.

Across the river, Stratford Academy was founded in 1805, its building erected the following year on Watch House Hill, thereafter known as Academy Hill, on the site of the watchhouse in the original palisade, also the site of the third meeting house, which had burned down in 1785. On the same site today the Soldiers' Monument stands, nothing remaining of seventeenth century watchhouse, eighteenth century church or nineteenth century academy.

Chronologically after these academies in the Lower Valley comes the first in the Upper Valley. For the dignified, late colonial style and the size of its building, built in 1803, still prominent on the Main Street of the village and kept in spick-and-span condition, for the distinguished list of its graduates, and for its length of service, Lenox Academy makes a persuasive bid for the distinction of having been the best of its kind and, for all anyone can deny, the best of all the hundreds of secondary schools that have followed it in this region of famous secondary schools. It was given a good start by the state legislature, a township in Maine, the proceeds of which were added to its endowment fund. Its graduating examinations usually admitted to the sophomore class of colleges, and many of its students came from remote parts of the country. Its graduates included Mark Hopkins the educator, David Dudley, Stephen and Henry M. Field of Stockbridge, Yancey of Alabama, Alexander H. Stephens, vice-president of the Confederacy. At times the enrollment exceeded a hundred. It did continuous service from 1803 to 1910, except for the years 1866-1879 when its building was occupied by the high school. Since 1910 it has had no consistent occupancy, being used occasionally for purposes of miscellaneous private education, art exhibitions and other public functions of a quasi-intellectual nature. Fortunately, the village managers appreciate the unique interest of the building and it is not likely to be destroyed. Efforts are being made to find a use for it agreeable to its educational tradition.

Also in Lenox, though later chronologically, was Mrs. Charles Sedgwick's School for Girls which she ran personally from 1828 to 1864. Her husband, one of the Stockbridge Sedgwicks who "never considered himself as bright as his brothers," was clerk of the court in Lenox, the shire town during almost the same period. It is quite possible that his small emoluments may have strengthened his wife's humanitarian impulse to run what she called a "character factory." Among her graduates were Harriet Hosmer, Charlotte Cushman and Jennie Jerome, the mother of Winston Churchill. It is safe to assume that as Miss Pierce's Academy declined Mrs. Sedgwick's School took up and carried high the torch of female education.

In 1805 the newly founded Ellsworth Parish in Sharon was in financial embarrassment and authorized both a lottery for general purposes and a school to be run by the minister, the Reverend Daniel Parker, for his own better enrichment. He performed the remarkable feat of starting an academy from scratch and having two hundred pupils in three years, his charges coming "from Ohio to the seaboard, from Maine to Virginia." During the same three years, 1805-1808, Mr. Parker fell into a violent and quarterless controversy with his colleague, the Reverend David Perry of Sharon proper, one cause being that the Reverend Mr. Perry, being also a man of learning, was likewise desirous of starting an academy but was having a slow time of it. In the same period the energetic Mr. Parker was also attempting to improve his worldly circumstances by certain speculations in which he involved a number of his leading parishioners and so ruined several families. When this came into the open, through the helpful intelligence service of the Reverend Mr. Perry, the Reverend Mr. Parker found it necessary to depart into New York State, and his Academy, which had had such a sky-rocket beginning, came to an even more abrupt end. He proceeded, however, to establish an equally successful and more long-lived school in Greenville, New York. His son, born during the controversy in Sharon, subsequently passed the whole course of Union College in one year and became one of New York State's most distinguished lawyers.

Danbury Academy opened in 1814. Goshen Academy had unsteady beginnings much earlier, and did not get integrated with a well-organized corporation and a building till 1823. The building with its golden spread eagle under the gable survives in perfect condition today. Goshen Academy was unique in its chemical laboratory and policy of instruction in the natural sciences, especially geology and mineralogy. There being three terms, the tuition was either $7, $8 or $9 a term, according to what you took, the full curriculum with Greek and Latin being $9. The contract with the early principals provided that $100 of the income should be devoted to repairs and unkeep, that all assistant teachers should be paid, and the balance should go to the principal, provided it did not exceed $600. Goshen Academy drew widely from Connecticut but very little from outside. I find no record of its attendance, but if the students averaged $24 a year, it will be seen that it must have flourished. Besides, it got several moderate bequests. This academy, seemingly one of the best, survived till the mid-nineties.

In Stockbridge the village elementary school and the academy, separately incorporated in 1828, occupied the same building. In 1842 the name was changed to Williams Academy, in gratitude for a $3,000 bequest by Cyrus Williams. In 1866 a new building was put up and doubly entitled the Williams Academy and the Stockbrige High School. Though the Academy funds were used in the building, the public school promptly crowded out the semiprivate, especially as another good private school—Ferdinand Hoffman's—already existed in the village.

Salisbury's brick Academy building next to the post office was built in '33, Lee's in '37, but in '51 the Lee Academy leased the building to the high school and went out of existence.

Great Barrington had several early "select" schools, the only one of consequence being started by Miss Sarah Kellogg in the 1820's and becoming, probably in the forties, Rose Cottage Seminary, a long-lived girls' boarding school. Besides Miss Sarah, her sisters Miss Mary and Miss Nancy taught there, and eventually their niece Mary Frances Sherwood, Great Barrington's Cinderella, of whom more later. Great Barrington Academy's building was completed in '41, but it flourished only a few years. The building was eventually sold and became a private dwelling. In '54 James Sedgwick, the first and only successful principal of the Academy, started a private school of his own which flourished until 1865.

In 1846 North Woodbury, being long in schism from the rest of the town, built an academy building of which the church was to have the use of the second floor for a chapel. In '51 South Woodbury built the Academy building now used as the town library, and it was always called the Parker Academy, after its first teacher, already referred to as the master who would not remit tuition but would exercise himself to see that somebody paid the tuition of each worthy student. In '52 an old boys' school in New Preston was re-chartered as the Waramaug Academy.

It is sometimes difficult to distinguish between the true academy, which was usually financed by a private group but expressly in the interest of the community, and the private school, where the motive might be financial or, more often in the period being now considered, educational in a broader than local sense. The school that Frederick W. Gunn set up in Washington, Connecticut, in 1837, was rather a private school than an academy, and from the fact that it is flourishing today almost exclusively as a boarding school, it may be taken as the first in the long list of distinguished boys' boarding schools in the valley.

Mr. Gunn was an abolitionist, wherefore he had no sooner got his school going than he was excommunicated from the church, discriminated against and chased out of town. After teaching ten years in Pennsylvania, he returned in '47, when the antiabolitionist sentiment was softening, and revived his school which, with a few brief periods of decline, has flourished since. Because of his early abolitionist stand he got the children of Henry Ward Beecher, of Mrs. Stowe, and of John C. Frémont.

Gunn seems to have been one of the most beloved of all famous schoolmasters. "If you would get into a boy's heart," he said, "you must get the boy's heart into you." An account of some of his disciplinary methods is worth quoting:

> Boys found with their hands in their trouser pockets lost their pie at dinner. Those who made too much noise were ordered to take a horn to the village green and blow a blast at the four corners of the church, to hug a tree for two hours, or to take a three-mile walk in the moonlight. A youth who talked too much might have a chip put in his mouth, to be kept there till meal time. Two boys who had quarreled ,were ordered to sit in each other's lap by turns for an hour or two. A little boy caught ducking a cat, was seized by the seat of the breeches and nape of the neck and plunged in after the cat . . . Boys who were found to have indulged in drink or smoking were given an emetic. . . . Mr.

Gunn's scheme for training boys had for its central objects manhood, character, and physique. With these secured he believed that mental growth would follow. . . . In consequence, though his aim of strong character was opposed to that of modern teaching, his scholastic methods seem to have suggested progressive methods. As to scholarship, the general standard of the school was unquestionably low. There was no marking system and no direct incentives to purely intellectual growth. . . . His theory for teaching the dead languages was to learn the language first and the grammar afterwards. So a boy often found himself in Homer before he could analyze the simplest form of Greek verb, and reading four hundred lines a day of Virgil, without a question on the syntax or prosody. In composition, rhetoric, and oratory, the stand of the school was high, and a knowledge of public events was made almost a compulsory part of the course—Mr. Gunn himself reading the daily paper aloud to the school as soon as the afternoon mail brought it in.

On Sunday afternoon each of the forty—more or less—boys was supposed to confess his sins of the week. On Friday night there was always a party to which girls were invited. Gunn himself played first base on the ball team. I do not find what his tuition was in the early period, nor what was his attitude toward remitting it. But it is plain that he considered himself as primarily an educator of youth and not a representative of the town of Washington; in which important respect his school differed from the academies.

Another institution suggesting the private school rather than the academy was the Alger Institute, founded in Cornwall in 1847 and, after many vicissitudes and changes of name, going strong today as Rumsey Hall. Besides the schools named, every town had two to a dozen private or semiprivate schools between 1820 and 1870, many of them probably more snobbish than educational. From many hundreds of them I have tried, on little evidence but local reputation, to mention those schools, especially the academies, that seemed to do the best job of educating.

Although the valley did not produce either of the great reformers of the public school system in the first half of the nineteenth century, nor any secondary educator who has become immortal except Frederick Gunn, it did produce the two leading names in higher education for the period. F. A. P. Barnard of Sheffield was a distinguished astronomer, president of the American Association for the Advancement of Science, a charter member of the Academy of Sciences, and president of Columbia University. Dr. Mark Hopkins, great-nephew of Samuel Hopkins, the first minister of Great Barrington, was president of Williams from 1836 to 1872.

The Hopkins family had moved to Stockbridge, and Dr. Mark's generation was chiefly three brilliant boys, two ponderous and humorless, one debonair, all without the means of acquiring a formal education. In 1815, when Mark was thirteen, he had an opportunity to go out to Clinton, New York, and work on his uncle's farm in return for his uncle's tutoring him. Harry, the lighthearted youngest, then eleven, gaily agreed to stay at home and tend the farm. His letters to the two-years-older Mark are gems from the typical cultivated home of early nineteenth century New England. "Your absence," he wrote in one of the early ones, "renders it necessary that much of the management of business should fall to the agency of one particularly capable, and although my health has been much impaired, yet I rejoice that my uncommon abilities quite make up the deficiency of health as far as regards business." Mark replied with letters in Latin. Later Harry went to New York to study art and, along with his friends, Harry and Robert Sedgwick, lost everything he had scraped together in a venture for making bricks out of soft coal. Returning to Stockbridge, he refused big brother Mark's offer to put him through college and became an artist and a great letter writer of local gossip. The middle brother Albert settled into a solemn and moderately distinguished career as a teacher of mathematics and natural philosophy at Williams under Mark.

Another prominent educator of the period was Charles Grandison Finney, born in Warren. In 1835 he became professor of philosophy, at Oberlin, and was president of the college from '51 to '66.

A special institution, said to have been the first of its kind in the country, was the Cream Hill Agricultural School, operated by Samuel W. and Theodore S. Gold in Cornwall from 1845 to 1869.

Another memorable institution was the Berkshire Medical College which ran in Pittsfield from 1822 to 1869 and gave 1,138 M.D.'s. It opened in a remodeled stable next to the Town House on the present park and, to the horror of the community, only a few steps from the graveyard behind the handsome Bulfinch second meeting house. In those days there was no legal method of providing medical schools with cadavers for study, wherefore medical students were notorious for their "resurrecting propensities." The normal procedure was to open only part of the coffin and haul the body out with a big hook inserted under the chin. In 1822 Pittsfield was especially touchy on the subject, because the body of one of the town's favorite sons, only eighteen years old, had been snatched two years before the founding of the medical college. It was generally, though not necessarily, the prudent practice of medical students to collect their specimens from villages other than that of their school.

In 1830 two of the Pittsfield students retrieved a pair of bodies in the towns of Montague and Conway in Franklin County, and were identified as the ghouls shortly after their return. In the interim before the machinery of the law began to move, certain leading citizens of Pittsfield proposed to tear the college buildings down; but the arrests were made in time to prevent this action. In that same year—apparently fruitful of boldness—Pittsfield students were pursued home from the scene of another snatching. The body in this case was that of a small and emaciated girl. While the officers of the law and the relatives of the victim in hot pursuit were searching the college, they were conducted by a tall and courteous youth who all the time had the little body under his great camlet cloak.

A later episode had to do with the home graveyard, handy to the college, whence the relatives of one recently interred desired to remove him to some other resting place.

When the grave was opened and found empty, one of the relatives betook himself to the neighboring tavern for consolation so profound that when he returned he fell and lay in the open grave. A student standing by in the crowd suggested helpfully that he be buried there and left to replace the beloved lost one. The wag himself was instantly chosen by acclamation to perform that office, but he escaped on the legs of youth.

In 1850 most of the original college buildings burned down. A year later the institution was rebuilt on the terrace at the end of South Street where the Soldiers' Monument is. But it lived only seventeen years thereafter, when the building was sold to the town of Pittsfield, and served first as the high, and afterwards as a grammar school.

Besides the new and intense interest in man in his practical lot on the earth, the epidemic of strange sects and spiritual experiments which began about 1800 continued into the new period. In 1839 the Mormons succeeded in establishing in West Stockbridge a congregation, which, after causing much local uproar, joined the general move of the Latter-day Saints westward in the next six years. In January, 1843, the whole town of Orange was converted, the weather abating miraculously to that of Indian summer, the ground being warmed so that it did not chill the prostrate penitents, the nights being bright as day, and a comet shining "from the zenith to the horizon" like the eye of God searching out sinners.

In 1850 the famous "Stratford Knockings" occurred in the great Phelps Mansion on Elm Street, at approximately the center of the original stockaded village. The massive structure, which survives today as a rooming house, consisted of a six-chimney, Georgian main body to which had been added divers wings and on the front a two-story portico of enormous Corinthian columns. At the time of the excitement, which began on Sunday morning, March 10, 1850, the occupant of the house was the Reverend Dr. Eliakim Phelps. Returning from church with his young wife and child, the minister was astonished to find his front door hung with crape and in one of the rooms a corpselike form was laid out and shrouded for the grave. Many of the manifestations that followed had a similar element of broad comedy, but most of them were only startling and irrelevantly miraculous. An account by a pious lady of the time gives the general flavor of the doings and of their effect on the community:

> During the early period of the unearthly possession the entire village was convulsed with excitement and lost its character for sobriety; crowds poured hither by every train; editors, reporters, spiritualists, skeptics explored, watched, investigated, interrogated, and gave an unwelcome publicity to the scandalous details. There were rappings—not merely rappings—but thumpings—as if a giant's strength were behind them; there were marvellous noises, with reverberations like thunder up and down the staircase and along the walls; there were apparitions, strange figures in strange places; there were messages from the unseen land of the spirits, not only spelled out in hard knocks & vibrations on the head-boards of beds, on ceilings, doors, and floor, but written out fairly on slips of paper, which floated down from the invisible like the leaves of the Cumaean Sybil.

Other accounts multiply the wonders: The vegetables from the cellar on being pared were found to be written over with indelible characters. Ornaments on mantel sprang from their places to alight unbroken on the floor. Pokers jumped up of their own accord and went crashing through windows. The doings in Stratford's haunted house were reported daily in newspapers throughout the state.

All the investigators agreed that the Reverend Dr. Phelps and his family were obviously distressed by the uproar and innocent of any hoax in the premises. Dr. Phelps sent a long article to the New York *Observer* stating that he had observed "hundreds and hundreds" of the manifestations and was convinced that they were genuine and "the work of wicked spirits in a state of torment seeking mitigation of their torment by redressing the wrongs of which they were guilty in life." Although there seems to be no certain proof of the cause of the rappings, tradition has accepted the view that the "wicked spirits" were found in the pious minister's very young and very playful wife who was a city girl and inordinately bored with Stratford. What is certain is that the racket stopped when Dr. and Mrs. Phelps moved away; also that there were labyrinthine passages inside some of the thick partitions of the mansion.

Expressive of the current humanitarianism that underlay the creation of the modern public school system was the famous Cornwall Mission School. One day in 1810 Edwin Dwight of Stockbridge, grandson of General Joseph Dwight of Great Barrington, having quit Williams because the discipline was too lax and being about to enter Yale, found a peculiar, foreign boy weeping on the college steps because they would not take him. It appeared that under royal Hawaiian auspices a number of youths had been sent to the United States to be educated, that the captain of the ship had stolen the money he was entrusted with for their benefit, that this boy, whose name was Henry Obookiah, had found his way to New Haven, and that others of his party were in Boston. Young Dwight took the youth home to Stockbridge, had him provided for there and taught a little English. During the next seven years he lived successively, as did the other Hawaiian boys, with various ministers, mostly in Litchfield County, getting a little education and earning his keep by farming.

Meanwhile the American Board of Foreign Missions became aware of the presence of the heathen boys and decided to found a school for the purpose of training Indians and Asiatics to be missionaries to their own people. After much and contentious consideration of various locations for the school, it was settled in 1817 on land donated in Cornwall; the old academy building which was its central structure, stood approximately where the chapel in Cornwall village stands today. At the opening there were seven Hawaiians, one Bengalese, one Hindu, one American Indian and two white Americans. The year after the opening, little Henry Obookiah died, "a heavenly smile upon his countenance and glory in his soul," according to his tombstone. Edwin

Dwight wrote a memoir of him which was translated into at least four languages and was a best seller pretty much all over the world.

This fantastic little institution exactly suited the eager and rococo humanitarianism of the times. From the beginning the school received contributions from everywhere, and the story of Obookiah increased them. The federal government became a regular contributor. Among the distinguished white missionaries trained there were Hiram Bingham, and the Ruggles mentioned before as originating in New Milford. In 1822 the school had thirty-four pupils, of whom twenty-nine were heathen, hailing from Sumatra, China, Bengal, Hindustan, Mexico, New Zealand, the Society, Sandwich and Marquesa Islands, the Isles of Greece, Azores; and of American Indian tribes, the Cherokee, Choctaw, Osage, Oneida, Tuscarora, Seneca and St. Regis (Canada). At one time twenty-three languages, including the classical ones, might be heard at the school. Hebrew, Latin, Greek, French, rhetoric, navigation, surveying, astronomy and theology were the normal fare of the advanced students.

The demise of the Mission School in 1827 was due chiefly to the fact that since its foundation several teaching missions had been established both in Polynesia and among the American Indians, and it was found that better results were thus obtained than in expatriating natives and training them as missionaries. This was the real cause, but at the time and afterwards it was popular to attribute the end of the school to two major tragedies which grew out of it. The following is the contemporary account—slightly digested and paraphrased—of a lady who knew all the parties intimately and was related to most of the local ones:

They were never allowed to go beyond a certain limit from the school, never into people's dwellings without an invitation, or for an errand from headquarters. When they embraced Christ as their Saviour, they had a written permit to go two or three miles as the permit stated, and talk with people, and tell them what Christ had done for them. We always laid aside all our work when the scholars came. They talked and prayed from the heart. It would revive us, so solemn and yet so joyful. It was a great wonder to them why every one in the town were not Christians, when they had heard of Jesus all their lives.

Among the students was a Cherokee, John Ridge, son of a Chief, a noble youth, beautiful in appearance, very graceful, a perfect gentleman everywhere, who was confined at Mrs. Northrup's house two years with a hip disease. Mrs. Northrup had so much work and care that she would send her daughter Sarah into John's room to take care of him. One day Dr. Gold . . . said to Mrs. Northrup, "John now has no disease about him and I do not think best to give him any more medicine, but he has some deep trouble and you must find out what it is."

That afternoon Sarah spent away from home, and Mrs. Northrup, taking her stockings to darn for the students, went in to sit with John. She said to him, "John, you have some trouble and you must tell me; you know you have no mother here, only me, and you have always confided in me as you would your mother."

He started up in wild amazement, and said, "I got trouble, No!"

She said, "John, I can not leave you until you tell me all."

"I do not want to tell you," he replied.

She said, "You must tell me."

"Well," he replied, "if you must know, I love your Sarah."

She said, "You must not."

"I know it," he replied, "and that is the trouble."

She said, "Have you ever mentioned it to her?"

"No, we have not said one word to each other; I dare not, but how could I help loving her when she has taken such good care of me these two years?"

As soon as Sarah came home Mrs. Northrup said to her: "Sarah, do you love John Ridge?"

"Yes, I do love John."

Mr. Northrup took Sarah to her grandparents in New Haven; . . . wished them to make parties and introduce her to other gentlemen, and try every way to get her mind off John Ridge. She stayed three months; would take no notice of any gentleman, or any company; no appetite for food, lost flesh and they soon thought she would be victim of consumption. They . . . brought her home.

Well, something must be done; John was dying for Sarah and Sarah was dynig for John. Finally Mrs. Northrup told John to go home and stay two years and if he could come back without his crutches, he might marry Sarah. He did so, came back well. His

father, Major Ridge, came with him; came in the most splendid carriage . . . that ever entered town, had their waiters in great style.
Maj. Ridge's coat was trimmed with gold lace. On the Sabbath he
could not be seen by strangers as "it was the day to worship the
Great Spirit, and if he went to Church they would worship him."
He would see people every day, during the two weeks he remained,
except on the Sabbath.

John and Sarah were married and went to the Cherokee Nation, then located in Georgia, there to live in splendor, but not
as missionaries. John was sent several times to Washington to trans-
act business for his nation. Sarah remained at home taking care of
her servants, for she had thirty living in the back yard. She simply
said to this one, go, and he goeth and to another come, and he
did so. She dressed in silk every day.

After the Town of Cornwall had become quiet over the marriage of Sarah and John, there arose another tumult, and the social
life of the parish, usually so quiet, arose to fever heat over the announcement that "Elias Boudinot (John's cousin) was about to
marry Harriet, daughter of Col. Gould," one of the fairest, most
cultured young ladies of the place, a very pious, amiable girl, the
nearest perfection of any person I ever knew. She was the youngest
of fourteen children; the others all married except two brothers.
One brother was a Congregational minister. Her sisters all married
in high rank; some rich, one a Cong. Minister, one a lawyer, another a Judge, &c. All had married so well that it was a dreadful
stroke to have Harriet marry an Indian. She was the idol of the
family; they tried to persuade her not to marry him, but all in
vain. . . . She would say, "We have vowed, and our vows are
heard in heaven; color is nothing to me; his soul is as white as
mine; he is a Christian, and ever since I embraced religion I have
been praying that God would open a door for me to be a missionary,
and this is the way." She thought she could do more good to be
one of them; they would not be jealous and think she looked down
upon them.

After it was known that she must and would go, the "roughs"
in town burned her and Mrs. Northrup and Sarah in Effigy; they
used a barrel of tar. While they were burning, Harriet's friends
carried her one mile away; the house, in which she was, stood on
a high hill, she looked out the window and said; "Father, forgive
them; they know not what they do." Sure enough, for they afterwards repented of it; could not forgive themselves . . .

Six months after the engagement was publicly known they were married. Excitement ceased and he came into town unmolested; had a splendid wedding at two o'clock p.m. . . . After they went to the Cherokee Nation Col. Gould and his wife went all the way in a one horse carriage to Georgia, to visit them; found them living in a two-story house neatly furnished with everything needed in a family. Mrs. Gould told us after their return "that she never had such a store of provisions" (and Col. Gould was wealthly and a good provider). . . .

Sarah and Harriet lived almost within speaking distance; ran into each other's door any time of day. Boudinot was educated for a Minister, but when he went home, his people wanted he should teach them, so he taught school and edited a newspaper in their dialect; had a good salary (he was a charity scholar in Cornwall). I have read many compositions written by his scholars.

(It will be remembered that the removal of the peaceful and highly civilized Cherokees was one of the blackest passages in all our dark treatment of the Indians.)

Everything passed off very smoothly for several years, until the Indians were removed beyond the valley of the Mississippi; then Boudinot and Ridge lived a mile or so apart. Sarah had three children; Harriet had six children and died when the last child was born. Her husband went to Vermont and married Harriet's cousin. Boudinot lived about two years after their marriage. After his death his wife went home to Vermont, and Harriet's children were sent back to Cornwall, Conn. My mother visited at Mrs. Northrup's after her return and Sarah related to her the following sad story, and my mother told me the same:

Ridge and Boudinot were in sympathy with the arrangement by which the tribe were removed to Indian Territory, but a strong party was opposed to leaving the burial place of the tribe, after the settlement in the Territory, denounced Ridge and Boudinot as traitors and untrue to the traditions of their people, and one night when Ridge and wife were in bed, quiet as usual, two hundred Indians surrounded the house; John looked out the window; said, "They will kill me; it will do no good to say one word; keep still." They dragged him out of bed into the dooryard, stabbed him thirty times; such doleful groans he gave; his wife went to the door and begged them to kill him quick. They told her to go back in the house and be still; they would not hurt her or the children, "but John Ridge we kill him, then we are going over to Boudinot's and kill him"; they did so the same night.[1]

The founding of missions, home and foreign, was only the more obvious expression of the humanitarian surge. Just as widespread was sympathy with the democratic revolutions abroad, or any kind of revolution that could be interpreted as opposing tyranny. All the towns contributed to subscriptions for the new Greek government, part of the upshot of which was to present it with two frigates. Robert Sedgwick took the case of the Greek government against certain New York firms, and Henry Dwight in Washington defended its rights in neutral shipping. Timothy Field—of a new family just settled in Stockbridge—went over and joined the Greek Army. In the fifties the suffering Hungarians were very fashionable. In Stockbridge a fair was given for Kossuth, his portrait in the Academy was hung with laurel, and six young ladies solemnly banded together to learn Hungarian in anticipation of a patriot from that country who was going to be sent to Stockbridge. Through some error, the Hungarian patriot turned out to be a German who spoke only his native tongue. His name was Ferdinand Hoffman and when, in '54, he had overcome the linguistic difficulty, he bought Henry Carter's school—whose building included what remained of Jonathan Edwards's house—and became one of the best schoolmasters Stockbridge ever had.

In this international connection, it is interesting to find Stockbridge in '53 coming out for better guarantees of peace with foreign nations:

To the Honorable Senate and House of Representatives of the United States.

The undersigned citizens of the town of *Stockbridge* in the State of Massachusetts, deploring great and manifold evils of war, and believing it possible to supersede its alleged necessity, as an Arbiter of Justice among Nations, by the timely adoption of wise and feasible substitutes, respectfully petition your Honorable Bodies

[1] Account of Mrs. Ellen M. Gibbs, in *A History of Cornwell*, Connecticut, by Edward C. Starr, B.D.

to take such action as you may deem best for this most amiable end, by securing, in our treaties with other nations, a provision for referring to the decision of Umpires all misunderstandings that cannot be satisfactorily adjusted by amicable negotiations.

[Signed by 41 citizens in three columns]

The forties and fifties were the greatest reform period New England ever had, with formidable attacks on small as well as great abuses. The valley had little share in the rise of feminism, the movement for prison reform, the founding of the S.P.C.A., or the improvement in insane asylums generally—though Lakeville could make the proud boast of having a school for imbeciles.

It was in this period that conscious village planning and landscaping got under way. In the 1780's Oliver Wolcott, Jr., son of Connecticut's governor, depressed by the desolation in Litchfield and impressed by efforts to remedy the same condition in New Haven, planted thirteen sycamore trees, one for each state in the Union. Twelve of them soon died of disease, and the surviving one—naturally the one representing Connecticut—stands today in what was then Meeting House Street and is now the East Park. This experiment having been unsuccessful, Oliver Jr. and his brother Frederick set out about 1790 a good many of the elms now magnificent along South Street, eliciting much local complaint on the grounds that "we no sooner get the woods cleared than you start fetching them back." John C. Calhoun of South Carolina, while a student—1803-1805—at Tapping Reeve's Law School in Litchfield, set out a few elms in front of each of the two houses where he boarded. The Misses Pierce, building in 1803, seem to have been the first to set out trees on North Street, their choice being maples. In 1825 two prominent citizens gave North Street its real start, with a row of elms for about twenty rods on the east side. In 1855 another private individual had Calhoun's habit of planting elms in front of the places where he lived. Since he moved frequently, the result was pretty well to complete the array on both North and South streets and start the village toward its splendor of fifty years later, a splendor which is erroneously accredited to the colonial period. There are only three elms in Litchfield Center that are supposed to be primeval. One is the Whipping Post Elm on the Court House Corner, which is thought to be older than the town and which did serve for the punitive purpose that gave it its name. The second is the Beecher Elm on the former Beecher property. The third—and most doubtful for antiquity—is the Sign-Post Elm at the corner of South Street and the park, which for at least a century and a half served as a signboard for town notices.

Such other towns in the Valley as have trees of more than a century's antiquity owe them, as Litchfield does, to the probably unpopular ideas of a few individuals in the late eighteenth or the early nineteenth century. In Stockbridge the first impulse of the sort seems to have been that of Theodore Sedgwick, Jr., who in 1834 bought Laurel Hill and presented it to the town for a park forever. In 1853 the Laurel Hill Society was formed for the purpose of keeping clean and beautifying the village generally. It was the first village improvement society in the valley and, by local claim which stands unrefuted, the first village improvement society in America. During the rest of the nineteenth century most of the villages in the valley followed suit. Well-kept and parked greens under monumental elms replaced the barren and filthy wastes of a century before. With the help of the now universal fashion of painting houses white—also an early nineteenth century development—and the beginning of modern sanitation, there emerged in fifty years the neat and quaint, "old-time" villages of New England.

To the great temperance movement the valley, especially Litchfield, made a memorable contribution. In 1789, when every town had one or more stills, and the consumption of hard liquor, chiefly rum, was more than a quart a week per man, woman, child and baby, when even farmers who did not drink bought barrels of whisky for their laborers to keep up their vitality, and when "consociations" of ministers were jovial, noisy affairs whereat "the sideboard, with the spillings of water, and sugar, and liquor, looked and smelled like the bar of a very active grog-shop," in this state of things Litchfield, chiefly moved by the degradation of two of its ablest and most alcoholic citizens, formed a local Temperance Association. It didn't accomplish much, for there continued to be frequent brawls in Deacon Bradley's tavern and grocery store wherein salted codfish was the favorite missile. Nor, in this same period, was temperance doing very well in Woodbury, where beloved Deacon Sherman, for advocating it, first suffered the burning of his buggy, then the shearing of his horse's mane and tail. At last the opponents of his master's views went so far as to tar and feather the poor beast.

In 1810 Lyman Beecher was installed as minister in Litchfield, and for sixteen years he took no stronger position than that of temperance. But his observation at church consociations, the reports to him by Deacon Bradley's sister, the wife of the deacon's partner in the tavern, and especially the scruples of one of the local distillers began to persuade him into a stronger position. This stiller was Hezekiah Murray, and he lived in "The Pitch." Observing the effects of liquor on other youngsters, he first forbade his own boys to drink his output. Then he went to Dr. Beecher and asked him flat if he thought he ought to sell to others what he forbade to his own. That was in 1826. Twenty years before, Beecher had first shown his talent as a reformer by leading the campaign against dueling following the Burr-Hamilton meeting. Now he went all out again: ". . . I wrote under such power of feeling as never before or since. Never could have written them [the famous six, successive sermons on total abstinence] under other circumstances. They took hold of the whole congregation. Sabbath after Sabbath the interest grew and became the most absorbing thing ever heard before. . . . All the old farmers that brought in wood to sell, and used to set up their cartwhips at the groggery, talked about it, and said, many of them, that they would never drink again." The sermons were distributed over the country, and largely through their influence the American Temperance Society was organized the same year, 1826. Five years later there were in the country three thousand total abstinence societies, with three hundred thousand members.

Great as was the effect abroad of Dr. Beecher's sermons, the result at home was not all that could be asked. In 1829, after Dr. Beecher had gone west, the third meeting house of his own former church was built. For the first time—so far as appears—in the history of New England, it was boldly proposed to accomplish the raising without a suitable provision of spirits. All that was available around the cellar hole was "a hogshead of small beer." There were plenty of men standing round, but not enough hands came forward even to set the long sills in place. When the strike had continued some time, "Dr. Buel asked William Norton and some other boys to go to his store and bring over a certain box, which the lads found to be very heavy." It contained several cases of liquor. Instantly the great frame rose, and the experts, running along the plates, pegged it together. On the last day, for the raising of the spire, there were "three Shaker tubs of rum punch . . . with little tin cups near by." The temperance movement in the main was far from a failure; but a church raisin' was too important and too traditional an event to be meddled with.

As elsewhere in New England, the great and significant and emotionally charged reform in the valley was abolition. And equally deep in the people was the sacredness of the Union. As early as '35, Catherine Sedgwick, a very dove of gentleness, informed Harriet Martineau with heat that "the Union must be preserved at any cost." The certainty of alienating the South—incidentally losing the southern market!—was the chief cause of the emotional unpopularity of abolition before the issue began to be clear in the fifties. In the early forties Frederick Gunn, having founded the Gunnery School in Washington, Connecticut, was hounded out of town, largely from the pulpit, because he was an abolitionist.

In '38 in Danbury, which had a flourishing hat trade in the South, an abolitionist organizer, the Reverend Nathaniel Colver, was announced as a speaker in the Baptist church on a certain evening. An hour before the lecture a trumpet sounded near the courthouse where a large crowd gradually assembled. As soon as the lecture had started, the mob proceeded to the Baptist church and bombarded it with stones. With the windows crashing round him and his audience slipping out to safety, the prophet finished his lecture, and afterwards was conducted to his lodgings by the military. In spite of the demonstration, an abolitionist society was formed.

A similar fracas in Stratford was more colorful. The occasion was a meeting in a private house of the already formed abolitionist society. In this case the ammunition of the mob was selected rotten eggs, and the attack opened while the faithful were assembling and unprotected. Afterwards the bombs burst mostly against the house and windows with no more than ornamental effect. In this case the assailants were tried and properly fined for assault and breach of the peace. The trial, the most fiery in the history of the town, was held in the Academy Building, because it was the largest available. Afterwards the building became a Negro Baptist church.

Because Lenox was the county seat of Berkshire, temperance and antitemperance, abolition and antiabolition, and every other kind of meetings were forever being held there. The first memorable abolitionist sermon in the valley was preached by William Ellery Channing in the *Church on the Hill* in Lenox in '42. Incidentally it was the last sermon of the great Unitarian. The immediate interest being the remote one of emancipation in the West Indies, Dr. Channing uttered his mind with a precision and a force that Berkshire County never forgot. The abolitionist societies in almost all of the towns, being for immediate and blanket emancipation, never included more than a small minority of the population because, outside of the equally small group of emotional antiabolitionists who were interested in the southern trade, almost everybody quietly understood and sympathized with the economic dilemma of the South.

Like the rest of the young Republican party, the people

of the valley wanted only to exclude slavery from the new territories, otherwise to let it die gradually in the old South by such means as the South itself might support. As the South got more insolent, the people of the valley got more extreme in their views. There are only two underground railroads of record, but as both of these were in Stockbridge it is probable that there were many more. In '52 Harriet Beecher Stowe, identified with the valley only because she was born in Litchfield and spent her first fourteen years there, published *Uncle Tom's Cabin.* In the next five years it captured the North and became one of the immediate causes of the Civil War. By '57 the Reverend George Uhler could preach an unequivocal emancipation sermon in Curtisville (now Interlaken) and meet with no open resentment. When the South chose to secede on the issue of the extension of slavery to the territories, the overwhelming majority of the valley rose as one man.

The tradition of the valley is one of idealism, taking various forms, and has little to do with physical action, let alone organized military action. Yet in contrast to the second- and third-rate Union generals who have been given an undeserved immortality because they commanded an army unsuccessfully for a month or so, it is impossible to avoid mentioning two great soldiers from the valley who are not generally known. The brother of President Barnard of Columbia, General John Gross Barnard of Sheffeld, West Point '33, had a voluminous record of service as an engineer, including command of Washington and its defenses when it was in danger, and culminating as chief engineer of Grant's Army of the Potomac, after which General Barnard declined the office of permanent chief of engineers of the army.

The valley's other Civil War general of first distinction was General John Sedgwick of Cornwall ("Uncle John" to his soldiers), grandson of the Revolutionary general of the same name. Graduating from West Point in '37, he served in the Indian and Mexican wars, being promoted for bravery in the latter. In '55 he was promoted to major in the cavalry, and served in the West chasing Indians until '58 when, upon the burning—this time by lightning—of the second Sedg-wick homestead on the same foundation, he returned to his native Cornwall Hollow, retired from active duty in the army and, in '59, let the contract for the third Sedgwick mansion on the same site. During the rest of his life his only expressed wish was to settle down for good in the Hollow, which he called the most beautiful place in the world. Called back into service for the war, he soon rose to the command of a division as a brigadier general. His first conspicuous service was at Antietam where, by foolhardy heroism when foolhardy heroism was the only method left, he was more responsible than anyone else for staving off defeat. Sent into a large-scale ambush on the collapsed right flank, with his three brigades he stood off, long enough for heavy support to arrive, at least twelve Confederate brigades which out-numbered him three to one, had him almost surrounded and held all the defensible ground, while in their divisional and corps command there were such fearsome names as Jackson, Hood, Hill, Ewell, Early and Jeb Stuart. In the half hour before he was relieved, he lost half of his five thousand men, was himself twice wounded but refused to leave the field. His convalescence from these wounds gave him his only chance to live in the mansion he had had built in Cornwall. Meanwhile he was promoted to major general and put in command of the 6th Corps. In the Chancellorsville campaign he carried Marye's Heights easily, where Burnside the year before had slaughtered two thousand boys and wounded nine-teen thousand to no purpose. When Hooker was foolishly routed on the other end of the long line, Sedgwick was left alone on the west side of the river, faced with four or five times his numbers under Lee. By a celebrated withdrawal he got his whole corps back across the wide river with slight casualties. From Frederick, Maryland, to reach the field at Gettysburg, he made the record forced foot march of his-tory, due entirely to his men's affection for him, and arrived in time to supply a new backlog at the end of the Second Day when the original backlog was gone. At the famous council of war after the Third Day, he was the most vehement in advising an immediate pursuit of Lee. Here there are two significant "ifs," either one of which going in the opposite sense would have ended the war then and there in July, '63. One is "if Sedgwick's advice had been taken by Meade." The other "if" came a little earlier. Sedgwick twice declined the command of the Army of the Potomac, the second time being just before Gettysburg, at which time he is supposed to have said to Lincoln, "Mr. President, I am a soldier, not a politician." If he had accepted the command, the war likewise would have ended after Gettysburg. Through

the rest of '63 "Uncle John" did a few spectacular things with his corps, but they were not at critical moments. The following year, while inspecting some artillery emplacements opposite the Bloody Angle at Spotsylvania, he was warned that there were Rebel sharpshooters in the woods across the ravine. With the absurd nonchalance of high generals, he paid no attention to the warning. The bullet left no mark but one drop of blood on his cheek where it entered. He fell dead instantly.

Among the Civil War generals, on both sides, if you would exceed Sedgwick in the combination of personal popularity, leadership, courage, moral integrity, decisiveness and tactical ability which makes a great general you have to reach up to Jackson, Sherman, Grant and Lee. He belonged in their company. Sedgwick and Lee always remained close friends. Not long ago there was in existence a correspondence between them, carried on right through the war, in which they recall old comrades who have been lost on either side and reaffirm their personal regard for each other. Though his work was not of the kind characteristic of the valley, he is among those natives of the region who best deserve to be remembered with respect and with love.

The Lord's Prophets

THE EDUCATIONAL and otherwise humanitarian trend
in the valley in the first half of the nineteenth century was
no more than a part of the larger trend in the country generally, and its attainments in the Housatonic region can be
equaled, perhaps exceeded, elsewhere in New England. It is
true that the Hopkins family, long identified with Berkshire
County, produced in Mark of the mid-nineteenth century
the leading collegiate educator of his age; and it is equally
true that Mark's near rivals for the honor would include
Sheffield's President F. A. P. Barnard of Columbia. Yet,
though both of these men were products of the tradition of
the valley, they actually did their great work elsewhere.
Ultimately, the distinction of the valley is less in the men
than in the actual works it has bred.

In the literary movement of the first half of the nineteenth century, related to the humanitarian trend in that
both arose out of a new interest in man as man, we find the
valley taking a prominent place, not as a nursery of the
great writers of the time but as a workshop where many
of them came to do their mature work. Like migrant birds,
they flew in among the mountains, there to rest a few years
and hatch a few of the great books of the world. Then they
flew back to the cities, some to the foreign countries of their
birth, leaving their legends as contributions to the tradition
of the valley.

Between 1816 and the Civil War the banks of the
Housatonic produced a literature that cannot be rivaled by
any other region during any other American forty-five years

except by the production along the Charles River in the same period, the Charles with its ostentatiously literate shores of Cambridge and Boston. Many of the figures of the day nested for a time on each of these rivers, and to make comparisons you would have to inquire minutely into just what was written where, and whether under the mountain or the urban influence. Without claiming precedence for either region, the plain fact is that on the Housatonic and the Charles we have the two largest gardens in the "flowering of New England," probably the two largest gardens in the literary flowering of America to date. In this early period of its cultivation, the Housatonic garden was more concentrated in space and time than it later became. Its greatest extension was from Lanesboro down through Great Barrington. Its strongest and richest blooms were in the three towns of Pittsfield, Lenox and Stockbridge, and its prize flowers matured in the single *anno mirabile* of 1851.

The literary tradition of the valley, as distinct from the religious tradition from which it derived, was younger than the tradition of greed and industry. Thomas Lamb began operating his forge at Lime Rock in 1732; but Jonathan Edwards did not begin *The Freedom of the Will* in Stockbridge till twenty-one years later. By the Revolution and continuously thereafter, the oxcarts were drawing pig iron in large quantities out of Salisbury over to the Hudson, and in 1800 the saws at Marbledale began to rasp. But, after Edwards, there was literary silence in the valley till 1817. In the intermediate period we can point to only a few premonitory events and constructions which were fraught with consequences.

Even before the Revolution we find that Judge Oliver Wendell of Boston had retained some 280 acres of the original 24,000 owned by his father Jacob in Pittsfield; that, fearful of Boston's going over to the Tories—being himself a prominent Whig who might be harshly treated—he made preparations with his tenant farmer on the old place in Pittsfield for himself and his family to retire there in case of emergency. He called the place "Canoe Meadows" because it contained a river flat which went by that name, a wide low flat of perhaps two hundred acres through which the Housatonic flowed, flooding it every spring. The only thing in the Canoe Meadows that was never flooded was a level-topped mound, an old Indian burying ground that was a mine of arrowheads. The local account of the name Canoe Meadows was that seasonally hundreds of Indians assembled there in their canoes to visit the graves of their fathers. Along the southwestern edge of this flood plain an embankment rose a safe twenty feet to the level of the cultivated part of Judge Wendell's farm. Having once turned his mind to the place as a possible refuge, the judge formed the habit of visiting it more or less regularly in the summer, riding in a fabulous carriage with green blinds, buying chickens at one inn and hanging them under the carriage until the next, in order to avoid eating them freshly killed. Thus Judge Wendell became the first of the summer residents—the "cottagers," as they were later called—in Berkshire County. After his daughter Sally married the Reverend Abiel Holmes and inherited Canoe Meadows, she and her husband continued the annual pilgrimage.

A second bed in Berkshire's literary garden was plowed when in 1785 Theodore Sedgwick built on the terrace close to the river in Stockbridge the mansion which, because of the fabulous hospitality soon established there, became a mecca for distinguished people, literary and otherwise, from all over the world.

A third preparation of the land occurred at about the same time when Henry Van Schaak, lately a Tory, built a mansion—now the Pittsfield Country Club—on the westernmost of the three Lenox-Pittsfield roads—now Route 7. In 1816 the place was bought by Thomas Melville, gent., down-at-the-heel gent. who did his own work. He called it Broadhall and presently began taking selected boarders.

That same year of 1816 a young lawyer, George H. Ives of Great Barrington, wanted a still younger partner and, after investigating several who had recently entered the bar, sent a proposal to a twenty-two-year-old youngster who had just set up practice in Plainfield, just out of the valley in Hampshire County, and whose father was a doctor and a state senator. "The offer was accepted with alacrity" by the young man, who throughout his life showed a flair for moving from the smaller to the bigger puddle. In October of 1816 they set up practice, under the firm name of Ives and Bryant, in the office of Mr. Ives's father, who had been that General Thomas Ives of the Revolution who fed the jailed Shaysites after their last battle on the Sheffield plain.

Not long after the firm of Ives and Bryant hung out its shingle—possibly as late as 1820—a tiny farmhouse was built and painted red in the northeast corner of Stockbridge. Its outlook from the rear was down over Lake Makeenack—now called the Stockbridge Bowl—across it to Monument Mountain and beyond it in the haze to "The Dome" of Mt. Everett. The house was about 200 yards from the Lenox boundary, and only two miles from Lenox Center, and Lenox is correct in its claim that the inhabitants of that corner considered themselves part of Lenox, where they shopped and got their mail.

With these five foundations—Canoe Meadows in Pittsfield, the Sedgwick house in Stockbridge, Broadhall in Pittsfield, the law office of Ives and Bryant in Great Barrington, and the little red farmhouse in Lenox—the five main batteries of the valley's literary artillery were in position. Bryant was the first of the big guns to be heard from. In December of '16 he was still such a newcomer in Great Barrington that in a list of the subscribers to the refreshments for a dance his initials were not known. Five months after this party, in April, 1817, Lawyer Bryant had been successful enough to enable him to buy out his partner, himself retaining the office and the business. That fall the *North American Review* published a poem called "Thanatopsis" which made the literati of two continents look around toward the western wilderness. It was the beginning of American poetry independent of British standards.

At first the people of Great Barrington were a little confused over the fanfare about their young lawyer who was still a good deal of a stranger. It was embarrassing to have in town somebody who had never claimed to be a poet and who didn't try to entertain all comers with doggerel in the fashion of Emanuel Hodget, the Hessian veteran and local genius, someone whom you saw every day and who suddenly, so they claimed, was tooted higher than a kite by the newspapers of Boston and New York and every other place. Fittingly they bestirred themselves to honor him in their fashion. Within a year they gave him the high offices of justice of the peace and town clerk.

Up in Stockbridge the Sedgwicks, who already had a habit of entertaining celebrities in their mansion on the natural terrace by the river, were a year slower in honoring the new local star. The recognition came through Charles, the youngest son of the great Theodore, the lovable one who "never thought he was as bright as his brothers." Being just about Bryant's age and likewise a young member of the bar, he introduced him to his two New York lawyer older brothers, Harry and Robert, who immediately set about finding him a suitable place in the big world. That fall of 1818 Bryant was twenty-four, a practical success in the town where he earned his bread, and a *succès d'estime* in the outer world. But since he had settled in Great Barrington he had written no more verse. For a year the effect of the valley, if any, had been to stifle his creative impulse and limit him to the use of what he called the "barbarous pen" of a lawyer. Now, on the wings of success—doubtless also on the wings of aspiration toward one Miss Frances Fairchild, the "fairest of the rural maids"—he began to write again.

In the late teens of the young century there were other premonitory activities in and relating to Berkshire. In 1810 the Reverend and Mrs. Abiel Holmes of Boston had been blest with a somewhat frail boy whom they had christened Oliver Wendell after his maternal grandfather. Among his earliest memories were those of his parents' annual pilgrimage to some region in the far West where there was a house called Canoe Meadows.

In this same decade Pittsfield's leading lawyer, Thomas

Gold, who late in the preceding century had built the mansion called Elm Knoll on East Street where the high school now stands, died leaving the house to his daughter Maria Theresa, wife of the wealthy Boston merchant Nathan Appleton. The Appletons began to use the house as a summer place. It was the normal eighteenth century mansion, with the wide central hall and grand stairway with a landing running across the rear. As in many houses so designed, a tall clock stood prominently in the back corner of the big landing, visible from both upper and lower halls. It was a substantial, big clock of the type later called "grandfather's," a type then being turned out both in Pittsfield and in Lanesboro. Like most such clocks, it had performed more or less conscientious pendulum duty for a generation or more, and was prepared to continue the service through eternity. This particular clock, however, was destined for something more than physical immortality.

A minor event in the valley in 1818 was the birth of Henry W. Shaw in Lanesboro. The event was minor from the local viewpoint, not because "Josh Billings," America's leading humorist of the mid-century, is of little consequence, but because he, like Mark Hopkins and the several Barnards, was of the class of distinguished men whom the valley produced but who emigrated to do their work elsewhere.

Of more bearing on the local record than Shaw's birth was the fact that in 1819 Charles Sedgwick married Elizabeth Dwight of Northampton. Beyond adorning his environment with an unusually gentle and beloved personality, Charles himself was of little consequence in the valley. Of more importance was this wife, who shortly was going to establish her famous school, and his sister Catherine, two years his senior, who one day was going to maintain the valley's chief literary salon in his home.

In 1819 Catherine was already thirty years old. Six years before, after the death of their father, Theodore I, she had written to her favorite brother, Robert, two years older than herself: "I am satisfied . . . that I can never love anybody better than my brothers. . . . Notwithstanding the proverbial mutability of a woman's inclination, the probability is in favor of my continuing to stamp all the coin of my kindness with a *sister's* impress, particularly when you consider that every year depreciates the coin in the market of matrimony." Notwithstanding the depreciation, Miss Sedgwick in that year rejected an unidentified "Mr. B———" whose mind she describes noncommittally as "noble."

From her childhood, and especially after the death of their mother in 1807, it had been plain that Catherine was cut out to be the focus of the family, starting with what we in our cruder vocabulary would call a fixation on her father. A contemporary report has it that on his deathbed he forbade a certain marriage because the swain in question lacked moral stamina. After his death in 1813 Catherine scattered her passionate affection among her four brothers, with a specially tender tentacle around Robert, who was next senior to her. Now, in 1819, Theodore Jr., the eldest brother, was already long married and settled down to practicing law in Albany. Harry, the second son, was likewise married and practicing in New York. Robert, in partnership with Harry, was not yet married. The two sisters, both older, were married and established elsewhere. Charles had been the last chick at home at whose board Catherine could preside. To be sure, he brought his Lizzie back to the mansion for the time being, and there is no scrap of evidence that dear Lizzie and dear Kate ever suffered any visible or invisible friction. Nevertheless, dear Kate's authority and responsibility were now at best shared. The length of her winters' visits to Harry and Robert in New York began to increase.

Early in this year of 1819 there had chanced into Stockbridge a minister who gives the lie to Lyman Beecher's reputation of being "the father of more brains than any man in America." This man of thirty-eight had just completed a preaching tour on the frontier of western New York and was on the way back to Haddam, Connecticut, to fetch out his large family. The diminutive Reverend Stephen West was now eighty-four years old, had completed sixty years as Stockbridge's pastor, and recently had survived with sweetness a malicious church trial brought against him for wine-bibbing. The pioneering preacher, whose name was David Dudley Field, was invited first to substitute a couple of Sundays for Dr. West, then to act as his assistant. Stockbridge in hand looked better than the frontier in the still wintry bush. Field accepted, departed for Haddam and returned with a caravan of oxcarts containing lares and penates, six children and wife including child expectant. In May dear old Dr. West departed this life and Mr.— later Dr.— Field became the fully accredited pastor. Presently the seventh child was born and christened Cyrus West. The older children, in order of age, were David Dudley Jr., Emilia Ann, Timothy Beals, Matthew Dickinson, Jonathan Edwards, and Stephen Johnson. Henry Martyn and Mary Elizabeth were to follow. Of these nine children, five were to achieve greatness in their own right; two were respectively to bear and beget greatness; and one—Timothy—was to be lost at sea; only Mary Elizabeth, the youngest, was to enjoy the distinction of a simple, local life. Mr. Field founded the New Year's sunrise services in Stockbridge, which were continued for a century. When later his house burned down with all his sermons he said, "Now they give more light to the world than as if I had preached them." He usually took with him into the pulpit two of his boys; and during the last long prayer would keep a hand on each of their big promising heads, "just to be sure they were there."

Meanwhile, through 1818, '19, '20 and '21, Town Clerk Bryant in Great Barrington had recaptured his muse and turned out some dozen poems destined for his collected works, including "Green River," the tributary of the Housatonic in Great Barrington. Bryant considered this poem his best, it being the poem in which he complains of wielding a "barbarous pen" in the contentions of the courts. From this period also came the famous Harvard Phi Beta Kappa poem "The Ages." In 1820 we find Bryant, on the way back from Lenox, stopping in Stockbridge to call on Miss Sedgwick and to receive through her a request from a New York publisher, stirred up by her brother Robert, for contributions to a collection of hymns. Apparently this was the first meeting between Miss Sedgwick and Bryant, for she wrote enthusiastically about him to Robert and hoped he would return.

In 1821 Bryant, being twenty-seven, had three important experiences. Back in Cummington his father, to whom he owed his literary interest, died. His first book of poems apeared. And he married Miss Frances Fairchild of Great Barrington. The latter ceremony took place in the gorgeously paneled southeast room of the old Dwight mansion, at that time occupied by the bride's sister and her husband Captain Henderson. From the fact that the couple were married there, and because of Mrs. Henderson being Mrs. Bryant's sister, a legend has been concocted to the effect that Bryant lived in the Dwight mansion, and modernly it is known as "the Bryant House." For this legend and the misnomer of the house there is no basis whatsoever. With the exception of a few hiatuses of a month or two, the successive locations of the Bryants during their four years' residence in Great Barrington are well known. These four years, incidentally, were the most poetically prolific of Bryant's life.

Early in 1821 Charles Sedgwick was appointed to the office of clerk of the courts for Berkshire County, an office which he exercised thereafter with dignity and local fame for thirty-five years. In June, Catherine Sedgwick writes Mrs. Channing of her distress that his new office confines him most of the time at Lenox, the shire town, six miles away. At the same time she wrote brother Robert of the emptiness of the "still and solitary" old mansion, now that Charles stays in Lenox almost every night. "Oh, my dear Robert, this place is dreadfully changed without him. . . . My imagination is continually filled with those looks and voices that animated every part of the house—that beamed with love and rung with joy. Elizabeth is very pleasant and kind, and the baby a sweet little creature, but those beloved ones whose hearts responded to mine . . . are all gone, or far away." It is the cry of "Snowbound," the cry of the old agrarian civilization with its big houses, big families and big hospitality, now in its death agony in the war with the new, industrial cities. As events turned out, neither the Sedgwick house, Stockbridge nor the Housatonic Valley was in death throes, as the drama of this region was in the long run to go counter to the epic of the age. But for Catherine Sedgwick it was a cry of death in the scattering of her beloved family. A little while after these letters to Mrs. Channing and to Robert, Charles and his Elizabeth and baby are settled permanently in Lenox. Catherine bows her head to fate and writes to him: "Wherever you are I must have a home, and Lenox must be to me, when you and yours are there, the dearest spot on all the earth."

Actually, it is difficult to understand why Miss Sedgwick's repining should have reached such a pitch yet a while. As Charles and his Elizabeth moved out of the old mansion, eldest brother Theodore and his Susan moved in from Albany, and from that time they lived there as moderately opulent country gentry, approximately restoring the hospitable largess of Theodore Sr., for the first time since his death. For a good many years more Catherine did in fact spend most of her summers in Stockbridge, passing only a very few weeks with Charles in Lenox, and spending most of three seasons of the year with Harry in New York. It was not until the mid-thirties that her visits with Charles and Lizzie began to exceed in length those with Theodore and Susan, and it was not until the forties, after Theodore's death, that she actually settled in Lenox and called it home and "the dearest spot on . . earth."

In 1821 there could hardly have been more contrast between two upland villages six miles apart than that between Stockbridge and Lenox. Stockbridge was a valley village on a plain through which the comfortable river moved on an indolent great S. Lenox was on a bleak hilltop where the trees of the first destruction were not yet well replaced. Lenox's hill was in fact the edge of the first titanic step down the center of the valley, a step of two hundred feet down and six miles' tread, Stockbridge snuggling at the bottom of it. Stockbridge looked up everywhere to surrounding mountains. Lenox looked down over Stockbridge to the limit of sight,

past Rattlesnake, Monument and Everett, down between Bear
and Canaan into Connecticut. An eagle or other glider taking
off from Lenox Center or from the Church on the Hill could
without winging have alighted on the river forty-five miles
below in southern Kent at the foot of the last great step
where the river was thunderous with powerful rapids and
falls, and divers Lowells and Patersons were being prophesied.

Lenox was high and bleak, Stockbridge low and comfortable. Stockbridge was relatively old, with houses whose
wings were the growths of generations, and the legends ran
back to Edwards and Sergeant and the Indians. Lenox was
young and raw, intolerably noisy on court days, and possessed
hardly two mansions that could be compared with a dozen in
Stockbridge. But what it did have was five public buildings
to be proud of, at least three of them the best of their kind
in the valley. It had its courthouse whose two-column façade,
delicately columned, floating belfry, and arch-ceilinged court-
room rendered it, as it remains today, unique in its combination of the charm and the magnificence that were possible in
the Greek revival style in architecture. Next door on the
corner, it had the tavern which was as yet nothing memorable, but shortly, in '29, was to be replaced by the Berkshire
Coffee House whose columned double verandas and hospitality were to become famous. Across the street stood the old
courthouse, become the town hall, built in 1792 and still a
handsome, square building with pyramidal roof and belfry,
probably in 1820 the handsomest town hall building in the
valley. Across the street and twenty rods to the north was
the Academy, also probably the best of its kind. And beyond
and above rose the Church on the Hill whose only rival for
the palm for ecclesiastical building in Berkshire County was
Pittsfield's new Bulfinch church replacing the original, tiny
sanctuary on the park. Such, with the addition of a couple
of mansions, three or four other substantial houses and a
dozen hovels, was Lenox Center where dear Charles and dear
Lizzie in 1821 put down their stakes. Just where they put
them down at first is not clear, but within a year they owned
a substantial house on the corner of Walker and Church

streets with a story-and-a-half wing running along the latter. Behind the house, between it and the tavern, there was an oblong, characterless building which dear Lizzie a few years later was going to bring to life.

Meanwhile, six miles down the hill in Stockbridge, Susan, the wife of Theodore, was in charge of the old mansion and Catherine, apparently having less authority than in Lizzie's regime, was in despair. Now she had more both of time and of inclination to reconsider the truths of Unitarianism into which the great Dr. Channing had liberated her after the death of her father. And she had time to transcribe those truths into her vast correspondence, with Dr. and Mrs. Channing and all others who would reply. But beyond these activities she had still further time and, if not inclination, at least the very specific importunities of her brother Theodore to try something new and frightening. In that summer of 1821, sitting at the little desk in her bedroom at the southwest corner of the second floor of the mansion, looking out over the beloved lawn to the edge of the terrace where the Plain dropped to the meadows along the beloved river, listening to the voices of the beloved servants in the kitchen below, sitting thus in loneliness with time on her hands, great love in her heart, and her brother's importunity in her ear, Miss Sedgwick's fancy began to wander beyond the patterns of both eternal contemplation and eternal letter writing. In place of tender aphorisms and syllogisms she began to compose a fiction about people who acted or failed to act in accordance with tender aphorisms and syllogisms. In the fall, when she went down to stay with brother Harry —always the useful, as he was the most distinguished, member of the family—she took along the finished long-short story. She intended it only as a Unitarian tract. But Harry, having an acquaintance among publishers, took the manuscript in hand, determined to accomplish its publication as a novel.

Theodore Sedgwick's wise direction of his thirty-two-year-old little sister into fiction came just in time. For, while Harry was still negotiating for publication, in February,

1822, she received the greatest shock to her family love since her father's death. Her favorite brother Robert got engaged! The girl was Elizabeth Ellery of Newport. Immediately Catherine is writing busily to her sisters and sisters-in-law, commanding them to write Robert instantly because he "feels his happiness very incomplete till he has the expressions of his friends' sympathy." Robert himself failed no whit in fraternal love and duty. Apparently in response to his sister's first expression of "sympathy" he writes her: "You will never know, my beloved sister, so long as the obstructions of sense stand between heart and heart, how mine has been melted by your kind and generous conduct." Three months later, in May, 1822, and long before the full blow of Robert's actual marriage, Bliss White published Catherine's story under the title *A New England Tale*.

Instantly the letters began to pour in and overwhelm her. In less than a month Miss Sedgwick, writing to Mrs. Channing, reveals that sense of public ravishment experienced by all successful first authors who are more sensitive than vain: "If all poor authors feel as I have felt since obtruding myself upon the notice of the world, I only wonder that the lunatic asylum is not filled with them. I hardly know any treasure I would not exchange to be where I was before my crow-tracks passed into the hands of printer's devils." Without question this sigh for lost literary virginity was sincere. But just as deep in her there surely was the satisfaction of being a person of recognized accomplishment, an accredited champion of Unitarianism in the big world. Competent big brother Harry gloated, urging her to plunge into religious controversy "as you are so much of a Bibleist," and nothing suited Catherine better than to play the devout radical on the side of the dangerous Unitarians.

But by its literary merit alone *A New England Tale* raised Miss Sedgwick at once to the level and into the society of the leaders of a new and independent American literature. Whether she knew it or not, her distinction, like that of Bryant, lay in the fact that she dared—as Bryant himself said of her—to publish and enjoy success "without asking . . .

permission from the citizens of Great Britain." Following the
initial, best-seller flurry in New York, she divided the summer of 1822 between brother Theodore in Stockbridge and
brother Charles in Lenox. She was well fortified for the great
blow when in August it fell. And dearest brother Robert
measured up magnificently. On the eve of leaving New
York to be married in Newport, he remembered to write her:
"Though I am in the greatest possible confusion and hurry, I
can not leave town without telling you that my heart never
turned toward you or leaned upon you with more pure,
faithful, ardent, and confiding affection than at this moment.
. . . I know nothing that would alarm me so much for
myself as a consciousness that I was losing my love for you."

And so, with enough talent to take a high if transitory
place in awakening, independent American literature, with
the radical flair of Unitarianism to make her interesting,
while at the same time safe respectability dripped from every
natural curl of her upkempt head, above all with the support
of the four most loyal brothers any old maid ever mothered,
Catherine Sedgwick, never losing sight of the harbor of family affection, launched out on the sea of fame. In the next
thirteen years she published six more novels, all of which were
republished in England, most of them translated two or three
times on the Continent, attributed to Cooper when they
were anonymous, and generally rated with the top literature
of the day. In the winters in New York she was high in the
intellectual oligarchy of Halleck, Irving, Cooper, Morse in
his original role of artist, and others now forgotten. In the
summers increasing droves of lions, many of them foreign
and colorful, prowled around her court in New York, in
Stockbridge, or in Lenox.

Meanwhile events, some important in themselves, some
pregnant with future import, occurred among the people of
the valley. In 1824 Mark Hopkins, the great future president
of Williams, graduated there, followed in 1825 by David
Dudley Jr., the eldest of the great generation of Fields. In
the latter year Stockbridge's church burned down and was
replaced by the one that still survives, the western portion

of the congregation, dwelling in Curtisville, taking the opportunity to secede and build its own church. Catherine Sedgwick, frequently called on by Daniel Webster in New York, was in his party as orator of the day at the dedication of the Bunker Hill Monument. Harry Sedgwick, who had kept in touch with Bryant in Great Barrington, got the law-hating young lawyer a New York job on the projected "New York Review and Athenaeum Magazine." One of the big lights of the age went out in the valley, and Bryant's best years of poetry were over. On the other hand, he laid down his "barbarous pen" for good, and the seed of the *Tribune* was planted.

In '27 came the first real crack in the Sedgwick family, with Harry's first attack of insanity. In '28 David Dudley Field entered the Sedgwick law office in New York; and in Lenox Mrs. Charles opened her school for girls in the building on Walker Street between the tavern and her home. The next year the tavern came down and was replaced by the Berkshire Coffee House with its handsome columns and double piazza. Likewise in '29, Stephen Johnson Field, the second son, and, like David Dudley, destined for a distinguished legal career, went out to Smyrna with his sister Emilia Ann, wife of the missionary Josiah Brewer of Tyringham; Stephen Johnson was at this time thirteen years old, and his sole purpose in the arduous trip was to improve himself in Oriental languages. In '31 Harry Sedgwick died, generally conceded to have been the star of his generation in the family.

In 1832 an event of future importance for the valley was the landing in New York from a sailing ship of the famous English actress Fanny Kemble. She was promptly recognized by a call from the great Catherine Sedgwick, and a friendship was founded that never ended. In '33 Catherine is inditing doubts as to the wisdom of Frances' marrying a certain young southern planter, Pierce Butler—and the following year they are married. The same year a third Field, Cyrus, not destined for higher education, goes to New York, takes a job as clerk at $50 a month, gets home-

sick and is taken in by big brother David. Later the two great men owned adjoining houses in Gramercy Park and had a passage cut between them for closer communication.

In '34 Harriet Martineau started her celebrated American tour, and was naturally pounced upon by Catherine Sedgwick. The following year she visited in Stockbridge for six weeks, and in a solemn, evening walk along the river collided with Catherine's firm ideas about the necessity of preserving the Union. In '35 also, Washington Irving visited the Sedgwicks, and Catherine published her last novel, *The Linwoods*. She continued, however, more prolific than ever, pouring out a flood of short stories, children's stories, sketches and tracts.

In '36 Webster stopped by in Stockbridge to fish, on his way to make a speech in Pittsfield. That year is important in the valley as marking the first visit of Fanny Kemble Butler, who spent a month, not in Stockbridge but up at Charles' and Elizabeth's house in Lenox, where Catherine was by now spending at least half her Berkshire time. "I never looked abroad," wrote Mrs. Butler, "upon the woods and valleys and lakes and mountains without thinking how great a privilege it would be to live in the midst of such beautiful things." It would seem that the deeper friendship was founded between Fanny and Elizabeth, for it was with Elizabeth that she corresponded more extensively and intimately in the trying years that followed; and it was especially against Elizabeth and her gentle husband Charles that Pierce Butler later laid his obstinate taboo upon Fanny's Sedgwick association.

In 1837 Mrs. Anna Jameson, chalky complexioned and auburn curled, was a house guest for a long stay in the Stockbridge house. In the fall of '38 Fanny Kemble was back in Lenox again, apparently under her own steam, for she stayed at the Berkshire Coffee House—the "Red Inn" as she called it—inditing raptures about the grand view southward down over Stockbridge. After this she was in Lenox for a while almost every summer. From the beginning, the striking ex-actress was considered peculiar by the local people, galloping about the country, usually astride, on the biggest saddle horse she could find—"The death I should prefer would be to break my neck off the back of a good horse at a full gallop on a fine day." Less fiery than herself, her riding companions often included Mary and Fanny Appleton of Boston and Pittsfield. In the winter following the 1838 visit, Mrs. Butler was going for the first time to grace her husband's plantation in Georgia. She was already profoundly distressed about slavery, and Elizabeth Sedgwick urged her to keep a journal of her observations. She did, and it later became at once a best seller and a document of diplomatic importance.

At some time in the late thirties young Dr. Oliver Wendell Holmes, finding himself in Albany, ran over on the Western Railroad to view the place called Canoe Meadows which his parents had visited regularly in his childhood, and which he had either just inherited or was about to inherit, his father dying in '37. He was pleased with the old farm and from this time visited it every year. An incidental association with Pittsfield was through the now very ancient Major Thomas Melville who had been Pittsfield's member of the Boston Tea Party and had since moved to Boston, was reputed to be the last man in America to wear a cocked hat, and had already been celebrated by Holmes in the poem "The Last Leaf."

Throughout the thirties Catherine Sedgwick's Lenox sojourns were lengthening at the expense of those in Stockbridge. In '38 her beloved Robert had a slight stroke, and in '39 she went abroad with him and his family for two years. Not long after their departure Theodore died of apoplexy in Stockbridge. And soon after their return, an age ended for Catherine in the death of Robert. She wrote to her friend Dr. Dewey: "I have had praise and flattery, and I have not been insensible to them; but God knows they never weighed for one moment against affection, and I would give all the world could offer to me of them for one tone of Robert's voice." Charles was now all she had left, and Lenox henceforth was "the dearest spot on earth." The story-and-a-half wing of the big house on Church Street was her exclusive domain, equipped inwardly with all perquisites for small-scale hospitality and outwardly with beds of flowers which she herself planted and nurtured into life.

It was probably in 1840 that Longfellow began his twenty-seven-year flirtation with the valley, which never quite jelled into a marriage. In '37, while in Switzerland, he had met and been much taken with Miss Frances Appleton, daughter of Boston's rich merchant Nathan Appleton. As already mentioned, Mrs. Appleton had inherited the mansion Elm Knoll on Pittsfield's East Street, with the grand staircase and the tall clock on the landing. Mr. Appleton himself had bought just west of Stockbridge village the big loop of the river known as the Oxbow, where it first turns north out of its westerly course through the village, then west again, loops southward and back to form the oxbow, then swings definitely southward through Glendale, having completed almost three-quarters of a circle. This peninsula, less than half a mile in diameter at any point, enjoyed seclusion behind the moat of the alder-lined river, and it contained a small farm—as it still does—and patches of woodland free of underbrush, theatrical with nooks, shadows, knolls and grots. Fanny Appleton and her sister passed most of the summer of '40 in Stockbridge at the old Red Lion Inn. Thither Longfellow came wooing and, being already smitten by Miss Fanny, was now in addition smitten by the Oxbow. It may be assumed that he courted them both in a boat, the river's languid current here and the numerous retreats in the bushes along its banks comprising an invitation which no lover could neglect. At that time young Henry Dwight Sedgwick was one of Longfellow's students at Harvard, and throughout the ensuing winter the professor revealed his preoccupation by customarily addressing young Sedgwick as "Stockbridge."

In '43 Longfellow and Fanny Appleton were married and spent the longest of several wedding trips visiting her mother at Elm Knoll, "the old-fashioned country seat" in Pittsfield. Two years later Longfellow wrote "The Old Clock on the Stairs," using a French poem for pattern and Elm

Knoll's big timepiece for material. In '46 he is back again with his wife and two babies and complains that "It is difficult to write in this house, so closely is it shut in with trees. We lounge on the doorstep through the morning. . . ." A few days later he records in his journal that he "strolled along the banks of the Housatonic, through fields and pastures and meadows; a shallow brown stream, not very clear."

Two days later—August 22nd—he "drove to Stockbridge" and "came upon the Oxbow," whose beauty he proceeds to celebrate. "After dinner," the entry concludes, "it began to rain and we turned our faces homeward without calling on the Sedgwicks. Up the hill we went from which the view is so fine; beneath wound and circled upon itself the slow Housatonic through the meadows fair, forming the Oxbow. We stopped a moment to see the Lowells [James Russell] who go back [to Cambridge] Monday, as we do. I shall not soon seek country air again. Give me the sea-side in summer, and the town in winter." Longfellow was forever grumbling in this vein about Berkshire, yet he kept coming back, even without his wife. The fact seems to have been that he liked the valley but, unlike the rest of the writers who were attracted by it, he could not work here. Even after a long stay, the mountain air made him drowsy.

Returning to Berkshire in mid-July of '48, the Longfellows by-passed Elm Knoll and tried the genteel boardinghouse Broadhall on the Lenox Road, where Thomas Melville, son of "The Last Leaf," was host. Longfellow celebrates the landscapes in his diary, but three days later, on the 20th, he is already complaining that he cannot "pour from my drowsy brain a thought or two on paper." The entry continues: "After the dinner Mrs. Fanny Butler called. Then we walked down a pleasant lane and through the woods, to a little lake, very deep and dark."

Two days later he is back at the Oxbow:

"22d. We drove to Stockbridge, by the Lenox lake [probably Makeenack, the Stockbridge Bowl]. The air embalmed with mint and clover. Passed an hour at the Oxbow. What a lovely place! On three sides shut in by willow and

alder hedges and the flowing wall of the river; groves clear
of all underbrush; rocky knolls, and breezy bowers of chest-
nut; and under the soil, marble enough to build a palace. I
build many castles in the air, and in fancy many on the
earth; and one of these is on the uplands of the Oxbow, looking eastward down the valley, across this silver Dian's bow
of the Housatonic." (This handsome view—from approximately the location of "Southmayd" today—was partly
southeastward and so more or less "down" the valley, though,
the river making here its northern sweep, its "Dian's bow,"
to flow opposite to its general trend, the view is *up* the river.)

The journal continues with miscellaneous daily adventures, mostly geared to the children. At the end of the month
there is an adventure which affords a fleeting contrast between the intellectuals, who, consciously or not, were trying to save the valley, and the industrialists, who, consciously
or not, were trying to destroy it:

29th . . . To Lanesboro . . . Found a smelting furnace
for iron, which tempted us to see the casting of pig iron. Out
of the glowing furnace it ran, a river of fire, into the large
sand-mould, shaped like a comb, the bars being the teeth.
. . ." (A description which clarifies the common idiom of
the "sow and pigs.")

"August 1. I find it quite impossible to write in the
country, the influences are soothing and slumberous. In coming here I hoped to work successfully on *Kavanagh*, and as
yet I have written scarcely a page . . ." He describes going
down to Lenox to call on the Charles Sedgwicks and being
"entertained by Mrs. Butler singing German and Scotch
songs."

On the second the family drove up to Lebanon—"How
lovely the valley is, as one drives down into it from the Berkshire hills!"

"3d. The capacity of the human frame for sleep in the
summer is very great. . . ."

On the 5th he drove over to see Holmes in his new
house, or "villa," just completed overlooking the Canoe

Meadows, and found it "a snug little place." On the 8th he went down to call on the Stockbridge Sedgwicks and, observing that everything was Sedgwick thereabout, confided to his journal: "The grasshoppers in the fields chirp, 'Sedgwick! Sedgwick! Sedgwick!' " On the 21st he was back in Cambridge where he finished *Kavanagh* which, in spite of Longfellow's complaints earlier that summer, may be claimed as a production of the valley, since it was conceived and largely written there and most of the scenery is from Berkshire.

The next year, 1849, Longfellow was back at Broadhall with his children but not his wife. In '50 his father-in-law, who had already bought him Craigie House in Cambridge, presented him with his beloved Oxbow in Stockbridge, that he might build there a "castle on the earth" such as he had dreamed. To Mr. Appleton's gift Longfellow added a separate purchase of his own. Yet he actually spent that summer at Nahant by the sea, in the Appleton customary summer seat. Sometime he would build at the Oxbow, but not just yet.

Meanwhile, during the forties miscellaneous lions and lionesses were prowling for varying periods in Stockbridge and Lenox: Miss Sedgwick's court of Italian liberal refugees; two poets, William Pitt Palmer, the native one, and N. P. Willis, the dapper one; the latter's sister "Fanny Fern"; Lord Morpeth; Macready, the actor; George William Curtis, who after the demise of Brook Farm spent his summer vacations in Stockbridge; Dr. Channing, frequently in Lenox where in '42 he delivered his valedictory from this world in the pulpit of the Church on the Hill; James Russell Lowell; Harriet Beecher Stowe; Emerson, who had a daughter in Mrs. Sedgwick's school and was an occasional guest at the Coffee House in Lenox, as was his great friend Agassiz.

In the summer of '44 Charles Sumner came out to recuperate from an illness, and the Appletons entertained him at Elm Knoll, for he had been best man at the wedding of Longfellow and their Fanny. One day he borrowed a horse and rode out to Lenox to call on the Sedgwicks. There he discovered Fanny Kemble Butler, with whom he had been much taken twelve years before when he was a law student in Harvard and she made Boston on tour with her father. Sumner was now thirty-three, and Fanny was thirty-five and the unhappy wife of Pierce Butler. For several weeks they rode and loitered together along the lanes and paths of the mountains. Mrs. Butler had introduced archery in Lenox. ". . . We looked on," wrote Sumner to a friend, "while in a field not far off, the girls and others were engaged in the sport of archery. Mrs. Butler hit the target in the golden middle." The next day he wrote to a friend that he wished he were there to help him "bear the weight of Fanny Kemble's conversation. . . . I confess to a certain awe and sense of her superiority . . ." Two years later Fanny left Pierce Butler's persecutions and went abroad, and in '49 he divorced her. She and Sumner continued to see each other frequently. Yet her great abolitionist friend was officially never more than her financial adviser. There is no positive evidence that she hit him fatally "in the golden middle." He married late in life and was promptly divorced.

During Fanny's two years in Europe (1846-1848) she met a certain Mademoiselle Desportes who, having been governess of the children of the Duc de Praslin, had, in a recent *cause célèbre,* been tried for instigation of the duke's murder of his wife. Although she was acquitted, it was established that she "had turned the hearts of her pupils against their unfortunate mother," and established her position and authority in the family at the duchess's expense. The meeting with the charming and intelligent Miss Desportes was an ordeal for Fanny; the outrage that had finally driven her from her family was the same as that the duchess had suffered, Pierce having hired a governess and given her complete authority over the children. Years later there was a Berkshire sequel to this meeting.

With a few exceptions, such as Fanny Kemble and Longfellow, Channing with his great sermon on emancipation, perhaps also Lowell and Palmer, the bulk of the occasional visitors was passing froth on the tradition of the river. But increasingly through the thirties and forties Oliver Wendell Holmes was becoming a regular summer resident on his property along the Canoe Meadows on the river in Pittsfield, and he is charged with having said at about this time that "the best of all tonics is the Housatonic." Less excusably he proclaimed in Cambridge, with characteristic snobbery, that the river where it ran through his property was about the size of the Cam in England—a comparison flattering to the Cam, as to both size and beauty of natural surroundings. By '44 Holmes had well identified himself with the region, and was invited to deliver a speech and poem of welcome at the famous Berkshire Jubilee of that year when hundreds of natives of the county returned from all over the nation, the New York City committee including Bryant, David Dudley Field and Theodore Sedgwick. Holmes's speech, and especially his poem in playful satire of country life, made a hit. Fanny Kemble contributed an ode which was read for her. And Macready rendered a poem of Leigh Hunt's.

From this time on, Holmes was continuously pestered for occasional poems for various Pittsfield doings. Beginning with this Jubilee poem, most of the verse he wrote in Pittsfield was first published in a local paper. An exception was "A Vision of the Housatonic River," which he wrote as an epilogue to a lecture on Wordsworth, and which is not one of his more successful efforts. His best entirely local poem is "The Ploughman," composed for the Pittsfield Cattle Show of '49 and delivered while standing halfway up the steps to the pulpit of the then old Bulfinch church. That same year he watched this sanctuary burn to the ground, and the following year wrote in "The Astrea":

> The oriole drifting like a flake of fire
> Torn by a whirlwind from a blazing spire.

The verse which Holmes wrote in Pittsfield was, of course, a small proportion of the large quantity of it which, like "Astrea," he wrote elsewhere but in recollection of the Berkshire scene.

In 1848 Holmes had strengthened his roots in the valley

by building what Longfellow, riding over from Broadhall in August to see it, described in his journal as "a snug little place with views of the river and the mountains." 'Forty-nine was Holmes's first full season there, beginning what he later called "seven sweet summers, the happiest of my life." The farmhouse remaining as the functional center of the estate, Holmes called his retreat a "villa." Actually it was a fair-sized, pyramidal-roofed house of the period, with four large rooms on each floor, besides a story-and-a-half wing on the north side and a covered terrace on the south. It stands immediately on the bank above the Canoe Meadows, and Holmes used to go down and collect arrowheads from the old Indian mound. Legend says that the only shade tree on the estate when he took it was the pine still standing near the highway and known as the Holmes Pine. He himself wrote: "I planted seven hundred trees for somebody to sit in the shade of." Holmes's personal hide-out from such as his great dissenting son, at this time seven years old, was his library or study in the wing, commanding an open view northward to Greylock and eastward over Canoe Meadows and the river to the slope and horizon of Mt. Washington. From the semicircular, paved and covered terrace—an early form of piazza—on the southern side of the ground floor, he had a superb view southeastward along October Mountain, and southward and southwestward across houses of friends to the peaks of Yokun's Seat, South Mountain, Bald Head and the other hills of Lenox. At twilight he loved to take guests by the elbow and point out along the hills the shapes of birds, beasts and men, especially "General Taylor on his horse." Nobody ever identified these phantasms except Holmes himself!

Besides the settlement of Holmes as a regular summer resident, the perennial presence of Catherine Sedgwick and her court, and another summer's visit by Longfellow, the year '49 was significant for the permanent establishment of Fanny Kemble in the valley. In Pierce Butler's suit for divorce against her for desertion, her pathetic and unexaggerated story of his cruelty was excluded from evidence as irrelevant under the law as it was then. Since she had in fact run away from him, she lost her case and—what really mattered—she lost her two little girls, Sally for seven years and Fan for nine, after which they would respectively be twenty-one. Under the settlement she could have them with her that one last summer. In Lenox she bought a house with three lofty, pointed gables, standing between the Old Stockbridge Road and the Stockbridge Road, and having a long, southeastward view in that relatively treeless period down over Laurel Lake and the river. She called it "The Perch," and with her daughters by her, with her irrepressible capacity for enjoying the present, with Catherine and the Charles Sedgwicks a mile up the road in Lenox Center, with Longfellow and Holmes four or five miles beyond in Pittsfield, each genial in a proclivity for riding down to Lenox and foregathering with the always numerous transients at one of the houses or the Berkshire Coffee House, with more Sedgwicks and a miscellaneous assembly of highbrows five miles down the road in Stockbridge, and among all these and the surrounding farmers an infinite menagerie of children to play with her daughters, it is certain that Fanny filled with great joy that last summer before the knife of separation fell.

In September the knife did fall, when her girls went away to boarding school and into the darkness for what then seemed forever. Doubtless her first reaction was an increasing expression of her violent emotion: driving the famous black horse she acquired about this time into a wilder gallop and a fiercer lather; herself climbing more dangerously the cliffs of Monument Mountain; indulging more frequently her habit, when on foot, of running and jumping up on the box beside any farmer passing in his wagon, chatting with him till they crossed a brook, then jumping down and whipping off her shoes and stockings to stand in the running water. Doubtless there was at first an increased tempo in these evidences of her own neuroses now exaggerated by thwarted maternity. But, just as characteristically, she presently had herself soberly in hand and set out on her remunerative career of Shakespearean readings, with which she more than pieced out the piddling allowance she got by the settlement with her rich husband. By midautumn she was reading in Cambridge, entertained of course by the Longfellows in Craigie House, her "old friend Fanny" Longfellow giving her a bouquet, and Longfellow penning her a sonnet for the occasion which Charles Sumner carried off and published in the *Transcript*.

From this time "the Perch" remained for twenty-four years the focus of Fanny Kemble Butler's several orbits: her eyebrow-raising local orbit, gallivanting about on her charger or pacing the highway on foot, clad in anything from bloomers to full evening dress; her American orbit, earning her living as a reader of Shakespeare unrivaled in this country or in Europe; her world orbit, which took her every few years abroad to water her English roots, while reading before imposing audiences of royalty and nobility.

In Lenox she did not read for money but always for some worthy purpose or other. The usual purpose was the instruction of Mrs. Sedgwick's girls whom, along with a few invited guests, Mrs. Butler would entertain with Shakespeare either on the veranda or in the parlor, according to the weather. Once she gave the proceeds of a reading to the Lenox Library. On another occasion she proposed to the local authorities that she give a reading "for the benefit of the poor," at which she was airily informed that "we have no poor." She gave the reading just the same, and with the proceeds donated a big town clock, whose recent successor would still be watching over the whole village from the steeple of the Church on the Hill were it not, as in so many other Lenox affairs, for the unreasonable, modern interposition of jungles of treetops.

For twenty-four years the Perch remained the anchor of this incomparably vital woman who thought that New England's "Puritan farmers" were "the most intelligent men of their class in the world," and who meanwhile was piling up the letters and the journals that would keep her immortal. In the distant future the Perch would be torn down and its foundation more than covered by the garage of a rich man of a very different period. But the Stockbridge Road, renamed Kemble Street by the local people who finally came to love and honor her, would remain as a more enduring monument of her long residence.

With the establishment of Holmes and Fanny Kemble Butler in 1849, the literary current of the river, which had been rising steadily for more than a quarter of a century, reached a new high; the following year it was going to become a flood. Back in '36 Herman Melville, then eighteen and a native of New York City, had visited his father's brother, Uncle Thomas, proprietor of Broadhall in Pittsfield, had learned something of farming and had taken to it. Since then he had had his major adventures rounding the Horn and in the South Seas and, beginning in '46, had published *Typee, Omoo* and some smaller pieces, all moderately successful but not successful enough to support his new wife in the manner to which she was accustomed. By midwinter of '50 he owed his publishers $700 in unearned advances, and realized that the time had come for a major gesture. In March, being thirty-two years old, he moved his family up to Broadhall, which his uncle had recently sold. While prospecting for a less costly establishment, he found in the barn the old desk of his grandfather—Holmes's "Last Leaf"—set it up in his room and went to work on nothing that proved of consequence.

In April *The Scarlet Letter* appeared, enjoyed an immediate fanfare, and some chance made Melville read it. He had always had an inexplicable prejudice against Hawthorne that had kept him from reading his previous work. Now, on the wings of enthusiasm for *The Scarlet Letter*, he devoured all of his earlier books and made a god of this man who was fourteen years his senior. Immediately he wrote an unreservedly favorable criticism, and their mutual friend Evert A. Duyckinck published it in the New York *Literary World.* There is no evidence that Hawthorne ever acknowledged this praise. In the strange relationship between these incompatible men, all the discourtesy was on Hawthorne's side, though it was a discourtesy he regretted and tried to suppress.

When Melville wrote his full-souled effusion about Hawthorne, he did not know that the better writer and smaller mind, having lost his customs job in Salem, was already by way of becoming his six-mile-away neighbor. In May the Hawthornes—Nathaniel and Sophia and the two attractive youngsters Una and Julian—moved into the tiny red farmhouse built about thirty years before on the westernmost of the Lenox-Stockbridge roads, the one passing the Stockbridge Bowl. The cottage, just over the line in Stockbridge, was the property of the Tappans, who had not yet built on their estate, most of which was across the road. The trim little building was about half a mile from the lake, looking down to it over a wide, cleared slope. In the background was the most rugged profile of Monument Mountain, frequently covered with Olympian haze or adorned with the sunset, "like," said Hawthorne, "a headless sphinx wrapped in a Persian shawl." On the right, or north, was the orchard, and beyond it Baldhead, which was to prove easy climbing. All around were other big hills. From the beginning Hawthorne was frightened by the static grandeur of the mountain scene and believed he would not be able to work there. The nicely furnished farmhouse had four tiny bedrooms, and Hawthorne chose for his studio one looking out to the lake and mountain, fearing the power of the natural landscape, but fearing it less than he did the human power on the road that passed the front of the house. The substantial secretary on which he worked is in the Pittsfield mansion. Once a day he braved the human power on the highway by walking the mile and a half up to the Lenox post office.

Halfway down from the house to the lake there was a glen full of brush, vines, rocks, roots and a stream, which Hawthorne frequently explored with the children. He called the place "Tanglewood," coining a name that was bound for a distinguished history. The first transference was to the little property occupied by the Hawthornes. Later the Tappans took it for the name of their entire estate after they built the mansion. Modernly, after the donation of the estate to the Berkshire Music Festival, the name has stuck to the property, and to the general ear "Tanglewood" means this great Music Shed where the festival is held every summer. Another coinage of Hawthorne's was "Shadowbrook," the name first of the little stream that flowed through the glen Tanglewood, and afterwards of the great Phelps estate through which it flowed on its way down from the heights of Baldhead.

At this time Hawthorne was forty-eight, broke, jobless, his previous books dwindled to a piddling income, and he had a wife, two children and an expected third to support. According to his wife, he was himself a "bunch of rags," she writing her father to buy him "two linen sacks, well made and good linen"—apparently for smocks. Under these circumstances Hawthorne blithely devoted the months of May, June, July and most of August to playing with the children, his probably valid excuse being his depleted health. Both Una and Julian always remembered him as the most perfect playmate they ever had. Together they explored the glen Tanglewood, waded and tried to swim in the lake, fished, built toy boats, flew kites, walked for the milk down the road which Papa called the Milky Way, climbed to the top of Baldhead, scampered and roughhoused, all the excitement interfrosted with wonderful hours when they would sit down on a wall or a big rock and Hawthorne would spin stories out of his fancy, stories many of which the world would later hear from *The Wonder Book, Twice-Told Tales* and *Tanglewood Tales.*

Every day he walked up to Lenox for the mail, and his social terror seems sometimes to have left him the courage to drop in on the mild Charles Sedgwicks. Fanny Kemble was a different article. When he met her does not appear. But presently she was galloping down to Tanglewood at any hour, snatching up little Julian and galloping off with him for a wild ride through the woods, at length returning and handing him down to his papa with the command, "Here, take your Julian the Apostate." Hawthorne must have cringed before her. Of all the conflicting personalities that clashed in and around Lenox that year, those of Hawthorne and Fanny Kemble had the least in common. Throughout May, June and July there is no evidence that either Hawthorne or Melville was aware of the presence of the other.

Meanwhile two changes in the literary stage scenery were going on. That summer Charles Sedgwick's house in Lenox was moved from the corner of Church and Walker streets across the latter, out and down Kemble Street a little way, a move of only a hundred and fifty yards but shifting the house from a relatively enclosed location in the village to an open situation on the very edge of the big hill, where it enjoyed all the tremendous view southward and southwestward, an eyrie of a site, perhaps the grandest for view anywhere south of Lanesboro. On the southeast end a new wing was added to the house for the school. On the northwest end Miss Catherine's old wing came along with the house, but it was now enlarged and got a veranda on the back, or view, side. On the front, or Kemble Street, side there was plenty of almost level ground for the gardens, including Catherine's flowers. Miss Sedgwick was now sixty-one and settling into a routine which may not have had an irresistible appeal for the biggest lions roaming the surrounding hills. Her favorite pattern of entertainment became the breakfast party, where it is safe to assume that visiting lion hunters rarely or never got glimpses of Holmes, Melville or Hawthorne. Her favorite form of entertainment became the word game, which sounds equally terrifying. And actually Miss Catherine was by this time better pleased to tell stories to children or write letters to her own droves of nieces and nephews than to entertain visiting firemen.

A second move that summer was fraught with more consequence. Melville was fortunate in his father-in-law, Chief Justice Lemuel Shaw of Massachusetts who, in the present crisis of the half-successful author's affairs, made him a loan and took back a friendly and never-foreclosed mortgage which enabled Melville to buy a big farmhouse he coveted and which fitted his plans. It stood on what was then called the Middle Road out of Pittsfield for Lenox, now called Holmes Road, and was about a mile from Broadhall and half a mile from Dr. Holmes's villa. It was of the usual one-chimney farmhouse plan, only larger than most, approaching the area of most two-chimney mansions. Eastward it faced the road, then, a quarter of a mile across open pasture, the willow- and elm-bordered river, and beyond, Mt. Washington and October Mountain. Northeastward was Holmes's house, not then hidden behind a hedge. Northward and northwestward in the distance beyond the spires of Pittsfield rose Greylock, the northern bulwark of the valley. In exploring toward the river Melville picked up many Indian relics. Wherefore he called the place Arrowhead. For his studio he took the big north bedroom facing Greylock, but, as in the case of Hawthorne, there is no evidence that he got down to serious work until some time in August.

Melville's excuse for literary indolence was less picturesque and more practical than Hawthorne's. His plan had been to write for about a five-hour day and devote the rest of his time to light farming, raising just enough for his family's subsistence. As in the case of hundreds of other writers and artists, the plan was feasible on paper. But unlike most other cases, the failure in this case was not Melville's own. His wife Elizabeth, daughter of the judge, had not been raised to housewifery, let alone farm housewifery, and she lacked natural capacity for management. One of Melville's biographers says, perhaps too cruelly, that her equipment for that first year was "an admirable set of party dresses and slippers." From the beginning of their residence in the house that summer of '50, Melville was doing the cooking and most of the housework, besides the farming. By August, his mother and two sisters were in residence, freeing him from much domestic labor, but also living from his larder. Elizabeth's reaction to this arrangement is not of record.

At some time, possibly now, possibly later, Melville [1]

---

[1] All the inscriptions in and about the big fireplace are repeated in or from Melville's later writings. One plausible account of them is that they were much later copied out by his brother Allan.

began to inscribe on his big kitchen mantel and fireplace those strange saws and legends whose sophomoric eccentricity contributes to the eternal suspicion as to his sanity. A point to be noticed is that there was nothing remarkable about this chimney. It was not, as one biographer says, a "vast brick structure." As fitted a big house with big rooms, the flues were large and the stone chimney enclosing them correspondingly large. It was twelve feet square in the cellar, something larger than the average chimney of this type of house, but only because the house was larger than average. The biographer's statement that "the rooms that were left were none too large" is an uninformed deduction from Melville's queer musings. Actually the usual keeping room, parlor, kitchen, north pantry and downstairs bedroom were larger than those of most houses of the type in about the same proportion that the chimney was larger than most chimneys. Of course *any* colonial farmhouse chimney is a gigantic thing. If guessing is to be indulged in, the feasible inference is that at the time Melville wrote at least some of these several saws, his imagination was already occupied by a different embodiment of a vast, implacable, wide-mawed, subhuman force that was trying to press mankind out of the world.

Here are the inscriptions, as far as I can read them, all in and around the kitchen fireplace and all neatly printed in black, white, brown, red, white or green paint:

The root of the matter. This is a most remarkable structure, Sir. Yes, said Levery, one says so. The Magnitude of this foundation, Sir! Twelve feet square, one hundred and forty-four square feet! Sir, This House would seem to have been built simply for the Accommodation of your chimney. Yes, my chimney and me.

I and my Chimney as Cardinal Woolsey used to say I and my King. Yet this egotistical way of speaking, Wherein I take precedence of my chimney is hardly born out by the facts in everything except the above phrase. My chimney takes precedence of me. My chimney is grand seigneur here, the one great domineering object of the house Which is accommodated not to my

wants but to my Chimney's. He has the center of the House to
himself, leaving but the odd holes and corners to me.
    I and my Chimney are Settling together. A Mighty Smoke
we two Old Philosophers make. I resolved that I and my chimney
should not budge.
    I and my chimney like to have a quiet smoke together. [?]
chimney the [?] host.

Mrs. Sophia Peabody Hawthorne, originally a society
girl, was less than an inspiration to Hawthorne in only one
respect. She loved people in bunches and he feared them even
singly. By midsummer Sophia was being trotted all over the
place, while helping Nathaniel to avoid the ordeals she enjoyed. On August 1st we find Mr. O'Sullivan, who was on
bail for some "movements with regard to Cuba," showing
up in a double carriage and taking off the whole family to
visit "Mrs. Field"—possibly Mrs. Matthew Dickinson Field—
in the center of Stockbridge village at the foot of Laurel
Hill. "We were received with the most whole-hearted hospitality," wrote Mrs. Hawthorne to her mother, "and Una
and I stayed all night, and Mr. O'Sullivan brought Mr. Hawthorne and Julian back, because Mr. Hawthorne did not
wish to stay." After many civilities with the Sedgwick
widows in the old Stockbridge house, the evening ended with
what was its chief object, to watch the annual torchlight procession emerge from the Ice Glen just across the river. "It
looked," wrote Mrs. Hawthorne, "as if a host of stars had
fallen out of the sky, and broken to pieces." She goes on to
describe the departure for Lenox in a big omnibus of Mrs.
Sedgwick's girls who had been in the procession and "were
all lighted up by the burning torches, and were dressed in
fantastic costumes of brilliant colors, scarlet being predomi-
ant. . . . Poor, dear Mrs. Charles! She looked so warm and so
flushed—just like a torch herself!—and so lovely, kind, and
happy, in the midst of her living roses." Although Mrs. Hawthorne does not mention it, it may be assumed that after the
innocent scarlet torches were out of the way there followed
the big bonfires, stimulating refreshment and dancing in the

village street that was the culmination of this annual Stock-bridge festival.

Four days later, on August 5, 1850, there occurred one of the most fruitful collisions in American history. David Dudley Field, Jr., already New York's most distinguished lawyer for having rewritten that state's *Code of Civil Procedure*, was living in little Laurel Cottage on the Plain. On August 5th he gave a stag affair which began with an all-day walk up and down Monument Mountain and ended with a dinner. The guests were Henry Dwight Sedgwick—the only one present who had not published a book—Dr. Holmes, Cornelius Matthews, Melville, Evert A. and George L. Duychinck, the friends and advisers—especially Evert—of Melville, James T. Fields who was Hawthorne's publisher, and —literary triumph for Fields—the saturnine Hawthorne himself. It is reasonable to assume that Fields was the bait that caught Hawthorne. It is even safer to assume that if he had known Melville was going to be there, nothing would have brought him. Melville had complimented him highly in print, and Hawthorne liked it of course. But there were ancient taboos upon flattery, and especially upon being pleased by flattery which not New England's severest critic, so long as he was himself New England, could well transgress.

As the nine men crept up the trail at the snail's pace of mountain climbing, it is further reasonable to assume that eight of the snails were continually losing their breath talking, sparring with their sensitive antennae darting out to touch each other's minds and rebound. Not so Hawthorne. While Melville doubtless looped circles round him, tapping at him, trying to reach his mind from every side, Hawthorne crawled grimly along, his black tentacles drawn close in, his responses, if any, formal and monosyllabic. But even with his tentacles in, Hawthorne knew that he was being assailed by a unique and powerful, creative mind. It both delighted and frightened him. Gradually an external thunderstorm rolled up from the west and slowly crossed the mountain. The rain and lightning broke so suddenly that everybody ran for what rocky shelter he could find. Hawthorne and

Melville found themselves together in a crevice under a ledge that barely gave them both cover.

There for an hour Hawthorne was trapped, and the dark, shy recesses of his own soul began to open to the darker, deeper and franker recesses of Melville's. There is no doubt that during that hour a vast amorphic seed in Melville's imagination for the first time was fertilized and began to grow, and from subsequent events it seems probable that the same was true of Hawthorne. "I met Melville the other day," he wrote to his friend Bridge, "and liked him so much that I have asked him to spend a few days with me." Two days later Mr. and Mrs. Melville called and were treated to champagne and biscuits. About two weeks thereafter, both Melville and Hawthorne were hard at work.

Meanwhile Melville was forever "tumbling down in my pine-board chariot" from Pittsfield to Lenox. Una and Julian called him Mr. Omoo, and Julian loved to ride on the huge St. Bernard that he always brought along and that was such a good caricature of himself. On September 4th Mrs. Hawthorne wrote one of the most brilliant of her always vivid letters to her mother:

> Today, Mr. Hawthorne and Mr. Melville have gone to dine at Pittsfield. Mr. Tappan took them in his carriage. . . . This would have been no particular courtesy in some persons, but for this shy dear, who particularly did not wish, for some reason, to be introduced to Mr. Melville, it was very pretty. I have no doubt he will be repaid by finding Mr. Melville a very different man from what he imagines, and very agreeable and entertaining. We find him so. A man with a true, warm heart, and a soul and an intellect . . . with life to his fingertips; earnest, sincere, and reverent; very tender and *modest*. And I am not sure that he is not a very great man; but I have not quite decided upon my own opinion. I should say, I am not quite sure that *I do not think* him a very great man; for my opinion is, of course, as far as possible from settling the matter. He has very keen perceptive power; but what astonishes me is, that his eyes are not large and deep. He seems to see everything very accurately; and how he can do so with his small eyes, I cannot tell. They are not keen eyes, either, but quite undistinguished in any way. His nose is straight and rather hand-

some, his mouth expressive of sensibility and emotion. He is tall and erect, with an air free, brave, and manly. When conversing, he is full of gesture and force, and loses himself in his subject. There is no grace nor polish. Once in awhile, his animation gives place to a singularly quiet expression, out of these eyes to which I have objected; an indrawn, dim look, but which at the same time makes you feel that he is at that instant taking deepest note of what is before him. It is a strange, lazy glance, but with a power in it quite unique. It does not seem to penetrate through you, but to take you into himself. I saw him look at Una so, yesterday several times. He says it is Mr. Mathews who is writing in "The Literary World" the visit to Berkshire. Mr. Mathews calls Mr. Hawthorne "Mr. Noble Melancholy," in the next number of the paper. . . ."

Whether or not this reveals a difference of opinion between the Hawthornes about Melville, it is a clear indication that already Nathaniel at least had his reservations about this odd bird whom his wife "was not quite sure" she did not consider "a very great man."

But whatever worms may have been at Hawthorne's soul, he kept up his end of the friendship throughout this early period. Frequently he rode up to Arrowhead, where one of their practices was to lie in the hay in Melville's barn and discuss the universe, Hawthorne the unkempt artist with the wild, black hair, Melville the really wild man with the handsome face and bearing and the respectable beard. By the end of August both, while still in frequent communication, were well away on their new books, and Melville at least was sharing every turn of his story with his friend. The book Hawthorne was doing he would call *The House of the Seven Gables*. Melville would call his *Moby Dick*.

In that summer of 1850, literary "society" as usual centered around the Sedgwick houses, both in Stockbridge and in Lenox, and everybody appeared at one or the other with regularity except the lone bear in the Little Red House called Tanglewood, whom everybody called on whether he liked it or not, and the great lone whale in the big house called Arrowhead whom few if any called on though he might have appreciated it. A new arrival in Stockbridge was the successful English novelist G. P. R. James, a kindly and attractive man who had the assurance of the high second-rate. He dictated his novels to three or four secretaries simultaneously and was a vigorous snuff taker, being the last of the local literati so addicted, and to the last to carry a large red bandanna as a pocket handkerchief. He was one of the ominously increasing number of callers at the Little Red House, his companion being a big black Newfoundland which satisfied Julian as a horse even better than Mr. Omoo's brown one.

September passed and the piles of manuscript deepened at Tanglewood and at Arrowhead. The seasonal birds flew away, and gold and crimson autumn lay along the ranges of the valley. Melville called the eastern range across the river October Mountain, and the name has stuck. His friend Evert Duyckinck sent him from New York an occasional word of cheer and case of champagne.

October passed. The leaves blew away. The long, naked vistas of November opened to view the lesser valleys and secret nooks that summer hid. The first snow came and melted. More came and stayed. The piles of manuscript were formidable now, Melville still telling, and with increasing abandon, all the secrets of himself and his work to Hawthorne, Hawthorne telling Melville less and less at each meeting or exchange of letters.

January came and Hawthorne went at final correcting, with his wife's help. On the 27th he wrote the preface to *The House of the Seven Gables,* and that was that. By the middle of February the proofs were coming in. In March Ticknor and Fields published it, and the roar of applause began.

Hawthorne was now in good fettle, and he did not rest for long. Perhaps he built a few extra snowmen with the children, and at least once in this period he drove to Pittsfield to see Melville. But he was soon back at work, either on *The Wonder Book,* which he was to finish the following summer, or on any of several miscellaneous tasks. Among the latter was one he must have been busy on soon after *The*

Seven Gables appeared, a short story that stands in American letters as the type of tragedy of authors who are friends. While he was seeing Melville frequently and accepting his adulation, Hawthorne was planning and actually setting on paper a repudiation of him which, if Melville had known of it, might well in his then mood have brought the White Whale to an abortive end. Hawthorne at least did not personally reveal to Melville the murderous intent in his heart, and for this he can be thanked, for he was no coward and never secretive about his dislikes. But at the same time he was a creative artist, and what truth he saw he must set down. By May of that great year of '51 Melville could, if he had been unlucky, have read his own sentence to hell. But he did not see it. Privately, Hawthorne let him stay in his productive delusion. And the Great Whale churned on toward birth.

Melville's eventual destruction by Hawthorne was the necessary consequence of his incorrigible position as a noble savage against the world. To him Hawthorne was the good, kindly, intelligent, sympathetic external world he had always been looking for to complement his own imaginative power and absorb his passionate, profound, uncompromisable, fearless, defenseless demand for absolutes. Hawthorne was the first ear the world had turned to him that could hear the tragic secrets of man on earth, to which he could speak out of his vulnerable soul without reserve. Hawthorne was the first mind he had known that could understand, among other things, Melville himself. Throughout that autumn, winter and summer of their close acquaintance, it is plain that in his celebration of Hawthorne's genius he is at the same time usually celebrating himself. More precisely, he is celebrating the sad truth of the world that, so far as he knew, only they two could understand.

And Hawthorne's response was indeed that of the world, the external environment that he represented and for the moment justified to Melville. At the outset and for many months he did return appreciation and understanding of his young friend. There is no reason to doubt that in his deepest perceptions he agreed with his wife that Melville was "a very great man." But on the surface of Hawthorne's understanding and sympathy there was a shell of civilized, Salem wisdom to the effect that you must never look other than obliquely into the pit; that it was safe to acknowledge its existence, even to whiff and describe some of its upper vapors, but that having done so you must scamper back into the sunlight to lighten your mind with simple virtue and with play. Wherefore Hawthorne, while playing the friend to Melville, must keep his skirts clean of the stench of evil that exuded from the White Whale. It was as if he knew that he was its "only true begetter," but at the same time, at first privately and then before the world, he must deny the monster. He must announce that he knew it for an evil thing from the beginning, as any right-minded citizen of Salem would do. Hawthorne could snub the world. But, having declared his independence, he found that truly free souls, like Melville and Emerson, were too strong medicine for him.

Lenox and Stockbridge put on their summer green and their summer population of 1851. On the Fourth of July, G. P. R. James writes Hawthorne that Mrs. Charles Sedgwick sent him some bundles of her pupils' essays to correct and that "to give up reading *The House of the Seven Gables* for the purpose of reading a packet of seventy gabbles was like tearing the flesh from my bones." By the end of July, Melville had his manuscript in shape to show something he called "that book" to Hawthorne. Hawthorne commented on it with friendly reserve. And there followed one of the greatest and saddest letters in the world:

My dear Hawthorne,—
    People think that if a man has undergone any hardship, he should have a reward; but for my part, if I have done the hardest possible day's work, and then come to sit down in a corner and eat my supper comfortably—why, then I don't think I deserve any reward for my hard day's work—for am I not now at peace? Is not my supper good? My peace and my supper are my reward, my dear Hawthorne. So your joy-giving and exultation-breeding letter is not my reward for my ditcher's work with that book, but is the good goddess's bonus over and above what was stipu-

lated for—for not one man in five cycles, who is wise, will expect appreciative recognition from his fellows, or any of them. . . . Is love appreciated?

Your letter was handed to me last night on the road going to Mr. Morewood's, and I read it there. Had I been at home, I would have sat down at once and answered it. In me divine magnanimities are spontaneous and instantaneous. . . . So now I can't write what I felt. But I felt pantheistic then—your heart beat in my ribs and mine in yours, and both in God's. A sense of unspeakable security is in me this moment, on account of your having understood the book. I have written a wicked book, and feel spotless as the lamb. . . .

Whence come you, Hawthorne? By what right do you drink from my flaggon of life? And when I put it to my lips—lo, they are yours and not mine. I feel that the Godhead is broken up like the bread at the Supper, and that we are the pieces. Hence the infinite fraternity of feeling. Now, sympathizing with the paper, my angel turns over another page. You did not care a penny for the book. But, now and then as you read, you understood the pervading thought that impelled the book—and that you praised. Was it not so? You were archangel enough to despise the imperfect body, and embrace the soul. Once you hugged the ugly Socrates because you saw the flame in his mouth, and heard the rushing of the demon,—the familiar,—and recognized the sound, for you have heard it in your own solitudes.

My dear Hawthorne, the atmospheric skepticisms steal into me now, and make me doubtful of my sanity in writing you this. But, believe me, I am not mad, most noble Festus! But truth is ever incoherent, and when the big hearts strike together, the concussion is a little stunning. Farewell. Don't write a word about the book. That would be robbing me of my miserly delight. I am heartily sorry I ever wrote anything about you—it was paltry. Lord, when shall we have done growing? As long as we have anything more to do, we have done nothing. So, now, let us add Moby Dick to our blessing, and step from that. Leviathan is not the biggest fish; I have heard of Krakens.

This is a long letter, but you are not at all bound to answer it. Possibly, if you do answer it, and direct it to Herman Melville, you will missend it—for the very fingers that now guide this pen are not precisely the same that just took it up and put it on this paper. Lord, when shall we be done changing? Ah! it's a long stage, and no inn in sight, and night coming, and the body cold.

But with you for a passenger, I am content and can be happy. I shall leave the world, I feel, with more satisfaction for having come to know you. Knowing you persuades me more than the Bible of our immortality.

What a pity, that, for your plain, bluff letter, you should get such gibberish! Mention me to Mrs. Hawthorne and the children, and so, good-by to you, with my blessing.

Herman.

P.S. I can't stop yet. . . . [He goes on into a figure expressing his necessity to communicate with Hawthorne. Then he ends with the lover's pathetic combination of wile and fake declaration of independence.] P.P.S. Don't think that by writing me a letter, you shall always be bored with an immediate reply to it—and so keep both of us delving over the writing-desk eternally. No such thing! I shan't always answer your letters, and you may do just as you please.

What a letter for a mild, sensitive person like Hawthorne to receive! What ultimate criticism of "the book," of Melville himself, of Hawthorne! Mostly, what an expression of all the pantheistic exaltations, the groveling timidities, and tendernesses, the fond delusions and the swift, realistic perceptions of the lover! What a fetching down to date of the *Symposium*, in terms of works and men yet so familiar in the record that they might as well still be seen among us! Hawthorne of course could understand and was capable of feelings like those Melville reveals and glories in, only in his case they were subdued under gentle feelings, normal diluted feelings, such as enriched the everyday lives of his wife and children. They were not feelings which a good citizen of Salem could acknowledge otherwise than obliquely. Already, the previous May—though Melville was still unaware of it— Hawthorne had in print condemned his friend and all such destructive frankness. He had published in the *Dollar Magazine* a story called *Ethan Brand*, or the *Unpardonable Sin*. The unpardonable sin was the introverted overintellectualization of which Captain Ahab, and by inference Melville himself, had been guilty. Stealing some of Melville's own language from the early description of Ahab, Hawthorne sends

Ethan Brand on a long quest which terminates in the drying up of the springs of human love and the transformation of him into a fiend. It was a fair enough reportrayal of Ahab, but in so far as Ahab was a fictional character Melville had done him, and Hawthorne would not be interested in such a complete steal. It was Melville himself whom his beloved friend was identifying with evil and secretly flaying, Melville who two months and more after the appearance of the sentence of death could belie Hawthorne's charges with that letter of trust and affirmative love.

It is not known when Melville read *Ethan Brand*, and the fact that "the book" continued to its end without signs of an explosion implies that it was not until after publication, or at least completion. At about the time of the letter he took time off to build a piazza on the north side of Arrowhead, under his study window. Then he went to New York to see the beginning, the head, of Moby Dick through the press before he had created the tail. New York bored him and he returned to Arrowhead, driven now by the fury of the final chase. The chores of the farm again became too much for him, and he returned to New York where, writing to Hawthorne all the time, he finished the job in October in a third-story room, still a month and more ahead of the printers.

Meanwhile Hawthorne was getting increasingly restless in Lenox, the overt and sufficient reason being that he was daily more closely attacked by lion hunters to escape whom had been one of his reasons for coming there. "It is very singular," wrote Mrs. Hawthorne, "how much more we are in the center of society in Lenox than we were in Salem, and all literary persons seem settling around us. But when they get established here I dare say we shall take flight . . ."

Also, as he had predicted, Hawthorne was fed up with the static grandeur of the view and longed for the movement of the sea and the smell of dock mud. On the day that he received Melville's great letter he had sent off the finished *Wonder Book*. *The Blithedale Romance* was planned, but he shrank from tackling the work with another winter in the mountains in prospect. All of these are sufficient reasons to explain Hawthorne's departure from the valley. But we are left to wonder how much of the flight from "literary persons" was a flight from the naïve and lumbering affection of the wicked whale who could not let him alone.

Misanthrope that he was, it is difficult to find on Hawthorne's part any evidence of special friendliness toward any of the literary folk, great or small, who were increasingly swarming the hills and driving or riding up to his house for no purpose that he could see except to interrupt either his work or his play. He did seem to have a genuine affection for Longfellow. In fact—and this is a wholly gratuitous guess—Hawthorne may have felt toward Longfellow a smaller degree of the unrequited affection that Melville lavished on him. In May of '51 he writes Longfellow that he longs to see him and "I hear that you are coming to reside in Berkshire, and I wish with all my heart that you could make it your summer house." This was before Hawthorne had got Melville's effusive letter and had himself determined to move. Actually, Longfellow spent his summer vacation of '51, as he had spent that of '50, at Nahant on the ocean. Still he held on to the Oxbow, and did intend to build there.

Oustide of the absent Longfellow, Hawthorne surely cared little or nothing for his literary neighbors. Whatever he thought of Holmes, his fondness for him was hardly increased by a faux pas on the worldly little doctor's part when he drove up to Tanglewood one day, left a boy holding his horse, went into the house for some purpose, when he came out found Hawthorne himself holding his horse, and attempted a glittering Holmesism. "Is there another man in all America," quoth he, "who ever had so great an honor, as to have the author of *The Scarlet Letter* hold his horse?" This was in September, '51, almost a year and a half after the publication of *The Scarlet Letter* and six months after the appearance of another book of Hawthorne's which had been a greater success and which Hawthorne himself preferred. Perhaps Holmes was making a not too subtle comment on *The House of the Seven Gables*. More probably he had not read it and got befuddled about its title. In either case Hawthorne would be, not incensed, but bored.

At last, in November, the Hawthornes took their departure, and presently there appeared a new volume of *Twice-Told Tales,* and *The Blithedale Romance* was started. Melville at Arrowhead was left spiritually alone, while the Great Whale was slapping through the presses. Late in November it was published by Bentley in England, and a little later by Harper's in America. The criticism ranged from condescending to weakly favorable. The sales were disappointing. Melville knew he had done his best. Perhaps at this time he read *Ethan Brand* and came awake to Hawthorne's spiritual disloyalty. Without waiting to relax from the tension of *Moby Dick,* he plunged into *Pierre* which, like all of his subsequent work, was inferior to most of his earlier. From his old five-hour schedule he began to work all day, and without eating. The whisper increased that he was mad. Yet he was a long way from technically insane. For forty years more he turned out passable poetry and competent stories. But with the birth of *Moby Dick* and the flight of Hawthorne the best of him went out of this world.

The year 1851 was the apogee of literary production for the valley, with *Moby Dick, The House of the Seven Gables, The Wonder Book, Twice-Told Tales,* a few novels by G. P. R. James, a few poems by Holmes, Lowell and bevies of forgotten geniuses, Fanny Kemble's continuing journals, articles by Miss Sedgwick, and a golden treasury of correspondence back and forth from everybody to everybody. The magazine publication of *Uncle Tom's Cabin* in the same year was related to the valley only in so far as Mrs. Stowe was a native of Litchfield and later would be a seasonal visitor in Berkshire. For seventy years from this time the intellectual history of the valley is a clock running down, though it will never altogether cease to move. An event of this year cast into the future a legend which in the long run would help maintain the continuity of the tradition. The little minister Henry Martyn Field married in France and brought to Stockbridge the ex-governess Henriette Desportes whose alienation of her

charges from their mother had so closely paralleled the behavior of the governess put over Fanny Kemble's children by
their father Pierce Butler. Ninety years later Henry Martyn's
great-grandniece, Rachel Field, born in Stockbridge and
always faithful to it, would base an excellent novel, *All This,
and Heaven Too*, on her great-granduncle's successful sally
into the most un-Fieldlike society of France.

The year '52 passed without any important event or
production. In '53 Melville tried to get a consular appointment to the South Seas or anywhere, and failed. A fire in
Harper's destroyed the plates of all his books and most of
the books themselves. During the year his whole production
was two short stories. Longfellow's father-in-law, Nathan
Appleton, sold Elm Knoll in Pittsfield and "the old clock
on the stairs" went to his house in Boston. In '53 Harriet
Beecher Stowe published *The Minister's Wooing* whose hero
was Samuel Hopkins, the first minister of Great Barrington.
In the same year her brother, Henry Ward Beecher, who previously had summered in Salisbury, bought a hilltop farm
above Lenox Furnace, looking down on the river where "by a
mere roll of the eyeball I can look from Greylock on the
north to the dome of Taconic Mountains [i.e., Mt. Everett]
on the south, a range of sixty miles . . ." The Reverend Mr.
Beecher asserted proudly that he bought the place not to
work over but to "lie down upon"; nevertheless, during the
three or four summers he spent here he wrote the *Star Papers*.

In '53 Thoreau came to the edge of the valley, spending
a night in the observatory on top of Greylock, reading the
old country newspapers he found there, while mice ate his
shoes. That year the David Dudley Fields, Sr., were given a
golden wedding celebration by their children, of whom seven
were present, along with twenty-eight grandchildren and
great-grandchildren. A room was added to the house on
Stockbridge Main Street for the occasion, still known as the
Golden Wedding Room. David, Stephen, Matthew, Cyrus
and Henry were all well launched in their distinguished
careers. Cyrus's crackpot cable company had got a charter
to lay a cable to England. Matthew had built the famous

suspension bridge over the Tennessee River. Henry was now editor of the *Evangelist*, and he had his charming and dangerous Henriette at the family gathering. Jonathan had moved back to Stockbridge to live and was practicing law in the little office at the foot of the Prospect Hill Road. He was the only one of the six surviving brothers who was not destined to startle the world; but his son Stephen Dudley was already in college.

In '54 Melville was producing better, but with none but commercial purposes. Fanny Kemble went to England to be at her dying father's bedside. In '55 Melville had an attack, reportedly of sciatica developing out of chronic rheumatism contracted through early exposure, especially while rounding the Horn. Dr. Holmes came up the road to attend him, but did not think it essential to leave to the world any diagnosis or general appraisal of this strange genius. Since Holmes was shortly to begin contributing the *Autocrat* papers to the almost-born *Atlantic*, it is reasonable to assume that he was at work on them this summer. Also he probably wrote in Pittsfield and about this time *The Wonderful One-Hoss Shay*. The shay in question had been built some time before 1814. At this time the big two-wheeled vehicle was the property of one Amasa Rice of Pittsfield, and Holmes often visited it, not only contemplating it but taking measurements. It was indeed an impressive work, being all of wood except for the axle ends and a few bolts, and having magnificent wooden springs, big wheels, embroidered upholstery, and a top of leather so heavy it will still swing up without cracking. Perhaps the reason for Holmes's frequent inspections of it was that he did expect it someday to disintegrate before his eyes. If so he was disappointed, for, enjoying a protected retirement in the Pittsfield Museum, it still shows no signs of collapsing. Though he did not know it then, when Holmes drove out of his gate that September he looked back at the house and the pine and the Canoe Meadows for the last time, ending what he later called "the seven happiest summers of my life."

In '56 Melville, having long before finished his north

piazza, published *Piazza Tales*. After that he slumped into a sense of failure and refused to be drawn into talk about the sea or philosophy or anything that used to be his lifeblood. He went abroad and to Liverpool, where Hawthorne was now a consul. He called on him and they had a last walk together along a gusty sea beach. Melville raised all the old questions—Time, Eternity, Free Will—and as always he got sympathy but no answer. They parted, never to meet again.

In '56 Fanny Kemble returned to the Perch from Europe, and her Sally, now twenty-one and free of the divorce decree, came to visit her and went on tour with her in the fall. Longfellow bought another strip of land in the Oxbow of the river, almost completing his ownership of the peninsula in Stockbridge. In '57 he wrote interestedly to his caretaker about finances, repairs and the color of the paint to be put on the barn. Still he came there little if at all, and when he came he stayed in the old farmhouse and showed no sign of building. The dramatic event of '56 was the death of Charles, the last of the Sedgwick brothers of that generation, the last of Catherine's beloved brothers, beloved also by both the high-brows and the low-brows of the county, for thirty-five years clerk of the courts of Berkshire.

In '58 Melville was lecturing regularly, and his health was poor. Fanny Kemble's Sally married Owen Wister of Philadelphia. The other daughter Fan came of age. Though she was always on good terms with her mother, her sympathies were with her father and the South. In '58 Cyrus Field's company completed the cable to England; Queen Victoria and President Buchanan exchanged felicitations, there were numerous celebrations and messages, and after a few weeks the line went dead. Cyrus started again.

In '60 Melville went on a sea voyage with his young brother Tom. By the death and will of his father-in-law, Judge Shaw, he got a clear title to Arrowhead. Melville and Hawthorne reacted typically to The War. Melville went into ecstasies about freedom. Hawthorne said the North and South always were two different peoples and he welcomed the secession.

Fanny Kemble spent the winter of 1860-61 at the Perch, the thermometer once touching thirty-two below. In the spring she went to New York and did miscellaneous volunteer work. Her Sally had a baby boy, Owen Wister, Jr., who was going to make his mark. Fanny and her daughter Fan went abroad, where for almost two years she was oppressed by the preference of the English for the South and the callous attitude toward slavery. During her one winter on her husband's plantation she had kept a "Georgia Journal" in which she had recorded with awful literalness the horrors of slavery which he saw under a not excessively cruel planter and overseer. In '63 she published it, as deliberate propaganda, in May in England and in July in New York. There is no doubt that it caused a stir in England, for anything Fanny Kemble wrote or did was news in the highest circles. It is possible, though, that when her biographers imply that *Georgia Journal* was chiefly responsible for England's final rejection of the idea of recognizing the South, they may be guilty of overenthusiasm. After all, Gettysburg was only six weeks after the English publication and a few weeks before the American.

In this same year of '63 Melville finished his long turn in the valley. He swapped Arrowhead for his brother Allan's house in New York and moved back to the city. In the same year Stephen Johnson Field went from chief judge of the Supreme Court of California to the Supreme Court of the United States.

In '65 David Dudley Field completed the revision of the civil and criminal codes of New York and the legislature accepted his work, thus superseding the common law. In '66 Cyrus again got a cable across the Atlantic. This time they had rigged up a special line to the little law office of Jonathan Edwards Field in Stockbridge. Henry Martyn was the lucky one who happened to be there when the message came in, before the official one to Washington, the first message of the intercontinental cable service which has never since been interrupted. At one of the parties for Cyrus in New York Mrs. Cyrus said audibly to the lovely Henriette, wife of Henry Martyn, "Where is dear Henry?" Said Henriette in the same audible tone, "Dear Henry is upstairs writing dear Cyrus's speeches." In this year of '66 Melville got a customs job in New York and fades off into twenty-five years of physical life in mediocrity.

The literary age of the valley was now definitely over. Holmes, Melville and Hawthorne were gone for good. In the fall of '67 Longfellow sold the Oxbow and ended his seventeen years of equivocation about building there. There remained only the fitting resolution of the play, and then the epilogue in the form of a recessional diminishing into silence. Catherine Sedgwick had, more than anyone else, been the heart of the period, the one who, while making her contribution to the general output, was also the only one who was entirely local in feeling, who, though she wintered in New York, yet always thought of Stockbridge and Lenox as home and entertained all comers as the literary hostess of the Berkshires. As she had opened the era, it was proper that she put the period on it. Within her family, which was the center of her world, she had outlived all her brothers and sisters and all their wives and husbands. She died in Lenox on July 31, 1867. "Early in my acquanitance with Miss Sedgwick," wrote Fanny Kemble Butler, "my admiration for her became affection, and the love and respect with which I soon learned to regard her increased and deepened to the end of our intercourse. Her memory remains to me as that of one of the most charming, most amiable, and most excellent persons I have ever known."

Mrs. Butler herself had now given up Lenox as her center, for at fifty-eight she no longer found it necessary to invite death "from a good horse at a full gallop on a fine day." This year of '67 Pierce Butler died, which removed the last shadow from her intimacy with both her daughters. Henceforth she lived with or near one or the other of them for the rest of her life. Fan was now married to an Englishman, and all of them lived with equal ease on either side of the Atlantic. In '73 Mrs. Butler sold the Perch, but she continued to come for a few years to the Curtis Hotel for a while in the summers, and Bret Harte was prominent in her drawing room there. In '75 Charlotte Cushman built a modest cottage near the Center, but she died the next year, and it is doubtful whether she and Fanny Kemble were there together. Fanny learned to type out her memoirs for the *Atlantic* on an odd little printing press which you manipulated merely by pressing the lettered keys. In '77 she took her last look at the Berkshires and crossed the ocean for the eighteenth and last time. She insisted on going back to the Alps, and, recalling her earlier wish to die by breaking her neck from a fine horse at a full gallop, she expressed a new one: "Surely if I had been a man I should have lived on a peak, died in a crevice, and been buried in an avalanche."

The first literary period of the valley was also the early Victorian period, and all of the group were Victorians except the greatest of them, Melville, who was without age. Dr. Holmes was the most Victorian of them all, the most elegant in wit, the most worldly, the most effusive in sentimentality. As it was fitting for Miss Sedgwick to ring down the curtain on the local play, it was fitting that Holmes should recite the epilogue and outlive all the rest. His last word is contained in a series of excerpts from his letters. In 1880, declining an invitation to speak at a banquet of Berkshire journalists, he writes: "Seven of the happiest summers of my life were passed in Berkshire with the Housatonic running through my meadows and Greylock looking into my study windows." In '85, now seventy-six years old, he writes to a personal friend: "It seems too bad to take away the town's [Pittsfield's] charming characteristics; but such a healthful, beautiful, central situation could not resist its destiny: and you must have a mayor, aldermen and common council. But Greylock will remain, and you cannot turn the course of the Housatonic. I cannot believe that it is thirty years since I said 'Good-bye', expecting to return the next season. As we passed the gate under the maple which may stand there now, we turned and looked at the house and at the Great Pine which stood—and I hope it still stands—in its solitary grandeur and beauty; passed the two bridges to the railroad station—and, Good-bye, Dear Old Folks!"

In '93 he is close to eighty-four. Three years before, on June 6, 1890, Hawthorne's Little Red House had burned down. Melville, the next to the last of the old literary crowd, had died in '91. "Dear old Pittsfield!" writes Holmes. "Shall I ever have spunk enough to take another look at it? It would be both a pleassure and a poignant ache. The old outlines are there. The trees I planted would look kindly down upon me. But alas! how much would be missing! And then, you are getting so grand and New Yorky, I should be lost in its splendor and wealth."

July 24, 1894—he is two weeks short of eighty-five: "It tires me to write now. I cannot give your letters to my secretary. My eyes are dim—my fingers crampy.—Were I forty years old, instead of three-score and twenty-four, I would try to buy my old place, *just as it was,* and be once more your summer neighbor. My habits are fixed. I am ill. Write and aid my convalescence with a lively manifesto from our blessed city of Pittsfield. The pendulum has a very short range of oscillation." Five months later it ceased to oscillate.

The Falling of the Idols

O F ALL THE niggardly preparation the Lord made for His Chosen People in New England, the most niggardly was in the Naugatuck Valley, just over the divide to the east from the Housatonic. It was a pretty valley originally, of diminutive dimensions. But its little rocky hills were too steep to hold the soil, and its river had never been large enough to smooth out a wide, central plain where the earth could settle and be fertile. It was an early saying that "You couldn't grow a nettle in the Naugatuck Valley."

Moreover, the mineral resources of the region did not exist. The water power was negligible in comparison to that of the Housatonic Valley. And railroad transportation was ten to twenty years later in getting through. Yet from 1820 to 1870 the people of the Naugatuck Valley solved their difficult problem by developing what continues to be the greatest brass industry in the world, along with dozens of other manufactures that brought true for them the prophecies of the new Patersons and Lowells that had originally been made—and with reason—for the Housatonic Valley.

In the same period of 1820-1870, the industrialization of the Housatonic reached an early fruition and declined. The closing by 1850 of the twenty-three marble quarries in Washington, Connecticut, was ominous. By 1855 the industry was dead also in Sheffield, Egremont and West Stockbridge. Huge blocks from the quarries at the last-named place were left piled beside the railroad, vainly waiting to be loaded. Within a few years the marble works at Lenox, Pittsfield and Lanesboro likewise were abandoned. An old quarryman, accounting for the death of the industry in his town, said with finality, "Quarrying stopped at West Stockbridge because Italian and Vermont marbles were better and cheaper." As to "better," the remarkable durability of the West Stockbridge marble front on the New York City Hall might be put in evidence. As to "cheaper," the statement is absurd. The West Stockbridge quarries were on the Hudson & Berkshire Railroad, a short haul from tidewater at Hudson. Each of the other Housatonic quarries could have been reached by a railroad spur of six miles or less.

The fact that the Housatonic quarries never developed modern methods of quarrying is a result, not a cause. If they had been profitable, and had there been a will to continue them, they would have adopted modern methods. Why they did not do so, why one after another their great white cliffs were left to vines and erosion, that is part of the major mystery of the Housatonic Valley. The big quarry at Lee is still running profitably. Otherwise, the only remaining industrial exploitations of the "marble bed" of the Housatonic, still hardly scratched, are the lime works and the gypsum plant in North Canaan.

Of more importance than the decline of marble was that of iron, because, while marble might here and there blanch a village or a cluster of farms with ghostly dust, it was iron that carried the high promise of burying the valley under soot, slum-filthy cities and piles of slag. The deliberate demolition of the Lakeville furnace in 1843 and the "freezing" and abandonment of that at Mt. Riga in '47 have been mentioned as significant events, especially significant because they were the work of Alexander Hamilton Holley, third in the dynasty of Salisbury, and reputedly the biggest ironman in the valley.

The fifties and sixties were dramatic as representing the climax, the turning point, in the competition between ideas and greed, the Lord and the Devil, for possession of the valley. In '51 the big ironworks of Horatio Ames at Falls Village is said to have been employing eight hundred men, and in spite of the loss of the two old Salisbury furnaces, the industry was at its zenith. But in that same year literature likewise made its strongest gesture. Pittsfield put out *Moby Dick* and several poems of Holmes; Stockbridge and Lenox produced *The House of the Seven Gables, The Wonder Book* and numerous items of secondary importance. This blast of literature seems to have left the iron industry groggy. Throughout the fifties Melville, Holmes, Lowell, Miss Sedgwick, Beecher, James and others continued to roll up the score. In the same decade six new iron furnaces[1] were built; but two of them[2] went out of blast within two years, while six of the older furnaces[3] were abandoned. The volume of nocturnal flame from the valley's chief industry was not quite holding its own with the flicker of notable candles and midnight oil.

The Civil War was an artificial stimulant to iron. The 10- and 12-inch Rodman and Columbiad cannon manufactured at South Boston and the big Parrott guns made at West Point both used Salisbury iron. The Richmond Iron Company made cannon and so much of the iron plating for the navy's monitors that its mine became known as the Monitor Mine. Horatio Ames invented and manufactured in his works at Falls Village what, in '64, a military and naval board found to be the strongest guns ever made. He proved them by shooting shells into the hill back of the plant, thus bringing the war home to the natives. The Ames guns were appreciated by the army and navy too late in the war to justify a large order, and Ames had invested so much in special machinery to produce them that he failed. His big plant went out of business, was subsequently sold to the Housatonic Railroad for repair shops, and was eventually abandoned and torn down. In spite of the stimulant of the war, no

[1] The Benedict and one of the Millerton Iron Company at Millerton, New York, the Pomeroy and two of the Berkshire Iron Company of West Stockbridge, and the Weed furnace at Sharon.

[2] The Benedict and one of those of the Berkshire Iron Company.

[3] The Briggs at Lanesboro (the one Longfellow admired), two of the Stockbridge Iron Works at Housatonic, the Buena Vista at Huntsville in Canaan, the Beckley in East Canaan, the Dover Station at Dover Furnace, New York.

new furnaces were built in the sixties, but the big Macedonia furnace in Kent went out of blast in '65.

The gradual abandonment of the rest of the valley's forty-odd furnaces continued through the nineteenth century and into the twentieth. At some time in the seventies the Lenox mine, which was in the Center, though the furnace was down on the river, undercut a house on Main Street until one fine day it solemnly settled to the second story. The Lenox works was abandoned in '81. Half a dozen others were also abandoned in the eighties. Another half dozen in the nineties. And so it went.

The demise of the Roxbury mine was farcical. It was just beginning to work profitably with modern methods, when the ghost of a former company that had abandoned a lease rose to claim the profits it had not earned. The rails of the little ore cars were soon snarled in litigation and have remained so for about sixty years. The heir of the property recently tore down part of the excellent retaining wall of the furnace to build a modern library for the town. The Columbia School of Mines now uses the property for demonstration purposes.

By the time of World War I only Canaan No. 3 Furnace in East Canaan and the Richmond Iron Company were still doing business. By chance, and for different reasons, these last vestiges of a once great industry closed in the same year, 1923. In Salisbury, where the Ore Hill of two centuries before had been replaced by a conversely huge hollow, the pumps stopped for the first time in a century and a half, and a million dollars' worth of machinery slowly disappeared under a lake fifty feet deep. But for the little constellations of village windows, the nights over the valley went back to darkness and the vigil of the stars. Only a few of the more than forty furnaces that once roared in the valley have been torn down. Most of the old stone towers, shorn of their one-time wooden housings, still stand on their abandoned premises in varying degrees of ruin at the hands of frost and rain. The Mt. Riga furnace, granddaddy of them all, sprouted an enormous mane of hanging grass that transformed it into a colossal lion's head, an object of curiosity and whispers of backwoods superstition for miles around. Typically, the rest are surrounded by the rust and rot of village dumps and by groves whose age is the measure of the time since they last poured red. They are all cold now, and funereally crowned with soil brought by the wind, and with drooping grass and goldenrod and weeds.

Along with the decline of iron and marble went the gradual failure of most of the miscellaneous factories that for a time had flourished along the river in the main valley between Pittsfield and Derby. One by one the manufacturers of shoes, hats, buttons, shears, textiles, pottery, farm implements, and the rest of life's gadgets succumbed to bigger, mass production mills in Pittsfield, Derby, Danbury and great cities outside the valley. The Lenox Glass Works, to be sure, was in the mass production category, claiming to be the largest factory in the world under one roof. It first failed in '72, was bought in the nineties by Theodore Roosevelt I, father of the president, and operated unsuccessfully for a few years. Today, what is left of the big building is a flattened and filled foundation beside the railroad and the river, where children still pick up contorted whorls of discarded glass. What remains of its machinery is sometimes grotesquely visible in the river, where it was jettisoned.

A less complete and more picturesque ruin is that of the once large and booming Bridgeport Wood Finishing Company which adorns the spectacular natural scene in New Milford where the Still flows into the main river just above the Great Falls and the Lover's Leap Rapids. In the 1920's this plant was bought by du Pont, and presently demolished. A part of one wall with large openings, suggesting a classical colonnade, remains under a load of vines. Beside it at intervals lie the big, broken millstones that used to grind the silex for the wood filler. With the rumble of the falls that used to turn its shafts, the ruin seems a symbol of man's failure to translate natural into industrial power in the valley.

The summary record of the failure of industry in the valley is contained in the fact that its railroad never carried

THE GREAT FALLS, FALLS VILLAGE

enough freight to show a profit. From the time in the forties
when the Housatonic line lost to the New Haven & Hartford
the franchise to extend to New York, it was a frail enterprise,
operated by trustees for the stockholders. In spite of its example, railroad building continued in the valley, and the story
of the main local line continues well into the next period. In
'71 the Connecticut Western Railroad, later part of the Central New England, passed through Salisbury and Canaan and
connected with Rhinebeck on the Hudson. In '72 work was
started on the Shepaug line from Newtown across the river
and in through Roxbury and Washington for forty miles
with 147 curves to Litchfield.

But already the main Housatonic Railroad was in its
death throes as an independent line. In 1889 its President
Starbuck, Wall Street banker, got a hearing in Hartford
on a petition to run a line from Norwalk to New York parallel to that of the New York, New Haven & Hartford.
Mr. Starbuck complained pathetically of the horrors of the
New Haven's monopoly, but the whole proceeding smacks of
an effort to run up the value of the Housatonic stock and
compel the New Haven to buy. The petition failed, and with
it the last financial hope of the valley's railroad. In 1892
the New York, New Haven & Hartford leased it, and in '98
bought it, maintaining it thereafter as a luxury line, a mere
branch that justifies itself financially only during the summer vacation period, but must be maintained on a skeleton
schedule under the carrier's duty to the public. The New
Haven likewise bought the Shepaug in 1898 and the old
Connecticut Western in 1904, gradually reducing the service
on each to the present state of virtual abandonment, with
grass growing between the rusty rails.

For the failure of any particular furnace, foundry,
quarry, factory, railroad or other business in the valley, plausible immediate causes can usually be found—some form of
incompetence, some kind of hard luck. But why the *whole region*, highly blessed with resources and transportation, should
fail at the time when all the rest of the East was developing,
that broad question remains a mystery which no ordinary

reason seems to answer. Several efforts have been made to explain the failure of the whole iron business, the largest local industry; but none of the reasons given stands close examination. It is generally supposed that the ore ran out; but actually it has never been determined whether the subterranean veins at the more productive mines have been exhausted or not. A second reason suggested is that, once the surface ore was gone, modern machinery was never introduced to make it possible to work profitably the underground veins; but this begs the question, for there was nothing to prevent the introduction of modern machinery if anyone had had the enterprise to do it. A more impressive explanation is the failure of fuel, that is, charcoal, which means forests. Yet, when I offered this explanation to the best qualified local ironman I could find, he assured me that fuel need not have destroyed the business, in spite of the axiom that it is cheaper to haul ore to fuel than fuel to ore. He insisted that reforestation would have provided a constant supply of charcoal, sufficient to maintain production a little below the peak; and that a very little addition of imported coke or coal would have maintained high and profitable production.

The one explanation which everyone agrees had something to do with the decline of iron in the valley was the discovery of the Bessemer process. Under this method, especially as improved in America, low-grade, cheap ore could be made into steel as well as Salisbury's high-grade ore. On the principle that the supply of fuel, not of ore, determines the location of the plant, it would seem inevitable that the Pittsburg area, once it was armed with the steel formula, should become the center of the industry to which the cheap, still surface-mined, low-grade ore could be shipped from the shores of Lake Superior.

But even this explanation fails of persuasive finality. While it was true that the Mesabi ore was cheaper to mine, being still found in quantity near the surface, yet it had to be shipped by boat to Cleveland, then transshipped for a railroad journey to Pittsburg about the equal of that from

Salisbury. It is hard to believe that proper deep mining in the Salisbury region would have cost as much per ton as did the thousand miles of extra transportation from upper Lake Superior, plus the cost of transfer to the railroad at Cleveland. One mine in the valley, the Millerton, did profitably ship ore to Pennsylvania, but it was a small mine and was exhausted in 1915. Why could not the big mines, the Davis and Ore Hill, have done and still be doing the same thing?

Another objection to the notion that it was the Bessemer process that destroyed mining in the valley is even more obvious. The early steel plants were not all concentrated in Pittsburg or anywhere else. They were mostly small plants, and many of them were set up at scattered points where somebody was willing to make the necessary investment, and for some of them *both ore and fuel* had to be hauled in from outside. Why, the main question remains, was no such early plant established in the valley, in the presence of plenty of ore and almost enough fuel? Why did the heirs of the half dozen big fortunes already made out of Salisbury iron turn their attention elsewhere and let the land that enriched them return to a state of agriculture, even a state of nature?

I am examining rather fully the possible causes of the failure of iron in the valley, because what I take to be the real cause may support a historical thesis that would explain the unique resistance of the whole Housatonic region to the forces of industry. This thesis would be that the forces of idealism—in this case the readapted Puritan, or Yankee, tradition—may sometimes triumph over those economic forces which modernly are supposed to control history. Where there is a state of general poverty and hunger, doubtless the economic forces will triumph. Also, even though the poor are not suffering acutely from want, yet if the display of wealth above them is very great indeed, their vanity may conquer their idealism and lead them to emulate it. But where there is little real want, and where the wealthier people are few or not much wealthier than the rest, then, it would appear from the history of the Housatonic, that the forces of idealism may prevail.

Throughout the general population, the "ideas" that resisted the new industries were a few simple Yankee and human
prejudices. First, there was the deep prejudice of an ancient
agrarian society against working for wages, and the contempt
for any able-bodied man who did. Second, while there was
no prejudice against making money, and admiration undoubt-
erly existed for any particularly clever deal that fetched in
some profit, yet there was a profound suspicion—partly a
jealousy, but mostly something democratic, a recollection connected with the British—of anybody who really *had* and held
a lot of wealth in the bank; it was a condition somehow alien
to the known agrarian virtues; certainly it was a bad thing
to inherit such money, and any youngster who did was certain to turn out no good. Third, as a corollary there was the
prejudice against "foreigners," in this case the original Swiss
and Lithuanians and the later Dutch and English brought it
to run the furnaces, and the Irish to build and run the railroads—all of course made necessary because the Yankees
wouldn't work for wages. Add these three prejudices together, and combine them with a little leadership, either by
village improvement societies that wanted to save their baili-
wicks or by enlightened individuals who wanted to save the
whole valley, and you will get a conservative deadweight,
quietly resisting the developments.

But after all, Yankee prejudices and enlightened leadership were not limited to the Housatonic Valley. There must
have been local conditions that favored the triumph of idealistic over economic motives there. What these conditions were
is evident from a comparison of the Housatonic with the
Naugatuck Valley which, as already observed, was by the
nineteenth century a rocky desert whose farms had gone
down the swift little river to Derby and the sea. The people
had either to emigrate or to find other than the old agrarian
methods of survival. Here the economic motive was so strong
that it overcame the idealistic one. The first-rate minds of
Waterbury, Naugatuck, Thomaston, Torringford and the
rest were compelled to set to work to build up local enterprises at the expense of all other interests in life; and the

people rushed in to work for them in the mills, because hunger was more persuasive than prejudice.

In contrast, the economic compulsion into industry in the Housatonic Valley was almost nonexistent. Though most of the upland farms had run down into the valleys, yet these were wide and flat between the distant hills, and still afforded support for a large agrarian population. With the West and the cities drawing off the surplus, those who remained settled into a comfortable, almost a voluptuous subsistence economy, rich with cider and applejack and every imaginable viand and vegetable and local wine. There was time on Saturday night and Sunday to exchange prejudices and other ideas round the cracker barrel with the independence that goes with the guarantee of a full belly. This was a farming population that still admired book learnin' and could afford to traffic in ideas, ideas of politics and theology and the Union and slavery, ideas about that book the Litchfield minister's daughter wrote, ideas about these books people were writing up in Stockbridge and Pittsfield, ideas about still other books that people outside the valley were writing, ideas about cities and railroads and factories, and conclusions that we who live here can do as well without these newfangled riggins, whose purpose is money, and the foreigners with their strange ways who come in to run them. The Housatonic Valley was not a place where the leading minds would find much impetus into iron and factories. Rather, if they were factory minded, they would be aware of the local opposition, and like as not would look outside the valley to apply their bent. The element of necessity was not present, and ideas, abetted in some cases by a love of the land and its beauty, were stronger than the stark itch for power.

It is only upon some such basis as this that it is possible to explain the conduct of a particular native son of the valley, who, precisely in the critical period in the struggle between the Lord and the Devil for local control, was perhaps the best qualified man in the United States to build up a great industry, especially an iron or steel industry. This was Alexander Lyman Holley, son of Alexander Hamilton Holley and fourth in the Salisbury iron dynasty, without question America's leading metallurgist and mining engineer of the period, himself the inheritor of a great iron fortune and having easy access to unlimited capital among his friends, a great inventor, a man of enterprise, leadership and the "vision" of an industrial genius. Add the great personal charm which he possessed, the complete devotion to science and industry to the exclusion of self-interest, the literary talent which clarified his epoch-making reports, and Holley emerges as one of the paragons of his day. If he had wanted to develop his home town, as he did many others, by installing the latest methods in mining, smelting and transportation, he was the best qualified man in the world to do it.

Holley was born in Salisbury in '32, and in boyhood learned the machinist's trade while being given classical preparation for Yale. By his own preference he did not go to Yale, but took a scientific course at Brown, where he graduated in '53. For a year thereafter he worked as an engineer, a real, locomotive engineer, on the Stonington Railroad, and it was during this period that he won his famous bet that he could drive a locomotive for a level mile without fire, water or steam. A condition was that he and his cold engine be hauled some way out to a level stretch, and while this was being done young Holley, innocently riding in the cab, adjusted the valves so that the cylinders were charging the boiler with compressed air.

His career as a scientific writer began with some articles in '55. In '56 he bought the *Railway Advocate* and edited it for a year. In '57 he went abroad to study railroads and his book, *European Railways*, published in '58, effected many changes in America, including the introduction of coal-burning locomotives. For the next two years he acted as a technical correspondent for the New York *Times*, being sometimes in America and sometimes abroad, acting during part of the time also as an editor of the *American Railway Review*, crossing the Atlantic on the maiden voyage of the famous *Great Eastern*, prophesying immediately thereafter that screw-driven ships would replace side-wheelers, all the

time preparing his *Railway Practice,* which was published in
'60 and became standard, and incidentally composing about a
thousand engineering definitions and several hundred illustra-
tions for Webster's Dictionary. (Where all this time was
the needed little railroad from the Hudson over the mountains to Salisbury and the valley, the little railroad that somebody else built presently and called the Conneciticut
Western?)

At the outbreak of the Civil War Holley, already at
twenty-nine having the highest position among civil engineers, offered his services to the government and was ignored.
By a lucky stroke of fate Edwin A. Stevens of the "Stevens
Battery" sent him abroad to investigate ordnance and armor.
The resulting *Treatise on Ordnance and Armor* remained
standard on the subject for many years. But the importance
of this turn in his career was the direction of his chief
attention upon metallurgy. In '63 a Troy iron company sent
him back to England to look into the new Bessemer steel
processes.

His relations with Sir Henry Bessemer remained always
cordial and intimate. Holley suggested acceptable improvements to him, and bought his patents for use in America. In
'65 he built the first experimental steel plant at Troy, New
York, and improved it in '67. In the same year he built
the Harrisburg, Pennsylvania, works and superintended their
use for two years. Subsequently he planned the works at
North Chicago and Joliet, the Edgar Thomson works at
Pittsburgh, the Vulcan works at St. Louis. This was what I
called the critical period when the Salisbury region might
have blackened into Pittsburg. What was Holley up to,
enriching Troy and the West, neglecting his home town
where he frequently spent long periods in his father's house,
neglecting the whole valley with its moderate supply of fuel
and its iron superior to that available to any of these outlying
furnaces?

Immediately after his initial practical experience with
steel in '65, Holley surpassed the English methods in facility
of operation and quantity of output. He continued to im-

prove the methods of steel production while he lived, and was greatly beloved in his profession, forever being president or vice-president of one or other of the engineering societies. After much difficulty he overcame a native shyness and grew to be a witty speaker. At a big banquet for him in Pittsburg, in acknowledging a handsome testimonial that was given him, he said extempore:

Among us all who are working hard in our noble profession and are keeping the fires of metallurgy aglow, such occasions as this should also kindle a flame of good fellowship and affection which will burn to the end.

Burn to the end! Perhaps some of us should think of that, who are burning the candle at both ends. Ah! well, may it so happen to us that when at last this vital spark is oxidized, when this combustible has put on incombustion, when this living fire flutters thin and pale at the lips, some kindly hand may turn us down, not underblown—by all means not overblown—some loving hand may turn us down, and that we may perhaps be cast in a better mold.

That was in '79, and Holley undoubtedly had his suspicions already. A year later he almost died in London. In '82 he did die, overwork being the basic cause. His pallbearers were the leading editors, educators and industrialists of metallurgy in America.

It is not possible to say with certainty why Holley neglected the local industry that had made the fortune he inherited, why, when he went to England to study and buy the Bessemer patents, he was willing to represent the Troy company rather than the iron producers of his home region. Knowing the revolution he had in his pocket, and being at bottom a railroad man, he did nothing to complete the little farther transportation that the valley needed. With his resources and connections, he could have inaugurated a system of forest conservation by which his home region could have been kept in moderate production; and he could have transformed a sufficient number of the old iron furnaces into steel furnaces. But instead of doing any of these things, he developed half a dozen big and little plants elsewhere, and let the fairest industrial hope of the valley die.

Always on the lookout for the real reason for the failure of Salisbury iron, I got what seems the best answer when I asked a surviving kinsman of Holley's who remembered him. "Why," he said, spreading his hands as if it were obvious, "Cousin Alexander killed it."

And why, then, did he kill it? To that nobody has a certain answer. Possibly, for his own secret reasons he did not want a Pittsburg or a Youngstown in his home valley. He was certainly a man of sentiment. It is a reasonable guess that he loved his old town. Let the smoke and the battle for money go somewhere else.

As already suggested, the reason why the people of the valley could neglect the oportunities of industry was that their own population was now stably adjusted to the capacity of the soil to feed them. When a family outgrew the old farm, both its most and its least enterprising youngsters would wander off to the omnipresent lure of the new cities or the new West. Likewise, when the hilltop farms and settlements were at last eroded down to rock, the emigrants from them did not crowd the good farms in the valleys but set out to find better farms beyond the sunset. The result of this steady movement out of the valley from the higher, often the older, settlements was a general decrease in population. In the agricultural, central stretch between Pittsfield and Derby, the population had been comparatively stable after the readjustments, both of emigration and of immigration, that followed the Revolution. In 1800 it had been 50,-039 for the thirty-seven towns. In the forties and fifties the increase in both industrial and literary activity caused a jump to a peak of 62,471 in 1860. From that time, with the failure of local industry, along with Vanity Fair's invasion of the Berkshires, driving out the Yankees, there was a steady decline till 1920 when the figure of 51,332 was close to that of 1800. After 1920 new forces began to fill the region, till at 60,761 in 1940 it was almost at the maximum of the mid-nineteenth century. This apparently is the healthy saturation point for the valley.

By 1870, the desertion of the old hill settlements was well under way. In 1848-1850 Kent had built its new church at the new Center on the railroad, and in the original settlement up in the hills, already called Flanders, the steeple was pulled off the pre-Revolutionary church with ropes and the church demolished.

In Cornwall's Dudleytown there were only three or four farms left where there had been three or four dozen. Gables were sagging around chimneys. Some buildings had already fallen into their cellar holes and been collected for firewood by the half-wild remnant of population. Thousands of cleared acres were going back to brush. In the village of Cornwall Bridge, at the foot of the Dark Entry Road that came down through the perpetual night of the great ravine, the legends of Dudleytown ghosts were already growing.

Dodgetown in Lenox was entirely a ghost village of walls and cellar holes, already gone back through the brush phase into "weed forest" of poplar and birch.

From Washington Township to the northeast, where the railroad crossed the divide, the descendants of the first settlers had left the bleak region to the Irish immigrants who had come in to build the railroad, and some of them had now settled as railroad men, handling the switching at that point where the booster engines left the trains.

On the bleak summit of Mt. Riga, whence the keeper of the famous department store had carried off $200,000 when Holley and Coffing had let the furnace die, the old Pettee mansion still stood, and the now useless dam still held back the lake. Back in the tall brush the families of the old furnace men who had refused to give up hope were being wrought into that special race of proud, cunning, and essentially honorable wild animals known as "Raggies." There were only eight or ten families of them—mostly Dutch or English importees—and already they were inbreeding as rapidly as possible. Half sheltered still in their shacks hidden in the bush around the great, decaying furnace, they subsisted by a little farming on the barely existent soil, much hunting and fishing at all seasons, and some artisanship—usually first-rate carpentry—for the more fortunate citizens down in the valley. It was possible but difficult to make them accept gifts. They would never fail to steal liquor and small sums of money, and they were never known to commit any greater crime, except incest. Their sexual relations were extremely vague, and one old character went so far as to swap his wife for a cow. During the Civil War they were either very patriotic or very adventurous, for the number of G.A.R. flags in the little Mt. Riga cemetery is far out of proportion to its size. The Frink family contributed seven brothers.

A typical story is that of the Salisbury man who hired a Raggie to do some extensive carpentry in his cellar, and congratulated himself that he had not tapped the barrel of hard cider there, for surely no Raggie would do anything so crude as openly to tap a barrel. Every night the householder went down and found the keg undisturbed. In due course the work was well finished, paid for, and the Raggie departed. When the time came to tap the barrel, it was found empty. Years later the loser of the fifty gallons accosted the Raggie in the village and asked him how he did it. "That ain't hard," said the Raggie. "Ye tap a hoop to one side, bore yer holes, draw off what ye require, plug the holes and tap the hoop back."

But while the population was decaying and vanishing from the hilltops, life in the valley cities, crossroads villages, and farms continued as usual to the end of the period, perhaps a little more prosperously than usual. Derby, at the lower end of the valley, had added guns, organs, pianos, and was about to add typewriters to its output, and the river below it was foul with its sewage and that of the Naugatuck flowing between the gorgeous bluffs. Pittsfield also was beginning to darken the river with urban filth, though Pittsfield, having become the county town in 1869, and suffering less of a concentration of industry than Derby, still kept a rural flavor and in interest in ideas.

In the ninety miles between Pittsfield and Derby life

continued to turn, as it had for two centuries, around the churches and the town meetings. But it can be assumed that, where fifty years before there had been a sense of economic and political importance at every little crossroads and in the breast of every farmer, now, with the transfer of power from the agrarian to the urban population going on rapidly, the desiccation of the former had set in. Life in the typical farmhouse began losing its intellectual quality. The old balls that had been patterns of grace and dignity began moving in the direction of animated, backwoods "square dances." Even dress boots began filling with hayseed. With the loss of a sure sense of importance, the prejudices deepened and the little jealousies became more possessive and more shrill.

During the past fifty years bridges in most of the towns had been removed by ice or freshets, and had been replaced by the handsome, covered Towne bridges that came into vogue about 1821. Of these only two—one at Bull's Bridge and another at West Cornwall—remain.

Public buildings had continued to burn down or be torn down and replaced. Stratford's new town hall, built in 1844, had one of the spots of playing cards, in the form of a hewn stone, set in each of the walls, the heart in the north wall, the club in the east, the diamond in the south, and the spade in the west. In 1821 the primitive beacon on Stratford Point, consisting of a basket of burning wood, had been abandoned and the first lighthouse was built. It burned whale oil behind an expensive lens.

In '56 Bridgewater Parish was set off from New Milford as a separate town.

The temperance movement had its effect on the propaganda of a tavern in Salisbury which put a sign over its bar, "Drink little and often."

In '68, at the mouth of the river, the draw of the George Washington Bridge between Stratford and Milford fell on the small steamer *Monitor*, injuring twelve boys. What was remarkable about the accident was that the draw remained unrepaired, blocking the river, for four years. With deep-draft, steam shipping now carrying the world's trade, Derby was already dead as a port, and was flourishing on its factories.

In '69, when the seat of Berkshire County moved to Pittsfield, Lenox tore down its jail and used the materials to build the dam at Lenox furnace. This dam proved useful for the still-existing furnace just below, and for the paper mills downriver in Lee. Lenox was now deserted, forgotten by civilization, open to any kind of "foreign" invasion.

By 1870 both the great literary period and the peak of

the iron and marble industries were past. But although industry was going downhill and out of the valley for good, ideas of one kind or another were going to continue to flourish, with the hope of more golden ages to rival the decade between 1845 and 1855. By '70 the general aspect of the countryside had changed chiefly in a slight increase in the size of the town centers and other villages. The extremes of Victorian architecture, being largely urban in conception, had not much affected the appearance of the houses. The highways between the old walls were better only in so far as they had been used longer and more of the rocks and ledges had been worked out. Along the river and the large tributaries the little wooden factories were still standing, perhaps half of them still operating, the other ·half, already un-windowed, serving as "forts" for boys and hostelries for tramps. Of the great stone furnaces, the symbols of the industrial age, about half also were still groaning with their bellows and occasionally glaring red in the night. The other half stood cold on the hills and in the hollows, nibbled at by frost, rain and the roots of weeds, beginning the long process of crumbling, like the turrets of ancient castles gutted in wars lost long ago.

PART IV

The Devil's Rear-Guard Action
(1869-1929)

Tallyho - Crescendo

A CONVENIENT date at which to mark the beginning of the Fourth Act of the Drama of the Valley is 1869, the date of the shift of the seat of Berkshire County from Lenox to Pittsfield. Since Pittsfield was already a flourishing city, the moving of the courts there added little to its importance; it was merely a recognition of a fact already accomplished, the shift of power to the industrial cities from the country towns. But as for the latter, the change "took out of Lenox the core of its culture," and left it open to the latest and subtlest attack of the Devil on the integrity of the region. Having failed to make the valley a hell of factories and slums and local new-rich, the spirit of evil sent in floods of new wealth from outside, a wealthy class interested, not in the physical destruction of the valley but, as they supposed, in its beautification, a class dedicated in the main to the parade of wealth and genteel manners that, as they supposed, were the mark of aristocracy. The attack was formidable, and reached its highest intensity about 1900. Its beginning being placed in 1869, its end may be put for convenience in 1929, both dates being arbitrary and subject to overlapping with the ages before and after.

The coach horns of the new era in the valley, the age of "The Switzerland of America," can be heard as far back as the forties when Samuel G. Ward bought and built expensively on a large property—later divided into the Tappan, Bullard and Stokes estates—looking down over Stockbridge Bowl, the Tappan purchase included the Little Red House of Hawthorne, and when Oliver Wendell Holmes built his "villa" in Pittsfield for summer use only. The approaching flourish of brass was stronger in the fifties and sixties, with the establishment of the Aspinwall Woolsey, the Haggerty and the Schermerhorn estates, the sale of Henry Ward Beecher's farm to General Rathbone, of Longfellow's Oxbow to Charles Southmayd, of the property of Lenox's Judge Walker to Judge Pierpont—Grant's minister to Great Britain—who presently resold to Richard Goodman, and half a dozen other purchases by rich, summer invaders, of real estate formerly belonging either to local Yankees or to survivals of the shrinking literary colony. The nature of the new trend was evident enough before 1869. But it was only after that date that tallyhos in force poured tooting down into the valley beyond the mountains, when the tanks of new wealth began to knock down the old farms all over the place, and the Puritan tradition seemed to be dangerously threatened.

In a certain sense, the scattering attack before '69 had in it more potential danger than the full charge of the seventies and eighties. Among the early invaders there was a large percentage of responsible people who had no sense of inferiority and were not interested in display. Their houses were moderately large, but there were not many of them, and they were American houses that fitted into the landscape. The Tappans were among America's chief philanthropists and humanitarians. Mrs. Schermerhorn became Lenox's principal benefactor, adding numberless smaller gifts, most of them forgotten, to her principal one, the purchase of the threatened old courthouse and the donation of it to the town for a library. Mr. Goodman left the reputation of having done more good privately than any of the other "cottagers," as the builders of the châteaux were called. These early invaders, or most of them, were in fact gentry. They did good without asking for a receipt and public notice of it. They saw to the education of promising children, both on and off their estates. They retired their aging servants honorably, and concerned themselves with poverty anywhere. Their major gifts were not monoliths, towers and chimes that chiefly perpetuated their names, but they kept their generosities as anonymous as possible and intended them to be of actual, objective value to somebody else.

Such possessors of native virtue, now strengthened by great wealth, would, if they had prevailed, have conquered the valley and the rest of America. They were not only a force of destruction, but also of affirmative change. They and their descendants would have destroyed liberty, but they would have maintained the valley as a place where ideas flourished. They would have changed the status of the farmers to that of peasants for whose welfare they, the rich, were responsible. They would have patronized the intellectuals, would have made it easier than under the commercial system for them to write, compose, paint, teach or invent. For good democracy they would have substituted, not meaningless plutocracy, but good aristocracy. If the real responsibility of most of the early invaders had characterized most of those who poured in after them in the seventies, eighties and nineties, the valley and America would have suffered a counter-Jacksonian, a counter-Jeffersonian revolution. And the establishment of a real, hereditary aristocracy, with escutcheons of banks and mines couchant, of railroads and factories rampant, might have offered compensations for the loss of liberty.

But most of the people who rose to power after '69, and most of their children and their grandchildren, were either not of the American tradition that might have changed from good democracy to good aristocracy, or their wealth dazzled them into forgetting their background. In spite of notable individual exceptions, they did not as a class assume the responsibility to the valley and the nation that is the condition of vested power. Actually, they knew themselves to be less civilized than the run of the local farmers. Wherefore, their chief interest was in parade; parade in terms of palaces, horses, carriages, clothing and costly entertainment;

parade also in terms of a code of manners that it took leisure to practice well, the code of Victorian genteelness that had no courtesy but only pattern and pretense, the code whose purpose was to cover up the ignorance that underlay it and give its adept a false assurance of the importance he did not possess. Most of the invaders of the seventies, eighties and nineties were, or fain would have been, of Ward McAllister's Four Hundred.

The Stockbridge Sedgwicks, maintaining the intellectual tradition of the valley now in the fourth generation, were not of the new magnificence, and Nathalie Sedgwick Colby speaks with adequate scorn of it:

> Palaces that housed flashy wives of captains of industry; women who powdered their hair with gold dust, and were buxom counters for jewels: whose parties were prepared . . . by imported chefs and served by flunkies in knee breeches. The livery of admittance for their guests was a flamboyant appearance that advertised a rising bank account. No manners were required in these houses; no intellect. . . . The new society moved rapidly from New York to Newport [to the Berkshires and back again] so a changing environment would give them the illusion of thinking.

This was the way the great families began. Actually, by the time the Berkshire castles were built, most of them had risen to the illusion that Victorian propriety represented the pattern of courtesy and the mark of power.

Vaguely the new rich, or the ignorant majority of them, knew that there was some incongruity between them and their money, that somehow it made them smaller instead of larger as human beings. It did not occur to them to consider their farmer neighbors and their servants as their human equals and economic wards, because that would have taken self-confidence. Instead, knowing themselves for foxes and wild boars, they saw the people as the hounds that might one day take after them, whom they must therefore keep in their kennels. Wherefore, the people, who would have preferred to worship and imitate them as gods, at length saw them for what they were, and became indeed the hounds that eventually dug them out of their lair.

By the seventies the attack of the jangling coaches and the uniformed footmen was on in full clatter, and the knights of the financial round table were pitching their tents of stone and brick and oak all over the hills on properties of a few hundred to a few thousand acres bought at skyrocket prices from the farmers. The crowded tents of the new knights were spectacular piles such as might, in a truly feudal, medieval economy, have graced kings and dukes ruling hundreds of thousands of acres. There was something askew at the outset in the erection of imitation castles and manor houses whose only function was to parade power, when the power they vaunted had no relation to the local economy, and there was no need for so many or so large chambers within such powerful walls. The Victorian barons did not know that the houses they caused their architects to imitate had had a function in the economy of their day, that their owners were bound to entertain enormously, not for play but by necessity, and that their crenelations and bastions were built as a military retreat for their vassals for miles around. Where the original Gothics built to administer authority and protect their thousands, the Victorian Gothics built only to display power, without relation even to the few dozen hirelings they liked to believe they owned.

The golden invasion boomed on. Land rose to $500, $1,000, ultimately in one case to $25,000 an acre, doubling and trebling in value every few years. The great houses bulged out of the knolls where the views were, the Louis XIV château, the Norman manor house, the Tudor and Stuart manor house, the manor house of Queen Anne, of the late eighteenth century, the Petit Trianon perfectly reproduced, the great Gothic castles among which was the largest house ever built in the United States, the many places that mixed two or three styles, as the Georgian manor house with the Renaissance Italian gardens, the vast "shingled palaces" that had the validity of being natively American in the ugliest style America ever produced, the flimsy, comfortable, wide-verandaed, light-painted, sometimes pseudo-classic, frame mansions of the nineties.

A crisis arose in the construction of one of the biggest manor houses, when it was proposed to move off and across the street the previous house that occupied part of the site. A five-foot hedge intervened. Rather than cut out part of the hedge, the owner asked if the house couldn't be hoisted over it. And this was done.

A lady, native of Great Barrington, was not impressed by the millions her husband left her. While building a major castle at the command of her second husband, she was wont to hover nervously about the scene, most of the workmen being her childhood friends. One day when the foundation was just above the ground she addressed one of them. "Mercy," she said, "I hope it doesn't cost a million dollars." "Mary," said the man, "you've already spent more than a million dollars."

Around the houses the landscape architects laid out the baronial terraces, the poplared vistas and box mazes, the mirror pools and lakes, the waterfalls and fountains. Somewhere on each estate sprawled the regal stable, and somewhere else the glass village that was the greenhouse. And through the pruned and cleared woods the drives and the paths, often of crushed marble, wound out to the great gates that blazed with fake escutcheons. And somewhere in the corner of the property was hidden the model farm of a hundred acres or so. So the palaces rose and the grounds were laid out, usually under the eye of the wives, who rarely hesitated to shift towers, trees and bridges, after they had already been placed at a cost of many thousands of dollars.

From all over the world came on ships the many-colored marbles and other rare stones for the great halls, the columns and the fountains; the mahogany and teak and sandalwood for the panels and moldings; the heavy furniture from the royal châteaux of Europe or imitations of the same; the statues, flowerpots and sundials of Greece and Rome, and the arms and armor of the medieval world; the great built-in organs; the fancy staircases of stone and mahogany lifted out of their origins or meticulously reproduced; the materials for rooms completely walled and ceiled in convoluted gold leaf, for rooms completely walled and ceiled in Renaissance leathers, silks and brocades; the foreign workman to put all these things together. From France, Switzerland, Italy, England came the droves of trained servants, the higher ones born of generations of servitors: the awesome Butler who ruled the house staff and knew the combinations of all the lofty safes in the pantry where was kept the plate—silver or gold—and the more valuable china; the Coachman who ruled the population of the stables where no untoward speck must ever be found, where the colored sand of the coach houses was arranged in fancy designs and must be perfectly rearranged after a carriage was rolled out or in; most powerful of all, the Superintendent who was in command of everything except the stable and the actual service of the house, who kept the accounts and paid out the money, carried the title of "Mr." and stayed on the premises the year round, was in command of the farmer, was the functional chief gardener who planned the beds, saw to the maintenance of acres of putting-green lawn that some refused to touch with a power mower. He governed all the other gardeners and the greenhouses where were nurtured the twenty, forty, sixty thousand prize buds that were later set out to flower in bulk, and the young fruit trees, including the figs, dates and the tropical fruits raised under glass. Came the prize horses and dogs, cats, pea fowl, guinea fowl, swans, cranes, pheasants and doves to strut, float and coo round the terraces as patterns for their owners.

Through the seventies and eighties and nineties the palaces rose in fitting situations against the forest and the sky and were named with tasteful names—High Lawn, Cliffwood, Erskine Park, White Lodge, Twin Elms, Shipton Court, Oberlee, Interlaken, Elm Court, Yokun, Allen Winden, The Maples, Wheatleigh, Clipston Grange, Venfort Hall, Bellefontaine, Coldbrook, Wyndhurst, Blantyre, Beaupre, Groton House, Bonnie Brae, Shadowbrook, Lakeside, Bonnie Brier Farm, Stoneover, Ethelwyn, Belvoir Terrace,

Highwood, Birchwood, Eastover, Brookside, and dozens more. By '80 there were thirty-three estates in Lenox, and by 1900 there were seventy-five. There were fewer in Stockbridge, and still fewer in Great Barrington and Lee. The Lower Valley did not compete.

The great erections rose, the genteel frolics of the rich multiplied. It was the time of the double standard. The men tended to behave themselves in the country, and the frolics were for the most part as exemplary as they were supposed to be. Routine entertainment was the lawn party, New York's Sherry always catering; archery—with big bets by the gentlemen—being the accepted substitute for thought or conversation. Chronic larks were picnics, being excuses to use the coaches to haul the happy parties part way up Baldhead, Rattlesnake or Monument, leaving them to scramble the rest of the way and scream and revel in tiny misadventures. There were boating and fishing parties on Wood Pond down at Lenox Station, the river being set back by the dam below into the mysterious, mile-long, upper reaches of the pond, a region of islets, marshes, lost channels, reeds, shallows and water lilies, all swarming with fish, muskrats and waterfowl. Here, every spring, a select group of young ladies paddled up into the aquatic wilds to see the arrival of the white heron, an event of ornithological unorthodoxy which, on the testimony of credible witnesses, seems actually to have happened occasionally.

Autumn was the favorite time for parties. Then, whether for teas or dances, the big verandas would be muslined in, and the muslin, along with the whole interior of the house, covered with autumn leaves. Dances were often held in Sedgwick Hall, a place of local assembly given to Lenox by Mrs. Schermerhorn and Mrs. Auchmuty.

The great annual events of Lenox were equestrian. The Horse Show was usually held at Highlawn in Lee, the Races on the Lee track down on the flat by the river, between the hills that stand in close there and cast an early shadow. To both of these events the coaches and the carryalls rolled down from Lenox, tooting their horns, announcing their giggling freight of tons of costly clothing and jewels and parasols.

The famous autumn Tub Parade was originally the official closing of the Lenox season, when the coaches, tally-hos, landaus, surreys, carts and what not, along with their shining horses, were covered—wheels, harness and all—with hundreds of thousands of flowers the gardeners had provided, to march in sedate and colorful display before the applauding world. Shortly after the turn of the century the Tub Parade was discontinued in favor of the less original and more exciting run of the Berkshire Hunt.

The flower shows were usually county affairs, run by the superintendents, and there was keen competition in them among gardeners who were genuine artists, many of them spending their lives as specialists on one or two species or subspecies. For casual entertainment of the elect there was in time the exclusive Lenox Golf Club with its golf course. And for the equivalent of an expensive city club, there was the Lenox Club in the village.

Lenox and Stockbridge felt and expressed high contempt for one another. Since the village centers of both towns were near their respective southern boundaries, there were a number of large estates in northern Stockbridge—including the Tappans' Tanglewood, the Bullards' Highwood, and the Stokes' Shadowbrook—that were considered to be socially part of Lenox. Accepting this fallacy, Lenox excelled Stockbridge in wealth, and even without the fallacy it excelled in the display of it.

Stockbridge retained a good deal of the quality of a country town, where the relatively poor Sedgwicks held their own in leadership against the relatively rich Fields, and both conspired to keep the intellectual tradition of the town not far below what it had been in the previous era. The Stockbridge Casino was less of an exclusive club than a playground, theater, and place for art exhibitions, supported by the villagers as well as by the summer people. The dances held there were germans. The annual events of Stockbridge were not geared to great wealth. The torchlight procession through the Ice Glen with everyone in costume, followed by the big bonfire and dancing in the village street, went back to the 1830's. An innovation of the new age was the similar night procession of rowboats on the river, usually in August, each boat decorated with Japanese lanterns and the curves in the river marked by Bengal lights. As in the Ice Glen parade, everybody was in costume, and the occasion ended with dancing round a bonfire in the village street.

Southward through Great Barrington and Sheffield the invasion of new wealth captured less of the towns, though, between the Hopkins-Searles mansion and the Berkshire Inn, Great Barrington village lost its original quality, the inn functioning not only as an eyesore itself but as a screen to conceal the handsome old Dwight mansion, or Bryant House, which was moved back to make room for it.

Litchfield was the happiest of the valley towns in its adjustment to the new age. Its eighteenth century mansions were already too elegant to be plowed under by the forces of new wealth. A number of Litchfield's old families participated in the tide of industrial riches. The strangers who came in and bought were mostly people of intelligence. The result of the new era for Litchfield was simply that it got repaired, painted and polished, and the arboreal glories of North and South streets were completed. Not a single major monstrosity arose in the village.

In Lenox there was a sizable minority of the "cottagers" who were people of tradition older than their new wealth, who felt some responsibility for the town and had no truck with the more flamboyant goings-on. They had no truck with the lady who, ordering specially one of the earliest cars in Lenox, had it all lined in white velvet, and required that it be specially wide to accommodate a toilet. The same lady upholstered all her walls with satin or brocade; left her superintendent for several years without wall paper or electricity, then remembered and equipped him regally. She installed a golf course, swimming pool, bowling alleys, canals, bridges and fountains, the latter motor driven; every afternoon at certain hours the fountains played and the public was admitted. The outside of her house was festooned with red, white and blue lights. The parties there were magnificent with the most costly opera singers and magicians for entertainment. The lady never broke into the exclusive set of Lenox. Her husband, who was personally popular, and a man of high attainment, came to Berkshire one of the richest men in America, and he ended in the hands of the banks.

A different type of husband was the sissified one who each morning gave his superintendent the orders for the day on red, white or blue slips according to urgency. This man and his wife had been locked in a room in their New York house while thieves went through it; wherefore, he drove around Lenox in a bulletproof car. There is no record of Lenox having had a major burglar scare; but Stockbridge had a "gentleman burglar" in '93. He was most considerate in the ladies' bedrooms while taking their jewels, often leaving a particular piece when requested, and generally raising a flutter of expectation in the several wealthy, old-maidenly breasts of the village. When caught, because of carelessness in leaving around the bands of the fine cigars he had stolen and smoked, he turned out to be a workman whom everybody knew; and felonious romance faded.

Diamond Jim Brady was a frequent guest at one of the Stockbridge châteaux. He presented the house with a cutglass punch bowl so large that only a very strong butler could lift it even when empty.

One of the Lenox proprietors observed that his superintendent, an Irishman, was going to Albany regularly every week. There came a week when the owner himself was going to be away and he asked his chief agent to stay. "I know what you go for," he said. "I'm going west myself, and I'll stop in Albany and send you back a good woman." "That will do very nicely, Mr.————," was the reply. "I know you're a good picker."

Animals figured in the décor of the estates. One of the most sophisticated effects was that obtained at Groton House, the estate of Grenville L. Winthrop on the edge of Lenox village. But for a famous climbing hydrangea on the house, there was not a flower on all the spaciously parked and lawned property, where all but the open mowing was by hand machine. For color there were numerous tame peacocks and fancy pheasants, one or more of which were likely to appear on the right terrace at the right time. A little on the extravagant side was the idea of Mrs. Spencer, who required that her house and all the animals in and about it be white. How far the fancy went I am not informed. It included droves of white dogs and white pigs; a baby of the latter variety habitually functioned as a house pet, occupying the parlor with his mistress. Stockbridge would fain forget the story of the family that, buying an unobjectionable, minor place across the railroad tracks, had a few extra outbuildings set up, appeared with a zoo, complete with elephant, remained a short time, and vanished more abruptly that it had come.

A large private zoo, done in the grand manner and with taste, was that of W. C. Whitney, Cleveland's secretary of the navy, who bought almost all of October Mountain, fenced it all with steel, imported appropriate animals and released them in the vast park. As the crown and object of the whole venture, Mr. Whitney built on the summit of the mountain a hunting lodge or summer cottage for his son, who honeymooned there and afterwards was not interested. The property was under an English warden, with an outdoor staff of cowboys who conducted hunting parties on horseback. In the twenties the place began to fall into disrepair, many of the animals were shipped to the Bronx Zoo in New York, the hunting lodge burned, the warden settled in Stockbridge village, the park was abandoned and given to the state of Massachusetts as a picnic site. For years the wandering ghost of the dead preserve was Old Bill, a bull moose who escaped capture, emerged through the ruined fence, and presently became an accepted resident of the surrounding countryside. His most frequent calls were on his old friend the warden in Stockbridge. Latterly, he also favored the warden of the Pleasant Valley Bird Sanctuary established by Miss Mary Parsons in Lenox. Old Bill was friendly and whimsical, frequently held up the trolley without malice, and from timed reports moved with aerial speed from village to village in the application of his somewhat undisciplined ideas. One day an ignorant or ungentle hunter shot him dead. The warden of the bird sanctuary found him and buried him, first cutting off his feet, which are preserved in the sanctuary's museum.

The Pleasant Valley Bird Sanctuary, whose property has been increased by the accession of all of Bald Mountain, is the third largest in the country in number of species reported. It was the idea, and partly the gift of Miss Mary Parsons, she being of the second generation of the invasion and one of Lenox's more responsible benefactors. When she came to buy the land, she thought the price too high. In any event she was relying on a neighbor to pay for it, and so she wrote to her in California, quoting both the asking price and the lower price which she considered fair. The friend wired the larger amount, with a message, "Buy the place and keep the change."

The relations between the rich and the townspeople was at least superficially good, because the rich spent money. The Stokes family was one of those which felt some responsibility for the poorer neighbors. Mrs. Stokes, Sr., used to give Christmas parties for the whole town, both when she inhabited the Homestead in Lenox village and, afterwards, when she was mistress of the vast castle Shadowbrook. Not long after the completion of the latter, her son, Anson Phelps Stokes, Jr., wired her from New Haven, "Bringing ninety-six for the week-end," meaning that he was bringing his cronies from his class of '96 at Yale, in all perhaps a dozen boys. Mrs. Stokes, whether she understood or not, wired back with humor, "Can't you make it ninety-five house is already crowded?"

At least one of Lenox's townspeople was in a position to express himself candidly about the "cottagers." This was the professional cicerone who drove tourists around in a carryall, entering the private grounds, driving right up to the big houses, stopping at a close vantage point and sounding off about the glories of the property and its owner. At length the proprietor of the most picturesque of the palaces forbade him his grounds. The side of the house was visible from the highway at the end of a superb, straight drive beyond massive gates. Immediately inside the gates was the gatehouse, and just beyond a sort of secondary stable. After having been excluded from the grounds the professional guide changed his line about this particular property. Stopping at the gate with his gaping crowd, he would bellow so all the servants in the vicinity could hear him, "This is the estate of ————. He is the only man in Lenox who made his money all in one day." When one of the tourists would ask how he did that, the local authority would shout, "He married it."

Of more varied human interest than the plutocrats were the droves of employees who served and supervised their play. The smaller estates got along with as few as a dozen of them; the biggest properties had more than a hundred. The employees and their families comprised the majority of the population of Lenox, running to more than two thousand souls in the palmy days. What these people had in common was competence. They were the pick of the gardeners, butlers, chefs, footmen, coachmen, stablemen and maids of Europe, lured here by the highest wages in the world. In character they varied from minor racketeers who insisted on their cut from the local tradesmen, up through major racketeers who outdressed and outstrutted their employers, to men and women of distinction whose presence increased the inferiority complexes of the bosses.

The help comprised a society of their own, and gave themselves two or three balls a year. The superintendents organized among themselves the Lenox Horticultural Association which ran the famous flower shows, distributing cups and certificates. When the snobbery of the employers rose to the point of having a cricket team, the superintendents provided the best talent. All of them had their own wine cellars and the best of cigars—both essential perquisites of office —and most of them had a small stable assigned for their private use, with a few carriages, from the master's stable. "Lenox superintendents never die or resign" was their slogan, which a half dozen of their old guard are still supporting. One of the ablest, a Swiss who did forty years of service, was said never to have left the place in that time.

The most colorful superintendents were the pompous ones—usually English or Irish—and they shone to best advantage in the typical situation where their employees were ignorant and dependent on them. There was a remarkable series on what I shall call the Smith estate. The first of them was a big, handsome man I shall call Jones. Like most of the superintendents, he wore the loudest and most expensive tweeds, and otherwise he exceeded them all in grandeur. He frequently gave banquets for which he would kill a fatted steer, his guests including some of the wealthiest merchants from Pittsfield. When a neighboring superintendent asked him to lend him fifty feet of rope, Jones sent over a wagon with half a mile of it. One of the more expensive of gardening tools is the budding knife, and superintendents are careful to get no more of them than necessary—Jones used to order them by the gross. He started each day with a conference in the greenhouse which lasted as long as the cigars. His employer was forever complaining that the place had too many servants—it was one of the hundred-staff properties—and Jones would forever reassure him—"I'll tend to that, Mr. Smith, I'll tend to that, Mr. Smith"—after which he would hire a few more. One day they were discussing matters when Mr. Jones said, "Oh, by the way, Mr. Smith, I bought the X farm"—one of the smaller estates. "You and I are going to run it on shares." This was Mr. Smith's first knowledge of the plan. But he paid up, and Mr. Jones ran the farm as he proposed to. His most outrageous behavior had to do with one of the stablemen who was caught in the main house stealing from the master's wine cellar. Mr. Smith complained to Mr. Jones who said, "I'll tend to that, Mr. Smith." Instead of firing the culprit, he gave him two weeks' vacation with pay, then promoted him to be his private, uniformed coachman, and thereafter they missed no chance to give the family their dust. Greatness in the long run proved more than Mr. Jones could bear, and he ended his days in a semiprivate asylum.

One superintendent was a famous liar and grafter, boasting about the prizes he had won at other flower shows, casually informing his mistress that he had just cut three thousand roses when he had cut a dozen. On one occasion he rented the town's stone crusher for use on the estate, then asked the selectmen for a little graft on the side. The first selectman carried the matter to the proprietor, who put it up to his superintendent. "The damned old liar," said the latter, "it was just the other way round." He got away with it.

Another superintendent was charged by the New York papers with having absconded with certain of his employer's funds. He sued for libel, recovered $1,000 from each of thirty papers, and with the proceeds set up business in Pittsfield.

Most of the superintendents, while they did tyrannize over their employers, were honest and responsible. Typical of them was a Scotchman in Boston who was offered the post of command on one of the biggest estates, being informed at the same time that there were some hundred employees whom the proprietor desired to keep. Two days later the prospect called and said, "I came to tell ye I'll no take your position." When asked for his reasons he said that he would come only on condition that the entire force be fired, after which he would hire back such of them as he required. This was done. Actually he hired back every one of them at once, and most of them stayed with him during his ensuing fifty-four years of service.

The invasion of the Upper Valley by the new rich after the seventies was an incidental action of the main campaign which in the same period was capturing the urban centers of America, substituting the standard of irresponsible wealth for the standard of right which was the tradition, creating a new economic stratification which had not existed on any scale since before the Revolution. It was a particularly dangerous invasion in the Berkshires, because there the worst horrors of the factory system were no longer even threatened. To the ignorant it seemed to set a tangible goal of aspiration in the great and impressive houses, the lawns and the marble columns and the peacocks, the supposedly gratifying ease of life among these things. It was particularly dangerous also because among its personnel were scattered individuals of responsibility and cultivation, who honestly desired to improve their towns and who disseminated among the rest strange ideas about books and music and the like.

These were the people who would have liked to change America into an aristocracy. But there were too few of them to characterize their economic class. And finding no congeniality among their peers, they failed to grasp the opportunity to further the American democracy out of which they themselves had risen a few generations before. They merely wrapped their refined skirts more closely around them, cutting out not only the plutocrats their neighbors but the simple Yankees whom they chose to think of as peasants. It is shocking to find that some of the most enlightened people in America in the eighties and nineties, while paying their help well and seeing to their physical comfort, were discouraging them from educating their children and sending them "off the place." Those who above all should have preserved the American tradition of opportunity became merely an insignificant and pompous group within the larger new-rich class which was trying to make itself a European landed aristocracy.

The rise of rococo wealth continued through the nineties and thereafter. Symbolic of its high tide was the completion, in 1902, of the huge Aspinwall Hotel on the highest point of the ridge that runs down the center of the valley, the point below which in cliffs the great downward step of the valley in Lenox begins, the highest point in Lenox except for the flanking mountains of October and Yokun Seat. The Pittsfield architect J. McArthur Vance designed the million-dollar, four-hundred-room pile whose four-hundred-foot length rose to its five-story height above the pines like a yellow and white crown on the mountain. Among the numerous outbuildings were dormitories with two hundred rooms for servants. The property comprised 447 acres on the deeply wooded mountain, threaded with bridle paths. In the hotel's ballroom five hundred could dance easily; the parlor was a perfect reproduction of one of the rooms at Versailles; all the furniture and appointments were of the richest. There was the State Suite where John D. Rockefeller stayed; the bridal suite where Lillian Russell stayed when she married Alexander Pollock Moore, editor of the Pittsburg *Leader;* the suite that Senator Chauncey Depew occupied for the month of August every year for twelve years. Other guests included President Theodore Roosevelt and Governor Franklin D. Roosevelt. The hotel was a great thing for Lenox. It was built by local contractors, and paid $5,000 local taxes every year. On the roof there were two lookout pergolas commanding the vast view southward across purple peaks to Canaan Mountain in Connecticut, and the shorter view northward to the beginning of the valley against a spur of Greylock. Barely perceptible with a glass in the foreground of the southern view, there nestled the microscopic house where *The House of the Seven Gables* had been written. The northern view included the tops of the trees round the birthplace of *Moby Dick*. The saturation of the Upper Valley with wealth was now about complete, and Lenox's fond historian described the completed scene as "Nature's inspiring canvas in a frame of Art. . . . More than half of the area of the township has passed into the possession of those who, with large means, have touched the olden picture of scenic charm only to adorn it." The literature and the architecture were all of a piece.

Fifth-Column Culture

THE INTELLECTUAL life of the tallyho days was a more serious attack on the valley than even honest philistinism. It pretended to encourage ideas. Actually it stifled them. A triumph of Victorian writing is the history of Lenox published in 1902 by the ex-Congregational minister, a man of real distinction who saw perfectly what was going on, though he must for his respectability seem to approve of it. In his nauseous vocabulary he proclaims himself a properly pious votary of the period, while, to anybody who can read, he occasionally states the truth accurately. ". . . The literary atmosphere once breathed in this old student-town has diminished. Another generation has arisen which knows not Miss Sedgwick, and which is a stranger to the intellectual and social prestige of the ancient Berkshire capital."

Having thus thrown the light on his rich friends, the good minister hastens to reassure them by returning them to the sickly half-light of sentiment: "Aside from the many inspirations to right living which an affluent class 'rich in good works' can and does present to those who are in less favorable circumstances, Lenox has enjoyed very many benefactions at the hands of those who have appropriated these heights as building sites." After going on to enumerate the gifts of the cottagers to the town, he works himself into the following purple sigh, appropriate to the several memorial gifts to the local churches: "If we might include the gifts to the churches in the list of gifts to the town, it would be difficult to stop the enumeration of gracious and fragrant alabaster-boxes whose sweet perfume is the memory of saintly lives."

The sweet alabaster boxes in question were mostly examples of sculpture, architecture, or both, and it would be hopeful to find that they added something to what man had already contributed to the valley in houses, churches and village landscaping. One of the saintly lives commemorated in Lenox was that of General Patterson of the Revolution, his shaft being a tall, stately, granite one, well placed on the edge of the great hill in the center of the village, well embellished with a bronze relief of a group of generals in council with the commander in chief. In two respects, both pretentious, it violates the tradition of the valley. First, granite memorials to individuals, no matter how tasty, have no place in a village whose white clapboards spell ancient democracy. Second, in terms of its inscriptions, this one is as much a memorial of the donor as of the supposed object of the donation.

A block away is another and smaller granite column, given as a combined road marker and lamppost at an important corner. The chiseled road indications being illegible, and the town having failed to equip the column with lights, its only purpose is to commemorate the donor, whose name is cut on it. The same individual presented the Episcopal church with a parish house, a gift presumably of consequence. Dozens of other expensive donations to the church of the better people would seem to be of little importance to a congregation that was sizable only during three or four months in the summer. Valid gifts to Lenox were the replacement of the now decrepit clock which Fanny Kemble gave to the Church on the Hill, the saving of the old courthouse from destruction and the donation of it to the town for a library, the erection of Sedgwick Hall as a general entertainment center. Most valid were the forgotten private generosities of too few of the rich, the old servants well pensioned, the children of servants sent to college, the poor and the sick of the town visited and cared for.

Practically every village in the valley got its numerous memorials to saintly lives between 1869 and 1929. Inevitable,

of course, were the Civil War monuments to the local sol-
diery, and they are harmless in the architectural landscape in
proportion that they are hidden or dwarfed within large
parks. A fine example of what a memorial of immortal materials can be is the stele to General Sedgwick, the valley's chief
soldier, in Cornwall. The granite terrace supporting the great
slab, with the cannon in front and piles of cannon balls flanking it, is large and pretentious. But placed in the center of
Cornwall Hollow, originally in a triangle of roads with a
wall of maple trees behind it, with no buildings near it, and
with the cemetery across the road where General Sedgwick
lies with his family, above all with a reposeful effect given
by the width of the terrace in proportion to the height of
the stele, this is a memorial that seems to be part of the earth
that supports it and the hills around.

In 1877 the Laurel Hill Association of Stockbridge presented the town with a monolith marking the burial ground
of the Indians, bearing a bronze plate inscribed: "The Burial
place of the Housatonic Indians, the Friends of our Fathers."
While the rough shaft is less objectionable than most, its chief
asset is contributed by the fact that the burial place was just
outside the village, where the site and memorial can be visited
for their own sakes, without awareness of their clash with
the general architecture. Less fortunate was the megalithic
chime tower which David Dudley Field contributed a year
later as a memorial to his granddaughter, locating it on the
site of the original Indian church and stipulating that the
chimes be played for half an hour every summer evening.
The thought is a tender one, but the chimes could have
played as effectively in the near-by church tower, and the
village could have been spared an eyesore. The provision for
sweet vesper chimes, quite unrelated to vesper services, is an
exotic one which could hardly have occurred during another
age. Near by stands the Jonathan Edwards memorial, erected
by his descendants. Down the street, the sundial marking the
site of his house on the present Riggs Foundation property is
small, conventional, unobjectionable, and therefore a suitable memorial.

When Lenox's historian said in 1902 that a generation had arisen which was "a stranger to the intellectual and social prestige of the ancient Berkshire capital" he was guilty of understatement. Between 1850 and 1855 Lenox had been one of the two principal greenhouses of the literary flowering of New England. Twenty-five years later its greenhouses and flowers served nothing but vanity. Its industrial tycoons entertained gladly all the braided diplomats they could get hold of—including Count von Bernstorff and Dumba, the Austrian ambassador, one of whose messages a newsboy heard ticking off on the Lenox telegraph set, copied it, and the newspapers decoded and published it, causing Dumba's dismissal. Also they frequently imported famous musicians because they had heard of music, and the opera was fashionable —Jenny Lind was a guest at Highwood, and her outdoor singing one evening gave its name to Echo Lake. It is claimed that Isadora Duncan gave her first recital at the Chapin place. There were two academicians of standing in summer residence: Professor Thomas Egleston of Columbia, who had a house in the village, and John S. Sargent, who had one north of Laurel Lake. Doubtless also in the eighties and nineties numerous artists of distinction came through and stopped obscurely at the Curtis Hotel. But for creative artists in even summer residence there were only Charles McKim the great architect, who was of the right set and did houses for them, a Miss Stebbins, a sculptor to whom Charlotte Cushman gave her house, and Thomas Shields Clarke, likewise a forgotten sculptor.

To carry the banner of literature in the wake of Catherine Sedgwick, Fanny Kemble, Hawthorne, Lowell, Beecher and the full galaxy of American writers of the former generation, there was only Edith Wharton. She married into Lenox, liked it and in due course built her house, the Mount, overlooking Laurel Lake, the place being a reproduction of a small country seat of an English peer. Mr. Wharton was accustomed to the society of Boston's best, but shortly after their marriage his wife took him to a literary gathering there, which by that time in Boston was something else again. Feeling out of place, he whispered to Edith, "At least, I'm the best dressed man here." "They won't know it, Eddie," she replied. Mrs. Wharton did much of her work in Lenox, and set at least one novel there. The respective residents of Court House and West Street hills—the two streets leaving the Center to the south and west—are still quarreling over which hill Ethan Frome took his last slide on. There being no evidence, I vote for Court House Hill, because it is more dangerous.

Besides Mrs. Wharton, James Barnes, a war correspondent and writer, was a summer resident of Lenox. Up in Pittsfield there was not even a James Barnes to succeed Melville and Holmes. It was a fitting period on the past literary age that in 1890 Hawthorne's Little Red House burned down. A few years later a bull gored a man dead against one of Hawthorne's trees, the horn leaving a wound in the tree that was visible for many years.

Besides that of Mrs. Wharton, the other literary name to conjure with in the valley in this period was that of Richard Watson Gilder, poet, editor of the *Century*, literary leader at the end of the century. He hid out in a house which he bought on the side of glorious Tyringham Valley and is little referred to in the annals of the right people of the neighborhood. Ex-President Cleveland and his wife, being friends of the Gilders, took a house near them for a summer, and delighted Lenox by appearing for a dance in Sedgwick Hall. Incidentally, adjoining Monterey had been the home of President Garfield, and after he was shot the town changed the name of its chief body of water from Brewer Pond to Garfield Lake.

Edith Wharton and Richard Watson Gilder in literature, Charles McKim in architecture—to which Stockbridge had one name of distinction in the creative arts to add, that of Daniel Chester French. In '93 his "The Republic" dominated the World's Fair at Chicago. A few years later he built a house and studio in Stockbridge. Around the turn of the century Stockbridge had also a group of resident or summer-resident painters of importance—Marie Kobbe, Lydia Field

Emmet, Walter Nettleton and Robert Reid. And besides
French there was the sculptor Augustus Lukeman.

Even more than Lenox, Stockbridge was now without
literary names of consequence. But Stockbridge, as distinguished from Lenox, kept its literary flavor without benefit
of great names, under a tradition carried by several families
but by none more than the Sedgwicks who—though they
had no cut-in on the new wealth—still kept the grand old
house and the grand old hospitality in the maturity of the
third generation and the youth of the fourth. In the Sedgwick house every transient of distinction stopped as a matter of course: Owen Wister, the grandson of Fanny Kemble,
Owen Johnson, William Roscoe Thayer, Mr. and Mrs. Booker
T. Washington—causing a near mutiny in the now all-white
kitchen where Mum Bett had presided.

Laura, one of the Sedgwick girls of this generation, had
flaming red hair. In the summer of '86 the Matthew Arnolds
came and lived in Laurel Cottage which their daughter Mrs.
Whitridge rented from Lady Musgrave, the daughter of
David Dudley Field. Arnold walked and drove with Laura,
read her his verses, gave her his picture which she kept on
her bureau, generally lifted many eyebrows, and when he
finally left in the late fall wrote her some love poetry. Early
in his stay a family that was not much given to entertaining thought it proper to throw a tea for the great man. All
the neighbors pitched in, contributing cake, sandwiches and
servants. "The smell of cake came out on the street." All the
coaches came down from Lenox, all the carriages from Pittsfield. Everybody came, and everybody waited and went.
Arnold forgot to appear. He and Laura Sedgwick were out
on a long drive to see a view. Some time after the Arnolds
left, Lady Musgrave sold Laurel Cottage on condition that
two trees Arnold had planted should not be removed.

In the same year as Arnold's visit, 1886, Stockbridge got
its Casino, designed by McKim, Mead, and White, and
painted yellow. Intended originally simply as a club offering
tennis and billiards, it shortly became the local art gallery,
and eventually the scene of uproarious local dramatics. Until

1926 it stood on the corner where the old John Sergeant house was moved in that year. Its adventures since then are part of the recent epoch in the valley.

Between 1869 and 1929 triumphant materialism expressed itself in all imaginable forms from abstract wealth to concrete health. Until the overlapping intimations of a new period, noticeable after World War I, it was a time of decreasing quantity and quality of literature and art, since they concerned themselves with the intangible elements in humanity. Likewise the aim of philanthropic endeavor changed from the invisible to the visible man. Hampton Institute, founded by General S. C. Armstrong, frequent summer visitor in Stockbridge, was less typical of the new time than of the humanitarian interest of the pre-Civil War period. More modern was St. Helen's Home, established at Interlaken—formerly Curtisville—by John E. Parsons of Lenox as a fresh-air farm for city children.

With the rise of science, the health of the body became the chief aim of life, and while literature and religion declined all kinds of therapy rose. Around the end of the century good hospitals began to go up, not only in the cities of Derby, Danbury and Pittsfield but also in some of the country towns that were too far from the cities for comfort, in Milford, New Milford, Sharon, North Canaan and Great Barrington. Shortly before 1910 Dr. Austen Fox Riggs, retiring permanently from New York to Stockbridge, started the work in psychiatry which has developed into the Austen Riggs Foundation with its two modern "inns" in the center of the village—one appropriately replacing Jonathan Edwards's house—and its hundreds of annual psychiatric or quasi-psychiatric patients who, with their visitors, contribute appreciably to the support of the town. An informal adjunct of the Foundation is Tom Carey, who drives patients up from the station in the last buggy functioning in the village. Once when he was taking a lady down to the station for her departure she began to cry at the necessity of leaving the place. "Cheer up, lady," said Mr. Carey. "You'll be back soon."

Equally appropriate, with health, to the age of scientific materialism was the matter of physical invention. The inventor, like any other scientist, leads a life of hypotheses which in psychological terms are ideas, *materialistic* ideas but ideas nevertheless. If there were enough inventors behind the hedges and at the dinner tables to flavor the thought and talk of the valley, the idealistic tradition would survive in a new idiom.

As a feature of the rise of industry in the first half of the nineteenth century, the amazing list of inventions attributed to the Shakers has been given.[1] Because of their communal life, it is difficult to associate any of these with individuals, or even to determine which of the contributions were made by the Shaker communities in the valley.

Probably the valley's first inventor of remembered consequence was Simon Lake of Milford who in the seventies and eighties made important contributions to the development of the submarine. Speaking of submarines, the first vessel to be sunk by one was the Union frigate *Housatonic,* torpedoed by a hand-propelled Confederate submarine in Charleston Harbor in 1864.

The valley's chief contributions to invention were electrical, and they were major.

Franklin Leonard Pope was born in Great Barrington in 1840, was an experienced telegrapher at seventeen, and at nineteen was taken on the staff of the *Scientific American* because of his talent both for painting and for mechanical drawing. In 1865 the Collins Overland Telegraph Company put him in charge of an expedition to explore British Columbia and Alaska, and to map out a telegraph line to Asia and Europe via Bering Strait, Pope was working his way up the Pacific coast with dog teams when, in '66, Cyrus Field of Stockbridge successfully completed the laying of his Atlantic cable, and the Bering Strait project was called off.

Many electrical devices combine several patents, so that each of several men may claim justly to be the inventor of them: Pope is one of two Berkshire men for whom it is

[1] See pp. 252-253.

claimed that they invented the stock ticker, and Pope in '67 and '68 was certainly superintendent for the Gold and Stock Reporting Telegraph, being at the same time editor of the *Telegrapher*. In '69 he took young Thomas Edison into partnership. Each of them seems to have wanted to run the show, and the partnership was dissolved in a year but not until they had together improved the regular telegraphic printer and invented the rail-circuit for railroad signals.

Pope subsequently was employed in various expert capacities, including that of patent lawyer, by the Western Union, the Bell Telephone, and the Westinghouse Company. In 1886 he was elected president of the American Institute of Electrical Engineers, and in '93 retired to his Great Barrington home, Wainwright Hall, built in 1766 and now disguised under double Victorian porches. But this puts us ahead of our story. Already Wainwright Hall had been the scene of a greater contribution to electrical science than any of Pope's.

The biggest star in Great Barrington's electrical galaxy, the inventor from whom stem all the electric light and power systems of the modern world, was William Stanley. In '85 he was a young man working for the Westinghouse Company. He asked to be financed to experiment with some notions about transforming a large electric current at low pressure into a small current at high pressure and vice versa. It was universally recognized that a gadget for such transforming was necessary if current was to be transmitted on the relatively small conductors that alone were practicable for great distances. George Westinghouse, however, did not think Stanley's ideas worth any appreciable risk, and thereby transformed his young employee into one of those great inventors who are also great heroes. Stanley retired to Great Barrington with his family, rented Wainwright Hall from the older and still absent Pope, and devoted all of his little fortune to setting up a laboratory there. Whether through kindness or rapacity, Westinghouse kept his eye on him and lent some useful apparatus.

It is a coincidence that the two biggest private mansions

of Great Barrington were identified with Stanley in some way. In 1885, when he made his hegira back to the valley from the outside world, Mrs. Mark Hopkins, widow of the railroad man, was building the enormous castle, Kellogg Terrace, which will be described later. Among other facilities it had a power plant that was ready for use early in '86, though the whole mansion was not completed till the fall of that year. Stanley got permission to transmit current from this private plant to a near-by, abandoned rubber factory where he installed his transformer and where, if successful, it would cut down the current and step up the voltage for transmission on small wire round the village. It is to the glory of Great Barrington that it had twenty-five heroes who were willing to risk the destruction of their properties by subscribing to the crazy scheme that Stanley claimed would give them light in their stores and offices. From the one-time rubber factory two number eight wires were strung through insulators on trees to the twenty-five guinea-pig hutches. On March 20, 1886, everything was ready. After supper some of the more courageous villagers went down to the rubber factory. The less courageous stood around the streets at great distances from the wires. Darkness fell. Stanley himself closed the switch. There was no sound. Suddenly and simultaneously twenty-five sets of windows along Main Street were seen to be alight. In prospect all the future nights of the world were alight.

The immediate result was, of course, that the two big electric corporations behaved in the then usual way of big industry toward small individuals. They both pounced on Stanley, hoping either to buy or to steal his patent and starve him. This part of the story, however, has a happy ending. Stanley beat both bullies in lawsuits and became himself a rich man. He bought the large farm south of the village called Brookside, where in '85 the supposedly largest barn in the United States had burned down. Much later, in 1904, the house burned, and in 1908 Stanley started to build a palace, but sold it to William Hall Walker when it was partially completed.

Meanwhile the efforts of Franklin Pope and Stanley had merged to the further enrichment of the world and the setting off of a tragic accident. In '93, as has been mentioned, being seven years after Stanley's great invention, Pope retired to his Wainwright Hall in Great Barrington where Stanley had perfected the transformer and which he had left when he bought Brookside. Taking over and equipping the laboratory in the cellar, Pope continued private experimentation. A year later, in '94, he supervised the installation of a system by which current, through a transformer, was transmitted four miles from a dam in Housatonic to Great Barrington for purposes not of light but of power. Thus was completed the electrical pattern of the modern world: transmission of light in '86, of power in '94. A year later Pope, returning home from an absence, went down to his cellar laboratory and was electrocuted by a transformer that had been improperly connected in his absence.

Besides the great lights Stanley and Pope, Great Barrington had four other distinguished electricians to complete its galaxy. Of Pope's two brothers, Ralph Wainwright was for twenty-six years secretary of the American Institute of Electrical Engineers and Henry William held numerous high executive positions in large light and power companies. There were also the two Tobey brothers both of whom became national authorities on the transformer, the elder, William, being an active associate of Stanley's until his death in line of duty in South America in 1896.

George Westinghouse was an inventor on whom the valley has a partial claim. He had produced his epoch-making air brake and his other important railway devices before he bought Erskine Park in Lenox and Lee. But thereafter, while a summer resident there, he made some of the earliest and most complicated applications of the principle Stanley had discovered. He installed the whole light and power system of the Chicago Exposition of '93, and built the dynamos for the power plants at Niagara Falls and for the municipal railways of both New York and London.

Although not accredited with any basic invention such

as Stanley's transformer, Stephen Dudley Field made the most varied contributions of any of the group of remarkable inventors of Berkshire County at the end of the nineteenth century. He was the son of Jonathan Edwards Field, local lawyer of Stockbridge and the only son of the first David Dudley who was not a man of national reputation. Young Stephen early became an employee of the Western Union Telegraph Company and as such lived in San Francisco between '63 and '79. During an earthquake in this period he was sending out messages to the firehouses from the City Hall tower when it collapsed under him, and he remained under the rubble miraculously alive for hours while they dug him out. While in San Francisco he made dozens of essential inventions for the telegraph and the then infant telephone. He rigged up the first long-distance telephone, covering sixty miles from San Francisco through twenty-four stations. His inventions and contrivances while in the West included the first police patrol telegraph, the electric annunciator for public buildings, and—perhaps his second most important contribution—the electric elevator. He is also credited with "the first central light and power station in America." It must have been a costly and impracticable system, for this was before the transformer.

In '79 Stephen Dudley Field came back to Stockbridge, where his uncles David Dudley and Henry Martyn were patriarchs in their great houses on the Hill. Henry Martyn's house was the now Victorianized and disguised "castle" of Ephraim Williams I. Stephen settled in a house on the Plain possessing a large garden. A couple of years after his return, he invited the neighbors out to his garden to see a horseless carriage, equipped with a brilliant headlight, run on narrow-gauge tracks. It clanked around the circle very nicely. Stephen sat on the single seat and explained how the current came in through a trolley from an underground cable between the tracks. Later he also invented the overhead trolley. And in '93 he demonstrated his completed streetcar at the World's Fair at Chicago.

Among Stephen Field's later contributions to the machinery of the modern world is modern stage lighting; and he sufficiently improved the electric stock ticker to base a claim made for him that he was its inventor. Among great inventors Field is interesting in that, although making major contributions to the age of materialism, he remained an old-fashioned antimaterialist in practice, quite in the tradition of the valley. In 1902 the inventor of the trolley car led and won a passionate fight to keep the Berkshire Street Railway Company out of his own village, compelling it to go down along the river on its way from Lee to Great Barrington. In 1908 the great electrician assisted an equally passionate but losing fight to keep electric lights off the streets of Stockbridge.

Altogether, in the period between the Civil War and the 1930's, Berkshire County domiciled an array of inventors who were as important in the world of science as had been the Hawthornes, the Melvilles and the Holmeses in the world of literature. And of these men themselves it can surely be said that they lived a life of ideas quite as much as the Puritans did, or the libertarians, or the writers. The difference, however, was that, while the great writer, the great reformer, the great mystic induces ideas in those around him, the great scientist has the opposite effect—in so far as he is a great scientist. Although his own life is in his mind, he strengthens in society around him the tendency to interpret the world in material terms. While his own imagination is as active as that of any prophet, the inference of his work is that all life is subject to physical law. Although Stephen Dudley Field had none but an intellectual interest in the gadgets he contrived and would not have one of his own streetcars passing his door for commercial purposes, yet the fact is that he did contribute the streetcar, the elevator and the rest to the modern world, and so helped to bury the human spirit under a weight of things.

It can hardly be claimed, therefore, that the Age of Science in the valley was one in which the ideational tradition was preserved. In so far as the life of the mind continued in any community, it was in terms of what little remained, mostly in Stockbridge, of the literary tradition. But, as was pointed out earlier, the literary tradition was now feeble and, being Victorian, was decadent. It mostly subserved the new-rich snobbery that was really the dominant idea of the time, the pseudo idea that almost everybody from richest to poorest entertained in some form. The really great men of the age, the men who inspired most admiration and emulation, were the leading men of the actual, material world, the men both of financial success and of social grace, whose intellectuality was that of things as sense and reason say they are, the intellectuality of "realism." The acknowledged great men of the valley were not the scientists but the journalists, the lawyers, the men of wit and wisdom who knew how to get along in the market place.

The valley's chief journalist was Frank Crowninshield, summer resident of Stockbridge, much beloved there, the established chairman of all local doings that needed to be amusing. Joseph Pulitzer was an occasional visitor in Lenox, but never bought or rented land there.

Theoretically at the top of the valley's lawyers were Stockbridge's two members of the United States Supreme Court, Stephen Johnson Field and his nephew, David Josiah Brewer. But they were not even summer residents, and their work was not in the valley. David Dudley Field, Jr., was now an old man and the emeritus leader of the New York bar, retired to his new big house in Stockbridge called Eden Hill, and given to local good works. On his property, incidentally, was the little mansion which Abigail Williams Sergeant had required her husband to build for her in 1740.

Field's legal mantle had now fallen on Joseph Choate, who had his friend Charles McKim build him a handsome castle, also on the hill in Stockbridge. High with Choate in legal glory were his partner, Charles Southmayd, who had bought the Oxbow of the river from Longfellow, John E. Parsons, of New York and Lenox, and Charles E. Butler, one of the first "cottagers" in Stockbridge; all four of them were responsible leaders in the towns of their summer residence. Joseph Choate was altogether the perfect great man of his time: leader of the New York bar who had successfully defeated the first income tax in the United States Supreme Court in '95; he was ambassador to the Court of St. James's; exemplary family man; philanthropist; pattern of perfect manners; internationally famous wit.

"Who would you wish to be if you were not Joseph Choate?"—"Mrs. Choate's second husband."

"I have decided to become a permanent resident of Stockbridge."—"How is that, Mr. Choate?"—"I have just bought a lot in the cemetery."

"It is hardly necessary to build the proposed fence around the cemetery, since no one who is in it wants to get out and no one who is out wants to get in."

"Most men have five senses, but Southmayd has a sixth —a sense of property."

Less well known is Choate's passage in court with his friend John E. Parsons, who lived, besides in Lenox, in Rye, Westchester County, New York. In his address to the jury Mr. Parsons cautioned them against being swayed by his opponent's "Chesterfieldian style and urban manner." Rising in rebuttal, Choate called attention to his learned opponent's "Westchesterfieldian style and suburban manner."

Choate, Parsons and Depew were of the real gentry, which, if it could have been reinforced by the raw majority of the plutocracy, might have replaced American democracy by genuine aristocracy. To the raw majority it seemed that all that they—or rather their children—needed was a little education, namely, some good manners according to the code and a little knowledge from books. With their usual lavishness upon themselves, they set out to provide this education in the best and most costly way, the provision of the best equipped schools, paying the highest prices for the best teachers.

In seriously founding, patronizing and perpetuating excellent schools, the plutocrats of the valley and the nation most nearly laid their ax at the roots of their country, and particularly at the roots of the valley. For this looked like the real thing. It was a bid for the mind. It looked like an interest in the humanitarian idea of education, which in the previous age had fostered the public school system and multiplied the quasi-public academies. Actually it was nothing of the kind. The purpose was to superimpose upon public, democratic education a better and more exclusive education for a privileged class, the possessors of economic power.

So far as the founding of fine schools went, the plutocrats of the nation succeeded. They employed the best teachers, those with English accents preferred. In choosing the valley for locale, they picked a perfect countryside, where the ubiquitously gorgeous natural scene was merged—everywhere except on the estates—with human tradition in the architecture of farms, villages, walls, fields, byways, and the always preserved woodlots. In contrast with the palaces, the private school buildings were economical and functional, designed to fulfill a vital purpose. On their spectacular hilltops, or in their parks or rugged hollows, they were all beautiful, whether their style was English collegiate Gothic or Georgian, American Georgian or the wide-front-porch-and-columns style that was fashionable at the time of their construction. At once they fitted into their sites, and nature accepted them and embraced them rapidly with trees and vines.

Beginning in the seventies and gathering momentum, the valley sprouted more private boarding schools than any other rural region or any city in the world. The neighboring Connecticut Valley was the runner-up for rural regions and New York for cities. During the past seventy-five years many excellent schools have arisen, flourished and disappeared because of the death or incapacity of a celebrated headmaster or headmistress. Of the valley's surviving boarding schools, I shall list only twenty here, postponing mention of several others to a later chapter.

The Gunnery School, opening before the present period in Washington, Connecticut, has been described as the father of the valley's private boarding schools. Next, and the first within this period, was the Curtis School, founded in Bethlehem in '75, but moved out of the valley to Brookfield in '83. In order there followed: Hotchkiss, at Lakeville, '92; Miss Hall's School, at Pittsfield, '98; Rumsey Hall, started in New York State in 1900 and moved to Cornwall in 1907; Salisbury, in Salisbury, 1901; Connecticut Junior Republic (exceptional in being partly public and charitable), in Litchfield in 1904; Laurelton Hall, in 1905 in Milford; Kent, at Kent in 1906; Berkshire, at Berkshire in Lanesboro in 1907; Milford, started in New Haven as Rosenbaum Tutoring School in 1907 and moved to Milford as a boarding school in 1916; Canterbury, in New Milford in 1915; Duncan, in New Milford in 1916; Crestalban in Berkshire in 1917; Indian Mountain, in Salisbury in 1922; Litchfield, at Litchfield in 1922; South Kent, in Kent in 1923; Wooster, in Danbury in 1926; Weylister Secretarial Junior College, in Milford in 1927; Forman, in Litchfield in 1930.

With very few exceptions these and the dozen or so other schools established in the valley were—and still are—excellently run, staffed and equipped. The pupils of most of them could have become educated if their parents had desired it. But for the most part the youth became what the parents were or wished to be. The children of the gentry went on getting educated. The scions of the plutocrats went on becoming snobs, differing from their parents only in that they lost the ability that had made the money and substituted for it a supercilious ease and facility in bluffing the breeding and wisdom they did not possess. It would have taken a great deal more than schools to have transformed into a genuine aristocracy a selfish power group which had no permanent function in the community, no landed, legal or customary obligations, no economic purpose except the bald acquisition of more power, and no other use for wealth and prestige but its display.

Puritan Retreat

W HILE NEW wealth from the outer world was appropriating half the land of Lenox, perhaps a third of Stockbridge, and smaller fractions in the rest of the towns down the river, the currents of the previous age thinned toward oblivion. In inverse ratio to the rise of expensive, private boarding schools, the local, semipublic academies petered out, and their buildings were taken over by public schools, libraries, historical societies and other institutions. The last of them, those of Roxbury and Canaan, opened their doors in the eighties and nineties respectively. By 1920 all their doors, academically speaking, were closed for good.

Likewise industry continued to retreat after its defeat in the fifties and sixties. While the cities at the ends of the valley—Derby, Shelton, Danbury, Pittsfield, and latterly Stratford—continued to swell in population and output, the villages in the ninety miles between gave up their ambition to rival them. New Milford was especially reluctant to surrender and remain a beautiful village and town. It was not until after the turn of the twentieth century that granite quarrying there was finally given up in the face of competition with concrete; that the New Milford Hat Company failed; and the Cold Roll Steel Company; and the vegetable button business which supported two factories in the eighties. In commercial farming, the New Milford region built up a million-dollar tobacco business, but unfortunately it was a "stogy quality" tobacco, and since World War I it has contracted to about a fifth of its original volume. In the Upper Valley an important local industry suffered an unhappy mishap in the suffocation of one of its leaders in a folding bed which closed on him in a New York hotel; the companion who had been with him managed somehow to save herself from the jaws of permanent sleep.

New Milford not only declined in industry, but in 1890 it lost to hated outside enterprise a picturesque and profitable custom. From time immemorial the top of the spring shad run had been the Lover's Leap Rapids and, at their head, the "Great Falls" of New Milford. At the foot of the rapids was the big, quiet pond, the "Good Fishing Place" that gave Chief Waramaug his name, the "Fishing Cove" of the white man's vocabulary. There for centuries both races gathered and fished side by side—always at night—during the spring run, when the dorsal fins of the big ones cut the surface in the moonlight and hundreds of thousands were taken, fetching normally twenty-five cents for a sugar barrelful. They were so common that the hired men in their contracts would stipulate that shad should not be served beyond a set number of times a week. A person looking poorly was described as looking like "the last run of shad." At some time in the nineteenth century the fishing was organized, and the abutting property owners made a good thing of selling "rights" to fish at certain spots between certain hours on certain nights of the week. A man having a right could, if he chose, hire another to fish for him.

Up through the decades the shad survived these efforts to exterminate them. Then a human force intervened to save them or direct them elsewhere. In 1890, after a bitter political fight, the first dam was built across the river for the generation of electric power. It was constructed between Derby and Shelton, halfway down the old rapids there. It was agreed that a fish-race would be built alongside the dam, but the dam engineers made it as a series of steps which no shad could negotiate. At any rate, no shad ever did. For years public-spirited Derbyites kept armed guards at the dam, until the threats of the New Milfordites to dynamite it quieted down. And the Fishing Cove passed into memory.

Between 1869 and 1900 the valley made a lurid contribution to American civilization which was probably the region's last successful effort to get rich locally. In the seventies Charles B. Thompson of Bridgewater started in his native town America's first mail-order business. He had the true modern spirit, being concerned only with salesmanship and not at all with the quality of the goods he distributed. His usual method of putting on the heat was through premiums that really were attractive. When he offered beautiful dolls to salesmen of toilet soaps and facial creams, the little girls of the nation sold so much that the manufacturers couldn't meet the demand, and Thompson had to set up a plant of his own in Bridgeport. At one time when lanterns were hard to get and Thompson needed half a carload, he ordered a carload each from five concerns. To his astonishment all the orders were filled. Undismayed, he hung hundreds of the lanterns around Bridgewater Center on the first clear night. Thinking the glow in the sky meant a fire, the farmers swarmed in, and at cut rates Thompson disposed of three or four lanterns per farmer. Because of his enormous mail business, Bridgewater became a first-class post office. Nevertheless, the postmaster would occasionally grumble at the volume he had to handle. Then Thompson would shift his business to New Milford and the local man would come to heel. In the nineties, at the peak of his successes, Thompson built himself fitting memorials in tiny Bridgewater Center: a house that was not extreme for Victorian décor; a stable that was, and well worth a trip to Bridgewater to see; and a business block with a stylish false front, provided at one corner with an octagonal tower in which Thompson had his office. On the ground floor of the building he employed twenty-five lady clerks. Storage was in the cellar, and wrapping on the second floor.

Thompson lived, performed his miracles, and died in his native Bridgewater. His early contemporary, Phineas T. Barnum, was born in Danbury, but he practiced his even greater wonders in other parts of the nation. One of Barnum's achievements was the importation of Jenny Lind who, as already noted, glorified the echoes of Stockbridge and provided the name of Echo Lake there.

Even while the fabulous C. B. Thompson was making the valley's last effort to get rich, its greatest means to wealth, the river, was finally abandoned to beautiful uselessness. In the eighties a diarist making a canoe trip down the river notes the "almost endless series of unused water privileges on the Housatonic easily capable . . . of being improved." At the same time he observes many abandoned dams, left from the efforts at industrialization in the forties and fifties. In 1883 a survey of the valley was made, looking to the addition of the Housatonic water supply to that of New York City. A favorable report was made, proposing to locate the great reservoir at Bull's Bridge. The plan, which would have ended the hope of hydraulic development below Kent, was not carried out, doubtless because of the opposition of Derby and Shelton. But the water privileges continued to tumble down their rapids undeveloped all the same.

The inexplicable, the mysterious neglect of the Housatonic as an industrial stream continued. Above Derby it was not even worth mentioning in a report, in 1911, by the Connecticut Rivers and Harbors Commission. This incidentally brings us up to date on the later state of navigation on the tidal reaches of the river:

At the mouth [that is, across Stratford Harbor] the government has constructed a jetty 915 feet long. Its chief tributary is the Naugatuck River which is noted for its great extremes of water. . . . The Housatonic is navigable to Derby and Shelton, where the Naugatuck has its juncture. The general channel depth to Derby and Shelton, where the Naugatuck has its juncture, is from 5½ to 6½ feet [in colonial days it was reported as 13], but on account of the crooked channel commerce is usually carried by tidal navigation, barges going up stream on flood-tide. There has been $297,450 expended on the river since the first appropriation in 1871 by the government. Even with the unsatisfactory condition, commerce to the extent of 81,485 tons was handled last year, valued at $472,088.76. If plans were devised for pooling or canalizing the Naugatuck River to Waterbury, the Housatonic would become an important stream. . . .

In other words, the commercial possibilities of the main river are not worth considering, and the lesser but developed ones of the tributary Naugatuck are the only commercial asset to the Housatonic watershed. Shortly after this report was made, Guy Nickalls, coach of the Yale crew, discovered the Housatonic; a handsome university boathouse was built a little above the Derby dam, and the wide reaches above, between the great bluffs, were devoted to a picturesque and supposedly agreeable purpose.

Miscellaneous developments sprinkle the valley during these years between the Civil War and the 1929 crash. Pittsfield got its Academy of Music, a sort of opera house where the best talent came on tour, and where memorable balls were held on a platform built over the seats. Staffordshire in England put out commercially an eighty-two-piece set of "Pittsfield Old Elm Ware," the design showing the tall, venerable tree standing in front of the Bulfinch church in winter. Because of the industrialization of Pittsfield, its Berkshire Agricultural Society and fair—inaugurated as a cattle show in 1810 by Elkanah Watson, predecessor of Thomas Melville in ownership of Broadhall—diminished in resources and in public interest; it expired in 1901. Meanwhile the rival Housatonic Agricultural Society, centering around its annual fair on the Great Barrington grounds, prospered right down to recent time. Both of these Berkshire fairs, for which 15,000 was a good attendance, were small potatoes compared to the Danbury Fair which, though not founded till 1871 along with its sponsoring Danbury Farmers' and Manufacturers' Society, rapidly became one of the big annual events of New England, which it continues to be. By '96 the grounds included more than a hundred acres, with enormous permanent buildings, a grandstand holding 5,000, and an annual attendance of 60,000. Besides their showings of hundreds of purebred animals and birds, and tons of prize vegetables and preserves, besides the usual horse drawings, ox drawings and all the seductive concessions, both the Danbury and Great Barrington fairs draw the best entries in the East for their horse races; and each of them offers all imaginable human athletic contests, including sack races, spoon and egg races, shoe races and three-legged races.

By 1911, the river traffic below Derby had diminished to tug-drawn barges, and small passenger steamers that plied between Bridgeport and Derby. At New Milford also there was a tiny, side-wheel steamer "not much larger than a rowboat." Numerous iron and steel bridges were built across the river, including a "very handsome chain suspension bridge" at Zoar's Bridge. Two of the bridges built between 1869 to 1929 were the fourth and fifth successively over the river's mouth between Stratford and Milford, connecting the points between which the giant Moses Wheeler had rowed the first ferry in 1648. His successor had rowed Washington across in 1775 on his way to take command of the Continental Army, the commander in chief referring to the ferry in his diary as "near half a mile; and sometimes much incommoded by winds and crosstides." From this event each of the later bridges built there was called either the Washington or the George Washington Bridge. The first, built in 1802, was carried away by ice. The second, 1813, served until '68, when its big draw collapsed on a little steamer. In '72 this was replaced by a third, using most of the old piers. In '92 the first iron bridge was constructed. In 1921 the modern bridge was completed, commemorating magnificently in the midst of industrial filth the passage of a man and horse between two tiny towns on a rowed flatboat a century and a half before.

In 1902 the Berkshire Street Railway Company, which Inventor Field kept out of Stockbridge that year, just missed changing history. Teddy Roosevelt, president by dint of McKinley's assassination and without any vice-president under him, came to visit Massachusetts's governor W. Murray Crane of Dalton and agreed to make a few speeches in Berkshire. On the morning of September 3rd he spoke in Pittsfield, whereafter the four-horse carriage, bearing the president, Governor Crane, the president's secretary Cortelyou and a secret service man, set out for Lenox and Stockbridge. A little short of the Pittsfield Country Club, established three years before in old Broadhall, the trolley track swerved out from skirting the road and crossed it. Through miscalculation by somebody a crowded trolley car whipped out just in time to hit the presidential equipage. The secret service man and a horse were killed, the driver badly injured, the president scratched, the Governor and the secretary unhurt. A little later T. R., mounting the steps of the Curtis Hotel in Lenox and still splotched with blood and dirt, snapped his teeth characteristically, saying, "A man has been killed."

In this sixty-year period rounding the corner of the century, the village improvement societies continued their aesthetic efforts into what now became mature results, and visitors began to think that the neatly parked villages they saw had some relation to "ye olden days." At a date which I have been unable to determine a gentleman of New Milford, being in his Sunday best and threading his way across the swamp that from time immemorial had been the focus of the village, inadvertently stepped on a half-submerged hog which rose with a snort, upsetting the intruder, and gave him a fast ride out to dry land. In '75 the Village Improvement Society was formed, took cognizance of the swamp, filled it, planted in and around it, and so transformed the old common land into the handsome, modern green. Litchfield matured into the most beautiful village in the valley, and one of the half dozen most beautiful in America. As already reported of Lenox and Stockbridge, all the villages blossomed with miscellaneous halls and monuments.

In 1886 Litchfield, in 1895 and 1896 Great Barrington, and in 1904 New Milford all suffered fires that eliminated most of their business sections. The generally foursquare brick reconstruction in Great Barrington and New Milford suited the clapboard construction of the villages. But a decade earlier in Litchfield, late Victorian ponderosity influenced some of the replacements, making them out of key with the architecture of the rest of the village. Generally, this sixty years suffered little from this architectural style, except in the several wooden Gothic churches of all denominations that may be found in the valley.

The last important surge of building in the period was

in the neocolonial style of the twenties, the boom time when neat brick libraries sprouted, along with handsome, neo-Georgian town halls, and schools with better plants than teachers or educational systems. Library buildings varying from the norm were the marble one given to Stratford, the stone one presented to Cornwall, the older and larger Victorian ones of Milford and Pittsfield. At the same time there was an epidemic of historical societies, establishing themselves in donated colonial houses, in abandoned academy buildings, or pre-empting sections of the library buildings. Meanwhile, the twentieth century was proceeding from telephones and trolley cars to electric lights and automobiles, and so to macadam roads and motor fire engines in all the towns.

As always, the valley exceeded its quota of men and money in World War I. Between the war and the crash of 1929 there was a transitional period, the end of Victorian snobbery and the rise of the new individualism which deified self-indulgence. While enjoying increasingly magnificent roads and multiplying gadgets, the whole country gyrated through a phase of restlessness and rootlessness greater than any since the age of emigration and immigration that followed the Revolution.

The population trend between 1869 and 1929 was mixed. While the industrial cities grew spectacularly, the greater, rural part of the valley declined, to reach in 1920 its lowest figure since 1800. The lowlands did better than hold their own, but the hilltop regions that man had first denuded of forest and soil continued the process, begun in the previous period, of denuding themselves of man. In Dudleytown in Cornwall the last house fell into its cellar about 1910, and in the brush in the cellar hole you can still find fragments of plaster and shreds of beams. Already the region, where there had been twenty farmhouses in a mile diameter, had gone back to forest growing in the highways and closing tall shade over the once cleared fields and pastures. The only living flesh and blood were birds and chipmunks, the only sounds their calls and the murmurs of streams. Nature was beginning the thousand-year process of restoring the topsoil which man threw away. Most of the big cellar holes were already partly filled, and the road and pasture walls were winding welts in the earth all overgrasped by the roots of trees. The road coming up three miles from Cornwall Bridge had always been called the Dark Entry, because it climbed a canyon under hemlocks and was in consequence always night-

bound. Now the name took on ominous significance, and the swelling legends multiplied the ghosts who would pursue you in Dudleytown, whistling and screaming at you and killing you if they could. The more literal minded said it was a great region for owls, and called it Owlsborough.

Another hilltop region in Cornwall was Dibble Hill, but since its slopes were not so steep as those of Dudleytown it was still in the transitional state of agricultural and human decadence. There, through the seventies, in their respective, slowly crumbling ancestral houses, lived two "witches," complete with beards and pipes, late daughters of Revolutionary veterans, the first inhabitants of the hill. Besides them, there were five families on the hill, three of hillbilly Yankees and two of more promising " '48 Irish" who had come in to build the railroad and had stayed. Everybody on the hill took his cider by the gallon, and the de luxe drink was metheglim, a fermentation of honey guaranteed to be anesthetic.

The men of one of the Irish families were gigantic. One of the sons was able to lift a full cider barrel—about 600 pounds—and set it on his shoulder. The inhabitants of Dibble Hill once reported patriotically at a church raising in the valley, their brawn being much counted on; but after a few minutes' fortification with metheglim they all sat in a trance, and the frame did not rise.

Between the last-ditch Yankee families on Dibble Hill and their Irish neighbors there were eternal feuds, leading sometimes to barn burning, sometimes to lawsuits. But against the valley people they were united, swooping down periodically to steal their cattle. They were let alone by the lowlanders with a frightened respect suggestive of medieval Scotland. On at least one occasion when the highlanders had driven off some cows and butchered them, they made the magnificent gesture of returning the valuable hides. It is said of them all that they watered their milk—"The spring was their best cow."

Yet among these final hillbillies some decency and some hope remained. In the midst of the wilderness, one of the youths in the best of the three Yankee families, while holding up his end of devilry with the rest, was all the time studying in the office of an attorney in West Cornwall. His first achievement of note was to get the gang off, the only time they were haled into court for cattle stealing. His personal reputation was for sharp dealing when you opposed him and for generosity when you didn't. The Honorable L. J. Nickerson eventually bought almost all of Dibble Hill, rose to be the strongest man in his town, the speaker of the Assembly of his state, and for years one of its most respected Superior Court judges.

Probably the largest, wholly desolate upland region in the valley towns is that of North Goshen, once a thriving community with a church and a couple of mills, but almost deserted by 1920 when the water company of Torrington bought it for its big pond—the drainage of that corner of Goshen is mostly eastward into the Naugatuck. The water company burned down everything that was still standing, creating in one stroke a desert which nature would have required another fifty years to complete. Because the main roads of the region—perhaps three miles square—were kept open up to within twenty-five years, and because some of the houses stood over their cellars until then, it is now a cemetery of a lost civilization better outlined, more Pompeii-like, than others in the valley. In 1923, the trustees of its old Methodist church, then still standing, solemnly met and voted to demolish the building already long bereft of services. For a monument they raised on edge the heavy, lunar doorstep that stands in the new wilderness, bearing its epitaph of a civilization: "This doorstep erected in memory of the original subscribers of the North Goshen M.E. Church which stood here 1840-1923." Near by the old mill pond still pours over and through the monolithic ruins of its dam. All around on the abandoned back roads the frost has thrust levers into the walls, and the bridges are leaning into the little streams. But wherever there was a farm the three or four, set-out trees along the road still tower over the rest of the forest, marking the place. Front steps remain, and the remnants of posts and gates. The ghosts of North Goshen are alive and friendly because they are young ghosts; because their bodies were there only a little while ago.

Contiguous to the North Goshen desert, and divided from it only in that its streams eventually reach the Housatonic, is another lost, upland region called Meekertown, partly in Goshen and partly in Norfolk. Originally most of the thousands of acres here were part of the property of the Sedgwicks of Cornwall Hollow, and the farmers were their tenants. By the eighties all these small farms were denuded of soil and deserted, except for one, owned by a wealthy farmer we may call Smith. He had 300 or 400 acres that made a level and fertile plateau on the top of the ridge. A good road led eastward to Norfolk and westward down a long steep hill to the Dogtown furnace at Huntsville in Canaan. One morning in the late eighties Mr. Smith drove out to Norfolk for the day. For his own reasons the hired man decided that this was the time for him to leave, and he told Mrs. Smith so. For her reasons she informed him that he was not going to leave. But he went up to his little room in the wing, wrapped his belongings in a big handkerchief, came down and started out. When he was at the front gate Mrs. Smith shot him from the house with the family shotgun. He crawled a mile down the road to the first cabin of a Huntsville furnace worker and died there. Mr. Smith devoted his entire property to the defense of his wife. He got her off with a life sentence and left the region a poor man. The substantial house was the last standing in Meekertown. As late as 1930 a hunter cut an old shot-gun slug out of one of the gateposts. The site is now covered by an artificial lake, one of a chain by means of which the present owner of the region, ex-United States Senator Wolcott of Norfolk, is transforming sixty years of desolation into well-drained, healthy forest.

Despite the return to wilderness of the once populated hilltops—and the instances I have given could be nearly matched on the hills of every town—despite this decline, the whole combination of tendencies in the valley between the Civil War and the crash of 1929 would not seem at first glance to indicate any general trend of special significance for better or for worse. The loss of population on the hills was almost equaled by the growth in the valleys where the amount of tillable soil was increasing. The relatively prosperous farms of the lowlands were outstripped as money-making concerns by the western farms; but the inhabitants of the valley had never farmed to get rich anyway. Their traditional, subsistence basis remained sound, and their increased returns were sufficient to pay for the new farm machinery that was now universal.

Almost everywhere along the river the little industries initiated in the previous age failed. But they had never employed so many local people as to effect much dislocation by their failure. The few Raggies of Salisbury were the only group that suffered noticeably because of the closing of an industry. Other unemployment was drawn off by the West and the cities.

The old academies disappeared, but they were presumably equaled or excelled by the new public high schools and private boarding schools. The literary output of the valley declined, but it did not cease; and in its place the valley had a population of lawyers and scientists who were as high in their respective fields as the great writers of the previous age had been. On the physical side, the villages were everywhere painted and parked. The old horse roads were replaced by automobile-carrying highways. The valley became ostentatiously healthy with hospitals, intellectual with libraries, and proud with historical societies.

Into this landscape of normal growth there intruded, to be sure, the army of alien wealth, setting up its castles and having itself carried about the landscape in its coaches. But this spectacular invasion was seemingly confined to four Berkshire towns, the amount of land it occupied was infinitesimal in the valley as a whole, and in most of the region no tallyho was ever heard. Related to the industrial wealth brought in from outside was the crop of private boarding schools which came up everywhere in the valley; but these too had seemingly little effect on the real life of the Yankees, the late Puritans, who went about their self-sufficient ways, apparently little concerned at the new rich and their antics.

This was the surface of the valley as it emerged into contemporary time. Actually the effect of wealth was more profound than was implied by statistics about how much of the land it pre-empted or how widely it vaunted itself. In the initial phase, the relation between the Yankees and the rich was illustrated by an anecdote of the beginning of one of the Lenox estates.

The first of two Rackemann brothers, German boys, came to America on a cattle boat, the second a little later and under more respectable auspices. For a while one of them taught music in the Sedgwick School in Lenox. Eventually they became prosperous architects in Boston, bought the Sedgwick property where Mr. and Mrs. Charles and Catherine had lived so long, tore it down, and let a contract to build for themselves a relatively modest cottage. Their contractor was William H. Clark, come from one of Lenox's oldest and most respected families, himself the salt of the earth and a good builder. While the work was in process he fell into doubt about a point, and to resolve it took the cars to Boston. The Rackemanns' office was on a second floor, with one of the first plate-glass windows in Boston looking out over the street. Mr. Clark and one of the Rackemanns sat at the window discussing their problem. Mr. Clark had a heavy quid in his mouth, and when Mr. Rackemann went back to the files, thinking the window was open, he let fly. Instantly he was up on the window sill, trying to wipe it off with his red bandanna. Whether maliciously or considerately, Rackemann stayed in the back office long enough for one of his young artists to draw a picture of Clark at work on the sill. Out of such incidents as this the Yankee, the bearer of the Puritan tradition, gradually became a "hick," a comic character who was outside the current of modern civilization.

In Lenox the invasion of wealth was so powerful as to change ethnically the control of the town. The Yankees, seduced by high prices, sold their farms and, being unwilling to work for somebody else, departed to the West or to the cities. By 1900, the retainers of the rich were a majority of the population, and almost everybody was in some way dependent on them. Here, as always at crucial points, the local historian lays aside his Victorian false whiskers and states the facts. After indicating the boom prices of land at the end of the century, he proceeds:

. . . A little of the old New England stock still survives, but it is a remnant. A different order has come about. In place of the New England yeomanry . . . [the most intelligent men of their class in the world according to Fanny Kemble] have come the summer residents and the caretakers of the great estates. The whole personnel in the public places, in the churches, has entirely changed. The character and nationality of the citizens of Lenox differ *toto coelo* from what they were fifty years ago. Municipal conditions have arisen more difficult to cope with. . . .

A few of the new rich, to be sure, were the peers of the best Yankee "yeomanry," because they were rooted in it themselves. But most of them were not. And none of the "caretakers" or servants were, at the outset. These became a majority at town meeting. Being of the European servant class, they were irresponsible and predatory outside their actual jobs, and their employers did not generally encourage them into a posture of independent citizenship.

Most of the Yankees who remained were likewise forced into an attitude of sycophancy, as either servants, artisans or merchants catering to the rich. It was generally a ruthless sycophancy, aimed at bleeding the conquerors of as much as possible of what they had first bled from the country. In some cases, where individual fondness appeared, it was an agreeable sycophancy. But whatever else it was, in the bosom of those Yankees, with two hundred and fifty years of breeding in independence, it was a bitter and an unhealthy sycophancy. Weakened as they were, the tradition of the Yankees was stronger than that of the new rich. The European servants presently became Yankees, bitter and twisted Yankees like their neighbors.

Today you may ask any one of the lower help on the remaining estates what he thinks of his employer, and you will usually get a sour earful. The higher help and the merchants who serve the rich will be more reticent. But at length you will find the same hatred in all of them. Like the Yankees who went to the cities, most of those of Lenox and many of Stockbridge, Lee and Great Barrington sold their birthright for something that glittered. They sold their independence on their own land and became renters and wage earners to a new and imposing system. Now they are a people of split personalities. Their native independence is not dead. But it is eaten by a bitterness. The bitterness is both a criticism of their employers who have not held their glitter, and it is more profoundly a contempt for themselves for having bowed to what their ancestors called "the world." They know now that plutocracy is not aristocracy, not even in the third generation.

So much for the effect of great wealth upon many of the citizens of Lenox, Stockbridge, Lee and Great Barrington. Before going on to the somewhat subtler effect of new wealth on the rest of the valley, I want to point out a partial degeneracy of the Yankees from Puritan standard that was going on irrespective of the invasion by impressive strangers. The Civil War generation was the last one that was motivated chiefly by what we might call great ideas. In the main, the first generation to mature after the Civil War succumbed to the materialism that was sweeping the country with the weapons of science, new wealth, machinery, factories and cities. The average Yankee still took his family to church, because it was sociable and the thing to do. But his idea of God, let alone old Congregationalist doctrine, was extremely vague, and he did not, as his ancestors until quite recently had done, spend a daily time on his knees trying to keep in touch with eternal truth. Like the rest of the Western world, he became an agreeable agnostic, a trifle condescending to his ancestors because of their piety.

The traditional independence of himself and his neighbors remained a powerful prejudice in him, and he would fight for it any time. Yet it was not often a conscious idea with him, as it had been in his Revolutionary and Jacksonian ancestors, a central conviction to which the rest of life must conform. Nor was the central focus of his life necessarily in any large and inclusive idea of any kind. He no longer dealt consciously in such notions as those of his fathers about the preservation of the Union and the fallacy of one man being compelled to serve another. He could say these things, he still had an admiration for book learning, but he did not seek it for himself. The leather library that all his grandfathers had accumulated dry-rotted on the shelves or in boxes in the attic. The intellectual tradition of New England faded in the country almost as much as in the industrial slums.

By the seventies, few Yankee men centered their lives any more about great ideas. The reason was that secretly, without admitting it even to themselves, they suspected that their great ideas no longer mattered, even if they had them. From the magazines and the papers they gathered the slow and troublesome impression that the smart folks who were running the nation were now city people, that they and their neighbors no longer had much to say about it, that the symposium in the grocery store was no longer going to direct the nation. Since they couldn't do anything about it, why worry about it? Why puzzle about highfalutin' notions that somebody else was going to apply, if anybody did. Every Yankee remained in pattern a Puritan. He still centered life about some idea. But now it became in most cases a little idea, a prejudice or a tough little complex such as could hold an uneducated mind. Being all he had, it was secret and sacred, but in fact is wasn't much, and he knew it. The compensation was to roll in an extra barrel of cider and keep up the courtesy and the humor. In his decline, the Puritan was more charming than ever. He didn't throw in the sponge. He'd play his game through. And he'd never admit his suspicions to anybody. Only, if his boy came to him and insisted on going to the city, he'd let him.

The effect of the change in the Yankee world was greater on the women than on the men. Traditionally, the woman expected the man to commune with God and report His requirements to the family. Or if he didn't do that, at least she expected him to pull down equally clear directives out of that mysterious abstract world of principle that was his special region. Now the woman knew as well as her man did that he wasn't doing either. He no longer occupied her soul, filled her imagination. She knew that anything he required was just his own notion, not God's—it might even be his drunken notion. The women lost respect for their men, and so grew contemptuous of everything, suspicious, malicious, destructive, shrill, all the things that the real Puritan women, even the recent Yankee women, had not been. Though the basic failure was in the men, the women approached the hillbilly stage faster than the men did. As the men weakened they grew tolerant, not necessarily opposed to change but indifferent to it. It was the women who developed the angry conservatism and the hatred of "foreigners." And in the new state of things, more often than not, it was the women who bossed the men.

Into this phase of early social decay in the valley came the forces of wealth and power. I pointed out the effects of the very rich, the new rich, the big rich in the four Berkshire towns they most thoroughly pre-empted. Ultimately, their effect may not prove to have been destructive. The bitterness and contempt in the consciousness of the local Yankees may presently lead to a conscious reassertion of their own importance, a revival of their individualistic tradition. More subtle was the effect of what might be called the little rich who at the same time came in to buy or build their little houses everywhere in the valley.

Salisbury got its "Gentleman's Driving Park." Litchfield was lucky and exceptional, in that several of its own old families were the ones to become summer people. Enough of them were there to dominate the rest of the rich and to form a real link between them and the Yankees who stayed at home. In the rest of the towns this was rarely the case. The summer people who came in were usually strangers. Usually these little rich were "nice" people, and their moderate wealth was often not new. They were often the old families of former villages that in the last two or three generations had become industrial cities from which they now wanted to escape. As part of the growth of their home cities, some of their ancestral properties had boomed in value and left them well off. Perhaps they had been prominent families at home for three or four generations. The reason they now came into the country to establish modest summer homes was

not any new rise to power but the simple fact that the multiplying railroads would now take them there easily. Also,
things were going well with their carefully watched invest-
ments; it seemed certain that the confusion of The War was
over.

These people were of the same stuff as the local Yankees
in the unchanged villages of the valley. If anything, that
made their influence more sinister. The local yokels could
not laugh at them and feel superior. Yet there remained that
fatal barrier of wealth. Though these people made no show,
the mere fact that they could migrate like the birds showed
that they were what a farmer would call rich. Here in his
very next-door neighbor whom he came to like, who did not
condescend to him, who indeed envied much of his rural
independence and admired his virtues, here more than in the
big rich who were remote and contemptible was a visible re-
minder to the old Yankee that he and his ideas were no longer God's special care, that the center of the universe had
moved out of town. The fantastic towers and palaces of
Lenox might fade and leave not a rack behind. But what
were you going to do about a summer neighbor who had only
one or two horses and took care of them himself, who liked
to do a little gardening, who greeted you civilly and could
make or take a joke, who liked to come in on chilly evenings
and have a glass of cider and put his feet on your stove and
talk about things you'd heard your father talk about, but
that somehow you hadn't kept up on? To be sure, your wife
kept sneering at his wife and telling you you ought to be
ashamed of yourself, guzzling cider with foreigners. All the
same, you liked this new summer neighbor better and better
the more you saw of him. The only thing about him that
bothered you was that you never left off talking with him
but you began to try to remember why it was that thirty
years ago you hadn't taken that chance to go to the city
when your brother went? Here, in the relations between the
little rich and the local farmers everywhere in the valley,
there might be a threat to Yankee independence more serious
than that in a part of the Upper Valley where the Yankees

had made fools of themselves by selling out and going to work for a lot of jackanapes that went around in fancy short pants and loud neckties such as no self-respecting man would be seen dead in. The Yankees of the Upper Valley were in a bad way, but at least the reasons for it were plain. The Yankees of the bulk of the valley seemed to be better off, but in so far as the attack on them was gentler and subtler, their retreat into uncertainty might be more significant.

Tallyho - Diminuendo

THE FATE of the Devil's last campaign in the valley had no relation to the moral quality of his troops, if "moral" is used in the usual way of relating to conduct. By the standards of the Ten Commandments, the "cottagers" were not any better or any worse than the general run of humanity. You get the impression that there were rather fewer scandals among the Berkshire rich than in most irresponsible groups, and in the second and third generations less degeneracy than is to be expected in the inheritors of great wealth. There was the smart pair of horses that broke themselves one bright morning going up hill to their stable at an extended trot, drawing the rubber-tired runabout where the young heir of their estate had passed out on the seat, keeping a slack hold of the reins. There is the story of a wife nagging her mild husband to the point where he threw a dinner knife at her at table just as an unexpected guest entered. There was the cottager who spent years plotting to buy the place nearest his in order to indulge the pleasure of tearing it down—the building so demolished was built around Lenox's best colonial house. The same demolisher went about sputtering with delight when a distinguished connection of his by marriage seemed in danger of going to jail for a slight inadvertence in the matter of the antitrust laws. There was the cottager who performed the exquisite and successful act of sadism of prescribing in his will that his wife and another lady he had introduced into the home must live together, at pain of loss of interest in the house by whichever one departed. There were the usual whispers of adulteries, both founded and unfounded. There were two or three cases where addiction to legal prescriptions taken with hypodermics suggested addiction to dope. By and large the Berkshire plutocracy differed from other groups of Americans only in its trappings and pretenses.

The defeat of the Devil's last legions in the valley was due to the fact that they neither adapted themselves to traditional American society and economy nor conquered them and transformed them into a going aristocracy. Their social failure appeared in the attitude of their children. In one house a music room was finished in gold leaf and a complete, ecclesiastical, pipe organ installed for the enthrallment of an invalid son. A few of the spoiled youths continued to live the lives of "gentlemen," without other interests. But most of the children were Americans in spite of their parents. They wanted to make their own way, and in several cases they broke their parents' hearts by not being sufficiently interested in the luxury to which they were born. They didn't have much time to spend in the hilltop palaces, and they didn't see the sense of keeping them up as expensive heirlooms.

A sad case was that of the two daughters of one of the most refined of the cottagers, and one of the country's major collectors. Because of a faint psychopathic taint in the young ladies' inheritance, psychiatrists advised the father to confine them from social contacts until they had passed a certain age. The prescription was enforced for several years. Then on the same day the unfortunately healthy American girls eloped respectively with the head chauffeur and the poulterer, the four of them going over the hill to Richmond where the Congregational minister tied the unfilial knots. The marriage with the chauffeur ended in divorce. For this reason, and especially because there were no children, the father would have welcomed that prodigal daughter back. But she was not interested and set herself up as a sculptor in another town down the valley. The marriage with the poulterer proved happy. The couple became responsible and respected citizens of Richmond, where they raised two admirable sons. Because of their happiness and successful life, no reconciliation with the father was possible. He finally gave his consent to one brief visit by his grandsons, stipulating that they call him "Mr." So-and-so. This was one of the men who had back of him the breeding that might have produced aristocracy. Perhaps the trouble was that his tradition, though ancient, was of Boston, that strange society which so conscientiously refused to rise above the bourgeois pattern.

On the economic side the defeat of the new rich was due to their failure to identify their wealth with real responsibility for the well-being of society, either in the valley or in the nation. They invoked the principle of liberty for purposes of accumulating their wealth, and denied the principle when they wanted to interfere with the liberty of somebody else. Instead of identifying themselves with society, they set themselves against it. Consequently, beginning in the nineties, society began to get after them. Joseph Choate of Stockbridge protected them from democracy's first counterattack in the income tax of 1894, persuading the Supreme Court to hold the tax unconstitutional. But in 1913 the Sixteenth Amendment meant the mobilization of the country to drive them from their strongholds. In 1918 they were paying 77 per cent on incomes of $1,000,000 or more. In 1932 the peacetime tax on the same was 55 per cent, and in 1935 it was 75 per cent. This was different from the eighties and nineties when you never got less than 8 per cent and had no income tax to pay. With local help in the shape of real estate taxes of between five and ten thousand dollars per estate, the country broke the ranks of plutocracy. By dodging from place to place, a few were able for a time to avoid having a residence and so any liability for the income tax; but this stratagem did not avail for long. Under relentless bombardment by the people whom their owners had ignored, the tinsel palaces began to crumble. Some held out until they were demolished. Some came to terms, being permitted to stand upon the reduced garrisons' undertaking to carry on in modest style. Thus, in the few palaces still occupied by their original families, with a staff of half a dozen where once there were a hundred, we see in dusty and threadbare grandeur the first intimation of that aristocracy which they failed to achieve in their palmy days.

With dramatic justice, the event that marked architecturally the high noon of Berkshire glory contained in it the first intimation of the decline. The location of the mammoth Aspinwall Hotel in 1900 on the top of the valley's central ridge was made possible by the sale of Cliffwood the Aspinwall-Woolsey estate, one of the oldest, and the demolition of its relatively modest house of the fifties. The next strong points to fall were also of the older vintage of cottages, Yokun that had been the property of Richard Goodman, and Interlaken that was built by D. W. Bishop. The surrender of Shadowbrook, greatest of the castles, in the year after World War I, was a major debacle; and in the manner of the surrender we see a pattern that was going to become familiar in the capitulations that were to follow. Shadowbrook was built by Anson Phelps Stokes in the mid-nineties, abandoned by him about 1900, and sold to S. P. Shotter. Mr. Shotter sold it about 1910, and it was used as a hotel for a few years before Andrew Carnegie bought it. He died there in 1919, and three years later Mrs. Carnegie sold it to the Jesuit Order for a novitiate. The biggest of the houses was thus the first to succumb to the tradition of the valley and to become a school, not a snobbish school aimed at fashioning the children of the rich into imitations of European, aristocrats, but a real seminary dedicated to the service of one of mankind's great ideas.

Probably the nearest to the type story of the rise and fall of new wealth is contained in the history of Kellogg Terrace, or Barrington House, the famous Hopkins-Searles château in Great Barrington. Here is the incredible success story; the generous and bewildered intentions; the entry of the artist who was also half brigand; the gorgeous $2,000,-000 pile signifying nothing; the curtain on the farce in proprietary wrangling; the epilogue in the consecration of the pile to a social purpose.

In 1851 Miss Mary Frances Sherwood was twenty years

old, penniless, and a teacher in the select school for young ladies conducted in Great Barrington by her three aunts, the Misses Sarah, Mary and Nancy Kellogg. The school building contained Bryant's former law office, the site today being under or near the southern end of the Berkshire Inn. The Kellogg homestead, occupied by the three spinsters and said to have been a beauty, was across the street where the mansion now stands. In that year of 1851 there appeared in town a successful young forty-niner named Mark Hopkins, descended from the original Great Barrington Hopkins and a remote cousin of the Mark Hopkins who was then president of Williams. Mark the forty-niner looked on Mary the schoolteacher with approval, married her, took her to California, became one of the "Big Four" with Crocker, Huntington and Stanford, and died in '78 leaving Mary a fortune of not less than twenty nor more than fifty millions, including palaces in San Francisco, New York and Paris.

In 1881 a firm of New York decorators sent out to Mrs. Hopkins a young salesman of theirs named Edward F. Searles, be being an architect and something of a musician on the side. He was twenty years younger than Mrs. Hopkins, and she liked him so well that she made him her financial adviser and kept him by her. In the same year Nancy, the last of the Kellogg aunts, died and left the old homestead to Mary. With a tender, homecoming sigh Mary, who seems always to have remained a local girl, abandoned her palaces and flew home to Great Barrington to nest.

Edward, however, had different ideas. To his credit be it remembered that his interest in the Hopkins money was little if any for personal aggrandizement and almost exclusively for the creation of beauty, according to his lights. He started modestly, inducing Mary to buy all of the present mansion grounds, demolish the old houses thereon and do a job of landscaping. Then he caused the erection of an elaborate, Gothic coach house out of the famous Great Barrington bluestone, a strange anomaly as an adjunct to the colonial mansion. Meanwhile Mary was devoting herself to good works. She made a very large donation to the church, and

soon afterwards got a bill for her pew. She had in mind to
endow a free school for girls.

In 1885 Edward revealed his hand, got Mary's consent
and went to work on what was probably the most luxuriously
appointed of the Berkshire cottages, this one a late Renais-
ance Victorian-French château of the local bluestone, containing, *inter alia*: a sixty-foot, marble atrium copied from
the Athenian Erechtheum, a Louis XIV drawing room which

was first built in Paris and afterwards imported; a two-and-
a-half-story, barrel-vaulted organ room whose organ—which
Edward played well—was set in a magnificent shell; two
underground stories of culinary and thermal catacombs, including a kitchen all marble to the drawers and an electric
plant; three equally complicated upper stories labyrinthine
with dark passages, mysterious, crossing stairways, gorgeous
bedrooms and circular tower rooms, all done in the fanciest
woods and marbles with intricate ceilings copied from famous
European buildings. While overseeing the construction of this
château Edward was building himself another one in his
home town of Methuen, Massachusetts.

During the Christmas season, 1886, Mary opened Kellogg Terrace with a reception. Thereafter, she lived there a few months, then married Edward who, after the wedding trip, took her to his own place at Methuen, where she lived four years and died. By the will Edward got everything, but he immediately settled out of court with the heirs, who sued claiming undue influence.

Paradoxically, he now moved back to Kellogg Terrace and renamed it Barrington House. He made friendly gestures toward the town, including the gift of a high school. At the same time he complained of his assessment, and bitterly opposed the passage of the Berkshire Street Railway Company down Main Street past his property. Failing to prevent this, he built the great wall round his place. At last, driven to desperation by a switching curve at the corner where the car wheels screamed, he moved the organ and other treasures to Methuen and abandoned Great Barrington. During this period, it should be remembered to Edward Searles' credit, he dickered a good deal and unsuccessfully with the town about endowing the place as a free school, with the emphasis on music, a plan which would have carried out his wife's wishes.

In 1920 Searles died, leaving Barrington House to his secretary, Mr. Walker. He also complained of the taxes, and one day in 1923 told the board of tax review that his assessment of $650,000 was absurd, that he would sell the place for a tenth of that. A few hours later a syndicate of local citizens called and tendered him $65,000, which he accepted. Since it has not been possible since to make a sale of the property appropriate to its magnificence and the interests of the town, the Barrington School for girls was established there in 1924, an institution having college preparatory standards rather than social ones. Mary Sherwood's dream of a free school has not been realized; but at least the great pile which she probably never desired is dedicated to an educational purpose—which puts it, incidentally, in the best tradition for Berkshire palaces.

By 1924 the casualties among the great estates and

houses had been Cliffwood, Interlaken, Yokun, Shadowbrook and Barrington House. In 1926, Sunnycroft of G. G. Haven and, next door, F. K. Sturgis's Clipston Grange, adjoining the Lenox site of the now long-demolished house of Charles Sedgwick, were combined into the partially endowed Lenox School for Episcopal boys of small means. At first the school was held in the Haven House, using its stable for dining hall. Later the house was torn down to save taxes and a more modest academic building was put up down the hill.

In 1929 came the financial punishment of the whole nation for the violation of economic law, the debacle which most precisely marks the end of the golden pseudo civilization produced by the industrial revolution after the Civil War. It would still be many years before the fallen giant would be wholly dead. Meanwhile, two years after the crash, there occurred in the Berkshires one of those Acts of God which, seemingly the work of chance, yet symbolized the trend of the times.

A little after midnight on April 25, 1931, Police Officer Timothy Dunn was returning from a tour of duty to his home in Lenox village when, as he came up on his front porch, he saw flames high on the hill to the northwest. It couldn't be anything but the big hotel, the Aspinwall, a mile from the village up there on the cliffs, empty at this time of year, and with all the water drained from its water system that had dozens of hydrants. Officer Dunn ran to the house of his neighbor, Fire Chief Oscar R. Hutchinson. The fire departments of Lenox, Lenoxdale, Lee and Pittsfield responded. The first hose line laid was 4,000 feet up from the nearest hydrant in the village, and all the other lines were longer. The big pumpers stood in series up the long, elegant drive, but all of them together could produce only fifty pounds of pressure up there on the cliff. The cause of the fire was never known. The great building was already doomed when the fire was discovered; could hardly have been saved if its own water system had been available. But the fire walls slowed the spread of the fire sufficiently to enable the firemen to make a stand on the equipment building which adjoined the main house and to save that, the four employees' dormitories and the big garage. It was the most spectacular fire in the history of the valley for location, and, for a single building, perhaps the most spectacular fire in the history of America. Lenox village below survived a five-hour shower of sparks. On its 1,400-foot eminence the actual blaze was visible twenty-five miles. The brilliant sky was seen from points three times as far away, from Albany, from the top of the Mohawk Trail on Jacob's Ladder, from far down in Connecticut. In the night thousands of people assembled along the great clifftop to watch the symbol of the age writhe and roar and growl like a dying titan. In five hours the acre of ruins was flat. On the dawn of that April day there was no vast, summer hotel up there on the forehead of the mountain. Instead, there was only the old Curtis Hotel in the village, the inheritor of the tradition of the Berkshire Coffee House.

Coming so soon after the crash of 1929, in the depth of financial depression, on the eve of the New Deal period when the people of the nation were going to declare that they were no longer impressed by the mirage of wealth, the destruction of the Aspinwall was a blow to the life of Switzerland in America from which it never rallied. With a recovery of $600,000 of insurance, the owners were probably lucky to get out when they did. The automobile had already put a term on the age of great summer hotels. It has never been thought worth the risk to rebuild. The remaining buildings were demolished, and the mountain was sold to a timber company. It is now a wild region, one of the pleasantest walks in Lenox.

From that summer of '31 the sound of the tallyho began to diminish, and fewer coaches were seen in the land. The end was certain, and throughout the thirties the only questions were, which property would go next, and how long it would take them all to go. In Stockbridge a syndicate of real estate agents bought the de Gersdorff place. Dr. McBurney's estate was sold to Massachusetts for a state forest. The Whitney Preserve on October Mountain was likewise

sold for a picnic ground. The David Dudley Field place became an Episcopal school, which in turn gave way to a school
for Polish priests. In '32 Mrs. William Crane opened the
Morning Face School on the estate in Richmond.

In Lenox, on the site of Henry Ward Beecher's house,
John Sloan had built the Scotch baronial Wyndhurst which
was too far from New York for his son to use enough to
justify keeping it. Through Mr. Sloan's daughter it descended
into her husband's estate, out of which it was sold to a Mr.
Cole. He was gathering in half a dozen estates for some
elaborate real estate promotion scheme, including the Schermerhorn property and Morris K. Jesup's Belvoir Terrace. He
adorned Wyndhurst with a golf links and organized it into
the Berkshire Hunt and Country Club. His scheme was
against the trend of the times, and as far as Wyndhurst was
concerned it failed. Edward Cramwell advanced great sums
to the inflated club, and ended by taking it over and selling
the whole property to a Catholic school for one dollar.

Next door to Wyndhurst, the widow of Robert W. Patterson is said to have refused $250,000 for Blantyre, wanting
$300,000. After paying taxes for ten years, she sold it for
$25,000. It is said to be one of the solidest built places in the
Berkshires. The grounds are neglected, and the greenhouse
is a ruin. There is gossip of its being sold for a camp or for
an inn for the parents of children in a neighboring camp.

The widow of Alfred Vanderbilt, who went down on
the *Lusitania*, bought the old Westinghouse place, Erskine
Park in Lee, tore down the house intending to build a bigger
one, couldn't get materials during World War I, did nothing
about it afterwards, and eventually sold cheap to the Fox
Hollow School. Edith Wharton sold the Mount in 1914, and
after going through two hands it likewise was bought by the
Fox Hollow School. Eastover, the Fahnestock place, was sold
to the Duncan School.

In '42 Brookside in Great Barrington, at one time owned
by William Stanley the inventor and afterwards by William
H. Walker, was taken over by Dr. I. M. Altaraz for his
school which had been running in Monterey since '26. The

aim of the institution is to develop the individual in terms of group consciousness. The social goals of this center of tolerance are antipodal to the class purposes, conscious or unconscious, of the people who built the palaces.

"Brookside" is the last I have record of as going academic. But there are rumors of the Tenure place, Beaupre, being taken over as a summer music school. Miss Georgiana Sargent's Twin Elms and the old Schermerhorn place Pinecroft are both in a run-down condition. The house on Overlee, the Frothingham place, and Stoneover, the Parsons', have been demolished. Ananda Hall of the late Cortlandt Field Bishop was torn down by his heirs, leaving the unique wall of selected green schists along the highway—said to have cost $18,000—to crumble. The entire Bishop property, with the Winter Palace, its last master dwelling, is reported to be in the hands of real estate dealers.

The above incomplete account covers the demise of twenty-two estates, nine going either to the state or into ruin, twelve into schools, most of which are of a genuinely cultural nature. Of the close to one hundred estates that once occupied so much of four townships, that leaves perhaps seventy-five unaccounted for. The houses on the majority of these are empty, and they are kept up in superficial fashion by estates in the testamentary sense, being held for suitable buyers, enjoying an occasional token and partial occupancy by members of the family.

A few, typically the former Allen Winden of Charles Lanier, and Belvoir Terrace of Morris K. Jesup, have recently been bought by private purchasers and are well kept up. A still smaller number, perhaps a dozen places, are still occupied with some regularity by the survivors of the families of the great days. These, it happens, are mostly of the original inner circle whose members brought to the Berkshires in the beginning, if not on the whole sufficient social responsibility, yet gentility of breeding that had nothing to do with new wealth. Most of these people are of a very great age, the majority of them kindly old ladies who fret gently among their maids or, if they are reduced, with their one maid.

Through 1944 the now antique prestige of this group was fittingly commemorated by an annual, formal party in that "cottage" which is not the largest or most costly in the Switzerland of America but, if you admit a wholly exotic and imitative architecture, is the most beautiful. This is Bellefontaine of the late Giraud Foster, being a perfect imitation of the Petit Trianon in all architectural details, to the point of possessing the same floating quality as the original. Built in 1898, the furniture, hangings and rugs of its three main downstairs rooms were of such quality that not an item has been replaced or repaired, now forty-seven years later, though the house has been constantly used. In its heyday the Bellefontaine gardeners set out 40,000 annuals.

Here in 1915, Mr. Foster, being then sixty-five, gave the first of his birthday parties, inviting sixty-five guests. From that time the festival was repeated every year, the day falling in November. If you were not of the original sixty-five, you would never be invited. But those who were of the original elect made an effort to return every fall, though it was a post-season event. The number had declined to about fifteen at the last party in 1944. Still, even through the war, all the original ceremony was carried out, the extra footmen dressed in livery, the gold plate taken out of the safe and polished.

Mr. Foster was ninety-four at his last party and while he lived and held his festival, it could be said that the Switzerland of America still lived. But when he died in September, 1945, the climax that was spread between 1929 and 1931 reached its final resolution. After Foster will come, not the deluge, but forgetfulness, the departure of the last of the ancient fold, the sale of more of the estates for one or another institutional purpose, the demolition of the rest of the palaces to save taxes.

After Foster there will be no more Switzerland of America, and a generation will arise that will assume that Shadowbrook and Kellogg Terrace and perhaps Bellefontaine were built for the academic purposes they serve. The very rich, what I called the big rich, will no longer be found in the valley, and their relics will be the descendants of their servants who will be most of Lenox and a fair share of Stockbridge and Lee and Great Barrington. These people will be complete Yankees, as complete as those of old lineage, for unlike plutocracy Yankee democracy is a civilization and whoever touches it is absorbed in one generation.

With the death of Foster the last remnants of the age of the tallyho are swept away; the last rear-guard action of the Devil against the idealism of the valley is over. It was also an age of science, and the contributions of the valley's great inventors was as valuable of its kind as the earlier contributions in theology, in libertarian ideas, in education and literature. Yet the general level of idealism among the local people, the actual strength of the Yankee-Puritan tradition, has declined. The big rich will be gone, but the farmers will still be subjected to the humiliating proximity of the little rich, the summer people who come and go and are agreeable and so much wider in their interests than the farmers are. From among these people, or others like them, a new creative wave must roll through the valley. And the hopes for the future will be brighter if it is a wave that will absorb and contain the old Yankees as well as the new invaders. Ultimately the economic, social and ideational traditions of the valley must all be shared by all the inhabitants. Else each of these partial traditions will be precarious.

PART V

The Land Repromised (1920-1946)

The Latter-Day Prophets

URING the rise, decline and fall of Berkshire, the underlying Yankee or neo-Puritan life of the valley continued more or less as usual. Its essentially mature quality was evinced in the "characters" that adorned every town, the queer birds whose right to be themselves and independent was recognized by all, so long as they fulfilled the original Puritan condition of minding their own business and not attacking the public peace.

One I recall weighs less than a hundred pounds and is tossed around like a chip when he plows. He owns his place, has farmed it alone since a boy, and is a bachelor. He has not in his life been in anybody else's house, nor taken a meal outside his own. When he goes to a neighbor's he waits in the shed. When his new city neighbor asked him if he might cross his land, the reply was, "I'd be right happy if you would." He is, in the words of the same neighbor, "Squalid and filthy and a gentleman." These characters still exist by the hundreds, and they are even growing up in the younger generation. They are not so much a sign of degeneracy as they are of the vitality of the tradition, everybody living according to his private ideas and the town leaving him to his independent ways.

More decadent than the spectacle of these vital people

is that of the churches. Many beautiful ones are abandoned, falling into ruin, being used for hay storage and other secular purposes—the Methodist church of West Goshen was sold for $20. Most of the churches that survive are inhabited by dead little congregations, custodians of hopeless, rural conservatism, blind opposition to any kind of progress, the people who in town meeting draw lines not on the merits of a question but on North Street against South Street, on East against West, on a long-standing feud between two or three old families, on the line—usually weaker than the others—between the old and the new people. Here is real decadence. Among such Yankees the idea by which they live has shriveled to the vanishing point, to the point beyond which there is only alcohol and nothing.

As I intimated earlier, one of the things that has brought these late Puritans, these heirs of the original Chosen People, to this timid pass is the presence among them, not so much of the big rich of the Berkshire castles as of what I called the little rich, the summer visitors who do not condescend to them, who even show honest signs of admiring them; yet by their very social proximity they remind the farmers and the villagers that the center and power of civilization has moved somewhere else, that the local people are a remnant, a forgotten eddy. I said that if the valley was to get a new lease on life it must come through these little rich, or people like them, and that whatever new vitality they might bring to the tradition would have to involve the established natives as well as themselves. What I meant by this last statement was that if the people who actually maintained the local landscape, namely, the farmers, were not presently restored in their self-respect, all their children would move out. The hills and the hollows would either go back to wilderness or be taken up for developments fatal to the tradition of ideas.

The recent immigrants who in their hundreds have streamed in to revitalize the valley may lift their eyebrows at finding themselves called the "Latter Day Prophets," the New Puritans, the latest tide of the Chosen People. Yet by the definition of a Puritan as a person who directs his life from a central, personal idea or vision, these new people are actually nearer to the original article than most of the valley's immigrants since the end of the colonial period. They are people who come into the valley in order to get away from the world of greed and to live, as far as possible, in terms of whatever may be the central conviction of their lives.

Their motive of immigration is, in other words, the same as that of the first Puritans. For the single dramatic-aesthetic idea of God they substitute the miscellaneous dramatic-aesthetic ideas of books and pictures and sculptural works to be made, of music to be composed or interpreted, of miscellaneous recondite matters to be examined. If in the seventeenth and eighteenth centuries it had been the aesthetic individualists—the poets and the dramatists—who had immigrated instead of the religious individualists, the history of New England would have been essentially what it has been, the same crusades and clashes of idealisms, the same decays and renaissances, the same concessions by some to the temptations of wealth, the same indifference to the temptations on the part of most.

The new age in the valley was on the rise while the Rome of the Berkshires was declining and falling. Actually the intellectual thread has never wholly broken. In the lowest ebb of the eighties and nineties there were Edith Wharton and Gilder and the Sedgwick house in Stockbridge, along with Arnold, James and the other big names who were more or less transient. Daniel Chester French connects the nineties with the new age, and for his greatest achievement belongs to the later period. When most of the modern Chosen People were still in the pioneering phase in the early twenties, French was already at work, in his studio in Glendale, on the colossal Lincoln for the Memorial in Washington.

Scouting for the new tribes began shortly after World War I, and by 1930 the immigration was in full swing. By the middle thirties tribes of miscellaneous writers, artists and musicians and their families were established in Sherman,

Kent, Cornwall and Canaan, about seventy-five in each, counting families, the populations of the invaded towns being respectively 477, 1,245, 907 and 555. Every town in the valley has its representatives of the new invasion, and New Milford, Washington (Connecticut), and Stockbridge have as many or more than may be found in the four first named. Yet those four contiguous towns on the river, being small in basic population, represent the area where the new invasion is most securely established, where the New Puritans bear the highest proportion in numbers to the old, where the largest numbers of them are year-round residents, where they are most thoroughly identified with the local life and have least the aspect of vacationists.

Besides the tribes that have infiltrated as individuals to revive the valley's tradition, there are those comprising institutions that have grown up partly locally and partly through immigration. Most of the actors and musicians are summer people, but at worst they are in the tradition of the valley in making a workshop of it, a place to come to express in some kind of action the idea they live by.

The Berkshire Playhouse in Stockbridge had the virtue of evolving naturally out of the community, and it has a good claim to being both the oldest and the best of the summer theaters. It began as the Stockbridge Casino, simply a tennis club with a stage in the building which was designed by Stanford White and built in 1886. From the beginning it was used for art shows and local theatricals, in which visiting stars from New York usually performed. Once a year there was a grand vaudeville show, a benefit for the Casino itself. It was usually entitled the "Follies of" whatever the year was. All this was essentially local, the jokes and the lampoons involving the people in the audience and the local scene—the healthy way to start a theatrical tradition. At the same time the acting and the production were good, sometimes first rate. It was at the high point of the tallyho age when actors from New York were forever turning up as guests in the palaces.

In 1928 Miss Mabel Choate, daughter of the great

Joseph and resident in his sound, Stanford White-built château on the hill, was determined to save the little mansion of John Sergeant and his wife Abigail Williams which was drooping into dignified ruin under a couple of big maples farther up the hill on the property of the Polish novitiate. Since this house—somewhat equivocally called "The Mission House"—represented the beginning of Stockbridge, both in its 1739 age and in its association with John Sergeant, the place for it was somewhere in the middle of the village. A suitable site was that of the Casino on the corner of Main and what was then called Casino streets. The Casino was already decrepit as a tennis club, for the Stockbridge Country Club was long in full swing half a mile away, but it was far from decrepit as a hall for art exhibitions and especially as a theater. It was too bulky to move, and since it was the work of Stanford White it must not be destroyed. Clapboard by clapboard, stud by stud, sill and post by sill and post, it was taken down, set up again at the foot of Yale Hill on the Lee Road, reorganized and rechristened the Berkshire Playhouse. A big barn was bought back of it, up the hill on Route 7, duly painted red and dignified as the Berkshire Dramatic School. Eva Le Gallienne brought up her company to open the playhouse with *The Cradle Song* on the evening of June 4, 1928. Since then the playhouse has presented about 350 actors in more than 100 plays, giving nightly performances and Wednesday matinees through a nine- or ten-week season. Professional summer theaters have opened and have run a few years in Salisbury, Sharon, Marbledale—in New Milford, Litchfield, Brookfield, and elsewhere. But the Stockbridge venture is the only one that has been consistently successful. Almost every town has its amateur dramatic association which puts on one or more performances a year with local talent.

The summer theaters at best are second string to Broadway. Not so of the musical institutions. Each of three of them is as good as anything under metropolitan auspices. In 1918 Mrs. Elizabeth Coolidge founded on South Mountain in Pittsfield the first music colony in the east, the South

Mountain Music Colony. An old church was bought and moved in to become the Music Temple, this building being fortunate and probably unique in having served the idealisms of two ages in the valley. Under its new auspices it offers chamber music every Sunday afternoon in July and August.

In 1930 money was raised in Litchfield County to found Music Mountain in Canaan, for the Gordon String Quartet, with Falls Village for its metropolis. On a hilltop in the center of an amphitheater of higher hills were built the concert hall, the separate house for each member of the quartet, the caretaker's house, storehouse and outbuildings, all in conformance with local architectural tradition. In the hall a fair part of Litchfield County assembles every summer Sunday afternoon to sit in the churchlike pews and hear as good chamber music as the world affords, sandwiched with concerts and special numbers by visiting artists.

Triumph of the new musical tradition in the valley is the big Berkshire Symphonic Festival and the Music Center in Stockbridge and Lenox. In 1934 Miss Gertrude Robinson Smith organized the festival, and she remains the president of it. For the first four years the Boston Symphony Orchestra, under Serge Koussevitzky, gave its series of concerts in a circus tent on a hilltop on the Dan Hanna estate in Stockbridge. The acoustics were surprisingly good, and the sides of the tent were not used, so many of the audience heard the concert sitting on the grass outside under the stars. The moon and stars did not always oblige, and on two or three occasions the orchestra found itself competing with tempest and thunder; but there was no catastrophe.

In 1937 Mrs. Dixey, heir of the Tappans, gave the old family estate Tanglewood to the festival. Mrs. Gorham Brooks of Boston presented the Music Shed whose wooden hugeness rose and took form across the road from the site of the tiny Red House where *The House of the Seven Gables* was written, and where Hawthorne and Melville spent many hours lying in the grass looking down over Stockbridge Bowl to the distant, hazy magnificence of Monument Mountain.

The great shed, with its seating capacity of 9,000, its perfect acoustics, and its outer promenade opening on all sides to the lawn, was finished for the concerts of 1938. In 1940 the Berkshire Music Center was established in the Tappan mansion and in a theater and other new buildings that were constructed near the mansion and the shed.

Here every summer a six weeks' course for advanced students is given under Dr. Koussevitzky's direction, culminating in the festival. Dr. Koussevitzky himself has bought the small estate Serenak, a little way up the hill in Lenox. I first heard a concert in the Shed in 1942. As the vast audience assembled, I knew that a hundred yards away beyond the hedge was Hawthorne's site. I knew that two hundred yards away at right angles on the slope of Baldhead was the great castle Shadowbrook, now a Jesuit novitiate. In the Shed the great majority of the audience and student orchestra were not more than one generation from other parts of the world. Around me every language was being chattered. Koussevitzky entered, and the chatter changed to applause. When that quieted, still facing the audience, he raised his baton and they sang *The Star-Spangled Banner* with united power. I though that the tradition of the valley was a living organism, changing and growing, inviting the world.

A by-product of creative art in the valley was the inauguration of the Dalton Laboratory Plan of education in the Dalton High School in 1920, the plan being Miss Helen Parkhurst's and its effective supporter Mrs. W. Murray Crane, widow of the Massachusetts governor and senator. In its pure form the method was applied for only a year in Dalton; but, carrying the name of the town, it rippled out into the metropolitan world and became a movement in education. An improvement in education within the valley itself was the opening, in 1939, of the Housatonic Valley Regional High School on the river in Canaan near Falls Village. Combining in one school students from six river towns, it was the first regional high school in Connecticut.

Through the Berkshire Music Festival and Center, the

Berkshire Playhouse, and the scores of individual writers and artists who have immigrated in the past quarter of a century, the valley is picking up the qualitative thread of Melville, Hawthorne and Edwards—though it would be idle to speculate as to which of the separate works of the New Puritans was going to take permanent and classic place alongside *Moby Dick*, *The House of the Seven Gables*, and *The Freedom of the Will*. In quantity the output of first-rate work is probably greater even than in the days of Catherine Sedgwick, Fanny Kemble, Holmes, Hawthorne, Melville, Longfellow, Lowell and Beecher. Moreover, the work is growing steadily closer to the local soil, the New Puritans closer to the old ones.

Indeed, the best assurance for the long duration of the present phase of the valley's history lies in the mutual respect, frequently the friendship, that springs up between these recent immigrants and the older residents. They amuse each other, of course, but there is no condescension on either side. Probably the crux of the matter is in the fact that almost all of the new arrivals are more or less determined to make a partial subsistence out of the soil. They raise big gardens, and even keep a few animals. For all of this they are dependent on help and advice from their farmer neighbors, which is good for the latters' egos. Their long-humbled pride lifts its head and they feel secure, as their grandfathers did. In return they take an interest in the new people's concerns. Their hereditary Yankee interest in book learnin' comes down off the shelf. They don't mind exposing their ignorance of it, because the new people have exposed theirs about the farmers' specialty.

There are plenty of other hooks and eyes that connect the new Yankees with the old. Many of the immigrants are only two or three generations from the soil. They carry childhood memories of the last legends of the great agrarian America; they don't have to learn the thought and speech idioms of the farmers. Another point is that most of the new arrivals are not only of the little rich but of the littlest rich. They do their own work. The only reason they can buy or rent at all is that they are free-lance writers or artists, or teachers with long vacations. At the same time they are not in any usual sense vacationists. They do not wear sport clothes, or find the country and the people "quaint." They really love the valley and live there all they can, winter as well as summer. Their houses have furnaces and storm windows. They consider them as home, make the valley towns their voting residences and permanent addresses. An increasing number manage to stay the year round and to become active in local politics and social life.

Here the old and the new are becoming one people. The countryside is returning to its pre-tallyho state where each man is respected, not for his wealth, not even for his fame in the outer world, but for his locally observed character, industry and craftsmanship, his hard wit, above all his rights as an individual. Everybody recognizes that the other fellow's inner life, the idea by which he lives, is his private affair. Like the Puritans, their physical or spiritual ancestors, they all want to be let alone to their worship. They are all alike anxious that the Devil of greed and poverty and wealth shan't get in again.

Settlement with the Devil

WHEN I was recounting the slow death of the great iron and marble industries during the latter half of the nineteenth century, along with the failure of many and miscellaneous small factories that had run on the water power of the river or the tributaries, I implied that no other form of industrialization was rising in the valley to replace those which were declining. I said that the Devil's effort to conquer the valley in terms of greed had finally failed. Yet in the most recent period, while the New Puritans were coming in to reinforce the Old Puritans in the resistance to the growth of cities, there were built on the river four plants that at once violated the beauty of the river and represent the highest and most concentrated form of industrialization.

Least objectionable of these is the dam and relatively small power plant of the Southern Berkshire Power and Electric Company in Great Barrington, for it does little more than appropriate for generation of electricity the old dam and water power previously monopolized by the early Great Barrington industries. But in the Lower Valley the scenic havoc wrought by three big power plants is appreciable. At Falls Village, the Connecticut Power Company has with its canal raped the Great Falls, the biggest falls of the river, of all its water and left the naked rocks looking silly and humiliated in the sun, with their grooved channels worn by the plunging water tons of the ages now filling with blown soil, with village refuse and with brush. At Bull's Bridge Falls the huge twin flumes of the Connecticut Light and Power Company leave only a stream's trickle to cascade

FACTORY SITE AND GREAT FALLS, NEW MILFORD

down the water-smoothed ledges where the Great Falls used to shake the rocks. (Incidentally, this, the oldest power plant on the river, was at the time of its construction, 1904, the largest in the country, with 780 kilowatt capacity and a transmission voltage of 3,300.) At Stevenson the major dam of the Connecticut Light and Power Company, a dam comparable in height and imperial aspect to the show dams of the West, set back the river some eight miles in Lake Zoar, flooding for purposes of industry an average mile width of the valley. A dam such as that at Stevenson, with the drive across its hundred-and-fifty-yard length, with its dozen gates and as many separate falls mingling at the foot of their seventy-five-foot plunge, a dam such as this has a beauty of its own, comparable to that of any valley or mountain or natural waterfall. The beauty is real while the dam and its sightly little powerhouse stand alone, with nothing but the river and farming country around them. The danger is in the seed of a city that such an installation becomes. Only three miles below it the Shelton-Derby dam serves a dozen industries that, among dozens more, have vilified the most beautiful natural stretch of the river with human sewage and filthy and congested works and habitations.

Actually, these power plants represent the best bargain the Yankees could make with the Devil. The wild, primeval glory of the falls is lost, but in its place the great dynamos purr in the powerhouse below, an oil-smooth grace superior to that of the falls, a power as vast and romantic and more beautifully controlled. The generating houses themselves fit nicely into the landscape and the local architecture, for they are small and not adorned with chimneys. The worst concession to the Devil is the titanic files of high-tension cable conduit towers that loop away over the hills in a violation of the landscape for which there is no aesthetic compensation; there is only a hope in the fact that the power companies do intend eventually to accomplish the expensive feat of getting the cables underground. Yet withal, these aerial strings of cable represent a kind of insurance that is worth more than the price paid in their unsightly rights of way.

They carry the commercial power of the river out of the valley to light and drive the wheels of industrial cities and slums along the Naugatuck. Once this balance has been made, it is less likely that cities will grow up in the valley to make immediate use of this power. The valley has done well to throw one of its main commercial assets as an appeasement to the greed of the economy. With the power all in use, it is easier to discourage renewed efforts to develop the other assets.

A fifth recent power development involves no scenic violation of the river, indeed adds an element of scenic beauty to the valley and helps complete the job of sending the river's power out of the valley for use elsewhere. This is the Rocky River plant at the mouth of that little tributary northwest of New Milford village. The little stream is heavily dammed on the western hilltop about two hundred feet above the river, and at flood times water is pumped up from the combined pump- and powerhouse below, the power for pumping being the surplus at such seasons from the other power houses of the Connecticut Light and Power Company. In dry seasons the water is run back to the powerhouse to reinforce the waning power elsewhere. At the time of construction, 1928, this was the only pump plant in America, and the two pumps were the largest in the world, rated at 8,100 horsepower apiece.

The resulting reservoir up in the hills is Candlewood Lake, the largest lake in Connecticut, being about fifteen miles long and one to two miles wide, touching Danbury, New Fairfield, Brookfield, New Milford and Sherman, having a shore line of about seventy-five miles, and covering about 6,000 acres of former farm- and woodland, including several old-time mills on the Rocky River. The name of the lake is taken from that of Candlewood Mountain in New Milford, entitled from the profusion of pitch pine found there and cut into strips for outdoor illumination in the neighborhood in the eighteenth century before the days of lanterns. The lake itself is no blot on the landscape, but it is being utilized by those representing the only force that is today a menace to the tradition of the valley. By the enterprising people of Danbury and New Milford it is being used as the center of a pretentious real estate development, a development that was doubtless the bait used by the power company to enlist the support of the towns to be affected. The local realtors and publicists, who are interested in enriching themselves and the local merchants and destroying the quality of their towns, continue to carry on a seductive campaign whose purpose is to fetch in the most irresponsible type of vacationist and disfigure the countryside with summer slums. A member of the Sherman tribe of the New Puri-

tans, a man who really loves the region, asked me whether Lake Candlewood was a valid power project or whether it was somebody's private real estate racket. I don't see that it matters. Certainly it has proved a successful venture as a power project. And it is equally true that, racket or no racket, it is being used to hurry the destruction of another little slice of the Valley.

With the completion of the plants at Falls Village, Bull's Bridge, Rocky River and Stevenson, along with the older plant at the Shelton dam, the usable power of the Lower Valley has been about half developed in a fashion that does a minimum of harm. Meanwhile, and from far back in the industrial era, back on the average to the Civil War, the power of the Upper Valley has been much more fully developed, mostly for paper mills, a form of industry which, because it requires fewer men per factory, does not tend to produce great cities. The time has come when it is possible to hope that the 27 dams now functional on the 160 miles of the river are all the dams that will be built in any foreseeable time. Of the 27, 11 are in or above Pittsfield in the headwaters area, and 22—including the 11—are in or above Housatonic in the Berkshire paper area. In the hundred river miles between Housatonic and Shelton, where the lower industrial region begins, there is only one factory dam and the four more or less beneficent power plants.

United States Army engineers have located seven other possible sites for power developments in the valley, one at Webatuck on the Tenmile River, and six others on the main river, namely, at West Cornwall, at Kent Furnace, at Boardman, at Still River, at Shepaug, and a new development at Shelton. Yet, from authority close to the Connecticut Light and Power Company, which owns most or all of these sites, I have it that the construction of further hydraulic power plants is unlikely. The initial investment per kilowatt of capacity in a hydroelectric plant is two and a half to three times what it is for a steam plant. A few years ago this cost of construction was more than offset by the cost of fuel for the steam plant, requiring about two and a half pounds of coal per kilowatt-hour. But through modern improvements the amount of coal necessary to produce a kilowatt-hour has dropped to less than a pound. This about balances the greater cost of initial financing of a hydroelectric plant. And the overhead costs being about the same, the steam plant is superior to the water-power one because it can be adjusted to need, whereas the uneven flow of a river is always a hazard. Generally, the river is at flood in the spring when the electric load is lightest and the water power is lowest at the end of the year when there is the heaviest load due to early darkness.

The upshot is that the construction of more power plants on the river is unlikely and is probably limited to one possibility, that of a plant somewhere between New Milford and Lake Zoar—perhaps at Still River or Shepaug—to take full advantage of the Candlewood Lake Reservoir. Generally, there will be no more development of the river's water power. The possibility of further industrialization in the valley must rest in other causes, in the mineral facilities, which are not yet exhausted, and in the fact that land near the railroad is relatively cheap.

Against these advantages there is ranged, in most of the valley, a pretty well-integrated public opinion opposing the construction of any more factories. Roughly the alignment is between, on the one side, the farmers and the new intellectuals and, on the the other, the villagers who are still affected by the booster spirit of the twenties, who yet aim to make their attractive towns into ugly, rich-and-poor cities possessing the biggest something-or-other in the world. The time has almost come when it can be said with finality that the forces of spiritual progress in the valley are stronger than the forces of economic progress. A few years ago Mr. James F. Dickey, a road contractor of Bridgeport, got an option on the old Ore Hill mine in Lakeville and set about pumping out the deep lake that has covered the works for years. He had lowered the water level a few inches of the fifty feet or so he had to go, when one of the neighbors complained of the stream draining across his property. It seems clear that the mine carried with it the right of drainage across this land. Yet local public opinion was against Mr. Dickey, and between this and the hugeness of the project he lost heart and quit. I have heard of no movement to resurrect any of the other abandoned mines, or the marble quarries of Washington, Connecticut, Sheffield, Egremont or West Stockbridge.

From time to time new plants will be built in the valley, and old ones will go out of existence. The Riggi plant in New Milford has recently gone up and into operation on the shore of the river. The magnesium plant in Canaan, a war growth, may well continue in operation into peacetime. The little old Holley Cutlery Works plant in Lakeville has been buzzing with a new enterprise. But outside of Pittsfield, where the enormous growth of the General Electric Company has settled the city in the Devil's column, and Shelton and Derby, which seem permanently consecrated to urban filth, it is unlikely that the objectionable feature of industry, namely, the growth of cities, will spread further. To be sure, the tendency of most industry today is toward decentralization of plant, offering the workers homes in the country, and the valley will doubtless suffer some disfigurement from this decentralization. But the movement will hardly go to the paradoxical extreme of a new centralization, and because of the resistance it will meet from the population of the valley it may safely be assumed that in this region it will be at a minimum.

Generally a clear settlement of rights in the hundred and fifteen crow-flight miles of valley has now been reached between the Lord of Ideas and the Devil of Greed. The whole valley of the eastern or main headwaters, from Washington, Massachusetts, down through Pittsfield, has been acknowledged as under the Devil's control. From there for eighty-eight valley miles down to Derby, the Lord holds title, but with a qualified right in the Devil to maintain a smattering of industrial plants, though he must in no case construct a city or alter the basic agrarian economy of the people who work in the plants. From Derby and Shelton down to the sea the dominant rights are again in the Devil. Since there is no enforcing authority higher than the Lord and the Devil, a settlement of this kind is of course wholly dependent on the co-operation of these great powers. Actually, each is perpetually at work trying to exceed his agreement and to invade the precinct of the other. While the Lord still maintains a formidable underground in Pittsfield and an open, fighting organization in Stratford at the river's mouth, yet it can be said on the whole that it is not now foreseeable that the settlement will be substantially and effectively altered by either party for a long time to come.

A feature of the Devil's two concessions is the pollution of the river. The Naugatuck, joining the main stream at

Derby, "receives large volumes of raw sewage and untreated waste, as a result of which the river is the most polluted of any in Connecticut." In the beautiful basin between the bluffs where the two rivers and tidewater mingle, the contribution of the Naugatuck is a huge, nauseous, gray-green ribbon coiling out into the purer waters and discoloring them for the rest of the journey to the sea. Since the Naugatuck is entirely controlled by industry, all hope of curing this condition must be abandoned.

Almost as grave, but less hopeless, is the pollution of the Devil's upper concession from the sources of the East Branch down through Stockbridge. Here the Housatonic River Improvement Association, under the leadership of Lawrence K. Miller of the *Berkshire County Daily Eagle,* is waging a slow, relentless war against the forces of evil, a war that is almost certain to end in victory within a few years. One difficulty is that there are two entirely separate Devil's cohorts, each of which is able with some reason to point to the other as the chief culprit. On the one hand, there are the municipalities dumping their sewage into the river, which in these upper reaches is no larger than the Naugatuck at its mouth. On the other hand, there are the mills making their visible and sometimes colorful contribution of industrial wastes, the blue dye spreading down out of Dalton, the horrid big water lilies of soapsuds drifting in obscene stateliness down from the paper mills in Lee through the peace of the Stockbridge meadows.

The average citizen of Pittsfield is persuaded that the major pollution comes from the mills, but that the power of the rich owners, going as far as a threat to remove elsewhere, frightens the municipal authorities from trying to abate the nuisance. The industrialists put up two arguments. That of the Lee paper mills is that their waste in itself is colorless and nonpoisonous, but that mixed with the grease of the Pittsfield sewage it coagulates into the horrid globules which float down through Stockbridge. There is no doubt that the river reaches Lee already foul. From Hinsdale down it is black, and increasingly the sticks and leaves and grasses of its bed are coated with filth. The argument of the biggest interests in Dalton is that, while their wastes do contribute to the pollution of the river, yet the sewage of Hinsdale and Dalton is at least an equal and probably a greater factor. Shortly these controversial questions are going to be solved. Already Dalton has appropriated the money for a rectification plant. Pittsfield treats five-sixths of its sewage now, and has plans for new sewers to drain the remaining sixth into its big purification plant three miles south of the city. Lee has appropriated over eight thousand dollars to make a survey for a plant to rectify both municipal and industrial waste.

The hope of the Housatonic River Improvement Association is first to purify the river and afterwards to convert it and its bank into a recreation area, with canoes and fold boats available and a system of transport to return them from downstream stations back to upstream boathouses, with bridle paths along the landscaped and zoned banks, both riders and canoers being served by restaurants and perhaps amusement concessions at suitable points. From the point of view of offering healthy athletic and recreation facilities for the factory workers of Pittsfield, the plan is surely a desirable one. From the point of view taken by this book, the desirability of maintaining the valley as a cradle for creative work of all kinds, a workshop of ideas, the proposed improvements are not of much importance one way or the other. The area improved, covering most of the stretch along the river between Pittsfield and Lenox, would become virtually an extension of the industrial city of Pittsfield, swarming, if the development were successful, with urban irresponsibles whose first interest is to indulge themselves. Under these circumstances, neither the sound farmers nor the intellectuals who between them have the custody of the valley's tradition would be any more attracted to the area than they are now when it is dominated by the physical filth of the stream. It is more likely that they would be driven away, even farther than they are now.

The greatest importance of the strong movement to clean up the river in upper Berkshire is its evidence that in the leadership of Pittsfield itself there are still men who are putting ideas ahead of commercial success, who are willing to put the city and its chief commercial interests to vast expense, running into millions, in order to accomplish an ideal of cleanliness and health whose monetary return will be slow, inuring mostly to the remote future. Another encouraging thing about the Housatonic River Improvement Association is that, although its leadership is in Pittsfield, its interest is in the whole county. Indeed, there are in the organization leaders who are a little apologetic for the fact that Pittsfield has grown so big and successful. And indeed, Pittsfield does not have the fetid air of most industrial cities where labor and capital fight it out in grease, disease and degradation. In the movement to purify the river there is a serious attempt to apply an idea which is thought to be more important than commercial profit. The Lord is still a long way from giving up hope of Pittsfield.

Corresponding to the movement for purification among the filthy headwaters, there is a more pretentious movement which is aiming at the scenic preservation and improvement of the Lower Valley from the filthy tidewater all the way up through Connecticut to the Massachusetts line. This is the Housatonic Valley Conference, which assembled at the Housatonic Valley Regional High School in Canaan in 1941. The leader of this movement is Charles Downing Lay, a long-time resident of Stratford who has seen that town largely ruined by industry. As a man who for many years has enjoyed the whole valley and is probably as familiar with it all as anyone, and incidentally as one of the country's leading landscape architects, Mr. Lay's opinions are to be listened to with respect. Like most reformers, he has carried the burden of the plan for years now, with but indifferent help from the general citizenry of the valley. The movement now has progressed to the point where a bill is before the Connecticut legislature.

As originally conceived, the essence of the plan was the creation of a Housatonic Valley Authority for the purpose of preserving the valley against further despoliation.

The first duty of the authority was to have been to impose or recommend to the legislature proper zoning, to the end that industry should not further deface the landscape, that the shores of the river should be kept clean of refuse and vandalism, and that "summer slums" should be avoided by limiting all building to appropriate areas back from the river, under requirements of suitable distances between dwellings and of attractive arrangements around "greens" where proper water and plumbing would be provided.

So far the plan deserved the support of everybody in the valley. A little more industry might well be admissible if it were so located that it would neither encourage congestion of population nor deface the landscape. Summer slums are already appearing in several parts of the valley, notably along the magnificent reach of river between the Stevenson dam and Derby, the shacks there being those of the industrial workers of Derby and Shelton. The flimsiness and congestion of these shacks is due to the near-by existence of congested cities where the owners have their principal residences. If people began living year-round along the river, these shacks would soon enough disappear in favor of more attractive buildings. But the cities and the consequent trend toward cottaging being actually present, the only hope of real improvement—and of preservation in the still unspoiled northern reaches—is in zoning.

But Mr. Lay's plan goes beyond zoning into proposals that are liable to stir up real opposition. The landscape being preserved against destruction, he would then devote it to recreational purposes for the millions who, with the five-day week and the cheap cars or planes supposed to follow the war, will swarm out over the weekends from as far east as Hartford and as far south as New York. To serve them Mr. Lay would have fine parkways back among the hills, curving attractively instead of following the roller-coaster straight lines of many of the present superhighways. From these great arteries lesser ones would lead down to parks on or near the river, where and whence swimming, fishing (the river to be heavily stocked with everything up to salmon), canoeing, fold boating, horseback riding, hiking and, in winter, skiing and skating would be available, all to be served, as in the northern project, by suitable restaurants, inns, cabins, shelters and camp sites.

Such a gay consummation would of course destroy the tradition of the valley. First the intellectuals, the New Puritans, and afterwards the farmers, or Old Puritans, would be driven out by the herds of urban ignoramuses in sport clothes oozing across their land, breaking down walls and fences, leaving gates and barways open, gushing in without courtesy to ask foolish questions, trying to bully the farmers because they are civilized, leaving picnic refuse all over the place, neglecting all "No Trepass" signs, fishing in posted streams, running the cattle, getting their cars stuck and having to be drawn out, ending each weekend by spraining their ankles and requiring the farmers to drive them down to the doctor's, patronizing the doctor, who knows more in one cubic centimeter of brain than most of their city practitioners. Before this most horrid of invasions the writers and miscellaneous artists will instantly decamp, and the farmers will follow them northward, with the additional incentive of getting good prices for their land. What the upshot would be it is hard to imagine. The whole valley might become a bigger Coney Island. Or, under regioning, part of it might rise to the status of Westchester, occupied, with airplane commuting, by the vacuous, more or less harmless, more or less rich.

Thus, in my opinion, Mr. Lay's original plan involved one excellent feature, namely zoning under a Housatonic River Authority, and a set of undersirable features in the various proposals for parkways and recreational areas. Unfortunately, the bill now before the Connecticut legislature provides only for the undesirable feature of the parkways. While the hope of zoning is not abandoned, it is for the moment postponed. The tendency of the present bill will be to transform the valley into an enormous weekend playground for city people, the expulsion of the farmers and intellectuals and the final disappearances of the Puritan tradition. It is to be hoped that this unhappy end can be avoided. A deaf ear should be turned to the sweet song of the realtor who will try to seduce us into supporting recreational "improvements" by promising us increased property values. The Coney Island droves of weekend trippers must at all costs be turned away, though under proper zoning rules any and all may be welcomed if they build even substantial summer homes. If they stay in the valley, even for the summers, the tradition will absorb them. But the transient brings with him the seed of death. The great trunk parkways back in the hills, even though not connected with pleasure areas on the river, will of themselves impair the region. The supporters of the present bill providing for these parkways seem to ignore the fact that most of the gorgeous views are precisely in the upland valleys back from the river, that it is in these upland valleys that most of the desirable people live, the ones who really love the region and want to preserve it from the mobocracy that is besieging the nation.

It is my conviction that somehow the local people of the valley will preserve its integrity for a long time yet. It is already true that the urban nonresident is found in increasing numbers as far north as New Milford. But just north of there runs the solid wall of Sherman and Kent, closely backed by Cornwall, Sharon, Salisbury and Canaan. In those six towns there is probably concentrated more creative intelligence per capita than in any region, rural or urban, in the United States. And in reserve behind them is all of Berkshire County which has a greater past and would rival the boast of its southern neighbors today. In all these towns the writers, the painters, the scholars and musicians are no transients. They have their feet down on their own hearths, and most of them are thoroughly integrated into their towns so that they and the farmers talk the same language and vote the same local votes. From these there will be support of the zoning plan, but there will be a roar at the proposal to invite in the city weekenders.

With improved commuting, the hope is that there will

be more permanent residents and fewer transient visitors, that the New and Old Puritans together will invite location by people of their own disposition, that the transients and the big rich alike will find more attractive haunts elsewhere. I can see in the future valley a type of citizenry that will be in every way a fusion of the farmers and the intellectuals, a stock that will carry on the Puritan tradition for a long time to come. I see these people as all founded economically in one- to two-thirds local subsistence. The remaining income—that is, the cash crop—may be made in any of an infinite number of ways. Perhaps half the people will still make it by selling milk—these will be farmers who incidentally have a knowledge of and interest in literature, painting, sculpture, music or several of these. Of the remaining half of the population, most will be people whose cash crop will be in one of the arts or crafts, but who at the same time will be as clever as the farmer at subsistence —the raising of vegetables, fruit, chickens, pigs, goats, and perhaps a fancy crop of some kind. They will all talk the same language and, while the routine of life will still be different for the two groups, there will be no self-consciousness or jealousy between them. This new population of the valley is already taking shape in the hundreds of children of the high-brows who are going to the local schools and who will undoubtedly marry among the Old Puritans on an appreciable scale. What stands in the way of this resolution is the inferior public school system, especially in Connecticut, which tends to make the New Puritans, during the period when they have small children to educate, take them back to the city schools and so resume the status of summer people very much against their will. That problem is in their own hands. While they vote locally, too few of them take a part in the local squabbles. They like the farmers personally, but they avoid embroilment in their feuds. Until they take hold and swing the balance in local debate, the schools will remain inferior, and too many of the New Puritans seasonal. In more obvious matters, though, they can be counted on. When told of an industrial threat to their peace, or of proposed superhighways and pleasure parks for the urban barbarians, they will join with their neighbors, the Old Puritans, to resist the world conqueror.

Baedeker in a Canoe

FOR A SUMMARY view of the river and the valley there is nothing better than a canoe trip from source to mouth, especially in gorgeous October when the hardwood is aflame. There must be two of you, traveling de luxe, stopping for dinner and the night at appropriate hostelries, taking light personal equipment, and bicycles for short amphibious operations. With the story of the region behind you, you can see the valley in the perspective of two to three centuries, filled with the battlefields and monuments of the war between the Lord of Ideas and the Devil of Greed. The people you will easily identify as belonging to one army or the other, either the custodians of the best, or Puritan, tradition of America—and mankind—or the more numerous but less sure cohorts of materialism who are interested at worst in getting rich and at best in providing for somebody else's physical health and comfort.

In the trip it will be well to remember in summary the five parts of the war, or perhaps the five separate wars:

First, the fight between religion and land greed from 1639 to 1760.

Second, between liberty on the one side, and greed and license on the other from 1760 to 1820.

Third, the great and climatic struggle between humanism and humanitarianism on one side and industrialism on the other, the great fight which most of America lost and which most of the Valley spectacularly won, between 1820 and 1870.

Fourth, the seductive Tallyho Age from 1869 to 1932, when the Devil was petty snobbery, and also masqueraded as the Lord in good private schools and brilliant science.

Fifth, and overlapping the preceding period, the modern age bringing a great immigration of intellectuals, the only enemy visible being the urban vacationists who are not yet a serious threat.

As you paddle down from one industrial end of the valley to the other, you will see in the eighty-eight crow-flight miles between these limits the undoubted victory of the Lord in the clean, forested hills, the clean, agricultural valleys, the clean, unindustrialized villages, the absolute absence of cities, great wealth or great poverty, the relative absence of chimneys, dumps and hillsides sliced ragged for quarries and mines.

The upper, or headwaters, part of the trip will have to do with mountain streams mostly too small for your canoe, which you will leave at a strategic point on the southern fringe of the city of Pittsfield. Following the map in identifying the headwaters of the river with the largest of its three upper branches, you will seek out its source in that of the East Branch, being desolate, beaver-dammed Mud Pond, located dramatically on the Appalachian continental divide in the town of Washington, Massachusetts. To view this bleak origin you need only be drawn up to the divide on the Boston & Albany Railroad either way between Pittsfield and Springfield. Keep an eye out a north window of the car when approaching Washington station, where the booster engines leave the transcontinental trains, and you will see these lonesome waters whose scrub-forested shores the beaver keep in flood. Or you may drive up seventeen miles from Pittsfield through the industrial busyness of Dalton and the abandoned busyness of Hinsdale to the same, high, gray desert region of Washington, and from this same Mud Pond you may trace its inlet back half a mile through two more tiny ponds to the very spring where the river begins. Driving back down to Pittsfield, you will notice the road and the little river braiding back and forth across each other, and here in its highest reach, where the waters are virgin to pollution, you will observe that they are the usual brown color of mountain-and-forest streams.

Longfellow said it flatly in 1846: ". . . a small brown stream, not very clear." Holmes, about the same time, said it with Victorian flowers: ". . . dark stream but clear, like lucid orbs that shine between the lids of auburn-haired, sherry-wine-eyed demiblondes . . ." When attacking the modern pollution of the river we must not ask too much of it in color. But we may properly ask it to be chemically pure. Fanny Kemble addressed this aspect of it in her super-Holmesian idiom. She put in the record her opinion that the Housatonic was so pure that "it should be used only for baptism." Fanny Kemble knew, none better. For she was forever whipping off her shoes and stockings to stand in the river and baptize her passionate little toes.

Having viewed the orthodox beginning of the river in the East Branch, you will next drive fifteen miles up into Lanesboro for the sources of the North Branch and the head of the great valley which the river has made and which in turn has made a great civilization. There, from Pratt Hill, you may look down the fifty miles of the Upper Valley between the walls of the autumn-tinted Hoosacs on the left and the taller, mostly evergreen Taconics on the right, while hidden among the convolutions of the central ridge between them there await you the Lilliputian relics of the squabbles and the triumphs of man and his God. If you wish you may go on over the spur of Greylock that Pratt Hill is and come to the real beginnings of this North Branch. Where it goes under Route 7 there live two brothers of uncertain age who typify the Yankees, the last of the Old Puritans, who are at the foundation of civilization all the way down to the sea. Being Yankees, they will be happy to take you up Brodie Mountain and show you the three springs where this branch of the river begins. And they will show you how it goes underground beneath the bridge and comes up in the cow pasture a hundred yards to the southeast.

Returning to Pratt Hill, you will descend southward by car, passing Constitution Hill where Lanesboro celebrated Massachusetts' adoption of the federal instrument.

From Constitution Hill you run down Route 7 past the birthplace of Henry W. Shaw (Josh Billings) and so along the beach of Pontoosuc Lake, the recreation waters of Pittsfield. It is of no significance to the river or the valley except that its name, derived from the falls at the outlet, perpetuates the Indian word for those "Poun-tuck-ucks" or Falls-Places which are more numerous in the Lower Valley where one of them, pronounced by the English "Pota-tuck," gave the river its earliest name.

Below Pontoosuc Lake, you close your eyes and drive through metropolitan Pittsfield, opening them at the park, originally as now the central hill of the town. Here the modern, stone Congregational church replaces the tiny first one whence Parson Thomas Allen led his congregation up to the Battle of Bennington, and the Bulfinch second one, and a plaque records the famous Pittsfield Elm that got itself immortalized on Staffordshire china. At the park you turn left, passing the Athenaeum, the courthouse that was built when Pittsfield won the county seat from Lenox in 1859, the "Peace Party House," named for the celebration there of the victory of 1781, and the high school which stands on the site of Elm Knoll, the Appleton place which had the Old Clock on the Stairs. Then you close your eyes again, until you reach Williams Street, where, if you have time, you turn left and run down .7 mile to view the site of Colonel William Williams's Long House which burned down in the memory of living men and has been replaced by the residence of Lawrence K. Miller of the *Berkshire County Eagle*. The location is no more than a knoll in height, but on the flat, Pittsfield plain it commands a clear view to the mountains in every direction, and near the house the orna-mental colonel placed one of the forts which he designed and built during the threats of the Old French War.

If you wish you may proceed two miles farther east to the remnants of the beginnings of Pittsfield, the first cemetery and the Brattle House, built in 1762. Then you will return to the corner where you turned off and go left on Holmes Road. A quarter of a mile down you will come to the first bridge over the river below the point where the three branches have met and given it a respectable forty- to fifty-foot width. Also it has by now picked up its first consignment of sewage and industrial waste, and is become a black rather than a brown stream. On the property adjoining the bridge you left your canoe and, in spite of the fact that Holmes's "villa" is only .3 mile down the road, you neglect it, leave your car and take to the contaminated water. You are just well away in the dirty, gentle current, when the river begins to wind in a whimsical maze through the flatness of the Canoe Meadows most of which Holmes used to own. After more than two river miles you swing right for the fortieth or fiftieth time, and there .3 miles from where you started, is Holmes's place, with its pyramidal roof and semicircular porch, the whole abetted by a modern, rearward, architecturally comformable addition. If you are able to spot it among the modern trees, you can see a little to the left the big Holmes pine, traditionally the only tree there when he built in 1849, and the lattice-covered windmill that also dates from his time.

All this is a glance while you whip back to the left and enter upon a slightly less tortuous reach between banks a little higher than canoe-seated eye line, banks lined with big willows and white maples, the sparse leaves wanly gay for the season, all the trees collared gray with flood marks and, where you can peep over the banks, flood terraces rising a rod or so back on each side. Back of the flood terraces is good pasture land, and there are cattle paths down to the River whose pollution, according to my informant, is perfectly filtered through any cow, leaving the milk of these sewage-fed beasts as pure as you could wish and the animals themselves no more than normally infected with bovine diseases.

On the left—when you happen to be facing south— the gold and crimson glory of October Mountain stretches ahead and down into Lenox, October Mountain the east boundary of the valley that the river hugs close down into Lee. The mountain is perhaps the unique monument of the

Tallyho Age, being itself in unspoiled, pristine glory but carrying the memory of the great Whitney preserve it once was, populated by all the world's beasts that the climate would support, controlled by the English warden from the neighborhood of the lodge on the summit, and hunted from time to time by the Whitneys' guests led by real western cowboys on real western ponies. Now the fences are down and October Mountain is native wilderness again. Old Bill the moose, its last veteran who escaped and for years was petted and spoiled by the countryside, Old Bill, like the local albatross, has been shot by some Ancient Hunter of ill omen. The ill omen, though, was for the Tallyho Age with which Old Bill was identified.

About a river mile below Holmes's place, stand up in the canoe or get out and climb the bank, and you will see the valley's best souvenir of the Literary Age that outweighed the Iron and Steel Age in the mid-century. There stands the solid, white bulk of Melville's Arrowhead, a quarter of a mile over yonder on Holmes Road, the nearest window on the north or upstream side being the one at which *Moby Dick* was written in 1850 and 1851.

Continue your doubling and returning course down the dark, dirty river. The next feature is the entrance of the jolly, laughing water that is the supposedly pure outlet of the sewage-disposal plant of the great city of Pittsfield. You paddle vigorously, swooshing around the curves and trying to keep your lower hand dry. For two or three miles all submerged sticks, all floating leaves, all forests of waving eel grass, are darkly coated, and occasionally there are long streaks of iridescent grease. Trees that have fallen and died in the stream are not only bathed in the fetid soapwater but are dumps of cans, bottles, tires, bits of clothing and other rubbish disposed from the banks by farmers, hunters, picnickers and what not. You go under an abandoned and broken bridge with a fallen farmhouse in sight on an abandoned road. There is here none of the sentimental charm of the true ghost farm—there is a whole ghost village up on the northern slopes of October Mountain—where man has

cleanly gone and nature is already taking over. Here is only
the blight of the industrial city reaching out over the land,
black, flowing horror beneath, and on both sides muddy
gray horror and death.

You cross the Lenox town line and go under the bridge
at New Lenox, a shabby group of houses and back-yard
dumps appropriate to the water that passes them. Yokun
Brook, having flowed across the town from the slope of the
western mountain Yokun Seat, comes in on the periphery
of one of the river's eastward loops. Not long afterwards
the stream gives up its eellike antics of now seven or more
river miles and straightens out to run for a docile mile of
relative straightness, pinched between the country road and
the mountain on the left and the railroad on the right. Off
to the right, here and there connected with the main river
by breaks through the former banks, there begins the long
lagoon or setback, caused by the first dam of the Smith
Paper Company, located below Woods Pond, which is still
a mile and a third downstream. The lagoon having been
created a long time ago, has settled its shore line and is
romantic with islands and reedy shallows and mysterious,
lost channels. It is the place where in the eighties, in the days
before pollution, the select young ladies of Lenox used to
row up to see the white egret. But today, like the main current that flanks and feeds it, it is a stygian and unhealthy
flood, though teeming with muskrat, fish, water snakes,
ducks in season, water lilies in season, and infinite marsh
blooms, all less squeamish than man. Here, they say, prodigious bass and pickerel lie, for no one disturbs their peaceful
growth. If some drink the river's milk via cows, none dare
eat its flesh in terms of game.

Cutting in from the main river, you paddle down the
lagoon, perhaps getting lost up a blind bay and having to
explore your way out. You come into Woods Pond into
which a lover, having killed his beloved some years ago on
October Mountain, threw her body. On the right, as you
paddle down the pond, is the Lenox Railroad Station, and
behind it the road running up the hill to the Center. You

put in at a little concrete pier opposite the station, pull out
your canoe and get permission from the people in the house
near by to leave it there. You have paddled down a river
that in its pristine state, for charm of water, banks, surrounding pastures, woods and mountains, incidentally for
easy paddling and for endless nooks where the canoe can
put in, conceded nothing to any river in the world, not to
the English Cam with which Holmes compared it. But the
river you have actually paddled down was a fetid artery of
death. You have now passed the worst. From now on the
stream is larger and for twenty river miles it is swifter.

Now on your bikes you undertake the first side journey. You pedal 2.4 miles up on the steep nose of land, part
of the valley's central ridge, on whose summit is Lenox
Center. Coming into the village, you pass on your right a
playground where the iron mine used to be. You come to
the Main Street and pause, looking at the old houses lined
up right and left. Far up to the right, more than half hidden by the modern trees, is the Church on the Hill, finished
in 1805, to which Fanny Kemble gave its first clock and
Morris K. Jesup the present one, which still keeps time.
Diagonally across to your right is the handsome, empty and
well-preserved Lenox Academy, 1803. To the left, just beyond the corner drugstore, is a small park where stood the
jail when Lenox was the shire town. Beyond it is the beautiful, second courthouse, 1816, now the library, with its floating, light-columned belfry. You walk up past it, pushing
your bikes, and fetch up in front of the big Curtis Hotel,
successor to the Berkshire Coffee House where Holmes, Melville and the rest used to assemble, and whose predecessor
went back to the Revolution. The monument out in the
middle of the crossroads is to Revolutionary General Patterson. The road dropping off to the left of it, continuing
Main Street, is Court House Hill where Edith Wharton's
Ethan Frome took his fated slide. Across Walker Street to
your left is the modern, neo-Georgian town hall, successor
to a wooden structure which was the first courthouse, 1792,
became the town hall when the second courthouse was built,

and, shorn of its belfry, still survives as moved to a corner
you passed when entering the village. Back of the Curtis
Hotel is the first site of Mrs. Charles Sedgwick's school, and
beyond it on the corner of Walker and Church the first site
of the house of Mr. and Mrs. Sedgwick and Catherine.

Facing across Main Street from the Curtis Hotel, you
look down West Street Hill, which wages a losing fight for
the honor of having killed Ethan Frome. Safely you coast
down it past several small estates, the site of Charlotte Cushman's house, Groton Place, the former estate of Grenville L.
Winthrop, Stoneover, the former estate of John Parsons,
and so out on the flat. Two miles from the Center you come
to Tanglewood, formerly the Tappans' estate. You don't go
in yet, but slide by, avoid a fork up the hill to the right
that leads to Dr. Koussevitzky's Serenak. You turn sharp
left round the Higginson place, leaving the great Jesuit
novitiate castle Shadowbrook behind you on the slope of
Baldhead, pedal ahead a hundred yards and find on the road
the bronze plaque marking the place where Hawthorne's
Red House burned down in '90. You take in his view down
over Stockbridge Bowl and up to Monument Mountain's
cragged summit whence the Indian maiden leaped when her
lover was killed in battle and where Hawthorne and Melville got acquainted in a rock niche, hiding from a rain-
storm for an hour. After locating the outline of Hawthorne's foundation you peer through the hedge across the
road at some of the Tanglewood buildings. You return as
you came, this time going into Tanglewood to prowl round
the now deserted Music Shed and theater, giving such account of yourself as may be required. Then you pedal hard
and long back up West Street Hill to the Center. From
there you may, if you are spending the night, take any
number of loops to pass half-empty palace after half-empty
palace.

Whether that day or the next, you will return to the
river by way of Walker Street, passing on the left the original Sedgwick sites, on the right the Freylinghuysen place,
beyond which down Kemble Street (Route 7) was the sec-

ond and final Sedgwick location. Passing Kemble Street, you leave the original Wharton house—not Edith's Mount—on your left, the Episcopal church on your right, the Morgan and Schermerhorn places on your right. Forking left from the state road that heads toward Lee, you coast down the country road past the Cramwell School with the old Patterson place in the background. And so down to Lenoxdale where, if you wish, you can find the once profitable Lenox furnace under a dump on the river to the right of the four corners at the bridge. Up to the left is the dam that was made from the stones of the old jail, and a quarter of a mile up the River Road, on the edge of the village, you pass the flattened and overgrown ruins of the Lenox Glass Works where you may find gnarled souvenirs from the production in the eighties under Theodore Roosevelt, Sr.

And so an easy two miles up the country road to Lenox station where you left your canoe. Just before you reach the station, when you hear and see the falls at the dam, dismount and climb over the railroad tracks to see the Lenox Frog by the river, an item of local pride. A big boulder, five or six feet long and almost as high, resting on another in a slanting posture, inspired a local sculptor to complete the head and eye sockets with a touch of concrete and to paint the whole green with yellow spots, leaving a lifelike, titanic bullfrog forever about to leap into the river just below the dam.

A hundred yards above you retrieve your canoe, push off, paddle down and out of Woods Pond, carry around the dam, and put off again in the light rapids that presently smooth out into a sluggish stream easing down to Lenoxdale which you recently left. Along the banks green scum is gathered. On the left there is a huge gravel pit. You pass the river side of the Glass Works, drifting over jettisoned machinery which you cannot see for the dark water. Carry around the Lenoxdale dam, bridge and mill, put in again, and slip down into industrial Lee.

At Lee Center there are two dams to carry around. Below the second you put it among the big floating white nodules of industrial waste and start down a five-mile run, with frequent riffles whereby the river is partially purified. It is a little sporty, the going, with a certainty of scratching and a possibility of stoving in the canoe. On the left the mountains are near the river, closely containing the inner valley. On the right you slip past the track where the summer rich of Lenox, Lee and Stockbridge used to hold their horse races. Up on the horizon is Highlawn where they used to hold their horse shows. If you want to see the famous Tyringham Valley, you draw into shore in the quiet water above the modern covered bridge over the river at South Lee. It's fifteen miles up to Tyringham village and back, recommended but not insisted upon. The village is unattractive, but the valley of Hop Brook is the finest for mountain magnificence of the many tributary valleys. It is Shaker country. The late Sidney Howard's house, up the hill to the right from the village, was a Shaker meetinghouse, and the pegs still remain high along the wall where they hung up the chairs when the dance started.

Back on the river, a little below the covered bridge, you must carry around another dam and mill, putting into fast water again, but not fast enough or lasting long enough to eliminate the new pollution. The current slows, and you float with the white bubbles of filth a river mile and three-quarters down to the concrete bridge where Route 7 crosses the river in Stockbridge village. Here you land, push your bikes up the bank and ride up the street to the main corner, where you are at the center of one of the two closest concentrations of history in the valley.

Within a half-mile radius you have one or more notable monuments from each of the five acts of the valley's drama. Two hundred yards to the left and across the wide Main Street stands the little mansion of John Sergeant and his wife Abigail Williams, built in 1740 on the Hill, which rises in front of you, and in 1928 moved to its present site and made into a museum by Miss Mabel Choate. A little nearer, under some leaning, white birches on the same side of the street, is the sundial in the front yard of the Riggs

Foundation, marking the site of Jonathan Edwards's house that long afterwards was Bernard Hoffman's School. On the edge of the village, out of sight down the street to the left, is the monument to the Stockbridge Indians, and a little nearer, on the green, the Field Chime Tower stands on the site of their log church. Out of sight up the hill to the left, the house of Henry Martyn Field contains remnants of "the castle" of Ephraim Williams.

For the Second Act, you have first the big Red Lion Inn immediately on your right, which was not so big in 1774 when in its ballroom a Berkshire county convention met and promulgated the first complete nonintercourse act with Britain, called the "First Declaration of Independence." Three doors down the street on the left—visible if you cross the street and look back—is the mansion Theodore Sedgwick built in 1785, where Mum Bett, the first slave to be emancipated by law, was in charge for many years and saved the family silver when Shays' Regulators came by.

For the Third Act, you have the same house, where Catherine, daughter of Theodore, began her literary career and subsequently entertained all the writers, and everybody else of distinction, who anywise passed that way. To the left your half-mile radius touches the edge of the river's Oxbow, whose loops contain the elphin woodland which Longfellow loved and owned for years though he never built there. Down the street on the left is the house of David Dudley, Sr., father of all the Fields, with its famous golden wedding room. For a monument of the industrial phase of the Third Act, you have to go 1.5 miles westward to the Monument Mills of Glendale.

Of the towers and palaces of the Fourth Act, the best of several near-by examples is the house of Joseph Choate, now occupied by Miss Choate, up the hill to the left. Properly belonging to the Fourth Act, though it happened in the Third, was Cyrus Field's successful laying of the Atlantic cable in 1866. Across the street from where you are standing is a small building, the former law office of Jonathan Edwards Field, where Henry Martyn, the pious brother, received Cyrus's first message on the first cable that held. It is now the office of Congressman Treadway. Down the street to the left, beyond the Riggs Foundation Inn, stood another Field house, now moved away, where Stephen Dudley invented the trolley car and a string of other electrical items. Up to the rear and right, obscured by the Red Lion Inn, is Laurel Hill, local park given to the town by David Dudley Field, Jr., inspiration of the Laurel Hill Society, the first village improvement society in America.

For the Fifth, and modern, Act you have up the street the Berkshire Playhouse, and until recently in the Sedgwick house lived the younger Ellery whose work on Melville has recently appeared. If you add to these monuments the knowledge that Hawthorne's cottage and Tanglewood are technically in Stockbridge, far up the hill road almost in Lenox, and Stockbridge's claim to be the center of valley history is impressive.

Most of these things you have seen without going more than half a mile from your canoe. Now you return and paddle on down with the soapsuds through the meadows where the Indians used to live. You pass the rear of the Sedgwick mansion resting comfortably on the top of the river terrace. You go by the mouth of Konkapot's Brook where the old Christian chief lived. You do the big loop of the Oxbow, viewing the house that Lawyer Charles Southmayd built on the eminence where Longfellow always talked of building. You straighten out with the river and slide out into three miles of fast water, sometimes sporty to the point of danger, with two dams to carry round. You come down through a gorge of rapids ending in the pond at the dam for the Monument Mills in Housatonic, over the line in Great Barrington. Here you make a quarter-mile carry, put in below the industrial village, and zip along a mile down to the Rising Mills dam, where you have to carry again. Now the industrial waste has been purged away, and from here on you are traveling a brown but increasingly clean river.

From Rising down to Great Barrington Center is a

three-mile run under Monument Mountain, leaving it behind on the left, the great summit cliffs where the pere-
grine falcon nests. You slow up in the pond of the dam below the modern successor of the ancient Great Bridge over
the modern successor (Route 7) of the ancient Great Road.
Here, taking to the left bank, you carry round the dam
of the old woolen mill and modern power company, passing Great Barrington's original common, graveyard, and
site of its first church. Putting in, you glide down a couple

of long village blocks and go ashore again near the high
school at the third bridge. The bridge crosses the point that
was the original ford for the Indian trail, and afterwards for
the Great Road before the Great Bridge was built. Generally,
all the ground you have passed on the right from the dam
down is the old Great Wigwam, or capital, of the Housatonic Indians. This indeed is the very "Housatonuk," the
very "place-beyond-the-mountains" whither they first came
over the Taconics and where the name was applied, first to
the place, then to the people, and finally to the river. Here
at the ford, presumably on the open ground along the west

bank between the river and the school, was where, one
foggy dawn in the fall of 1676, Major Talcott wiped out
a band of Eastern Indians fleeing after King Philip's War.
Leave your canoes where the Indians and then the English
crossed and walk up the street to the central corner at Main.
Here again in a small radius you have the history of the
valley.

The pre-white man history is down at the ford and in
the country up to your left as you face the river, where
hundreds of Indian graves have been unearthed.

Of the First Act there is the memory that the first Indian mission house stood for a year over there where the
Congregational church is today, before it moved up to
Stockbridge, and that Samuel Hopkins, the first minister
here and afterwards one of New England's top theologians,
used to preach to a none too reverent audience up there on
the old common across the river. If you are standing in the
center of the four corners, the General Dwight mansion—
which Madame Dwight, ex-Mrs. John Sergeant, ex-Abigail
Williams, caused her general to build her, 1756-1759—stood
down the street to your right and rear on a spot now covered
by one end of the great Berkshire Inn. When the inn was
built, the house was considerately moved back and is well
preserved.

Being in the middle of the corners, you are a little in
front of the middle of the first Berkshire County courthouse which stood out in the street just here, and where
some of the first action of the Second Act of the drama took
place. Here, after passing the nonintercourse resolutions at
the Stockbridge convention in 1774, the local Yankees pre-
vented by force the crown judges from holding court. And
here the Regulators of Shays later tried the same tactics on
the state courts with less sustained success. Along Main
Street just here stood the famous captured artillery train
of Burgoyne, while most of his surrendered army camped
in two detachments outside the village, and Burgoyne himself was entertained by the second Colonel Dwight in the
paternal mansion.

Coming to the Third Act, the site of Bryant's law office is down yonder to the right, behind the other end of the Berkshire Inn, and the Stevens house, where he lived for a prolific year, is on the high ground past the corner beyond. The old woolen mill at the bridge likewise belongs to the mid-century.

From the frou-frou of the Fourth Act there is the castle Kellogg Terrace, now become the Barrington School, with its wall along the street opposite the Berkshire Inn. Also the inn itself. South of the village there is Brookside, now the Altaraz School. For the scientific part of the Fourth Act, Great Barrington led the valley. Just out of sight down the street past the Bryant-Stevens house is Wainwright Hall where William Stanley perfected his invention of the transformer. For his initial experiment he got his current from the private plant over yonder at Kellogg Terrace, and all around this corner, on the evening of March 20, 1886, the first municipal lighting system in the world went on in a single flash.

In the current Fifth Act, Great Barrington is not carrying a distinguished role. Of known consequence in residence, only Albert Spalding the violinist.

After the respective central crossroads of Great Barrington and Stockbridge, there aren't any more spots in the valley where you can see a concentration of monuments recalling the whole drama of Yankee history. Putting in at the old ford, you set out down a labyrinthine reach of at least twenty-five miles of twisting and returning to make about fifteen miles progress. This region—southern Great Barrington, all of Sheffield and the central river plain of North Canaan, Salisbury and Canaan—is one of the two best agricultural sections in the valley, which is here at its widest between the mountains. Flat, fertile land, meandering river and long views of East Mountain on the left, and on the right Mts. Washington, Everett, Bear, Riga and the rest of the tallest Taconics. You have now emerged from the region of pollution, and all down through these meadows plenty of bass, pickerel and perch can be taken and safely eaten. You paddle past the mouth of the Green River, the spot being the northern Scatacook, the Place-Where-Two-Rivers-Join. Where the river loops in close to Route 7 in northern Sheffield, you can hop out if you want to and pedal three miles over to the scene of the last battle of Shays' Rebellion. Here, great Everett hangs close over you, the biggest of the Taconics, 2,624 feet, referred to as "The Dome" in upper Berkshire. On Mt. Everett, and westward among lower peaks, is the township of Mt. Washington, southwest corner of Massachusetts, scene of bloody feuds in the eighteenth century when the Dutch and the Yankees met there. Today the official population is 57. They all turn out before dawn on presidential election day, in order to maintain their standing as the first town in the country to get in their returns.

In southern Sheffield you drift by the rear of the house of General John Ashley, having passed just above it the original site of the house (1735) of his father, Colonel John Ashley, whence Mum Bett fled to gain her freedom. The latter house has been moved a half mile inland, is in perfect preservation, and Mr. Brewer the owner is generous in showing it. Without knowing it you float into Connecticut, and presently thereafter the previously bare, pastured banks begin to be lined with big willows, and the hills edge in closer. The Blackberry River comes in, flowing northward to a hairpin turn. You pass under Dutcher's Bridge, site of the ford on the ancient Hartford-Albany Turnpike. From here you may, if you wish, climb out and ride up the big hill and down five miles into Salisbury Center, and two miles more to Lakeville where you may view in a close group: the site of Ethan Allen's blast furnace, source of much Revolutionary ordnance, demolished in 1843 and replaced by the Holley Manufacturing Company; the site of Ethan Allen's house, now covered by the railroad station; between house and furnace, the pre-Allen dam still holding and supplying the head to run Local Industries, Inc., the little modern factory in the building of the old Holley works. Up on the Main Street and across it is the house of John Milton Holley, built in 1808 and reproduced as "The Connecticut House" at the 1932-1933 Chicago Fair. A half mile southwestward on the Millerton Road, the Victorian mansion of Alexander Hamilton Holley stands on Wononscopomuc Lake; and a mile and a half farther you come to the star-shaped lake that was Ore Hill. Returning to Salisbury Center, you may push your bikes two miles up Mt. Riga to the furnace that is the most romantic relic of the iron industry in its wild location and in the wild human beings who live round it in the bush, the Raggies whom it left flat when it went out of blast.

Whether or not you have made the Salisbury expedition, you go on from Dutcher's Bridge down a river that is sizable now, getting on to where big adjectives like "majestic" would sometimes suit it. For a way yet the current is slow, but the margin of farm land is narrowing. While the wider valley remains outside, two inner ranges of hills are containing the river in an inner valley. The Hollanbeck comes in, one of the many streams that flow north to empty into the main artery flowing south. You come to the dam at the top of tragic Canaan Falls, once the biggest waterdrop of the valley. Now the Connecticut Power Company's flume leads the whole docile river off to the left and dumps it down into the powerhouse a quarter of a mile below. You get out on the right, or Amesville, side, drifting over on the big pond's bottom part of the remains of the Ames Iron works that made such good Civil War guns, and afterwards failed and the plant was sold to the Housatonic Railroad for repair shops. You'd better get a lift for your canoe for the half-mile carry from Amesville down to the powerhouse. From the big dam down you see the ruin first wrought on nature by industry and afterwards made more desolate when industry itself withdraws. The great dry cascade is a ghostly exhibit. So, inland along the road in Amesville, are the numerous foundations and retaining walls of huge, cut stones well fitted, the bones of the early factories that brought "Canaan Falls"—now Falls Village—nearer than any other part of the valley to fulfillment of the prophecy of becoming a Lowell, a Paterson or the like. The ruins are now well buried in pastures and orchards, the place returning to a second state of nature. You coast down to the bridge, passing the tavern with its two-story columns of tree trunks, and noticing at each end of the bridge the ruins of a big furnace that used to pour out the pig iron. You can ride up into the village—Falls Village—and see the National Iron Bank that opened for business in 1847 and has not since closed its door, not even when ordered to in the bank holiday. Dwight Dean, the recent president, enjoyed the same age as the bank, went to work there five days before Lincoln was shot in '65 and never worked anywhere else. He died in 1945, missing his centenary by two years. Falls Village is the railroad station for Music Mountain, and again if you are ambitious you can ride the ten miles up and back. If it's Sunday when you come by, the trip is advised, for that's when the Gordon Quartet plays. All around these parts, beginning in Canaan and thickening down through Cornwall, Kent, Sherman and New Milford, the New Puritans, the recent high-brow immigrants, are at their most numerous, far too numerous to name here, and far too resistant to being visited by passing canoeists.

You go back down to the powerhouse and shove off on a run of some twenty river miles to Kent, one of the favorite runs in the east for canoe clubs and fold-boaters, the river, now capable of thundering rapids when it wants to, showing white water all the way and canoers having few moments when they can look up at the cliffs, the wooded shores, the occasional glimpses of the distant mountains. If your passage were earlier in the year, in the fishing season, you would annoy hundreds of fishermen in their waist boots wading far out into the stream to throw their flies and their lures. This reach, heavily stocked each year by Connecticut, is one of the best fishing regions in New England, the brown trout running up to two pounds and a half, the brook trout to a pound and a half. Between Falls Village and Swift's Bridge below Cornwall Bridge there is no ban on the native bass because they are death on the trout.

Starting down this twenty-mile reach, you are at first running at only a comparatively good clip between Sharon Mountain on the right and Cornwall's Cream Hill and Tarrydiddle on the left. If you plan to stop at West Cornwall, you'd better do it in the quiet reach above the covered bridge—the last of the original Towne covered bridges and itself already precarious and condemned, the town and the state dickering about a new bridge. From here it is three

miles up to Cornwall village where the approximate site of the Old Mission School is now occupied by the chapel of the First Church of Christ. If you take this side trip at all, it is recommended that you swing back by way of old Cornwall whence you get a view southward similar to that from Pratt Hill at the head of the valley, a view the actual length of which I do not know, but it is all the tops of mountains filling the valley southward to the end of sight, probably twenty-five miles or so into New Milford, where the higher hills end. From the Center you swing farther

north to visit North Cornwall Church, the prettiest and
best kept up of the old churches in the valley; also the un-
marked site of Ethan Allen's boyhood home, somewhere
across the road from the church in the open field in the
southwest angle of the three corners. The so-called Allen
cemetery is back near the old Center, but the stones are
crude and illegible, and it is not worth visiting.

From the smooth water above the covered bridge at
West Cornwall you put off and get set for the sporty riffle
under the right span of the bridge, a popular riffle to upset in. Once the academic Yelping Hill Association went
bumping down the river in inflated inner tubes and came to
divers nonfatal griefs in this riffle. A quarter of a mile below you go over the Dimsey Hole whose bottom has not
been found. On the right the cliffs are lofty, perpendicular, and shelved only as blown out to build the road. A few
streams make bridal veil falls far up the precipice among
the thinly rooted shrubs, and in wet seasons the freshets
make many more. On the left there are no cliffs, but good
farm land. You sweep along at top speed, the number of
dangerous rocks depending on the height of the water.
Four miles downstream you come in sight of the lofty,
modern, concrete span of Cornwall Bridge, replacing the
covered bridge that went out with the ice in '36. Again,
if you are planning to stop here, the best place to do it is
above the bridge, though it isn't easy to draw in and stop
anywhere.

The only reason for stopping at Cornwall Bridge is
to go up Coltsfoot Mountain to Dudleytown, the most famous ghost town in the valley. For the full effect you'd
better climb it on foot up the abandoned road known as
the Dark Entry. It's less than three miles up to the over-
forested three corners where you meet the Main Street of
Dudleytown. The Dark Entry is named for the deep, hem-
lock-roofed canyon up which the road winds. Dudleytown
itself is all lost in forest, though part of the road in from
the Warren side has been reopened for logging. You can
spend as much time as you want to crashing around among

the cellar holes, some of them of mansions, all lost under brush and big trees. A local guide is desirable. In spite of legends to the contrary, it is unlikely that you will be murdered, or even whistled at, by ghosts. Remember how the people came up here in the 1740's, seeking either God or liberty. How they burned down the trees and furrowed unwisely and let the topsoil run away. Wonder where their descendants are now, and whether they value either liberty or God.

Back to Cornwall Bridge and down seven or eight more miles of sporty water to Kent, passing Kent furnace and the village on the left, sighting Kent school on the right. Here the river smooths out into the five-mile-long pond down to Bull's Falls dam, the reach of quiet water where the famous Kent School crews row and where the fishing for large- and small-mouthed bass and for pickerel is excellent. On the right you paddle past South Kent School and the remains of the Scatacook Indian Reservation with its few mixed-breeds. Carrying down around the dam a good half mile, you put in below the biggest electric power plant on the river. Just above is the great bend where the Tenmile comes in—the original Scatacook—and where the primordial river rolled down from the far northwest. Eight more miles down, passing on the right the great talus slide known as Cat Rocks, the town of Sherman, the Riggi plant on the left at what used to be a scenic place with cliffs on the right. On past the Rocky River plant with the two big conduits lying like giant worms up the hill to Candlewood Lake. The Aspetuck River pours in. Fast around the bend Weantinock where the river doubles Green Mountain, with the Indians' old Fort Hill opposite up there on the right, the flat plateau where their village Weantinock was big and prosperous in the days of Waramaug. And so down the left side of the now mile-wide valley floor that was the Indian Planting Field. Nose in at the bridge at New Milford.

Here it is worth getting out and walking up to the green at the top of Bank Street, if only to look across the

mile of flat to Fort Hill on exactly the same level; to know
that the two races lived opposite each other here in dignity
and peace for thirty years; to see above Fort Hill over
there in the west the greater height of Guarding Mountain,
and to know that just east of the green behind you there is
an equivalent rise, here called Second Hill; to know that
once the Great River, immeasurably larger than any on
earth today, was between those two mountain bridges for
banks, that afterwards as it receded it was between Fort
Hill and Town Hill where you are standing by the New
Milford green. Here, at the top of Bank Street, was where
the town of New Milford gathered on a then cliff to watch
the first railroad train come in in 1840, keeping this dis-
creet distance in anticipation that "the thing would explode." Back of you the green itself was one of the prize
swales of the early villages, now as picturesque and well
kept as most and with a few fine houses. If you are ambitious ride your bikes nineteen miles up through Washington to Litchfield, the handsomest village in the valley, considered by many the handsomest village in America. See
the Congregational church that reproduces Lyman Beecher's exactly; ride out to the Beecher site on North Street;
go down South Street to Tapping Reeve's house and law
school. Coast back to New Milford.

And now paddle two quiet miles down the river between big, piebald sycamore trees, past the foundry and
the bleachery, and so to the dramatic corner where the
Still River comes in northward in a reverse valley, like
Konkapot's Creek, the Blackberry and the Hollanbeck farther upstream. Here, where the river widens and smooths
out, but with a big roar down yonder, you'd better pull
quickly into the left bank and do your sightseeing from
the shore. Opposite you the Still, having come up through
its famous, tobacco-fertile valley from Danbury, pours in
its filth—though there is now too much volume and speed
of water to be troubled by a polluted stream almost as big
as was the river itself up at Pittsfield. On the point between
the Still and the Main River are the Romanlike ruins of

the Bridgeport Wood Finishing Company, and just below
them the big pond formed by the union of the two streams
spills over in the "Great Falls" Metichawan which used to
be the head of the shad run. They are not great at all,
being perhaps eight feet drop. Just below them, where the
banks are narrowing and heightening, a red iron bridge
crosses, high enough for you to see under it. Beyond, on
both sides and hardly fifty feet apart, rise perpendicular
cliffs in a canyon, more than a hundred feet high on the
right, somewhat less on the left. On the top of the right
hill Waramaug had his palace, and there he died after the
Reverend Daniel Boardman and the local powwow, or medicine man, had tried to howl each other down for three hours.
On the top of the left hill he was buried, and his monument
was afterwards violated by people building a castle there.
Down from the palace ran Lillinonah, Waramaug's daughter,
escaping from the arranged marriage, and pushed out in her
canoe above the falls. Below, beyond the modern bridge, the
heaviest rapids of the river, here congested in the narrow
canyon, convolute in ten-foot whorls and terrific speed. Just
as the fair Lillinonah and her canoe having shot the falls,
were sucked into this awful funnel, her true, white lover appeared on the cliff by the palace above and leapt down to
join her. Since when the whole gorge, the cliff on either side
and the rapids are indiscriminately called Lover's Leap.

If you can you get a lift over the river-trembling left
hill, through nice hemlock woods with the roar of the rapids
below. You put in again in a whopping big pool into which
the rapids disgorge, a lake two hundred yards or more in
diameter. This was the famous Fishing Cove where elbow
room anywhere on the bank had rental value at the time of
the shad run. The island at the foot of it is Goodyear's Island,
where in the 1640's was a trading post, the first white pene-
tration north of Derby. From here down we are getting out
of two- into three-century antiquity. But before chuting on
into early colonial times, take a six-mile round trip to Bridgewater Center and view the curious house, stable and business
block of Charles B. Thompson's first mail-order house in

America, the valley's best contribution to the fake, publicity-driven economy of today.

Now fifteen miles of moderate rapids, at first between Bridgewater on the left and Brookfield on the right. Under the concrete bridge of Route 25, where the little picnic park on shore carries a fierce sign, "Bridgewater town park for town people." On between Newtown on the right and Southbury on the left, under the wooden bridge of the old Shepaug Railroad and past the bridged mouth of the fast Shepaug River. And so down with increasing speed between banks here not precipitous, indeed a road running just at high water along the left one, but steep and evergreen-wooded and shutting out any inland view of the tobacco land, a reach more like untouched wilderness than any other on the river. Abruptly you pour out into wide, quiet water, the head of Lake Zoar set back by the Stevenson dam eight river miles below.

Now for the first time you have to paddle a mile to make progress. On the right you pass the mouth of the Potatuck River coming down its romantic gorge from Sandy Hook where Goodyear discovered vulcanizing. You head in at the long Sandy Hook Bridge, and take a nine-mile run up to Woodbury, if for no other reason than to view the most romantic natural monument of early settlements to be found anywhere in America. Six miles along in Southbury village, you pass the schoolhouse of longest use in the United States, the Bullitt Hill School, built in 1788 and used as a school until 1941, a square, brick structure with pyramidal roof and fine cupola, the second-story hall having a dome ceiling and having been used originally for town meeting. Pedaling up Woodbury's long Main Street, stop when you reach on the right the neoclassic little Masonic Temple set up on Drum Rock whence, from the 1670's on, the drummer summoned the plantation to meeting, to announcements or to war. Across the street is a small red barn where the first meeting house stood, and near it a tablet to the sagamore Pomperaug is attached to an outcrop close to which he is supposed to have been buried. Take the side road running up behind

Drum Rock and, reaching the gates of Orenaug Park, take the footpath that leads you up the Orenaug Rocks, that narrow and lofty outcrop rising gradually under columns and ceilings of hemlock and pine. A half-mile easy climb up this sloping, cathedral aisle brings you to the summit and solitude like a mountaintop, a mountaintop scarcely fifty feet wide and dropping off in two-hundred-foot cliffs on both sides. In this summit there is a hollow, a little natural amphitheater with big rock fragments tumbled around for seats. Here the Puritans gathered to worship under the presidency of their minister who stood on Bethel Rock, a boulder on a shelf a little above them. To this eagle-visited, solemn place, just as it is today, came those men of distinguished mind, carrying their guns, to kneel among rocks under great trees and worship God in the way they believed He desired to be worshiped. Here also occurred the tragedy of the young Chief Waramaukeag and Miss Walker the daughter of the minister.

If you wish you may swing back to the Sandy Hook Bridge by way of Roxbury, the natal houses of Remember Baker and Seth Warner and the site of the infant house of Ethan Allen. On the right as you come down to the Shepaug, you see Ore Mountain, the famous Roxbury mine whose capacity is so much greater than its failure would indicate. Farther down are the ruins of famous Roxbury Falls, blasted down for the Shepaug Railroad.

From Sandy Hook Bridge you paddle about seven miles down Lake Zoar, which is the river widened to a half mile or more by the Stevenson dam. On the right is fertile, rolling land in Newtown, on the left mostly inferior, corrugated, sandy ridges and hollows in Southbury and afterwards Oxford. At Stevenson you carry down around the big dam, with its separate falls through the dozen floodgates mingling in a solid sheet halfway down their seventy-five-foot drop. You put out into the rapids below in the rain of the spray, and in a few hundred yards they flatten into a uniform, deep, seemingly irresistible flow. Here, a hundred yards wide between great, wooded bluffs, all the springs and rain squalls and rills of thousands of hills are at last mingled in an easy flood that sends by a point almost seventy thousand cubic feet in a second of time. You have come down with the water from those far inland hills where this current was called Housatonic and Weantinock to the place where it was called Potatuck and Great River and Stratford River, and newly arrived white men dreamed of the unknown northern regions whence it flowed.

But now the greatness and the mystery are both gone. For here paddling and boating are easy, and both shores in the shadow of the bluffs are lined solidly with cheap boat-houses and restaurants and shacks. An amusement park will be next. It is the beginning of the reach of the river that nature made most beautiful and that the industrial age has hastened to adorn with a slum. You drift easily in deep-moving water for five miles down between Oxford and Monroe, afterwards between Seymour and Shelton. It is a hinter-land, already out of the upper, civilized reaches where man and nature have long made and kept a good truce; yet the new thing here is not yet fully grown, and nature is neither altogether destroyed nor man altogether depraved.

Then you swing out and around a bend, and there a mile before you is a sight of red and black grandeur. There stand lofty chimneys of brick, rivaling the hills in height, and among them great brick structures recall the magnificence of Rome. Between and over the chimneys lies a quiet black cloud of perpetual smoke, and through and under the smoke there are webs of tiny filaments that are cables and wires. From this distance it all seems clean, peaceful and beautiful, just and powerful and right. And all the time there comes up from this powerful panorama a steady, low roar, not the free crashing thunder of falls and rapids, but the mingled rumble of thousands of contained and ordered bearings and wheels. This is modern America, Derby, a city, where the Devil is well established and long ago ousted the Lord.

Here your run down the true and unspoiled valley is ended. But if you wish you may get a lift round the long dam and the rapids, and put in again in the beautiful, turning basin where the foul Naugatuck joins the river and both meet the tide. You may go up into Derby and locate early colonial structures and sites. Returning to the river, you may pass on the left the abandoned flats, now covered with railroad cinders, where the great shipyards used to be; and if you go too close you will still scrape some of the piles that carried the wharves of Derby for two centuries of shipping days. You may paddle down past the site of the Hull house in

Shelton, whence Commodore Isaac went out to command the *Constitution* and where he returned, the whole situation now dreadful with dumps and slums on the hill behind. You may ease down on the ebb for thirteen miles, the last of it through salt marshes, to the ocean breeze, under the George Washington Bridge and out into Stratford Harbor that is the salt sea. You may bike it three miles eastward to Milford village and the green where the church and the town hall, the pool between them and its dam are placed as they were in 1642, and you may see the oldest house standing in the valley, the "Stockade House" of 1659, along with countless other relics and remains. You may ride down to Milford Beach and see Charles Island out there where Captain Kidd used to put in and where no treasure has been found. Along the beach you may see piles of clam and mussel shells left by the Indians before the white man came. You may return to Stratford Harbor and paddle across the salt water to tiny Mac's Harbor where the first settlers of the valley landed in 1639. From here you may walk up to the site of their first meetinghouse, to Watch House Hill, and round the outline of the first stockade. And you may find numerous later landmarks: the house of the famous, Episcopal Samuel Johnsons; the house, now the museum, that was connected with the watchhouse by a tunnel; the house of the Stratford rappings. Back in the little estuary of Mac's Harbor you can hear the outer surf pounding on Milford and Stratford points. If the surf is not heavy you may paddle out there where the incoming Puritans first passed, where Captain Block in 1614 saw the bluffs of Stratford Point and named the stream the River of the Red Hills.

All these things and the reminders of many other events and conditions that have been named in this book you may see by paddling on down below Derby to the Sound. But in this tidewater region, as to a less extent in the headwaters through Dalton and Pittsfield, these things are relics of a world that is gone, a world over which the modern, industrial one feels itself so victorious and superior that it can afford graciously to leave corners of itself as museums of forgotten time.

Yet in the country between tidewater and headwaters, in the ninety-mile valley back in the uplands above Derby, this is not the case. There the relics and the monuments commemorate a people and a civilization that yet survive, and the changes have been of surface and not of kind. This civilization is one in which the direction of life is prescribed by ideas in the minds of men, and it includes equally the lives of Edwards and Bellamy, of Sherman and Allen, of Hawthorne and Melville, of Field and Stanley, of Thurber and Van Doren.

To be sure, there are many who believe that this state of civilization is something ancient and lost, that the valley of ideas is vestigial and atavistic in a world that is aiming for the comfort of the senses and not of the mind, that those who look to the valley and love it are abandoned to nostalgia and far from the current of things as they are.

But those who are so criticized are pleased to take a contrary view. They believe that the life of the mind, traditional in their Valley and along their river, is the only life that is close to ultimate and satisfying reality. They remember that one branch of human civilization, in its highest expression, identified it with the life of ideas that is centered in the one idea of the True, the Beautiful, and the Good. They remember that another branch of human civilization, of which the original Puritans were one expression, identified it with the Love of God. However defined or assimilated, they believe that the life of the mind is the only life of human consequence, not only for three centuries gone but for all centuries to come. They believe that, though the valley is small on the modern earth, it is yet one of the repositories of a human secret of importance, a secret of understanding and insight that in many other places has been lost for a time. They hope that one day this secret will spread from the Place-beyond-the Mountains to enlighten America again, and through America the world.

In Acknowledgment

A LIST of those to whom I am indebted for help in making this book would start with the youth who found me standing on the bleak shore of Mud Pond where the river rises, told me about the beaver dams yonder, and led me back through muck and alders to the spring which is actually the beginning. The list would end with the boy who jumped on my car and guided me down to the ocean beach at Milford and the sight of Captain Kidd's Island a little way off shore. Between these two anoymous contributors to the book, I might properly include most of the population of the Housatonic Valley.

Before attempting a selection of those whose contributions to this particular book seem to have been the greatest, I want to put on record an acknowledgment that I have long owed to Miss Anne S. Pratt, Reference Librarian of the Yale Library, for invaluable help not only in this book but in others that have preceded it. I don't know how many hundreds or thousands of researchers, of all ages and degrees of stupidity, it is Miss Pratt's duty to keep spinning at once like so many tops. All I know is that one of the tops never asks her a question but the authority of the world on the point is instantly before him, and with a readiness that makes him feel that Miss Pratt had always been specially interested in the question herself and had been awaiting just this opportunity to go into the matter. And back of Miss Pratt stands a great library that is unfailingly generous to people whose requests are bona fide, no matter how unreasonable.

At the foundations of this particular book on the Housatonic River and its people lies the work of Mrs. Joseph Gangi, who was Miss Adelaide Starr at the time she did the research. Having agreed for a small compensation to do a little of the initial spade work for me according to a tentative outline I provided, she proceded to digest most of the town histories of the valley under my several headings, covering about two reams of typewriting paper in single space, a work approximately four times the length of this one.

From the scores of people who have given me formidable help, I have selected fourteen whose contributions, either in bulk or in originality, and usually in both, have substantially affected the book, shaping and coloring my ideas in definitive ways. Among the two score librarians of the valley who have helped me, the work of three bulks so large that I am sure that without their help the book would have been something quite different from what it is. These three were Miss Emily Marsh of Cornwall, Miss Irene Poirier of Lenox and Mrs. Graham D. Wilcox of Stockbridge. Not only did each of them permit me to keep inordinate tonnages of books for inordinate periods, but each of them also made independent researches into troublesome details.

Eleven other persons made definitive contributions, entitling them to a sense of partnership in the book. E. J. Amberg, Research Engineer of the Connecticut Light and Power Company, provided the data on the flow of the river and its present state of development for industrial and municipal uses. James Dixon, retired engineer of Lenox, active in the Housatonic River Improvement Association, paddled down the most polluted reaches with me, enlightening me on the causes of pollution and the proper remedies. Maurice Firuski of Salisbury lent me many books—which is not the business of a bookseller—and steered me in numerous useful channels of Salisbury history, especially among the complicated legends of the iron business. Professor R. F. Flint of Yale spent a day enlightening me on the geology of western New England. Frank C. Haggard of Lenox told me numerous stories of the town and vicinity. Charles Rufus Harte, engineer for The Connecticut Company and leading authority on Salisbury iron, taught me the history of the industry, and supplied me with his several rare pamphlets on different aspects of it. Edwin Jenkins of Lenox provided stories and atmosphere of the Tally-ho Age. Laurence K. Miller, editor of the *Berkshire Evening Eagle,* leader of the movement for the purification of the river in the Pittsfield region, dug out much data from the newspaper's files. Starr Nelson sent me valuable notes from the histories of the downriver towns. Holley Rudd of Lakeville supplied me with invaluable reminiscences of the Holley family, especially of Alexander Lyman Holley. Miss May Sherwood of Danbury Teachers College lent me as many books as most libraries did and wrote for me several useful accounts of little known events and conditions in Danbury, New Milford and the country between.

In addition to the above fourteen people whose contributions to the book were definitive, many others helped me with manuscripts, with personal recollections, with hospitality in houses and other buildings associated with the history of the valley, and in other useful ways. Twenty librarians, besides the three I have mentioned, gave me assistance beyond the requirements of duty: Miss Florence Brooks, Miss May Butler and Miss Julia Conklin of Lenox, Miss Fannie G. Clark of Pittsfield, Miss Elizabeth Dennis of Lee, Miss Mary B. Dillon of West Stockbridge, Miss Rosalie Ellis of Stockbridge, Mrs. Lois S. Exford of Dalton, Willard C. French of Sheffield, Mrs. H. W. Humphrey of Roxbury, Miss Nellie J. Hunt of Mt. Washington, Miss Lessey and Miss Kennedy of Derby, Miss Elizabeth H. Noble of New Milford, Mrs. O. K. Schulze of Great Barrington, Miss May Smith of North Canaan, Miss Ruth B. Smith of Washington, Conn., Mrs. Marion P. Whitaker of Dalton. Besides the librarians there were: Dr. I. M. Altaraz of Great Barrington ("Brookside" and modern school), Dr. Edward Andrews of Richmond (Shakers), Fred J. Bate of Cornwall (fish), E. S. Boyd of Woodbury (local history), Leverett Bradley of Salisbury (Housatonic Valley Conference), Edward A. Brewer of Pittsfield (Col. Ashley mansion), Frank Calhoun of Cornwall (local history), Malcolm Cowley of Sherman (local history), Albert Evitts of New Milford (local history), Miss Isabella Graham Foster of Wethersfield (the "Dower House" of New Milford), Lewis Gannett of Cornwall (Ezra Stiles mss.), Milton Glover of Hartford (data on river's flow), Mrs. Montgomery Hare of St. James, L. I., (recollections of Lenox and Stockbridge), James L. Hickok of South Kent (Appalachian trail) Town Clerk Hunts of Mt. Washington (local history), Mrs. May Hall James of New Haven (Indians and references to valuable authorities), Mrs. Agnes W. Johnson of Washington, Conn. (local history), John M. Johnson of Lenox (research for librarian), G. A. Kinley of the New York Central Railroad System, Charles Downing Lay of Stratford (plan for beautification of valley), P. V. D. Lockwood of the New York Central Railroad System, Mrs. Orrin W. Mills of Newtown (extended loan of local history), Leo T. Molloy of Derby (present of local history), Mrs. Charles R. Myers of Tyringham (local history), D. M. Neiswanger of the New York, New Haven and Hartford Railroad Company, John O'Donnell of Cornwall (Dibble Hill), Benjamin Sedgewick, formerly of Cornwall (Meeker Town), Mrs. Ellery Sedgwick of Stockbridge (Sedgwick Mansion), Mrs. Joel Spingarn of Amenia (extended loan of local history), Mrs. Ray Spur of West Egremont (local history), Dr. Lilian Stanley of Lenox (research for librarian), Paul Stoddard of Falls Village (references on education and other matters), Mr. and Mrs. Tracy of the Barrington School, Great Barrington, William Swift of Cornwall (local history), Miss Katherine H. Wead, Secretary of Connecticut Public Library Committee, Charles Williams of Cornwall (Dudley town), Mrs. Grace W. Wellwood of Bridgewater (local history), Alfred Worley of New Milford (local history). A number of Lenox people did research at the request of the Librarian.

In some cases I have not been able to use material supplied me by the people named and by others. Also, in matters of opinion, I have sometimes arrived at views different from those of my informants. Generally, all facts stated and opinions expressed in this book are presented on my responsibility alone.

Bibliography

I—LOCAL SOURCES

(Note: The author failed to obtain from local sources historical material upon twenty-one of the forty-seven towns in the Valley. In these cases, and in the cases of several other towns where the local material was inadequate, recourse was had to personal interviews and correspondence, acknowledged elsewhere, and to the frequently very full general sources. It will be observed that in some cases, notably that of Cothren's *Ancient Woodbury*, the history of a parent town contains, up to the time of secession and sometimes until much later, a full history of towns cut out of it.)

AMENIA, · N. Y.
Benton, Chales E., *Troutbeck*, Historical Monograph No. 1, Dutchess County Historical Society, Dutchess County, N. Y., 1916.

BETHEL, CONN.
The Connecticut Tercentenary—1635–1935—and The Two Hundred Fiftieth Anniversary of the Settlement of the Town of Danbury which included the Society of Bethel—1635–1935. Published by the Tercentenary Committee, 1935.

BETHLEHEM, CONN.
Cothren, William, *History of Ancient Woodbury*, Bronson Brothers, Waterbury, Conn., 1854.

BRIDGEWATER, CONN.
Orcutt, Samuel, *History of the Towns of New Milford and Bridgewater, Connecticut*, Case, Lockwood & Brainard Co., Hartford, 1882.

CANAAN, CONN.
Dean, Reverend Lee M., *mss.* of "Commemorative Discourse" at Falls Village, 1938.

CORNWALL, CONN.
Gold, Theodore S., *Historical Records of the Town of Cornwall*, Case, Lockwood & Brainard Company, Hartford, 1904.
Starr, Edward C. B. D., *A History of Cornwall, Connecticut*, Tuttle, Morehouse & Taylor Company, New Haven, 1926.
Stone, Reverend Timothy. *Mss.* record of, copied and arranged by Emily Marsh.

DANBURY, CONN.
Bailey, James Montgomery, *History of Danbury, Conn. 1684–1896—Compiled with Additions by Susan Benedict Hill*, Burr Printing House, New York, 1896.
Case, James R., *Tryon's Raid on Danbury*, Danbury, Conn., 1927.
Robbins, Thomas, "Century Sermon and Historical Collections of Danbury, January 1, 1801–1846" in Bailey, *op. cit.*, New York, 1896.
Sherwood, May. *Mss.* outline history of Danbury.
The Connecticut Tercentenary—1635–1935, and the Two Hundred and Fiftieth

Anniversary of the Settlement of the Town of Danbury, etc. 1635–1935. Published by the Tercentenary Commission for the State of Conn.: Committee on Education in Schools. State Board of Education, Hartford, Conn., 1933.

DERBY, CONN.

Molloy, Leo T., *Tercentenary Pictorial and History of the Lower Naugatuck Valley*, Press of the Emerson Bros., Inc., Ansonia, Conn., 1935.

Orcutt, Samuel, and Beardsley, Ambrose, *History of the Old Town of Derby, Connecticut*, Springfield, Mass., Press of Springfield Printing Co., 1880.

GREAT BARRINGTON, MASS.

Kellogg Terrace, Issued by Kellogg Terrace Associates, Great Barrington, Mass.

Taylor, Charles J., *History of Great Barrington—1676–1882*, (Part I.) *1882–1922*, (Part II.), Published by the Town of Great Barrington, 1928.

Extension by George Edwin MacLean. Published by the Town of Great Barrington. 1928.

Mss., Letter of E. J. VanLennep, 1938.

Ibid. 1940.

GOSHEN, CONN.

Hibbard, A. G., *History of the Town of Goshen, Connecticut*, Case, Lockwood & Brainard Company, Hartford, Conn., 1897.

KENT, CONN.

Atwater, Francis, *History of Kent, Connecticut*, Illustrated, Printed and Bound by the Journal Publishing Co., Meriden, Conn., 1897.

New Milford Times, October 26, 1939. Special edition on the bicentennial of Kent.

LEE, MASS.

Hyde, C. M. and Alexander, *Lee*, C. W. Bryan & Co., printers, Springfield, Mass, 1878.

LENOX, MASS.

Bartlett, W. J., *Half-Century Memories of Lenox, Mass. 1841–1891*, being an address at the dedication exercises of the Charles Sedgewick Library. Privately printed, Lee, Mass., 1894.

Mallary, R. DeWitt, *Lenox and the Berkshire Highlands*, The Knickerbocker Press, G. P. Putnam's Sons, New York and London, 1902.

One Hundredth Anniversary of the Founding of Lenox Academy, Press of the Sun Printing Company, Pittsfield, Mass. 1905.

Shepard, Rev. Dr. Samuel. Mss. "Fiery Sermon Preached to Lenox Sinner in 1806."

Mss. "Non-consumption and Non-importation Agreement Signed by the Inhabitants of Lenox, 1774."

The Valley Gleaner. January 23, 1884.

The Berkshire County Eagle, August 4, 1937.

LITCHFIELD, CONN.

White, Alain C., "The History of the Town of Litchfield, Connecticut, 1720–1920," Litchfield, Conn., *Enquirer*, 1920.

The Lure of the Litchfield Hills, Vol. VII, No. 2. The Litchfield Hills Federation (with the New England Council, Litchfield County), Winstead, Conn., 1929–1936.

Newton, Caroline Clifford. *Once Upon a Time in Connecticut*. Riverside Press, Cambridge, Mass., 1916.

MILFORD, CONN.
Ford, George Hare, *Historical Sketches of the Town of Milford*, Tuttle, Morehouse & Taylor Co., New Haven, 1914.
History of Milford, Connecticut 1639–1939. Compiled by the Federal Writers Project of Connecticut, New Haven, 1939.
Stowe, Nathan, *Sixty Years Recollections of Milford and its Chronology from 1637 Up to and Including 1910*, Edited and Revised by Newton Harrison, Milford, Conn., 1917.

MORRIS, CONN.
White, Alain C., "The History of the Town of Litchfield, Connecticut 1720–1920," Litchfield, Conn. *Enquirer*. 1920.

NEW MILFORD, CONN.
Orcutt, Samuel, *History of the Towns of New Milford and Bridgewater, Connecticut*, Hartford, 1882.
Two Centuries of New Milford—Bicentennial Celebration, The Grafton Press, New York, 1907.

NEWTOWN, CONN.
Johnson, Jane Eliza, *Newtown's History and Historian Ezra Levan Johnson*, Newtown, 1917.

NORTH CANAAN, CONN.
Smith, May. *Mss.* notes, "On Canaan Academy," "On the Public Schools of Canaan," "On Samuel Forbes."

PITTSFIELD, MASS.
Berkshire Jubilee, 1845, Albany—W. C. Little; Pittsfield—E. P. Little, 1845.
Boltwood, Edward, *The History of Pittsfield Massachusetts From the Year 1876 to the Year 1916*, Published by the City of Pittsfield, Pittsfield, 1916.
Smith, J. E. A., *The History of Pittsfield Massachusetts, From the Year 1734 to the Year 1800*, Published by Lee and Shepard, Boston, 1869.
Ibid., *From the Year 1800 to the Year 1876*, Published by C. W. Bryan & Company, Springfield, 1876.

ROXBURY, CONN.
Cothren, William, *History of Ancient Woodbury*, Bronson Brothers, Waterbury, Conn., 1854.
Humphrey, Helen Hunt Wheeler, *Christ Church, Roxbury Connecticut, Bicentennial Celebration*, New Milford, 1940.
Humphrey, Helen Hunt Wheeler, *Sketches of Roxbury, Connecticut*, The Times Print Shop, New Milford, Conn., 1924.

SALISBURY, CONN.
Historical Collection of the Salisbury Association, Inc., Vol. II, New Haven, 1916.
Landmarks, Salisbury Bicentennial, 1741–1941. Printed for Salisbury Bicentennial, Salisbury, Conn., 1941.
Rudd, Malcolm Day, *An Historical Sketch of Salisbury, Connecticut*, New York, 1899.

SHARON, CONN.
Goodenough, G. F., *A Gossip About a Country Parish of the Hills and Its People—Ellsworth, Litchfield County, Connecticut*, Times Press, Amenia, N. Y., 1900.
Sedgwick, Charles F. A. M., *General History of the Town of Sharon*, Charles Walsh, Printer and Publisher, Amenia, N. Y., 1898.

SHELTON, CONN.

Mallery, Leo T., *Tercentenary Pictorial and History of the Lower Naugatuck Valley*, Ansonia, Conn., 1935.

SOUTHBURY, CONN.

Cothren, William, *History of Ancient Woodbury*, Bronson Brothers, Waterbury, Conn., 1854.

STRATFORD, CONN.

Quarto-Millenial Anniversary of the Congregational Church of Stratford Connecticut, The Standard Association, Printers, Bridgeport, Conn., 1889.

Wilcoxson, William Howard, *History of Stratford, Conn., 1639–1939*, Published under the auspices of the Stratford Tercentenary Committee, Stratford, Conn., 1939.

STOCKBRIDGE, MASS.

Colby, Natalie Sedgwick, *Remembering*, Little, Brown & Co., Boston, 1938.

Eaton, Walter Prichard, *Laurel Hill Pageant*, Printed for the Laurel Hill Association, Stockbridge, 1941.

Jones, Electa F., *Stockbridge Past and Present*, S. Bowles & Co., Springfield, 1854.

Marquand (see Sedgwick).

Harriet Martineau's Autobiography, edited by Maria Weston Chapman, Houghton Mifflin & Co., Boston, 1877.

Sedgwick, Sarah Cabot and Marquand, Christina Sedgwick, *Stockbridge, 1739–1939*, Printed by the *Berkshire Courier*, Great Barrington, Mass., 1939.

Steele, Fletcher, *Stockbridge Mission House* (Reprinted from the *House Beautiful*, July, 1930).

The Tale of the Lion, Issued by the Red Lion Inn, Stockbridge, Mass.

Typescripts of Indian petitions:

1762—"Respecting alleged illegal sale of Indian lands."

1775—"Respecting temperance."

1783—"For appointment of receivers upon departure from Stockbridge."

Milwaukee Journal. Quotation from article respecting ancient Bible of Stockbridge Indians.

WASHINGTON, CONN.

Cothren, William, *History of Ancient Woodbury*, Bronson Brothers, Waterbury, Conn., 1854.

WASHINGTON, MASS.

Johnson, Agnes W., *Mss.* "History of Washington, Mass."

WEST STOCKBRIDGE, MASS.

Jones, Electa F., *Stockbridge Past and Present*, Springfield, 1854.

Sedgwick, Sarah Cabot and Marquand, Christina Sedgwick, *Stockbridge, 1739–1939*, Great Barrington, 1939.

The Berkshire Evening Eagle. August 29, 1938.

WOODBURY, CONN.

Cothren, William, *History of Ancient Woodbury*, Bronson Brothers, Waterbury, Conn., 1854.

Strong, Julia Minor, *The Town and People of Woodbury, Connecticut*, Mattatuck Press, Woodbury, Conn., 1901.

Wilcoxson, William Howard, *History of Stratford, Connecticut, 1639–1939*, Published under the auspices of the Stratford Tercentenary Committee, Stratford, Conn., 1939.

II—GENERAL SOURCES.

BOOKS AND PAMPHLETS:

Abbott, Katherine M., *Old Paths and Legends of the New England Border,* G. P. Putnam's Sons, New York, 1907.

Along the Housatonic Lines, Bridgeport Publishing Co., Bridgeport, Conn., 1891.

Anderson, Joseph, *The Old-Time Meeting-House and the Old Church Customs of New England,* Price, Lee & Adkins Co., New Haven, 1896.

Andrews, Charles M., *The River Towns of Connecticut,* Johns Hopkins University, Baltimore, 1889.

Andrews, Edward D., *The Gift To Be Simple,* J. J. Augustin, N. Y., 1940.

Andrews, Edward Deming and Faith, *Shaker Furniture,* Yale University Press, New Haven, 1937.

Armstrong, Margaret, *Fanny Kemble,* The Macmillan Company, N. Y., 1938.

Bacon, Edwin M., *Literary Pilgrimages in New England,* Silver Burdett & Co., N. Y., 1902.

Barber, John Warner, *Connecticut Historical Collections,* Durrie & Peck & W. Barber, N. H., 1837.

Berkshire Historical and Scientific Society, Pittsfield, Mass., Press of the Sun Printing Company, 1892 and 1895.

The Berkshires. Compiled by the Federal Writers Project of Massachusetts, Boston, 1938.

Bradshaw, Harold G., *The Indians of Connecticut,* New Era Press, Deep River, Conn., 1935.

Census of the Commonwealth of Massachusetts, 1905, Wright & Potter Printing Company, State Printers, Boston, 1909.

Clark, George L., *A History of Connecticut,* G. P. Putnam's Sons, N. Y., 1914.

Collections of the Berkshire Historical and Scientific Survey, The Historical Society, Pittsfield, Mass., 1895, 1899-1913.

Connecticut Vital Records, Barbour Collection, Connecticut State Library, 1927.

Considerations on the Practicality and Importance of Opening a Navigation to the Interior of the State, by the Housatonic River, A. H. Maltby & Co., New Haven, 1822.

Cook, Thomas A., *Geology of Connecticut,* The Bond Press, Hartford, Conn., 1933.

Day, Clive, *The Rise of Manufacturing in Connecticut—1820-1850,* Yale University Press, Tercentenary Commission, New Haven, 1935.

Dedication of the Equestrian Statue of Major-General John Sedgwick Erected on the Battlefield of Gettysburg by the State of Connecticut, June 19, 1913. Published by the State, 1913.

DeForest, John W., *History of the Indians of Connecticut,* Published with the sanction of the Connecticut Historical Society, Hartford, 1853.

Deming, Dorothy, *Settlement of Litchfield County,* Published for the Tercentenary Commission by the Yale University Press, New Haven, 1933.

Dewey, Mary E., *Life and Letters of Catherine M. Sedgwick,* Harper & Bros., N. Y., 1871.

Dictionary of American Biography, N. Y., 1928.

Dwight, Theodore, Jr., *History of Connecticut,* Harper & Bros., N. Y., 1871.

Dwight, Timothy, *Travels in New England and New York,* T. Dwight, New Haven, 1821-1827.

Faust, Clarence H. and Johnson, Thomas H., *Jonathan Edwards—Representative Selections,* American Book Company, N. Y., 1935.

Fellows, Henry Parker, *Boating Trips on New England Rivers*, Cupples, Upham & Company, Boston, 1884.

Flagg, Charles A., *An Index of Pioneers from Massachusetts to the West, Especially the State of Michigan*, The Salem Press Co., Salem, Mass., 1915.

Gazetteer of Berkshire County, Massachusetts, 1725–1885, Syracuse, 1885.

Guide to Lake Candlewood, The New Milford *Times*, New Milford, 1940.

Hart, Albert Bushnell, *Commonwealth History of Massachusetts*, States History Company, N. Y., 1927-30.

Harte, Charles Rufus, *Connecticut's Canals*, From the Fifty-Fourth Annual Report of the Connecticut Society of Civil Engineers, Inc., 1938.

Harte, Charles Rufus, *Connecticut's Cannon*, From the Fifty-Eighth Annual Report of the Connecticut Society of Civil Engineers, Inc., 1942.

Harte, Charles Rufus, and Keith, Herbert C., *The Early Iron Industry of Connecticut*, From the Fifty-First Annual Report of the Connecticut Society of Civil Engineers, Inc., 1935.

Housatonic River, Connecticut—House Document No. 246., Washington, D. C., 1932.

Hurd, Duane Hamilton (compiler), *History of Fairfield County, Conn.*, J. W. Lewis & Co., Philadelphia, 1881.

Johnson, Thomas H. *See* "Faust."

Keith, Herbert C. *See* "Harte."

Knowlton, Millard, "Connecticut Looks at Smallpox—Then and Now." Reprinted from the *Connecticut State Medical Journal*, January, 1941.

Lathrop, Rose Hawthorne, *Memories of Hawthorne*, Houghton, Mifflin & Company, Boston, 1897.

Lathrop, William G., *Development of Brass Industry in Connecticut*. Published for the Tercentenary Commission by the Yale University Press, New Haven, 1936.

Lay, Charles Downing, *Conservation and Recreational Development of the Housatonic Valley*. Published by the Housatonic Valley Conference, 1941.

Litchfield County Centennial Celebration, 1851. Published by Edwin Hunt, Hartford, Conn., 1851.

Lockwood, John Hoyt, *Western Massachusetts*, Lewis Historical Publishing Company, Inc., N. Y., 1926.

The Marble Border of Western New England, Papers of the Middlebury Historical Society, Published by the Society, 1885.

Mason, R. B., *Report of the Survey and Examination of a Route for a Railroad from Bridgeport, in the Direction of New York City to Sawpits Village—1838.* G. Mitchell, New York, 1838.

Memorial of Alexander Lyman Holley, C. E., L.L.D., Published by the American Institute of Mining Engineers, N. Y., 1884.

Middlebrook, Louis F., *Salisbury Connecticut Cannon*, Newcomb, Gauss Co., Salem, Mass., 1935.

Miller, Perry, *The New England Mind*, The Macmillan Company, N. Y., 1939.

Mills, Lewis Sprague, *The Story of Connecticut*, Charles Scribners' Sons, N. Y., 1932.

Moldenke, Richard, *Charcoal, Iron*, Salisbury Iron Corporation, Lime Rock, Conn., 1920.

Morrow, Rising Lake, *Connecticut Influences on Western Massachusetts and Vermont*. Published for the Tercentenary Committee by the Yale University Press, New Haven, 1936.

Morse, John T., *Life and Letters of Oliver Wendell Holmes*, Houghton, Mifflin & Company, Boston, 1897.

Mumford, Lewis, *Hermann Melville*, Harcourt, Brace & Co., N. Y., 1929.

Mussey, June Barrows (editor), *We Were New England: Yankee life by those who lived it*, Stackpole Sons, New York, 1937.

Niles, Grace Grelock, *The Hoosac Valley, Its Legends and Its History*, G. P. Putnam's Sons, N. Y., 1912.

Ogg, Frederick A., *Pioneers of the Northwest (Chronicles of America)*, Yale University Press, New Haven, 1926.

Olson, Albert L., *Agricultural Economy and the Population of Eighteenth Century Connecticut*, Published for the Tercentenary Commission by the Yale University Press, New Haven, 1935.

Orcutt, Samuel, *The Indians of the Housatonic and Naugatuck Valleys*, Case, Lockwood & Brainard Company, Hartford, Conn., 1882.

Osborn, Norris G., *History of Connecticut* (In monographic form), The States History Company, N. Y., 1925.

Peck, Epaphroditus, *The Loyalists of Connecticut*, Published for the Tercentenary Commission by the Yale University Press, New Haven, 1934.

Peters, Rev. Samuel, *A General History of Connecticut*, London, 1781. Republished by D. Clark & Co.—Baldwin & Threadway, Printers, New Haven, 1829.

Picturesque Berkshire, Picturesque Publishing Co., Northampton, Mass., 1893 and The W. F. Adams Co., Springfield, Mass., no date.

The Population of Massachusetts (from U. S. Census), Wright & Potter Co., Legislative Printers, Boston, 1940.

Purcell, Richard Joseph, *Connecticut in Transition—1775–1818*, American Historical Association, Washington, D. C., 1918.

Report of the Commissioners of the Housatonic Railroad to the General Assembly, May Session, 1843, Alfred E. Burr, Hartford, 1843.

Report of the Commissioners of the Housatonic Railroad to the General Assembly, May Session, 1844, Babcock & Wildman, New Haven, 1844.

Report of the Engineers upon the Preliminary Surveys for the Housatonic Railroad, 1836, Hitchcock & Stafford, New Haven, 1836.

Report of the Joint Special Committee to Whom Was Referred a Communication from a Committee of Citizens of Bridgeport Relative to the Housatonic Railroad—1840, Bryant & Boggs, New York, 1840.

Robinson, Henry C., *Argument Against the Housatonic Railroad*, no publisher, 1889.

Rosenberry, Mrs. Lois Kimball Mathews, *Migrations from Connecticut after 1800*, Published for the Tercentenary Commission by the Yale University Press, New Haven, 1936.

Rourke, Constance, Mayfield, *The Roots of American Culture*, Harcourt Brace & Co., N. Y., 1942.

The Schaghticokes—Published in Connection With the American Indian Day Celebration October 1, 1939, at the Reservation of the Schaghticokes, near Kent, Connecticut.

Schneider, Herbert Wallace, *The Puritan Mind*, Henry Holt & Co., N. Y., 1930.

Shepard, Odell, *Connecticut, Past and Present*, A. A. Knopf, N. Y., 1939.

Smith, Joseph Edward Adams, *History of Berkshire County, Massachusetts*, Pittsfield, 1885.

Smith, Joseph Edward Adams, *The Poet Among the Hills*, George Blatchford, Pittsfield, Mass., 1895.

Spek, Frank Gouldsmith, *Decorative Art of Indian Tribes of Connecticut.* Publication of the Canada Department of Mines, Govt. Printing Bureau, Ottawa, 1915.

State of Connecticut, *Register and Manual 1943*, Published by the State, Hartford, 1943.

State of Connecticut, *Directory of Connecticut Manufacturing and Mechanical Establishments*, Department of Labor, 1939.

Supplement to the Same by the Connecticut Chamber of Commerce, 1941.

Steiner, Bernard C., *History of Education in Connecticut*, Govt. Printing Office, Washington, D. C., 1893.

Transactions of the Housatonic Agricultural Society, 1879, 1883, 1892 and 1896. Published in Great Barrington, Mass., in years listed.

Trumbull, Benjamin, *A Complete History of Connecticut Civil and Ecclesiastical*, Hartford, Hudson & Godwin, 1797, and New Haven, Maltby, Goldsmith & Co., 1818.

Trumbull, J. Hammond, *Composition of Indian Geographical Names*, Hartford, 1870. (In Conn. Historical Society Collections.)

Trumbull, J. Hammond, *Indian Names of Place—In Connecticut*, Hartford, 1881.

Trumbull, J. Hammond, *The True-Blue Laws of Connecticut and New Haven and the False Blue-Laws Invented by the Rev. Samuel Peters*, American Publishing Co., Hartford, 1876.

Water Resources of New England—Publication No. 51, New England Regional Planning Commission, 1937.

Williston, Samuel Wendell, "Report on Rivers Pollution." From Connecticut State Department of Health *Tenth Annual Report, 1887*, New Haven, 1888.

Winslow, Ola Elizabeth, *Jonathan Edwards*, The Macmillan Company, N. Y., 1941.

Withington, Sidney, *The First Twenty Years of Railroads in Connecticut*, Tercentenary Commission, Yale University Press, New Haven, 1935.

Manuscripts:

Harte, Charles Rufus. *A Criticism of "Iron Chains Across the Hudson"* by Angelo P. Casella (see below).

Jefferson, Thomas. *Letter to Ezra Stiles.* Dec. 24, 1876.

Stiles, Ezra. *Diary, 1754-1787.*

Newspapers and Periodicals:

Berkshire Evening Eagle, August 29, 1941.

Bulletin of the National Society of the Sons of the American Revolution, April, 1944. (Article "Iron Chains Across the Hudson," by Angelo P. Casella.)

Century Magazine, August, 1895. (Article "Reminiscences of Literary Berkshire" by Henry Dwight Sedgwick, p. 552 ff.)

The Connecticut Magazine, vol. VIII, No. 11, Dec., 1903.

The Danbury News, July 31, 1934.

Engineering and Mining Journal, vol. XXXIII, No. 5, Feb. 4, 1882.

New York Times, May 17, 1937.

The New Yorker, July 9, 1938 (Communication of J. B. Price)

The New England Quarterly, December 1942. (Article "The Puritans and Sex," by Edmund J. Morgan.)

The Waterbury Republican, July 10, 1941.

Index